EUROPEAN ELITES AND IDEAS OF EMPIRE, 1917–1957

Who thought of Europe as a community before its economic integration in 1957? Dina Gusejnova illustrates how a supranational European mentality was forged from depleted imperial identities. In the revolutions of 1917–1920, the power of the Hohenzollern, Habsburg, and Romanoff dynasties over their subjects expired. Even though Germany lost its credit as a world power twice in that century, in the global cultural memory, the old Germanic families remained associated with the idea of Europe in areas reaching from Mexico to the Baltic region and India. Gusejnova's book sheds light on a group of German-speaking intellectuals of aristocratic origin who became pioneers of Europe's future regeneration. In the minds of transnational elites, the continent's future horizons retained the contours of phantom empires.

This title is available as Open Access at 10.1017/9781316343050.

DINA GUSEJNOVA is Lecturer in Modern History at the University of Sheffield.

NEW STUDIES IN EUROPEAN HISTORY

Edited by

PETER BALDWIN, University of California, Los Angeles
CHRISTOPHER CLARK, University of Cambridge
JAMES B. COLLINS, Georgetown University
MIA RODRIGUEZ-SALGADO, London School of Economics and Political Science
LYNDAL ROPER, University of Oxford
TIMOTHY SNYDER, Yale University

The aim of this series in early modern and modern European history is to publish outstanding works of research, addressed to important themes across a wide geographical range, from southern and central Europe, to Scandinavia and Russia, from the time of the Renaissance to the present. As it develops, the series will comprise focused works of wide contextual range and intellectual ambition.

A full list of titles published in the series can be found at:
www.cambridge.org/newstudiesineuropeanhistory

EUROPEAN ELITES AND IDEAS OF EMPIRE, 1917–1957

DINA GUSEJNOVA

University of Sheffield

CAMBRIDGE
UNIVERSITY PRESS

CAMBRIDGE
UNIVERSITY PRESS

University Printing House, Cambridge CB2 8BS, United Kingdom

Cambridge University Press is part of the University of Cambridge.

It furthers the University's mission by disseminating knowledge in the pursuit of
education, learning and research at the highest international levels of excellence.

www.cambridge.org
Information on this title: www.cambridge.org/9781107120624

First published 2016

Printed in the United Kingdom by TJ International Ltd. Padstow Cornwall

A catalogue record for this publication is available from the British Library

Library of Congress Cataloging-in-Publication data
Gusejnova, Dina, author.
European elites and ideas of empire, 1917–1957 / Dina Gusejnova (Queen Mary,
University of London).
Cambridge, United Kingdom ; New York, New York : Cambridge University Press, 2016. | Series: New
studies in European history | Includes bibliographical references and index.
LCCN 2016000257 | ISBN 9781107120624 (hardback)
LCSH: Europe – Politics and government – 1918–1945. | Europe – Politics and
government – 1945– | Supranationalism – Europe – History – 20th century. |
Imperialism – Social aspects – Europe – History – 20th century. | Transnationalism –
Social aspects – Europe – History – 20th century. | Elite (Social sciences) – Europe –
History – 20th century. | Intellectuals – Germany – History – 20th century. | Aristocracy
(Social class) – Germany – History – 20th century. | Germany – Intellectual life –
20th century. | Germany – Politics and government – 20th century. | BISAC:
HISTORY / Europe / General.
LCC D727 .G84 2016 | DDC 325/.309409041–dc23
LC record available at https://lccn.loc.gov/2016000257

ISBN 978-1-107-12062-4 Hardback

To my grandmother, Nadezhda Dmitrieva,

who always says: in this house, where everybody is a writer,

nobody seems to have a pen.

Contents

Contents

Figures

Preface

I belong to a post-nostalgic generation. A day before the coup that triggered the collapse of the Soviet Union in August 1991, I was on a brief return visit to Moscow, having recently moved to a unified Germany with my parents. What drew me to this topic was a wish to understand the way people feel about the disintegration of empires, and what the political consequences of such a feeling might be.

I was sentimental about friends, relatives, games, and certain tastes, but had no concept of states or nations at this point. For my parents and their circle of academics and publishers, on the other hand, the previous decade had been a time of interesting changes. The international 'Republic of Letters' had already become more permeable in the 1980s, as the Iron Curtain started to go. At the time, George Soros was supporting numerous academic initiatives in eastern Europe. One evening, he visited our appartment, and my mother took this as a welcome opportunity to provoke some doubts about things that I had been exposed to at school. 'Do you know who this uncle is?' she whispered. 'He is a capitalist!' More confusions were soon to come. In 1990, my parents were finally allowed to take up academic scholarships in Germany, which they had received in the late 1970s but were not allowed to pursue at the time. Now they were free to see the objects and hear the languages, which they knew in great detail from slide shows and books but never imagined they would see in real life. The formal dissolution of the Soviet state was a promise of freedom, which many understood in terms of geographical mobility and the opportunity to travel to places where, in a sense, European culture had been produced.

They began in northern Italy. During the odd four-hour visit to the Uffizi, I was puzzled by their exclamations like: 'Oh, I didn't know this Fra Angelico was so small. In the reproductions it always seemed very big.' In Florence, a policeman kindly let us drive the wrong way up a one-way street because he thought we were exotic. In Fiesole, on the way to the European University Institute, my father tried to order food in Latin only to find that nobody understands him, after which he had to resort to imitating the sounds of various animals that he wanted to eat. Even an elderly monk who got a ride up the hill with us told us that they 'only speak Latin in the Vatican'.

In Liguria, the great theorist of nationalism, Ernest Gellner, who had been our guest in Moscow in the 1980s, hosted us in his little house of stone, boiling water on an old stove that we call in Russian 'burzhuika', the 'bourgeois one'. Perched against a rock above the small village of Glori, near Imperia, the house boasted an incredible view of the Mediterranean, with the contours of Corsica somewhere in the mist. In 1992, Soviet Russia began to recede into the distance, like Corsica. Meanwhile, Moscow was taken over by rampant capitalist slogans such as 'Moscow property will always have value'.

In central Europe and the United States, ironic nostalgia for the lost Soviet civilization had become a commercial product and a successful model for making works of art. In another attempt at education, my mother decided to take me to *documenta X*, Germany's most celebrated modern art fair at Kassel, where I saw Ilya Kabakov's installation *The Soviet toilet*, perhaps the first piece of ironic counter-nostalgia that I am aware of. It was simply baffling to me at the time that someone could take an object of use that was still fresh in my memory, supply it with a neat German label, and have hordes of international tourists pay to visit it. Even disgusting toilets, especially those, had become important in this collective Anatomy of Nostalgia, which eventually saw numerous expressions like the Museum of Communism in Prague, Café *Das Kapital* in Moscow, books like Alexei Yurchak's *Everything Was Forever, Until It Was No More* (2006), and transnational post-Soviet Balkan fusion bands like Gogol Bordelo.

The first time I could try out my own version of a post-nostalgic story of a state that is no more was when I had to teach Marx's *Capital* in an introductory course in social theory called 'Power, Identity, and Resistance' at the University of Chicago. To a group of undergraduates from the American Midwest, China, and Nigeria, born after the Cold War, the fact that I was born in the Soviet Union suddenly began to form part of my package of curiosities in European culture. I even saw Ilya and Emilia Kabakov there once during an event organized by the Renaissance Society. But he no longer wanted to talk about toilets, his wife and manager asserted: his new subject was 'utopia'.

The political influence of people who, living in the aftermath of the First World War, imagined themselves as a rare, soon to be extinct, species from a past world interests me because I have lived in three societies in which 'leopard identities' – to allude to Lampedusa and Visconti – play an important role: Russia and the Russian community abroad; Germany, particularly East Germany; and the United Kingdom. In each of these communities, it is common for intellectuals to think of themselves as mediators to a bygone world, be it the Soviet Union, divided Germany, or the British Empire. At the same time, in Germany and later in Cambridge, people around me had grown up being unequivocally enthusiastic about the European Union. Looking back at the 1990s and early 2000s, European integration then seemed to hold a palpable promise of progress, untarnished by the crises of economic inequality and migration. The people in my book inhabited a world that combined impressions of Europe's imperial past with visions of its future, with all the ideological baggage that such a combination entails. Trying to understand them helped me understand the messy, contradictory connections between empire and utopia, which remain alive in Europe today.

Studying imperial memory academically unexpectedly opened up a humorous connection between the different kinds of memory and nostalgia I had encountered in German and Russian society. As a PhD student in Cambridge, I was once seated next to the wife of the master of Peterhouse, Lady Wilson, whose grandmother was the Baltic Baroness Moura Budberg. After I explained that one of the subjects of my research was a Baltic German nobleman called Hermann Keyserling, she exclaimed to her husband: 'Please meet Dina. I just found out that we are related!'

I began to reconstruct an image of Europe that I had only known from my own grandparents' accounts of their past. What they have in common with that of the nobles I studied is the international, or at least interregional, geography that underlies their memories. Two of my Jewish grandparents were nostalgic for the peripheral cosmopolitanism of central Europe, of Odessa on the Black Sea and Czernowitz in the Bukovina. My grandfather from Azerbaijan reminisces about the cosmopolitan city that was Baku, and his house, which used to belong to a Caucasian princely family, the Utsmievs, but after the Soviets took over, was filled with many different families of German, Armenian, Jewish, and Russian descent. My Russian grandmother, daughter of a *kulak* who lost everything in 1929 and saved his family by landing a job as an accountant for Moscow State University, also has an 'international' kind of nostalgia. She came to Austria with the Soviet military on 16 May 1945, at the age of 19. The four years she spent there working as a stenographer for the Allied Control Council gave her a very vivid sense of the imperial past that was still haunting the city. Somewhere between these two aftermaths of empires, the post-Soviet and the post-Habsburg, are the contours of this book.

Acknowledgements

I have had the good fortune of spending time in stimulating environments while working on this book. It began as a doctoral research project at the University of Cambridge, with additional stays at the universities of Groningen, Stanford, and UC Berkeley. Work on the book itself started at the University of Chicago and University College London and was concluded at Queen Mary University of London. I am grateful to my new colleagues and students at the University of Sheffield for providing a nurturing atmosphere in the final stages of production.

Martin Ruehl has shaped this project from its inception: without his inspiration to pursue aspects of European social and cultural history with Count Kessler's diary as a guide, this book would not have come into existence. The regular discussions I had with Raymond Geuss frequently pushed me to explore unknown avenues as well as alleyways of research. The memory of past conversations with the late Istvan Hont contains a rich, and mostly constructive, catalogue of criticisms, and I wish I could share my latest take on the twentieth-century 'feeble thinkers' with him. Eckart Conze provided me with a connection to German scholarship that I had missed. Chris Clark gave me the inspiration to look for structuralism whilst restructuring the doctoral project. As I followed this trail, John Searle's work on the construction of social reality inspired me to look at processes of imperial deconstruction; he went far beyond hospitality during my visits to UC Berkeley, and his appreciation of some of my work has been key to the progress of the book's central theme. Over the past years, Axel Körner gave me the creative resilience to navigate the book in its postdoctoral condition through the prism of transnational history.

Discussions with colleagues and mentors at all these institutions provided a rich palette of inspiration at different stages of work on the manuscript. For their advice at various stages of the project, I would like to thank Melissa Lane, Hubertus Jahn, George Joffe, Sarah Snyder, Michael Collins, Margot Finn, Keith McClelland, Jérémie Barthas, Richard Bourke, Saul Dubow,

Rüdiger Görner, Gareth Stedman Jones, Georgios Varouxakis, and Daniel Wildmann. Quentin Skinner provided me with a way out of an impasse with the book's title in a decisive moment. Discussions of the proposal and individual chapters have been vital for the completion of this volume, and I thank Tim Blanning, Brendan Simms, Kathy Burk, François Guesnet, Keith McClelland, Ira Katznelson, Richard Westerman, Adnan van Dal, Olga Smith, and Khadija von Zinnenburg Carroll, who have read parts of the manuscript and provided valuable feedback. I owe particular thanks to Peter Kovalsky, who has helped me to work on a more idiomatic style in English, an undertaking that involved venturing into philosophical terrain. I am yet to absorb the idea that '"to remember" in English, unlike in Russian, is a verb that contains no element of speech. Remembering happens entirely internally.' Or: 'A preoccupation is a thing that keeps you distracted from your occupation – it's a problem, not something pleasant.' The persistent infelicities preoccupy me, but such is life.

Generous funding from the AHRC, Peterhouse, the Kurt Hahn trust, the Marie Curie European doctorate, the DAAD, a Harper-Schmidt fellowship, and a Leverhulme early career fellowship enabled me to travel widely for purposes of archival research and academic exchange. I am particularly grateful to Philip Pattenden, the senior tutor at Peterhouse, and to Andreas Heiner from the Leverhulme Trust, for their support throughout this time.

This book relied heavily on the use of archives scattered across Europe and the United States. For bringing to life the documents, ideas, and images which helped me to imagine imperial decline as a social process, I thank Gabriel Superfin, Laird Easton, Sabine Carbon, Roland Kamzelak, Maria Amélia Teixeira de Vasconcelos, Daniela Stein-Lorentz, Ute Gahlings, Natalya Kolganova, Mieke Ijzermans, Otto Chmelik, Tatiana Chebotareff, Georg Rosentreter, John Palatini, and Marita von Cieminski. Maxim L'vov and Gert von Pistohlkors identified key visual sources from Estonia. I also thank Henrietta Garnett and Ben Anrep for allowing me to reproduce images from their family estates. Markus Lucke, Tanja Fengler-Veit, Sabine Carbon, Marlies Dornig, and Daragh Kenny provided me with visual reproductions from the German Literary Archive, the Austrian National Archive, the Kessler society, and the National Gallery in London.

Conversations about aristocratic memory, autobiographic thought, imperial decline, and elite sociability, which I had over the years with Friederike von Lukowicz, Harald von Keyserlingk, Charlotte Radziwill, Samuil Lur'ie, and Khadija von Zinnenburg Carroll, have served as vital threads connecting the documentary afterlife of my protagonists to the living memories and experiences of the present. I especially want to thank Natasha and David Wilson (Lord and Lady Wilson of Tillyorn) for allowing me to interview them at great length about the role of Natasha's legendary grandmother, Baroness Budberg, in shaping the cultural memory of imperial Russia, British imperial decline, and the transformation of systems of honour in modern Britain: these have inspired some core themes in this book. Her recollections of her mother's intuitively warm feelings towards Scotland – 'because the Scots can dream!' – have influenced my analysis of the Baltic borderers.

Being a member of the Society of Fellows in Chicago gave me access to a magical community of intellectuals who were working on their own first book projects – thanks especially to Richard Westerman, Sarah Graff, Leigh Claire La Berge, Nick Gaskell, Dorit Geva, Elizabeth Heath, Markus Hardtmann, Mara Marin, Nima Paidipaty, Emily Steinlight, Neil Verma, and Anita Chari. At UCL and at Queen Mary, I was given a golden opportunity to design courses in modern European history in which I learnt much from students, for which I thank Nicola Miller, Stephen Conway, and Miri Rubin.

I presented ongoing work on this book at conferences and workshops in Cambridge, London, Groningen, Lisbon, Paris, Stanford, Berkeley, Pittsburgh, Brighton, Marburg, Chicago, Fiesole, St. Petersburg, and Moscow. For sharing ideas in these contexts, I thank Beatrice Kobow, Ásta Kristjana Sveinsdóttir, Klaus Strelau, Trevor Wedman, Jennifer Hudin, Gary Herrigel, Jennifer Pitts, Moishe Postone, Tara Zahra, Alexander Etkind, Uta Staiger, Tim Beasley-Murray, Richard Drayton, Tatiana Nekrasova, Ilya Kukulin, Maria Maiofis, Nikolai Ssorin-Chaikov, Mikhail Kaluzhsky, Artemy Magun, Suzanne Marchand, Jan Plamper, Zaur Gasimov, George Giannakopoulos, Tom Hopkins, Damian Valdez, Sam James, and Hugo Drochon. I have also greatly benefited from the novel approach to intellectual life by preparing short lectures for Postnauka.ru, Ivar Maksutov, Anna Kozyrevskaya, and Julia Polevaya, an invigorating project run out of a small office on Arbat.

More thanks are due to people who provided key impulses for this book in a variety of ways. Thus I thank Olga Smith, Roxane Farmanfarmaian, Özlem Biner, Juan Cristóbal Cerrillo, Mara Marin, Alec Rainey, Bhismadev Chakrabarty, and Advaith Siddhartan. Tat'iana Berdikova has sustained the link to the Serapion brothers as well as to Ernest Gellner in Russian. Elena Tverdislova has advised me on the sections dealing with Polish intellectual history. Margarita Dement'ieva has given me an education in modern American literature as well as the theme of exile and revolution among the 'white' Russians. I am also grateful to Yascha Mounk, Philip Wood, Josephine von Zitzewitz, Amy Bell, Manuel Arroyo Kalin, Yulia Yamineva, Alessandro Zocchi, Brynn Deprey, Alessandro Giacone, Thomas Land, Amir Engel, Alexis Papazoglou, as well as to Elvira Amosova and Samuil Lur'e, Alice and Wilhelm Schlink, Flora Goldstein and Igor Golomstock, Nadya Bodansky and Andrei Arkhipov.

My parents, Marina Dmitrieva and Gasan Gusejnov, co-produced this book in many ways. In addition to reading drafts and discussing ideas, their own work has had an influence on me in ways that a footnote would not reflect adequately. My mother's study of Italian architects from the Renaissance in central Europe, *Italien in Sarmatien* (2008), was a memorable adventure in European cultural geography, which has been as indicative to me as her work on the art of the Russian and central European avant-garde and the periodical communities associated with it. My father's fieldwork on the language and culture of late Soviet and post-Soviet national identity, first begun in the journal *The Twentieth Century and the World*, which he co-edited with Denis Dragunsky in the years of perestroika, was as important an influence as his *The Map of our Motherland* (2005), a book about imperial phantom pains in the post-Soviet Russian cartographic imaginary. My grandfather, Chingiz Huseinov, helped me to organize my thinking about imperial decline, and provided me with inspiration on transnational and postcolonial imaginaries through his novel on the revolution, *Doktor N* (1998).

My very special thanks go to Andreas Vlachos for having trust in our common itineraries while the counts were taking over.

My grandmother, Nadezhda Dmitrieva, has been assembling an archive of aristocratic memory from our local newspaper, the *Leipziger Volkszeitung*, in the past years, upon my request. This model of cultural memory in a postsocialist state and other conversations with her have supplied this book with the most important, if less visible, arc to the present. I dedicate this book to her, the real historian in the family.

I am grateful to two anonymous reviewers as well as to the series editors for their constructive comments, and I thank Michael Watson, Amanda George, Maartje Scheltens, Mary Bongiovi, and Louise Bowes of Cambridge University Press, as well as Jeevitha Baskaran, for their encouragement, professionalism, and patience in producing this book.

The remaining faults are mine.

Abbreviations

AV	Archive of the Convegno Volta, Accademia Nazionale dei Lincei, Rome
Barch	Berlin-Lichterfelde, Bundesarchiv (Federal Archives)
CSA	New York, Columbia University, Special Collections
DA	Děčin, Czech Republic, Štátny oblastny archiv
DAG	Deutsche Adelsgenossenschaft
DLA	Deutsches Literaturarchiv Marbach
GSA	Weimar, Goethe-und-Schiller Archiv
HA	Stanford, Hoover Institution Archives
HKN	Hermann Keyserling Nachlass, Darmstadt, Hessische Landes- und Hochschulbibliothek
IISG	Amsterdam, Internationaal Instituut voor Sociale Geschiedenis, Archive
Kessler, *Diaries*	Harry Graf Kessler, *Das Tagebuch 1880–1937*, Roland S. Kamzelak and Ulrich Ott (Eds.), 9 vols. (Stuttgart: Klett-Cotta, 2004–10); Vol. 5, 1914–16, Günter Riederer und Ulrich Ott (Eds.) (Stuttgart: Klett-Cotta, 2008); Vol. 6, 1916–18, Günter Riederer (Ed.) (Stuttgart: Klett-Cotta, 2006); Vol. 7, 1919–23, Angela Reinthal (Ed.) (Stuttgart: Klett-Cotta, 2007); Vol. 8, 1923–26, Angela Reinthal, Günter Riederer und Jörg Schuster (Eds.); Vol. 9, 1926–37, Sabine Gruber and Ulrich Ott (Eds.) (Stuttgart: Klett-Cotta, 2010).

Kessler, GS I, II, or III	Harry Graf Kessler, *Gesammelte Schriften in drei Bänden*, Cornelia Blasberg and Gerhard Schuster (Eds.), 3 vols. (Frankfurt/Main: Fischer, 1988)
KN	Kessler Archive, Deutsches Literaturarchiv Marbach
LHASA	Hans-Hasso von Veltheim Archive, Ostrau; Depositum Veltheim at the Universitäts- und Landesbibliothek Sachsen-Anhalt, Halle (Saale)
MT	Mikhail von Taube archive, Columbia University Libraries, Rare Books and Manuscript Library, New York
MWG	Max-Weber-Gesamtausgabe, 23 vols. (Tübingen: Mohr, 1988–2015). Vol. I:15, Wolfgang Mommsen and Gangolf Hübinger (Eds.), *Max Weber. Zur Politik im Weltkrieg* (Tübingen: Mohr, 1984); Vol.I:16, *Zur Neuordnung Deutschlands. Schriften und Reden 1918-1920*, Wolfgang Mommsen and Gangolf Hübinger (Eds.) (Tübingen: Mohr, 1988); Vol. I:17, *Wissenschaft als Beruf. 1917/19.Politik als Beruf. 1919*, Wolfgang Mommsen and Wolfgang Schluchter, in collaboration with Birgitt Morgenbrod (Eds.) (Tübingen: Mohr, 1992); Vol. I:22–24, Edith Hanke, with assistance from Thomas Kroll (Eds.), *Teilband 4: Herrschaft* (Tübingen: Mohr, 2005)
Nansen/UNOG	United Nations Records and Archives Unit, Nansen Fonds, Refugees Mixed Archival Group, 1919–47, Geneva
RGVA	Moscow, Rossiiskii gosudarstvennyi voennyi arkhiv (Russian State Military Archives), formerly Osobyi arkhiv
RNCK	Richard Nikolaus Coudenhove-Kalergi Archive, Moscow, Rossiyskiy gosudarstvennyi voennyi arkhiv (Russian State Military Archives), Fond 554

All translations from foreign languages are my own, unless otherwise stated.

Introduction

In December 1917, delegations from Russia, Ukraine, Austria-Hungary, Prussia, Bavaria, Bulgaria, and the Ottoman Empire travelled to Brest-Litovsk in the prospect of peace. In this ruined market town, only the train station and the nineteenth-century citadel were still standing. Before the war, Brest used to link the inland colonies of the Russian Empire with its commercial veins. Now under German control, it served as a market for a different kind of commodity: political prestige.

On the table were not only issues of territorial integrity but the question of legitimate succession to Europe's vanishing empires.[1] The Russian Empire's losses in the war precipitated a revolution in Petrograd in February 1917, which enabled the Bolsheviks, a party formed in exile, to assume control over the state in a coup in October of that year. They saw themselves as the vanguard of a new humanity, which had come to replace Europe's bankrupt imperial elites. After the tsar's abdication and the failures of the Provisional Government, they handled the Russian Empire's defeat and initiated the peace talks.[2] Two years after the event, journalists

---

[1] For more on Brest-Litovsk before the war, see Kh. Zonenberg, *Istoria goroda Brest-Litovska. 1016–1907, etc.* [History of the city of Brest-Litovsk] (Brest-Litovsk: Tipografia Kobrinca, 1908).

[2] There is, of course, a very large literature on the Russian Revolution and Civil War. To indicate directions which are important to the present book, I concentrate on references to works which link the revolution to processes of imperial decline and war and put these in comparative perspective. See especially Mark von Hagen, 'The Russian Empire', and Ronald G. Suny, 'The Russian Empire', in *After Empire. Multiethnic Societies and Nation-Building. The Soviet Union and the Russian, Ottoman, and Habsburg Empires*, ed. Karen Barkey and Mark von Hagen (Boulder: Westview Press, 1997), 58–73 and 142–155; James D. White, 'Revolutionary Europe', in *A Companion to Modern European History. 1871–1945*, ed. Martin Pugh (Oxford: Blackwell, 1997), 174–193; for revolution as a consequence of war, see Peter Gatrell, *Russia's First World War: A Social and Economic History* (London and New York: Routledge, 2005); and Katja Bruisch and Nikolaus Katzer, *Bolshaia voina Rossii: Sotsial'nyi poriadok, publichnaia kommunikatsia i nasilie na rubezhe tsarskoi i sovetskoi epochi* (Moscow: NLO, 2014). For a comparative and theoretical perspective, see the classic by Theda Skocpol, *States and Social Revolutions: A Comparative Analysis of France, Russia, and China* (Cambridge: Cambridge University Press, 1979), and Charles Tilly, *European Revolutions, 1492–1992* (Oxford: Blackwell, 1993). For a more comprehensive literature, see Jonathan Smele (ed. and annot.),

such as the American John Reed presented the Bolshevik rise to power as an inevitable revolution with global potential.[3]

Nikolai Lenin, a pseudonym he derived from the river of his Siberian exile, considered the collapse of imperial governments in the war to be the final culmination of global capitalism. He noted that previous theoretical models of imperial crises, which he had studied in libraries in London, Bern, and Zurich, failed to predict the impact of wars between empires on the ability of revolutionary groups to gain control over states. Now that even the former Russian Empire with its tiny working class had Workers' and Soldiers' Councils, a revolution seemed more likely in the rest of Europe as well.[4]

However, this is not in fact what happened in most of central Europe in the decades between 1917 and 1939. Even if we compare the changes during this time with more critical, non-Bolshevik perspectives on the Russian case, central Europe experienced a less radical transformation in this interval. The societies west of the new Russian border did not change their social, institutional, and economic basis to the same degree. Some of the more radical changes, such as giving women the vote, which immediately increased the number of active citizens in Europe, were not the work of new republican governments. Thus in Britain, a surviving empire and a monarchy, national citizenship and women's suffrage also replaced imperial forms of subjecthood after the First World War.[5]

This remained so until the new divisions of Germany and eastern Europe, which took place in the aftermath of the Hitler–Stalin pact of 1939 and the Yalta Conference of 1945. Before this time, seemingly radical changes like the abolition of monarchies in twenty-two German princely states and in Austria were the effects of mostly liberal constitutional reforms. Acts of retribution against the old elites were also more moderate in central Europe than in Russia. Most members of the Habsburgs, Hohenzollerns, and other families survived in exile. There were no

---

The Russian Revolution and Civil War, 1917–1921: An Annotated Bibliography (London and New York: Continuum, 2003).

[3] John Reed, *Ten Days That Shook the World* (New York: Boni and Liveright, 1919); on the history of the revolution as a story, see Frederick C. Corney, *Telling October: Memory and the Making of the Bolshevik Revolution* (Ithaca: Cornell University Press, 2004).

[4] Lenin's commentary on Hobson was first published as Nikolai Lenin, *Imperialism, the Highest Stage of Capitalism* (Petrograd: Zhizn' i Znanie, 1917).

[5] For the intellectual and practical transition via 'imperial citizenship, see Daniel Gorman, *Imperial Citizenship: Empire and the Question of Belonging* (Manchester: Manchester University Press, 2006). See also Elleke Boehmer, *Empire, the National and the Postcolonial, 1890–1920. Resistance in Interaction* (Oxford: Oxford University Press, 2002).

twentieth-century Marie Antoinettes west of the Curzon line, even though writers like the Austrian Stefan Zweig did invoke her name in a bestselling biography.[6] Revolutionary situations did happen between 1918 and 1922 in various cities, like Munich, Berlin, Kiel, Turin, and Budapest. But in many cases, radical movements associated with disbanded officer corps of the old imperial armies were more successful there than the contemporary socialist and anarchist movements or the relatively local sailors' mutinies. Moreover, new leaders on the left and the right, including Mussolini in Rome, Friedrich Ebert in Weimar, Adolf Hitler in Potsdam, and Franco in Spain all sought public accreditation from the representatives of Europe's traditional elites.[7]

By 1924, the most charismatic of the revolutionary leaders on the left, people like Kurt Eisner in Munich, Karl Liebknecht and Rosa Luxemburg in Berlin, and Giacomo Matteotti in Rome, became victims of political assassination alongside liberal reformers such as Walther Rathenau; others, such as Antonio Gramsci, Béla Kun, and György Lukács, were imprisoned or went into exile. Among historians, there were only two brief moments when the events in Germany were discussed under the label of 'revolutions'. The first was when the Russian socialists such as Larisa Reisner and Karl Radek hoped to encourage a revolution there in the early 1920s.[8] The second time was in the aftermath of 1968, when historians who were disenchanted with the actions of the Soviet Union in their own lifetime sought to recover an alternative history of European socialism.[9]

This book argues that intellectual communities and transnational cultural networks played a key role in establishing a consensus against revolution in central Europe. Looking chiefly at the decades between the revolution in Russia in 1917 and the beginning of Europe's post-war integration in 1957, I suggest that during this period, the old elites of continental Europe managed to convert their imperial prestige into new forms of power. The limited degree to which the Bolshevik revolution was

---

[6] Stefan Zweig, *Marie Antoinette: The Potrait of an Average Woman* (New York: Garden City Publishing Co., 1933).

[7] Cf. Christoph Kopke and Werner Treß (eds.), *Der Tag von Potsdam* (Berlin: Walter de Gruyter, 2013).

[8] Cf. Larisa Reisner, *Hamburg auf den Barrikaden. Erlebtes und Erhörtes aus dem Hamburger Aufstand 1923* (Berlin: Neuer Deutscher Verlag, 1923).

[9] Cf. Richard Watt, *The Kings Depart: The Tragedy of Germany. Versailles and the German Revolution* (New York: Simon and Schuster, 1968). For a more balanced recent account of the revolutions in Germany, see Richard Evans, *The Coming of the Third Reich* (London: Penguin, 2003), and Christopher Clark, Introduction to Viktor Klemperer, Victor Klemperer, *Man möchte immer weinen und Lachen in Einem. Revolutionstagebuch 1919* (Berlin: Aufbau, 2015).

able to spread west, this book argues, had much to do with the existence of media in which some vocal members of the European intelligentsia could discuss their own implicated role in the process of imperial decline, and even share a certain degree of enthusiasm for the revolutions.

The post-imperial transition in central Europe between 1917 and the 1930s was closer in character to British imperial reforms between the abolition of slavery of 1833 and the Representation of the People Act of 1918 than to the revolutions in Russia.[10] Why did revolutions not gain more public support west of Russia? There cannot be any one answer to this question, but this book contributes something to this larger question by highlighting the factor of social prestige in the transformation of power. Recovering the transnational sociability and intellectual production of a group of, mostly liberal, German-speaking authors, it reveals the persistent authority of people who belonged to the former elites of multiple continental empires.[11] They considered themselves implicated in Europe's imperial past, even though, as one of them put it, they were 'historically speaking, dead'.[12]

Memoirs and autobiographic reflections were one domain in which their imperial memories circulated. But the German-speaking aristocratic intellectuals of interwar Europe also became political activists and theorists of internationalism in interwar European institutions such as The Hague Academy of International Law, newly founded academies of leadership like the Darmstadt School of Wisdom, or the League of Nations unions.[13] Joining voices with more radical contemporaries who criticized parliamentary democracies and bourgeois values from the Left and the Right, they formed a peculiar international from above, which had the power to give or deny recognition in Europe's informal circles of elite sociability. In this way, the old Germanic elites fulfilled a double function. In Germany, they helped to overcome Germany's intellectual isolation by mobilizing their international connections. Internationally, they embodied the 'old' world of Europe's continental empires. They also became self-proclaimed representatives of Europe in encounters with the new intellectuals of the non-

---

[10] See Gregory Claeys, *The French Revolution Debate in Britain: The Origins of Modern Politics* (Basingstoke: Palgrave Macmillan, 2007).

[11] Otto Neurath, *Gesellschaft und Wirtschaft. Bildstatistisches Elementarwerk. Das Gesellschafts- und Wirtschaftsmuseum in Wien zeigt in 100 farbigen Bildtafeln Produktionsformen, Gesellschaftsordnungen, Kulturstufen, Lebenshaltungen* (Leipzig: Bibliographisches Institut, 1930).

[12] Hermann Keyserling, *Reise durch die Zeit* (Vaduz: Liechtenstein, 1948), 53.

[13] Noel Annan, 'The Intellectual Aristocracy', in *Studies in Social History*, ed. John Plumb (London: Longmans, 1955).

Western world, including global stars such as the Indian poet Rabindranath Tagore.

The position of German intellectuals changed dramatically between the two peace treaties that ended the First World War. At Brest-Litovsk, Germany and Austria-Hungary were winning and dictating the terms. By contrast, the Peace of Versailles not only prominently marked Germany's defeat as a nation. It also identified the old German-speaking elites as the representatives of more than one dismantled empire. As this book will show, however, paradoxically, this gave Germanic intellectuals greater international reach. As figures of precarious status, they provided the post-imperial societies of Europe with a personal vision of transition that they otherwise lacked.[14]

As members of a transnational elite, they actively resisted thinking about their present in terms of 'old' and 'new' regimes, which many contemporary political movements tried to establish. Such attitudes to revolutions have been previously expressed in British political thought in response to the French Revolution and the anti-Napoleonic struggles.[15] In the new international situation emerging around the League of Nations and other international bodies, the association of the German elites with multiple vanished empires, offered a unique form of cultural capital.

Looking back at the decade which followed Brest-Litovsk, Baron Taube, a former Russian senator remarked: 'We are truly living in strange times. Former ministers, field marshals who had been dismissed and monarchs without a throne' are putting the work they had been trained to do to rest in order to put to paper in haste the things which they had lived and seen 'in happier days, when they were still in power'.[16] But even as memoirists, these *'subjective* witnesses of the first rank', Baron Taube argued, could not be trusted because in remembering, they wanted to expiate themselves. By contrast, he thought that his own memory of the events he dubbed the

---

[14] Clifford Geertz, 'Centers, Kings, and Charisma: Reflections on the Symbolics of Power', in *Culture and Its Creators. Essays in Honor of Edward Shils*, ed. Joseph Ben-David and Terry Nichols-Clark (Chicago: Chicago University Press, 1971), 150–171.

[15] Classic examples are Edmund Burke, *Reflections on the Revolution in France* (London: J. Dodsley, 1790), and William Wordsworth, *Tract on the Convention of Sintra* (1808) (London: Humphrey Milford, 1915), as discussed in Michael Hechter, *Alien Rule* (Cambridge: Cambridge University Press, 2013), 1. For a problematization of the conservative/progressive optic in the intellectual history of revolutionary periods, see Richard Bourke, *Empire and Revolution: The Political Life of Edmund Burke* (Princeton: Princeton University Press, 2015), 1–23, and an unpublished paper, 'Edmund Burke and the Origins of Conservatism' (2015).

[16] Michael Freiherr von Taube, *Der großen Katastrophe entgegen. Die russische Politik der Vorkriegszeit und das Ende des Zarenreiches (1904–1917)* (Berlin and Leipzig: Georg Neuner, 1929), 1.

'Great Catastrophe' had more public value, if only because many senior diplomats representing their empires at Brest-Litovsk were also soon removed from the political stage.[17] People like Taube were not just observers in the 'second row of the ministerial lodge of the Russian empire'. He belonged to a rank of past historical actors, who were also leading internationalists of their generation.

To reconstruct how the intellectual communities of Europe remained connected through shared imperial mentalities, I look at authors who were social celebrities or well known in these circles. Some of the most visible personalities in these circles of post-imperial sociability were authors and intellectuals of aristocratic background, often with connections in imperial civil service or international law. These included the diarist Count Harry Kessler, a committed internationalist who was a Prussian officer with Anglo-Irish roots; Count Hermann Keyserling, a Baltic Baron who became a philosopher of global travel and identity, and Baron Hans-Hasso von Veltheim, a German Orientalist with a cosmopolitan social circle. The Austrian prince Karl Anton Rohan, a lobbyist and founder of the organization that preceded UNESCO, was a more important personality connecting old Europe with intellectuals, bankers, and industrialists of the post-war era, as well as building some ties to the nascent fascist movement in Italy. Count Coudenhove-Kalergi, the activist of Pan-European unity, was equally well known in central Europe, Britain, and the United States. Baron Mikhail von Taube was an international lawyer from the Russian Empire teaching in Sweden, Germany, and the Netherlands. As individuals and members of a wider network of intellectual communities, these authors and others of similar background contributed to the growth of an internationalist mentality by sharing experiences of the First World War, as well as successive crises of European democracies and economies. Their family networks past and present gave them a personal connection to multiple processes of revolution and reform which took place almost simultaneously in Ireland, Russia, Germany, and Austria-Hungary. They were, to adopt Donald Winnicott's term, 'transitional' subjects for post-imperial societies.[18] Their family histories, connecting

---

[17] His own reflections comprise Michael Freiherr von Taube, *Rußland und Westeuropa (Rußlands historische Sonderentwicklung in der europäischen Völkergemeinschaft)*, Institut für internationales Recht an der Universität Kiel (Berlin: Stilke, 1928); and Prof. bar. M.A. Taube, *Vechnyi mir ili vechnaia voina? (Mysli o „Ligi Natsii")* (Berlin: Detinets, 1922).

[18] Donald Winnicott, *The Maturational Processes and the Facilitating Environment: Studies in the Theory of Emotional Development* (1965; London: Karnac Press, 1990).

them to the history of more than one empire, helped others make sense of the transition from imperial to post-imperial Europe.

Power, prestige, and the limits of imperial decline

Readers of international news were unlikely to have heard of Brest-Litovsk before the peace treaty. In 1915, the English-speaking educated public was interested in the region mostly because it was home to the bison, Europe's biggest animal, whose extinction was imminent because of the protracted war. 'But for the jealous protection of the Tsar it would, even here, long since have vanished', lamented the *Illustrated London News*, if it weren't for the 'zoos or private parks such as those of the Duke of Bedford, and of Count Potocky, in Volhynia'.[19] Few could foresee then that in 1918, Europe's last tsar and his family would vanish even before the last bisons.

But to more astute analysts of modern empires such as John Hobson, the war merely highlighted what he had already observed nearly two decades earlier: empires persisted despite the fact that the majority of their populations lacked a common interest in imperialism.[20] Instead, as complex systems of social and economic relations, empires brought benefits to particular, increasingly global, commercial, and financial enterprises, which included the old dynasties as the oldest holders of capital in their empires. These national and transnational minorities were the chief beneficiaries of empires, and as such Hobson's readers such as Lenin concentrated their critique on them.

Other theorists of empire agreed with much of this analysis but were more sceptical in their conclusions. They believed that cultural values such as prestige were just as significant in maintaining stability in empires, which meant that even the supposed enlightenment of imperial subjects about their true interests would not necessarily lead to revolution. What I want to underline is that intellectuals and civil servants working for empires were among those minorities who benefited from empires by enjoying the existence of special honours, cultural goods, and the benefits of a multicultural identity.

In this book, I look at one of the subgroups of these intellectual elites who could be described as a kind of European imperial intelligentsia. Like the Russian origin of this term suggests, this group comprised critics of

---

[19] 'Menaced with Extinction by War: European Bison in Lithuania', *Illustrated London News*, 4 September 1915, 299.
[20] Hobson, *Imperialism*, 35.

imperial governments who were simultaneously profoundly implicated in their imperial economic and cultural systems of prestige. They questioned the way ideas of the nation, of culture and civilization, were used to justify imperial rule, and yet they also questioned the way these were used by the revolutionaries.[21] In this capacity, they can serve as guides to a social and intellectual history of continental European imperialism that could build on the work of scholars of the British Empire and, more recently, expanded in the form of the history of international political thought.[22] In addition, their perspective on empire opens up new possibilities for a more modest form of global and transnational history of imperialism after the age of empire.[23] The theorists and witnesses of the twentieth-century revolutions engaged with modernist forms of narrative and contemporary traditions in philosophy to make sense of their particular condition. They lived in an age in which empires declined, yet imperialism persisted. Moreover, their ideas of empire had formed in a trans-imperial context, reflecting the character of elite sociability in the Belle Epoque as well as the cultural traditions of European education.[24] Yet their peculiar endorsement of imperialism without empires was frequently constructed in highly traditional forms of writing, which hearkened back to the idea of a united Europe. Their golden age was anchored in the 'non-radical' moments of the enlightenment, in the cosmopolitan nationalism of liberals such as Mazzini, in technocratic idealism of the Saint Simonians and Cobden, and the aesthetic reform movements of William Morris and the Theosophical Society.[25] The political thought of the twentieth-century internationalist configuration that is at the centre of my attention in this book takes the

[21] On the German distinction between *Kultur* and *Zivilisation*, see Raymond Geuss, '*Kultur, Bildung, Geist*', in *Morality, Culture, History*, ed. Raymond Geuss (Cambridge: Cambridge University Press, 1999), 29–51.

[22] See, notably, C.A. Bayly, *Imperial Meridian: The British Empire and the World 1780–1830* (London: Longmans, 1989); Jennifer Pitts, *A Turn to Empire. The Rise of Imperial Liberalism in Britain and France* (Princeton: Princeton University Press, 2005); David Armitage, *Foundations of Modern International Thought* (Cambridge: Cambridge University Press, 2013).

[23] For a much grander nineteenth-century global history of empires, see Jürgen Osterhammel, *The Transformation of the World: A Global History of the Nineteenth Century* (Princeton: Princeton University Press, 2014), esp. 419–468.

[24] On the transnational character of imperial formations, see Ilya Gerasimov, Sergey Glebov, Jan Kusber, Marina Mogilner, and Alexander Semyonov, *Empire Speaks Out. Languages of Rationalization and Self-Description in the Russian Empire* (Leiden: Brill, 2009).

[25] I take the view that the radical thinkers of the enlightenment were generally less characteristic of the concept, at least in the way it was received subsequently, than Jonathan Israel has tended to present it. For the original statement of the 'radical enlightenment' thesis, see Jonathan Israel, *Radical Enlightenment: Philosophy and the Making of Modernity, 1650–1750* (Oxford: Oxford University Press, 2001). For a critique of this view, see David Sorkin, *The Religious Enlightenment: Protestants, Jews, and Catholics from London to Vienna* (Princeton: Princeton University Press, 2011).

form of autobiographies, diaries, memoirs, and classical dramatic fiction, along with treatises and other works of theory.

As one French publisher put it in 1920: 'Que nous réserve le vingtième siècle? L'Europe pourra-t-elle maintenir son hégémonie exclusive sur le monde?' ['What does the twentieth century hold in stock for us? Will Europe be able to maintain her exclusive hegemony over the world?'] In times of 'dismemberment of the Russian, Austro-Hungarian and other empires', these questions worried even those who had been critical of previous imperial excesses.[26] In fact, things had been falling apart in Europe's other empires, too.[27] Calls for national self-determination and home rule reached as far as the telegraph cables and the imperial liners, from the Atlantic to the Indian Oceans, across the Mediterranean, the Irish, and the Baltic Seas.[28] Increasingly, imperial governments were perceived as holders of an oppressive, alien type of rule that went against the interests of the majority of their subjects – metropolitan, peripheral, and colonial.[29] For a short while, the Ottoman and German empires and Austria-Hungary survived; but by 1922, these powers also unravelled. In the period between 1916 and 1922, new national republics like Germany, Austria, Hungary, Czechoslovakia, Poland, and the three

---

[26] Mehemed Emin Effendi, *Civilisation et humanité*, Introduction G. Ficker (Paris: G. Fickler, 1920), i–iv.

[27] This phrase was first used in comparative perspective by W.B. Yeats in 'Second Coming', first published in W.B. Yeats, *Michael Robartes and the Dancer* (Dublin: Cuala Press, 1920). According to the manuscripts, Yeats's original draft of the poem included references to the French and the Russian revolutions, but in the final version, only the Irish one remains. For details, see Thomas Parkinson and Anne Brannen (eds.), *'Michael Robartes and the Dancer' Manuscript Materials* (Ithaca: Cornell University Press, 1994). Significantly for the literature on decolonization, the line 'things fall apart' only became appropriated in the anticolonial literary movement associated with Chinua Achebe's novel *Things Fall Apart* (London: William Heinemann, 1958).

[28] On the key sites where self-determination and home rule were discussed, see Mahatma Gandhi, 'Hind Swaraj', *Indian Opinion*, 11 and 18 December 1909; Woodrow Wilson, speech of 11 February 1918; the Bolshevik peace plan, 29 December 1918; for more context, see Alvin Jackson, *Home Rule. An Irish History, 1800–2000* (London: Weidenfeld & Nicholson, 2003). For the Wilsonian conception of self-determination and its global effects, see Erez Manela, *The Wilsonian Moment. Self-Determination and the International Origins of Anticolonial Nationalism* (Oxford and New York: Oxford University Press, 2007).

[29] The classic critique of imperialism deceiving the imperialists is John Hobson, *Imperialism*. On the concept of alien rule, see John Plamenatz, *On Alien Rule and Self-Government* (London: Longmans, 1960), and Hechter, *Alien Rule*. On decolonization in comparative perspective, see especially Martin Thomas, Bob Moore, and L.J. Butler (eds.), *Crises of Empire. Decolonization and Europe's Imperial States, 1918–1975* (London: Hodder, 2008); Frederick Cooper, 'Decolonizing Situations: The Rise, Fall, and Rise of Colonial Studies, 1951–2001', in *French Politics, Culture & Society*, 20:2, Special Issue: Regards Croisés: Transatlantic Perspectives on the Colonial Situation (Summer 2002), 47–76. See also Ronald Robinson, 'Non-European Foundations of European Imperialism: Sketch for a Theory of Collaboration', in Roger Owen and Bob Sutcliffe (eds.), *Studies in the Theory of Imperialism* (London: Longman, 1972), 117–140.

Baltic states, emerged, alongside new federations like the Kingdom of Yugoslavia or the League of Nations. Particularly in the lands formerly belonging to the defeated empires of continental Europe, the old land-owning, military, and political elites seemed discredited.

In Russia, dismantling the old elites went further than anywhere else in Europe. The Bolshevik party began its rise to power by calling into question the very basic hierarchies of rank inside the imperial army. A 'Decree on the destruction of estates and civil honours' followed, which proclaimed the abolition of all status of privilege alongside deprived statuses like that of a peasant. What remained were the 'free peoples of Russia'.[30] The Romanoffs, whose Russian-sounding name obscured their relation to the German houses of Schleswig and of Hessen-Darmstadt, had already been exposed as 'inner Germans' and enemies of their former subjects under the Kerenski administration. Under the Bolsheviks, they were executed without trial along with their valet, their cook, and their butler, away from the public eye, in the heart of the Urals, where many Russian socialists and anarchists had been spending their prison sentences since the 1880s.[31] Some among the Bolsheviks thought that such actions were necessary in order to achieve the kind of self-determination they were seeking for the former imperial subjects. Former inner peripheries like the 'Pale of Settlement', a large rural ghetto created by Catherine II of Russia, to which the Jews of Russia had been confined, were decolonized.[32] Their demand for self-determination also extended to the subject peoples of other empires, such as the Armenians, as well as the Baltic territories now claimed by the German Empire.[33] But to say that in tearing down the old regimes, the Bolsheviks became universal spokesmen for the

---

[30] 'Deklaratsia prav narodov Rossii' (2/15 November 1915) and 'Dekret ob unichtozhenii soslovii i grazhdanskikh chinov' (11/24 November 1917), in *Dekrety sovetskoi vlasti* (Moscow: Gosudarstvennoe izdatelstvo politicheskoi literatury, 1957), 39–40 and 72.

[31] On the changing image of the Romanoffs during the war, see Boris Kolonitskii, *Tragicheskaya erotika. Obrazy imperatorskoi sem'i v gody Pervoi mirovoi voiny* (Moscow: Novoe Literaturnoe Obozrenie, 2010).

[32] On the concept of internal colonization, cf. Michael Hechter, *Internal Colonialism. The Celtic Fringe in British National Development* (1975, new edition, New Brunswick: Transaction, 1999). As applied to the Russian Empire, see Alexander Etkind, Ilya Kukulin, and Dirk Uffelmann (eds.), *Tam, vnutri. Praktiki vnutrennei kolonisatsii v kul'turnoi istorii Rossii* (Moscow: NLO, 2012), and Alexander Etkind, *Internal Colonization: Russia's Imperial Experience* (Cambridge: Polity Press, 2011).

[33] Concerning the decree 13 'On Turkish Armenia', *Pravda* (29 December 1917), see Serif Mardin, 'The Ottoman Empire', in *After Empire. Multiethnic Societies and Nation-Building. The Soviet Union and the Russian, Ottoman, and Habsburg Empires*, ed. Karen Barkey and Mark von Hagen (Boulder: Westview Press, 1997), 115–128, and Michael A. Reynolds, *Shattering Empires. The Clash and Collapse of the Ottoman and Russian Empires, 1908–1918* (Cambridge: Cambridge University Press, 2011), 179.

world's subalterns would be misleading.[34] They were dismissive of the Ukrainian constitutional democrats, for instance, who were their closest rivals in imperial succession. Internally, they also unleashed a brutal civil war, now known as the Red Terror.[35] The 'Lenin' moment supported those post-imperial emancipation movements that helped secure the power of the party.[36]

Elsewhere in Europe, the most visible representatives of the old elites, that is, Europe's ruling dynasties, the officers of the imperial armies and other civil and diplomatic servants, also had to go. Most of the aristocratic families of Europe were of German background, but more recently, had closer ties to Britain. Their genealogies dated back to the Holy Roman Empire of the German Nation, dissolved by Napoleon in 1806. Three of the monarchs whose empires were involved in the First World War called Queen Victoria 'grandma', and English was spoken at home not only in the households of the British royal family but also in that of the Romanoffs and among the Baltic nobility. A popular desire to discredit these elites was the most visible effect of the war on post-war Europe. In Germany and Austria, members of the Hohenzollerns, the Wittelsbachs, and the Habsburgs, went into exile in 1918. In Austria, the Habsburgs were not only forced to abdicate but became a kind of *familia non grata*. In Britain, the ruling Saxe-Coburg Gothas had changed their name to Windsor, which was more rooted in national geography.[37] But even at a lower level of power, aristocratic families in the Baltic states and in Czechoslovakia were stigmatized and partially expropriated. For instance, family crests of the Baltic Barons were removed from Tallinn's cathedral in

---

[34] On shattered hopes in the Bolshevik party as a vanguard of emancipation, particularly as expressed among the European left in the 1920s, see especially Pyotr Kropotkin, 'The Russian Revolution and the Soviet Government. Letter to the Workers of the Western World', in *Labour Leader* (22 July 1920), reprinted in *Kropotkin's Revolutionary Pamphlets*, ed. Roger Baldwin (1927) (New York: Dover, 1970), 252–256; see also *Archiv für Sozialwissenschaft und Sozialpolitik*, 50 (1923), referring back to Robert Michels, *Zur Soziologie des Parteiwesens in der modernen Demokratie* (Leipzig: Klinkhardt, 1911). On betrayals of the party from within in the crisis of the First World War, Grigory Zinoviev, *Der Krieg und die Krise des Sozialismus* (Vienna: Verlag für Literatur und Politik, 1924).

[35] On the changing concept of terror in the course of the revolution, see Oleg Budnitsky, *Terrorizm v rossiiskom osvoboditel'nom dvizhenii* (Moscow: Rosspen, 2000).

[36] Manela, *Wilsonian Moment*.

[37] See National Archives, HO 342,469/13, Letter from Lloyd George to the Secretary of State of 29 August 1915, in 'Titles, Styles and Precedence of Members of the Royal Family: Relinquishment of German Titles in Favour of British Titles; Adoption of Surnames Mountbatten and Windsor; Principles of Entitlement to the Style "Royal Highness" and the Case of the Duke and Duchess of Windsor (1917–48)', www.heraldica.org/topics/britain/TNA/HO_144_22945.htm, accessed 5 July 2015. On the wider British context, see Alan G.V. Simmonds, *Britain and World War One* (London and New York: Routledge, 2012).

Estonia, and larger forests were nationalized in Czechoslovakia.[38] In continental Europe, the officer corps of the old imperial armies, a classic context in which the habits of the old elite were formed, were disbanded.[39]

However, at the slightly less visible lower level of their elite administration, the transformation of post-imperial central Europe was far less dramatic. Moreover, the Peace of Versailles shifted attention away from social revolutions and towards the intention to shame the German nation.[40] At Versailles, the German negotiators tried to develop a model, which the Bolsheviks had pursued in Brest-Litovsk: to dismantle their ruling dynasty and key military elites for the sake of saving the nation from the burden of defeat.[41] But the representatives of the surviving empires, Britain and France, decided to make the German nation and not the elites of the old German Empire appear as the only surviving defeated power, so that it had to pay compensation for losses and damages, focusing on recorded atrocities such as the ruthless invasion of Belgium.[42] The cost was exposing Germany as the chief culprit behind the war, which emerged as a common purpose in which the interests Bolsheviks, who were not invited to Versailles, were aligned with those of Britain, France, and the United States.[43]

---

[38] For a comprehensive account of this social history, see Lucy Elisabeth Textor, *Land Reform in Czechoslovakia* (London: G. Allen & Unwin Ltd., 1923); Eagle Glassheim, *Noble Nationalists. The Transformation of the Bohemian Aristocracy* (Cambridge, Mass.: Harvard University Press, 2005); for an overview of the aristocracy in comparative perspective prior to 1914, see Dominic Lieven, *The Aristocracy in Europe 1815–1914* (Basingstoke: Macmillan, 1992); for the later twentieth century, see Heinz Reif, *Adel im 19. und 20. Jahrhundert* (Munich: Oldenbourg, 2012); for sociological and anthropological perspectives, see Monique de Saint Martin, *L'espace de la noblesse* (Paris: Éditions Métailié, 1993); Sofia Tchouikina, *Dvorianskaia pamiat': 'byvshye' v sovetskom gorode (Leningrad, 1920e–30e gody)* (St. Petersburg: Izd-vo Evropeiskogo universiteta v StPb, 2006); Longina Jakubowska, *Patrons of History. Nobility, Capital and Political Transitions in Poland* (London: Ashgate, 2012).

[39] The best analysis is from a sociologist of the Weber circle: Franz Carl Endres, 'Soziologische Struktur und ihr entsprechende Ideologien des deutschen Offizierkorps vor dem Weltkriege', in *Archiv für Sozialwissenschaft und Sozialpolitik*, 58:1 (1927), 282–319.

[40] For a social liberal German perspective on the revolution, see Walther Rathenau, *La triple revolution*, transl. David Roget (Paris-Basel: Éditions du Rhin, 1921), esp. 332–333; for an anti-liberal global perspective, see Oswald Spengler, *Der Mensch und die Technik* (Munich: Beck, 1931).

[41] For a critical German perspective on this post-war settlement, see Maximilian Graf Montgelas, *Leitfaden zur Kriegsschuldfrage* (Berlin: De Gruyter, 1923); and *Das deutsche Weißbuch über die Schuld am Kriege mit der Denkschrift der deutschen Viererkommission zum Schuldbericht der Alliierten und Assoziierten Mächte* (Charlottenburg: Deutsche Verlagsgesellschaft für Politik und Geschichte, 1919).

[42] Cf. John N. Horne and Alan Kramer, *German Atrocities, 1914: A History of Denial* (New Haven: Yale University Press, 2001), ch. 9, 'The Moral Reckoning', 329–365; Isabel V. Hull, 'The "Belgian Atrocities" and the Laws of War on Land', in Hull, *A Scrap of Paper. Breaking and Making International Law during the Great War* (Ithaca, N.Y.: Cornell University Press, 2014), 51–95.

[43] For the best-known critique, see John Maynard Keynes, *The Economic Consequences of the Peace* (London: Macmillan, 1919).

Politics as conversion: the German elites after Versailles

By contrast to the unknown city of Brest, Versailles suffered from an excess
of symbolic significance. It was the place where the new German Empire
had been proclaimed after France's defeat by Prussia in 1871. That location
had in turn been chosen because of Versailles' historical place in French
history, as the main residence of the court of the former French monarch,
who had been deposed and later executed with his family in the course of
the French revolution of 1789–93. In 1919, it seemed appropriate for the
purposes of French and British interests to turn Versailles into the place
where the German nation, and not the German dynasties, was discredited
as the chief culprit behind the war. The result was that in most of
continental Europe, the empires saved face and avoided any radical redistribution of power, opting instead for a joint redistribution of Germany's
colonial possessions, along with those of Austria-Hungary and the
Ottomans. The surviving empires of France and Britain, and the moderate
successor regimes of imperial Germany and Austria, then embarked on
a more controlled post-imperial devolution in the rest of Europe.
In Germany, this involved even socialists like Gustav Noske in the violent
crushing of emerging riots and uprisings.

As a result, even though new, socialist governments did come to power
in Germany and in Austria-Hungary, the public dismantling of the old
elites did not proceed as ruthlessly as in Bolshevik Russia after Brest-
Litovsk. Instead, the former emperor, Wilhelm II, former officers of the
disbanded armies, and former diplomats managed to preserve and even
augment their prestige as holders of true national dignity which had been
betrayed by the rest of Europe. An influential strand of national German
history focuses on the way these dismantled elites paved the way to power
for Hitler and the Nazis.[44] But as I want to show, in transnational

---

[44] For 'special path' explanations of National Socialism in intellectual history, see Kurt Sontheimer,
Antidemokratisches Denken in der Weimarer Republik (Munich: Nymphenburger Verlagshandlung,
1962), which also contains references to significant scholarship in this direction from the 1940s, and
an earlier version in Kurt Sontheimer, 'Antidemokratisches Denken in der Weimarer Republik', in
Vierteljahrshefte für Zeitgeschichte, 5:1 (January 1957), 42–62. For the 'Weimar' context of this
argument, see Karl Mannheim, 'Das konservative Denken I. Soziologische Beiträge zum Werden
des politisch-historischen Denkens in Deutschland', in *Archiv für Sozialwissenschaft und
Sozialpolitik*, 57:1 (1927), 68–143. For statements of the 'special path' in social history, see Hans-
Ulrich Wehler, *Deutsche Gesellschaftsgeschichte*, vols. 3 and 4 (Munich: Beck, 1995, 2003), and
Norbert Elias, *Studien über die Deutschen. Machtkämpfe und Habitusentwicklung im 19. und 20.
Jh.* (Frankfurt: Suhrkamp, 1989). On reunification as return to normality, see Konrad Jarausch, *Die
Umkehr. Deutsche Wandlungen 1945–1995* (Munich: DVA, 2005). For critiques of the special path,
see David Blackbourn and Geoff Eley, *Mythen deutscher Geschichtsschreibung. Die gescheiterte
bürgerliche Revolution von 1848* (Frankfurt/Main: Ullstein, 1980). On German social and intellectual

perspective, some of these old elites also had other effects on European society and political thought, including strengthening a moderate consensus around liberal, moderately socialist, and internationalist values.

A set of two maps produced by Otto Neurath, an Austrian socialist, who briefly served as an economic advisor to the Soviet Republic of Munich, highlights the nature of the changes.

In the first map showing the year 1914, most European states, except France, Switzerland, and Portugal, are governed by monarchs. In the second map, in 1930, the landscape changed dramatically: the former exceptions became the rule. Now, Germany, a part of Finland, the Baltic states, Czechoslovakia, Ukraine, and Greece are marked with a Phrygian hat, a symbol of the Jacobin idea of national self-determination hearkening back to the French Revolution of 1789. The new exception is no longer west of the Rhine but east of the Bug: here, a hammer and sickle marked the peculiar union of workers and peasants, which distinguished it from the so-called 'bourgeois' national republics in central and western Europe.

But you can also imagine a third map in this sequence, in which the societies living under new 'Jacobin' hats nonetheless retain certain bonds which they had shared as subjects of monarchs and empires. In this book, I seek to draw attention to the role of a particular, mostly intellectual, network in fostering such bonds and crossing the boundaries between these new 'Jacobin' states.

It seems surprising at first that intellectuals of German origin would obtain such transnational visibility after the First World War, after Germany's humiliating defeat. One of the reasons, I would argue, is that some of the most passionate and prestigious defenders of imperial great games had themselves turned into cautious advocates of change. By making their conversion to a new political situation public without necessarily endorsing revolutions, they facilitated such moderate forms of conversion for others. In using the term 'moderate', I do not wish to make a normative judgement of this community; it is merely a term I use to describe the form in which they intended to transform empires into their successor states, in distinction from Bolshevik Russia.

In his famous lecture in Munich in 1919, Max Weber, recently arrived from Vienna, addressed a group of students on the subject of choosing

history in global perspective, Jürgen Osterhammel and Sebastian Conrad (eds.), *Das Kaiserreich Transnational: Deutschland in der Welt, 1871–1914* (Göttingen: Vandenhoeck & Ruprecht, 2004), 1–29. For an overview of the aftermath of the special path after German unification, see Helmut Walser Smith, 'When the Sonderweg Debate Left Us', in *German Studies Review*, 31:2 (May 2008), 225–240.

Introduction

Regierungsformen in Europa

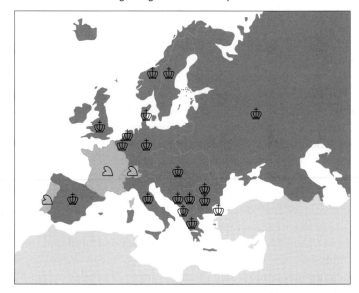

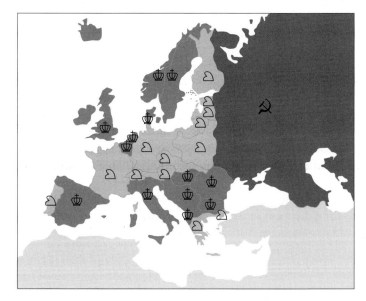

Krone auf Blau: Monarchien
Jakobinermützr auf Braun: Bürgerliche Republiken
Sichel und Hammer auf Rot: U.d.S.S.R.

Angefertigt für das Bibliographische Institut AG., Leipzig
Gesellschafts und Wirtschaftsmuseum in Wien   ©

Figure 1 Map after Otto von Neurath, *Gesellschaft und Wirtschaft* (Leipzig:
Bibliografisches Institut, 1931)

politics as their vocation.[45] Germany was discredited, and with it, his entire career, which he had devoted to building a Great German Nation. He had voiced this vision in his inaugural lecture on Political Economy in 1895. During the war, Weber moved away from the national liberal towards a more conservative and even colonialist position. Controversially, he joined the chauvinistic Pan-German League during the war to declare his commitment to German interests in world politics. Like many Europeans, and especially Germans, after the First World War, he reconsidered the foundations for his beliefs. He was no longer a theorist of a national political economy but, in a sense, an imperial thinker without an empire.[46] He even lectured on socialism to officers of the former Austrian imperial army. The entire intellectual community of which he formed a part devoted its attention to rethinking the consequences of imperial decline particularly for the cultural and political elites. This made eminent sense in a society without leadership, in a volatile, revolutionary Munich, where some of Weber's closest friends were socialists and in prison.

Alongside Joseph Schumpeter's comparative work on empires, Weber's *Politics as a Vocation* provided a theory of reconstructing government and reinventing legitimacy in the absence of power. In the long evolution of European thought about the state, this text provides a conclusive arc to the story of transformation by which the early modern mirrors for princes facilitate the emergence of the modern state. As empires had collapsed, the *imperium* of the state risked following suit. Weber's historical reconstruction of the Italian city states provided a recipe for *mantenere lo stato*.[47] This marked the moment which Quentin Skinner, speaking about Britain in the late 1950s, once described as 'that final gasp of empire'.[48]

Weber's solution was to forge a new elite from history, to give society a kind of collective biography according to which it would not depend on

---

[45] Max Weber, *Politik als Beruf*, Series Geistige *Arbeit als Beruf. Vier Vorträge vor dem Freistudentischen Bund. Zweiter Vortrag* (Munich: Duncker & Humblot, 1919). Hereafter cited as Max Weber, ,Politik als Beruf', from MWG I:17, 157–255.

[46] For a classic expression of this view, see Max Weber's inaugural lecture, *Der Nationalstaat und die Volkswirtschaftspolitik* (Freiburg: Mohr, 1895). On the relationship between economic and political theory, see also Max Weber, 'Die "Objektivität" sozialwissenschaftlicher und sozialpolitischer Erkenntnis', *Archiv für Sozialwissenschaft und Sozialpolitik*, 19 (1904), 22–88.

[47] For a historical reconstruction of this genealogy, see Quentin Skinner, *The Foundations of Modern Political Thought*, vol. 2, The Age of Reformation (Cambridge: Cambridge University Press, 1978), 352. See also 'From the State of Princes to the Person of the State', in Skinner (ed.), *The Foundations of Modern Political Thought*, 368–414.

[48] Quentin Skinner, 'The Art of Theory', conversation with Teresa Bejan (2013), in www.artoftheory .com/quentin-skinner-on-meaning-and-method/, accessed 4 March 2015.

the continuity of states and empires.[49] Weber, after 1918, was 'fabricating ideals on earth', to use Nietzsche's phrase, and did so by means of creative genealogy.[50] He was creating a new moral code by rewriting a genealogy of political morality. Weber's sources for comparative studies of empires were themselves imperial, but with an interest in perspectives from the periphery of empires: he compared the Prussian periphery of Ostelbia with Ireland, Bengal, and Poland, and looked at the transformation of aristocratic elites in all these different societies in comparison.[51] Seen in global perspective, the nobility was to him not only a reactionary class, as he had previously thought, but a 'politically recyclable social stratum' in the present.[52] The criteria he drew upon creatively combined traditional aspects of aristocratic habitus and the mentality associated with a Protestant ethic of work and commitment: the need for a certain code of honour, known as 'noblesse oblige', that would be independent from the prevailing ideologies of the day;[53] the preference of a life *for* politics over a life *off* politics; a special form of rule as 'territorial power' maintained through the division of spheres of right; and the feeling of noble detachment or *contenance*, which Nietzsche had praised as the 'pathos of distance', typical for aristocratic character.[54] He criticized the attempt some journalists made to place themselves seemingly above and outside societies, like 'pariahs'. Instead, Weber argued, engaged journalists should become more like Brahmins.[55] His 'analytical world history' was thus deeply implicated in post-war German politics.[56] By speaking of revolutions often in the plural, and distancing himself from them through inverted commas, he sought to ridicule the attempt at revolution which at this time was being undertaken

---

[49] For a more recent example of this approach, see Michel Foucault, « *Il faut défendre la société* », *Cours au collège de France (1975–1976)* (Paris: Gallimard, 1997).

[50] Friedrich Nietzsche, *On the Genealogy of Morality* (1887), ed. Keith Ansell-Pearson (Cambridge: Cambridge University Press, 2001), Essay 1.

[51] One of his key sources is Sir Henry Sumner Maine, *Lectures in the Early History of Institutions* (London: John Murray, 1905), dealing with Irish law, clan law, and spaces of law beyond Roman law.

[52] Weber, 'Politik als Beruf', 183.

[53] Cf. Eckart Conze, 'Noblesse oblige', in Conze, *Kleines Lexikon des Adels. Titel, Throne, Traditionen* (Munich: Beck, 2005), 88. See also A. Graf Spee, 'Adel verpflichtet (betr. Aufgaben des Adels in 1920)', in *Deutsches Adelsblatt*, xxxviii (1920), 115.

[54] Weber, 'Politik als Beruf', 227; see also Max Weber, *Wahlrecht und Demokratie in Deutschland* (Berlin: Fortschritt, 1918), in MWG I/15, 344–396, 374. On aristocratic honour codes and duels, see Hans Hattenhauer (ed.), *Allgemeines Landrecht für die Preußischen Staaten von 1794*, 3rd ed. (Munich: Luchterhand, 1996), XX, § 678–690. See also entires on 'Adelsrecht', 'Duell', 'Ehre', in Conze, op cit.

[55] Weber, 'Politik als Beruf', 242.

[56] This phrase is used in David D' Avray, *Rationalities in History. A Weberian Essay in Comparison* (Cambridge: Cambridge University Press, 2010), 5.

by Kurt Eisner and his followers.[57] He was also involved in it as the member of a delegation of German professors sent to Versailles to negotiate the consequences of German war crimes for notions of guilt and debt, and he co-founded the German Democratic party, a pro-republican liberal party which was only successful in the first years of the Weimar state.

The ideal type of a charismatic leader which Weber and his circle conjured up was to be a nobleman-cum-politician, a Brahmin-cum-pariah.[58] But Weber was adamant that in doing so he wanted neither to refurbish the old nobility nor to extend aristocratic status to the 'industrial barons' and bankers who became rich in the war. Instead, he demanded to ennoble the Europeans culturally through a theory of 'charismatic education'.[59] Charisma is not only rational but constituted by emotional regimes. It also partly overshadows its own subjects.[60] It can be depersonalized through blood ties but also by property relations such as primogeniture. Charismatic personalities through inspiration and empathy can change established social norms.[61] Similarly to Weber, Schumpeter believed that the core 'unit' of conversion and adaptation was the family. He called for a 'patrimonialization of elites', that is, the appropriation of old Europe by its purported modernizers. The former elites of Europe's empires continued to influence the nature of power, prestige, economic profits, as well as the cultural identity of post-imperial societies.

The history of aristocratic status in Europe served as a useful model for calibrating cultural identities in the age of conflicting national demands for self-determination. Already before the war, Georg Simmel had emphasized the ability of nobles to 'get to know each other better on one evening than regular citizens in a month', while remaining detached from the vernacular cultures of their nation. 'In England the Fitzgeralds and the Dukes of Leicester are from Florence, the Dukes of Portland from Holland, in France the Broglie are from Piedmont, the Dukes des Cars from Perugia, the Lynar from Faenza, in Poland the Poniatowski are from Bologna, in Italy the Rocca are from Croatia, the Ruspoli from Scotland, the Torlonia from France, etc.'[62] In different historical moments, such as during the French Revolution, nobles therefore could form a sort of aristocratic international or

[57] Weber, 'Politik als Beruf', 174.   [58] Ibid., 66–74.

[59] Max Weber, *Economy and Society*, ed. Guenther Roth and Klaus Wittich, vol. 2 (Berkeley, Calif.: University of California Press, 1978), 1143. On male fraternities and warrior clans, 1144.

[60] Ibid., 1135.   [61] Ibid., vol. 1 321.

[62] Georg Simmel, 'Zur Soziologie des Adels. Fragment aus einer Formenlehre der Gesellschaft', in *Frankfurter Zeitung und Handelsblatt* (Neue Frankfurter Zeitung), 52:358, 1, Morgenblatt, 27 December 1907, Feuilleton-Teil, 1–3, http://socio.ch/sim/verschiedenes/1907/adel.htm, accessed 25 March 2012.

'chain', a negative safety network. Conjuring up this past helped some intellectuals to transcend Germany's isolation after Versailles.

As Simmel himself was well aware, it was constitutive of aristocratic identity to form social networks and be part of familial associations that transcended national borders – aristocrats were 'superior' everywhere because everywhere they were thought of as being of different blood and cultural constitution than the majority of the population.[63] But this was before the war; like many others in his generation, during the war, Simmel now expected full commitment to the German cause in the same way in which the German princes in the age of Napoleon had formed an 'aristocratic chain' of German nobility seeking to defend their lands from the French invasion.[64]

Max Weber was a central figure at wartime gatherings of intellectuals in Castle Lauenstein, where he spoke about the 'Personality and the Orders of Life' and about the 'aristocracy of the mind' as concepts which would convert old into new elites.[65] The aim of such gatherings was to rethink the future of Germany from a post-war perspective even as the war was still going on, and to provide a new sense of community among intellectuals who believed themselves to have been wronged by international anti-German propaganda. A medieval castle, which had been restored in the historicist fashion in the late nineteenth century, furnished the setting for esoteric mystery plays in which all delegates were invited; the Holy Roman Empire was, in a sense, in the air. One of the themes of the 1918 conference was 'The Problem of Leaders [das Führerproblem] in the State And In Culture'. It was in these contexts that a new idea of aristocratic leadership was being developed, one that drew from examples of historical nobilities but disassociated the idea of aristocratic virtues from people with an aristocratic background.

Ideas about the future of elites in post-imperial Europe were also produced in Italy and in Switzerland during this time. Vilfredo Pareto, a proponent of moderate and liberal governments, saw the elite as a 'class of people who have the highest indices in their field of activity'.[66] By this token, elites prevailed in old regimes and in revolutionary societies

---

[63] Simmel, 'Zur Soziologie des Adels. Fragment aus einer Formenlehre der Gesellschaft', 1, Morgenblat, 27 December 1907, Feuilleton-Teil, 1–3.

[64] *Das deutsche Weissbuch über die Schuld am Kriege mit der Denkschrift der deutschen Viererkommission zum Schuldbericht der Alliierten und Assoziierten Mächte*, ed. Auswärtiges Amt [German Foreign Office] (Charlottenburg: Deutsche Verlagsgesellschaft für Politik und Geschichte, m.b.H., 1919).

[65] Marianne Weber, *Max Weber*, 611. Max Weber, 'Vorträge während der Lauensteiner Kulturtagungen 30. Mai und 29. Oktober 1917', in MWG I/15, 701–707.

[66] Vilfredo Pareto, *The Mind and Society*, transl. Arthur Livingston, 4 vols., vol. 3 (New York: Harcourt, Brace & Co., 1935), 1423.

alike.[67] Some revolutions involved constitutional change without radical distribution of resources, in a kind of 'revolving door' model of elite circulation. In other post-imperial societies, the elites had changed in a more vertical and radical fashion. But in all of them, the idea of the 'old elites' that were to be discarded in favour of new political communities was central, and they regarded themselves as a part of that configuration.

In this sense, Pareto's much-cited proclamation of 'history as the graveyard of aristocracies' and Robert Michels's contemporaneous 'iron law of oligarchy' were not just analytic statements, but performative interventions in an uncertain economy of values. According to both, progress depended on the permeability of classes and parties, and it could become stale when one's class position had become second skin, a type of cultural identity.[68]

A sympathetic but cautious observer of revolutions, the socialist Antonio Gramsci concluded that a 'new order' had been born. Its longevity would depend on the way in which the relationship between power and persuasion would be reconfigured. While the events in Russia showed clearly how power could be transferred by means of violence, he believed that the success of the revolution ultimately depended on the ability of intellectuals to persuade populations of a new ethics and the principles of a new, post-imperial world order.[69] Part of this process was persuading the old elites that the old rules of empire no longer applied.

One element of elite conversion involved the problem of recognition between the old elites and their challengers. Looking back at this period, the author of the Austrian constitution of 1919, Hans Kelsen, remarked that in addition to the classical theory of international relations, which knows recognition only among established states and their representatives, 'insurgents' with effective powers of governments, now had to be taken into account.[70] The problem of recognition also concerned

---

[67] Vilfredo Pareto, *Trattato Di Sociologia Generale*, 4 vols. (Florence: G. Barbera, 1916).

[68] Vilfredo Pareto, *The Mind and Society* (1916), transl. Arthur Livingston, vol. 3 (New York: Harcourt, Brace & Company, 1935), 1430; Robert Michels, *Political Parties. A Sociological Study of the Oligarchical Tendencies of Modern Democracy* (1911; New York: Hearst's International Library, 1915), 377–393. On class as second skin rather than position, see Gareth Stedman Jones's *Languages of Class: Studies in English Working Class History, 1832–1982* (Cambridge: Cambridge University Press, 1983).

[69] Cf. Antonio Gramsci (ed.), *L'Ordine Nuovo* (1919–22). On hegemony and the intellectuals, see Antonio Gramsci, 'The Formation of the Intellectuals', in Gramsci, *Selections from the Prison Notebooks*, Quintin Hoare and Jeffrey Nowell Smith (eds.) (New York: International Publishers, 2010), 5–17.

[70] Hans Kelsen, 'Recognition in International Law: Theoretical Observations', in *The American Journal of International Law*, 35:4 (October 1941), 605–617.

personal relationships among diplomats. Thus for instance, during the negotiations in Brest-Litovsk, the diplomats of the old empires lived in the immediate vicinity of each other for four months. But this close proximity made their heterogeneity apparent. In their conversations with the press and in memoirs which were soon published, for instance, they also tried to discredit each other in what could be called utterances of 'derecognition'.[71] British observers of the negotiations judged the representatives of the old empires very differently from those of their successor states. They held the aristocratic elites of the former empires, their chief enemies, in high esteem; by contrast, they had only contempt for the leading members of the Russian delegation, and described the Ukrainian representatives as youthful 'canaries' whose only function was to be entertained by the grown cats.

The Bolsheviks, on the contrary, not only discredited the old governments but also absorbed the ideas of their old critics. Thus in abolishing religion and private property, and in promoting national self-determination, the Bolsheviks assumed – and thus, declared – the existence of liberal values such as religious toleration that no previous Russian government had actually announced.

The process of calibrating levels of recognition among old and new elites took place in uncharted legal territory. Normally, only established states that mutually recognized each other could enter into negotiations with their respective representatives. Here, not all parties, which had effective control over territories, were actually representing internationally recognized states.

---

[71] In German, English, and American historiography, the social psychology of revolution on the left and the right has typically focused on the non-elite agents of revolutions. See the classic anti-liberal and anti-democratic view by Gustave Le Bon, *The Psychology of Revolution* (1911), Engl. transl. Bernard Miall (London: Allen & Unwin, 1913); Alexandre Kojève, *Introduction to the Reading of Hegel. Lectures on the Phenomenology of Spirit* (1947; New York: Basic Books, 1980); in the later twentieth century, structuralist theories of revolution moved away from psychological perspectives altogether, but continued to foreground patterns which enable revolutionaries to act. See, for instance, Skocpol, *States and Social Revolutions. A Comparative Analysis of France, Russia and China*. After this, theories of recognition replaced theories of revolution, but again focused on the recognition of formerly not recognized subjects, rather than what happened to the newly derecognized elites. Cf. Charles Taylor, 'The Politics of Recognition', in Taylor, *Multiculturalism: Examining the Politics of Recognition*, ed. Amy Gutmann (Princeton: Princeton University Press, 1994), or Nancy Fraser and Axel Honneth, *Redistribution or Recognition? A Political-Philosophical Exchange* (London: Verso, 2003).

Post-imperial phantom pain and its writers

In the aftermath of the revolution in Russia and the shaming of Germany at Versailles, many representatives of the German-speaking elites considered themselves to be connected to the political and cultural economy of more than one empire with their educational and professional background. After imperial decline, the choices they faced ranged from adaptation to the new national discourses of the post-imperial successor states, to nostalgia for past empires, or advocacy for a new kind of internationalism.

By the mid-1920s, aristocratic intellectuals of Germanic origin became recognizable as a new type of international celebrity. Their pre-eminence was rooted in the empires of Germany, Russia, and Austria-Hungary. They were considered odd but they were still sought after as public speakers. One of the most distinctive voices was the Habsburg count Richard Coudenhove-Kalergi. According to theorists of revolution, people like him should have been relegated to the dustbin of history, like the empire he had come from. Yet instead, Coudenhove became something of an international celebrity in mid-twentieth-century Europe.[72] In 1923, he popularized the idea of a Pan-European Union, which became widely associated with him in subsequent years, not just in German-speaking communities but also in international circles. Coudenhove argued that the world had to cease thinking in nations and to begin thinking in continents before a world federation of states would eventually be possible in the utopian future. In doing so, Pan-Europe would have to struggle side by side with the Soviet Empire, the British Commonwealth, and with Pan-America. He imagined that Pan-Europe would include the French and formerly German colonies of Africa and Asia, along with French Guyane, as territories to be held in common by the European nations.

Coudenhove has often been presented as a singular presence in post-imperial Europe. There was indeed something slightly exotic about his appearance to most Europeans, since he had a Japanese mother, which was quite unusual at the time, particularly in the relatively closed world of the Austrian aristocracy. But more important than this circumstance of his personal biography was the fact that he belonged to a larger network of continental Europeans, a voice from Europe's past whose judgement was sought by a surprising range of contemporaries. John Hobson, the old British critic of empire, wrote a sympathetic review of Coudenhove's book

---

[72] First formulated in 1922, it reached a wider English-speaking audience in the 1930s. See Richard Coudenhove-Kalergi, 'The Pan-European Outlook', in *International Affairs (Royal Institute of International Affairs 1931–1939)*, 10:5 (September 1931), 638–651.

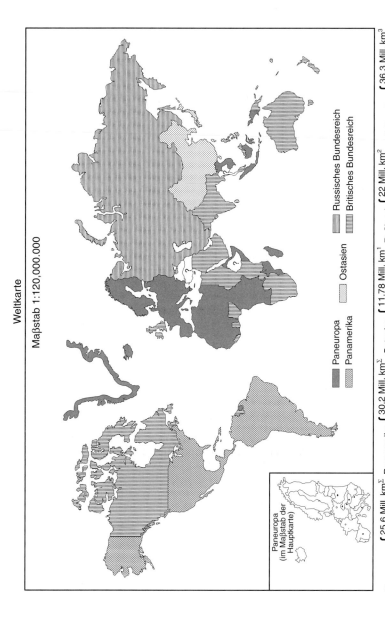

Weltkarte

Maßstab 1:120,000,000

Paneuropa
(im Maßstab der
Hauptkarte)

Paneuropa ☐ Russisches Bundesreich

Panamerika ☐ Britisches Bundesreich

Ostasien ☐

Paneuropa { 25.6 Mill. km^Σ 431 Mill. Einw Panamerika { 30.2 Mill. km^Σ 202 Mill. Einw Ostasien { 11.78 Mill. km[1] 408 Mill. Einw Rußland { 22 Mill. km[2] 145 Mill. Einw Britannien { 36.3 Mill. km[3] 445 Mill. Einw

Figure 2 Map of Paneuropa, designed according to plans by Count Coudenhove-Kalergi, in *Paneuropa*, 1 (1923)

for *The Manchester Guardian*, and Coudenhove had equal appeal among British conservatives, among Indian delegates to the League of Nations, and leading French socialists of his generation, like Aristide Briand.[73]

He saw it as his calling to start thinking globally and draw lessons from the collapse of Europe's empires on a universal scale. Against the backdrop of the discourse on self-determination, he made his own self the subject of his interventions, constructed less in terms of character and more in terms of its ties to the Byzantine and Holy Roman empires, as well as those of Russia and Austria-Hungary. His public persona seemed to give the new Europeans, which were not quite the Jacobins of the twentieth century, a sense of orientation.

Aristocratic intellectuals were, a recent historian of the Russian nobility-in-exile argued, the 'Former People' of Europe.[74] In fact, the category of 'former people' applies to the majority of twentieth-century Europeans. What distinguished the 'aristocratic authors' was their capacity to give this 'former' status a veneer of distinction.[75] The aristocratic intellectuals provided them with a biographical path through ideological contradictions and gave a personal face to elusive abstractions like 'Europe'. As Chapter 1 shows, even aristocrats whose families were less well known than the Habsburgs obtained a special charisma of decline between the wars, which had a cultural value of its own. The German officer class was another visible group among the former imperial subjects who remained connected transnationally. Some intellectuals who were former officers became mediators of a cosmopolitan memory of war, as the second chapter discusses.

Intellectuals belonging to the former diplomatic, military, cultural, and political elites of the Russian and German empires became important mediators for cosmopolitan cultural communities, maintaining prestige by virtue of their detachment from nations, as Chapters 3–5 demonstrate.

The Austrian journalist Karl Kraus had first identified a new social type among this group which he called the 'aristocratic writers'.[76] They were in a sense the opposite of Voltaire: not intellectuals ennobled by their writing but authors whose authority came from their nobility. The particular

[73] J.A. Hobson, review of Count R.N. Coudenhove-Kalergi, *Man and the State*, *Manchester Guardian*, 20 December 1938, 7.

[74] Douglas Smith, *Former People: The Last Days of the Russian Aristocracy* (New York: Macmillan, 2012).

[75] For a clearer understanding of the 'former people', see Sofia Tchouikina, *Dvorianskaia pamiat': 'byvshye' v sovetskom gorode (Leningrad, 1920e – 30e gody)* (St. Petersburg: Izd-vo Evropeiskogo universiteta v StPb, 2006). For social status and the construction of social reality, see John R. Searle, *The Construction of Social Reality* (New York: The Free Press, 1995), and Charles Taylor, *The Sources of the Self* (Cambridge, Mass: Harvard University Press, 1989).

[76] Karl Kraus, 'Der Adel von seiner schriftstellerischen Seite', in *Die Fackel*, XXVII (1925), 137.

charisma of the intellectuals of old nobility came from the context of imperial decline and revolution in which they lived. This gave their personal reflections on family history and autobiographic perspectives on European history, which populated newspapers, journals, and memoirs in the interwar period, more appeal. Many among them were of German descent, which did not necessarily mean that they were German or Austrian subjects: a large number included former Russian subjects like the Baltic Barons, a group to which Taube belonged.

As authors, the aristocratic writers of German background exercised a particular form of dilettantism that had been typical of nobility for a long time, but appeared in a new light in post-war Europe.[77] In the aftermath of the First World War, this dilettantism not only obtained much wider appeal among readers but also a new philosophical justfica-tion. Between the 1900s and the early 1920s, a strand of philosophy now known as 'vitalism', or the philosophy of life, an early form of existential-ism, had become fashionable in Europe. Its chief characteristics were a critical stance towards classical European philosophy and its systems, and towards traditional academic discourse more generally. Instead, phi-losophy was to become more personal, closer to the senses of life itself. In France and Germany especially, authors such as Henri Bergson and Georg Simmel focused on such ideas as the perception of time and the sense of self. Against this light, some aristocratic writers specialized in being aristocratic.

In the ideological formation of fascism and National Socialism, transna-tional elite communities played an ambivalent role. They were facilitators of these new ideological movements in their earlier phases, as Chapter 6 shows. But as discussed in Chapter 7, they were equally important for the cultural formation of dissident communities whose transnational ethos had formed from sympathy with causes such as the critique of the Versailles peace treaty, the republicanism of the Spanish Civil War, or international anti-fascism. The task of this book is not to evaluate the relative complicity of the old elites in revolutions or reaction. Rather, the transnational perspective served as a tool for elucidating the degree to which post-imperial transformation as

---

[77] On dilettantism, see Pierre Bourdieu, *Les règles de l'art. Genèse et structure du champ littéraire* (Paris: Seuil, 1998); With regard to the literature of the 1920s, see Boris Maslov, 'Tradicii literaturnogo diletantisma i esteticheskaia ideologia romana "Dar"', in Yuri Levin and Evgeny Soshkin (eds.), *Imperia N. Nabokov I naslredniki* (Moscow: Novoe literaturnoe obozrenie, 2006), 37–73. See also H. Rudolf Vaget, 'Der Dilettant: eine Skizze der Wort- und Begriffsgeschichte', in *Jahrbuch der deutschen Schillergesellschaft*, 14 (1970), 131–158, and Benno von Wiese, 'Goethes und Schillers Schemata über den Dilettantismus', in von Wiese, *Von Lessing bis Grabbe: Studien zur deutschen Klassik und Romantik* (Düsseldorf: Babel, 1968), 58–107.

a process crossed established political as well as geographic frontiers. The ideas and emotions of these Europeans belong to the cultural prehistory of European integration as it began with the Rome agreements of 1957.[78]

Towards a transnational and synaesthetic archive

My approach to the study of the survival of imperial and inter-imperial memory in post-imperial Europe was transnational in scope, which also meant that I sought to give equal weighting to diplomatic and government archives as I did to private archives and the archives of organizations such as the publishing houses. It was characteristic of imperial archives and their national successors alike to be extremely shrewd about controlling their own memory. The way to read against their archives is to look at archives gone out of control, in a sense: personal archives which contradict the logic of national and imperial borders, just as particular lives rarely coincide with state borders for instance. Fragments of multiple imperial and national archives have found their way by accident or by design to such places of purchased memories as the archives of the Hoover Institution and some American university libraries, or the archives which the Nazi government confiscated across Europe, which were subsequently confiscated by the Soviet army and are now housed in Moscow's special collections. In addition, the living memory of people today, accessible through recorded conversations and by email, is another source of knowledge about the past. This archive contains a multidirectional memory in which multiple empires blend into one concoction.

European political thought of this period was a product not only of rival political languages and philosophies but also of spontaneous speech and unfinished processes of thinking. It was also visibly synaesthetic, considering that thinking about post-imperial transformation happened in the age of new media such as radio and later film, as well as the illustrated press. These were not just new modes of reproducing and sharing

---

[78] For a genealogy of ideas about Europe, see Anthony Pagden (ed.), *The Idea of Europe: from Antiquity to the European Union* (Washington, D.C.: Woodrow Wilson Center and New York: Cambridge University Press, 2002). For an institutional history of European integration policy, see Wolfram Kaiser and Jan-Henrik Meyer, *Societal Actors in European Integration: Polity-Building and Policy-Making 1958–1992* (London: Palgrave Macmillan, 2013). On the intellectual history of European reconciliation in transnational context, see especially Vanessa Conze, *Das Europa der Deutschen. Ideen von Europa in Deutschland zwischen Reichstradition und Westorientierung (1920–1970)* (Oldenbourg: Institut für Zeitgeschichte, 2005); Guido Müller, *Europäische Gesellschaftsbeziehungen nach dem Ersten Weltkrieg das Deutsch-Französische Studienkomitee und der Europäische Kulturbund* (Munich: Oldenbourg, 2005); Mark Hewitson and Matthew D' Auria (eds.), *Europe in Crisis. Intellectuals and the European Idea, 1917–1957* (Oxford: Berghahn, 2012); Wolfram Kaiser, *Christian Democracy and the Origins of European Union* (Cambridge: Cambridge University Press, 2007).

information but also media for sharing emotions and common sensibilities. By the late 1920s, recorded sound and visual flashbacks of a reimagined historical past formed an irreducible part of not only present discourse but also ongoing political conflicts.

My interest in focusing on medium-sized periodicals was to capture the difference between the expression of uncertainty towards the viability of revolutions and the inability to express certain judgements about a political situation.[79] The intellecuals in the network whose importance I highlight were critical of empires and uncertain of revolutions, but there was no ambiguity in their judgement of politics or aesthetics. Politically eclectic, the periodicals to which they contributed created a kind of musée imaginaire of imperial memories in which one common theme prevailed: the idea that empires had offered them a multicultural way of life, which they were sorry to lose.[80] Here, emotions were shared and allowed readers and subscribers to form connections that only partially overlapped with ideologies.[81] These Europeanist journals reinterpreted the old German dichotomy of *Kultur* versus *Zivilisation* by reapplying it to Europe and its 'others'.[82] Journals of this kind are the closest non-oral medium which allows us to capture the importance of thinking in groups, and the fact that some ideas cannot be reduced to the work of individual authors.[83]

The contributions of the German-speaking elites of Europe provide the theoretical response to the works of fiction written in Europe, in which disorientation itself is the main theme. In these witness accounts and works of fiction, a clear hero is absent, traditional forms and scales of representation were replaced with new forms of representing sound and vision. They spoke of a 'dusk of humanity', of a 'decline of the West', and a European

---

[79] On affective contagion and trauma, see Jill Bennett, *Empathic Vision: Affect, Trauma, and Contemporary Art* (Palo Alto, Calif.: Stanford University Press, 2005). On the anthropology of memory and its transmission, see Paul Connerton, *How Societies Remember* (Cambridge: Cambridge University Press, 1989); Jan Assmann, *Religion and Cultural Memory: Ten Essays* (Stanford, Calif.: Stanford University Press, 2006); Marianne Hirsch, *Family Frames: Photography, Narrative, and Postmemory* (Cambridge, Mass.: Harvard University Press, 1997).

[80] See Maurice Halbwachs, *On Collective Memory*, transl. Lewis Coser (1925; Chicago: University of Chicago Press, 1992); on emotions and the affective turn, see Patricia Ticineto Clough and Jean Galley (eds.), *The Affective Turn* (Durham: Duke University Press, 2007); on the influence of neuropsychology and the isolated subject, see Jan Plamper, *Geschichte und Gefühl. Grundlagen der Emotionsgeschichte* (München: Siedler, 2012).

[81] On links between emotions and ideology, see, Michael Freeden, 'Emotions, Ideology and Politics', in *Journal of Political Ideologies*, 18:1 (2013), 1–10.

[82] On this subject, see Norbert Elias, *The Civilizing Process* (Oxford: Blackwell, 1994) (originally Basel: Haus zum Falken, 1939).

[83] Matthew Arnold, *Culture and Anarchy: An Essay in Political and Social Criticism* (London: Smith, Elder, and Co., 1896).

wasteland.[84] The newly found charisma of decline exhibited by the German intellectuals provided a kind of political facework in the age of imperial effacement.[85]

The book is organized around the moments and events, which are significant for the discursive sphere of these intellectual communities. These are determined by key moments of historical or remembered experience, when the European empires were under threat, and in which representatives of Germanic dynasties or German imperial elites emerge as central figures of decline. They do not necessarily correspond to a more familiar narrative of twentieth-century European history in this period. The first event is 1867, the year when the Habsburg 'puppet' emperor Maximilian loses his life to Mexican republicans. At the same time, in Europe, Austria concedes to a share of power with the Kingdom of Hungary, changing the constitution of rule in the Habsburg Empire into a Dual Monarchy. For the intellectuals discussed here, such events were remembered as part of their personal intellectual formation. Other post-imperial moments include the memory of public events such as the assassination of Franz Ferdinand, but also more personal experiences of revolution around the years 1917–20, when the Russian and German empires disintegrated. The analysis concludes with the immediate aftermath of the Second World War, when Anglo-American intellectuals and public figures propose a framework for reconstructing the idea of Europe in the wake of Germany's defeat. The book invites a new perspective on Europe in the period between 1917 and the history of Europe's institutional and economic integration associated with the Treaty of Rome of 1957. During this time, a German-speaking liberal fraction wove their experience of revolution into a common European memory of empire. In what follows, I hope to show what was characteristic of their mentality, how this network was formed, and the many individuals and groups belonging to this circle who were subsequently forgotten.

---

[84] I am thinking particularly of the poetry of the German expressionists like Kurt Pinthus (ed.), *Menschheitsdämmerung* (Berlin: Rowohlt, 1919), or T.S. Eliot, *The Waste Land* (London: Hogarth Press, 1923).

[85] Cf. Erving Goffman, 'On Face-Work', from Goffman, *Interaction and Ritual* (New York: Doubleday, 1967), 5–45; see also Peter Berger and Thomas Luckmann, *The Social Construction of Reality* (Garden City, N.Y.: Doubleday, 1966).

PART I

Precarious elites

How did contemporaries experience and explain imperial decline in continental Europe? Perhaps the most famous image of imperial decline in the twentieth century is the photograph of Franz Ferdinand shot on the last day of his life in Sarajevo. The Habsburg family did not just represent its empire but embodied it. This explains the particular shock caused by the death of Franz Ferdinand not only to Europeans but to a global readership of world news. A photograph shot just minutes before the assassination – such an utterance poignantly expresses the tint of celebrity surrounding this particular death.

The first chapter places the effect of his death in the context of a longer affective genealogy of dynastic decline. In the last decades of Habsburg rule, members of the Habsburg family, like those of other dynasties such as the Romanoffs, were plagued by fears of assassination. We can grasp imperial decline both from a first-person perspective of its rulers, and indirectly, by observing the changing function of dynastic families in the period of declining empires. From the intellectual formation of the last ruling Habsburgs in the climate of cultural globalization, we get to the odd wartime ethnography of aristocratic officers serving Germany and Austria in the First World War. In the same generation, they went from a sentimental education in the grand tours of the Belle Epoque to a very different kind of mobility. Their deployment as officers in the First World War gave them techniques and technologies of detachment from the theatre of war. Looking at imperial transformation through the eyes of the dynastic and military elites exposes the connections between imperial societies both during and after imperial decline. Whether empires ended gradually or abruptly, by way of partial devolution and decolonization, like Britain, or revolution, like Russia, they did not collapse independently from each other. The old imperial elites were mutually connected and remained so after the demise of their former rulers.

Figure 3 'Anniversary of the War's Origin', *New York Times*, 27 June 1915

CHAPTER I

Famous deaths
Subjects of imperial decline

On a December day in 1892, in Trieste, a young Habsburg Archduke boarded the steamer *Empress Elizabeth* to embark on a Grand Tour around the world. The Archduke originally planned to travel incognito, but throughout his journey, he was received and entertained by members of the highest nobility.[1] He was accompanied by three servants, two cooks, a gamekeeper, the adjunct custodian of the Austro-Hungarian imperial Hofmuseum for Natural History, and a taxidermist, who was also a photographer. The group included two consuls of the Austro-Hungarian Empire, and four military officers of the imperial Ulan Guards. One of the officers was the descendant of an old dynasty of Crusaders, and others belonged to the innermost circle of the Habsburg emperor.[2] It was impossible for the Archduke to hide his high standing with such an entourage.

Yet in some sense, in 1892, he was indeed unknown to the world. Few outside of Austria-Hungary, Germany, and the higher European aristocracy would have actually recognized him by first name. His trip around the world, for all its excesses in luxury, was typical of someone of his standing, as were many of his other activities. Before assuming the title of Archduke, the prince had been mostly interested in hunting exotic animals. He had purchased a hunting estate from a financially troubled Bohemian nobleman, Prince Lobkowicz. Here, at Konopischt, he displayed the spoils of his exploits shooting Bohemian deer to a select number of guests.[3]

---

[1] Franz Ferdinand, *Tagebuch meiner Reise um die Erde*, 2 vols., vol. 1, 1892–93 (Vienna: Hölder, 1895), 20.

[2] Regina Höfer (ed.), *Imperial Sightseeing. Die Indienreise von Erzherzog von Franz Ferdinand von Österreich-Este* (Vienna: Museum für Völkerkunde, 2010), 82–84.

[3] Wladimir Aichelburg, *Der Thronfolger und die Architektur* (Vienna: Neuer Wissenschaftlicher Verlag, 2003), 23.

His Grand Tour was organized using the same boat that had already taken one of his predecessors, Maximilian, on trips to Brazil.[4] By the middle of the nineteenth century, the educational tour around the globe had become one of the core experiences that prepared aspiring rulers for political power on an increasingly global scale. Between 1880 and 1912, several incumbents to the throne of the Romanoff, Wittelsbach, Hohenzollern, Saxe-Coburg Gotha, and Habsburg families all went on trips around the world. Even the route that Franz Ferdinand's group had taken was mainstream: they passed from the Mediterranean to Port Said in Egypt to India, from there to Singapore and Australia, then to Japan, North America, and finally, having crossed the United States, back to Vienna.

Global personal renown only reached the Archduke on the day of his death by assassination on 28 June 1914. As Emil Ludwig, one of his generation's most celebrated political biographers, put it, the assassin, 'under the doubly symbolic name of Gabriel Princip' had let loose a 'world-cataclysm' for all of Europe's remaining emperors.[5] The assassination signalled a famous chain of events that eventually put an end to four European empires. The shots resonated in European cultural memory decades after they were no longer heard in the streets of Sarajevo. The symbolic construction of this event was a major collective accomplishment of Europe's journalists and historians. Photographs of Franz Ferdinand, originally intended for celebratory purposes, marking the Archduke's state visit to one of his future domains, obtained documentary value because they were billed as having been taken 'just minutes before he was assassinated'.

There is hardly a political leader in European history whose assassination was as constitutive of his fame, in proportion to his lifetime identity and achievements, as Franz Ferdinand. This culturally constructed echo reached as far back in time as the French Revolution, when Empress Marie Antoinette had been executed, and as far away geographically as the remote Mexican city of Querétaro, the place where another Habsburg Archduke, Mexican emperor Maximilian, had been executed in 1867.[6]

---

[4] Georg Schreiber, *Habsburger auf Reisen* (Vienna: Ueberreuter, 1994).

[5] Emil Ludwig, *Wilhelm Hohenzollern, The Last of the Kaisers* (New York and London: G.B. Putnam's, 1927), 433–434.

[6] 'If one man's pistol shots had brought about the French Revolution and he had left the world for a prison to re-enter it after Waterloo, his eyes would not have looked at such a change as will Gavrilo Prinzip's in 1934 – or earlier, if the Allies win. True, Prinzip's shots were not really the cause of the war; the cause lay deeper. [. . .] But the assassination at Sarajevo was the signal gun': 'Anniversary of the War's Origin', *New York Times*, 27 June 1915.

Franz Ferdinand's significance as a symbol of the start of the First World War is so pervasive that it is still heard in the twenty-first century. A hundred years on, no historical analysis of the Great War can really do without some account of Franz Ferdinand's assassination.

The contrast between the rather local significance of Franz Ferdinand before his death, and the global fame of his decline, raises the question as to the reasons for this celebrity. On the surface, aside from the legendary Franz Josef I, who died in 1916, none of the Habsburgs who lived in the twentieth century had any significant political role. Even Franz Josef himself ended up witnessing the gradual devolution of his powers: first, in 1867, to Hungary, then, in the defeat at Solferino, to the rising Italian nation, and finally, around the time of his death, to the other components of his empire. The last Habsburg emperor, Karl, tried to preserve his own power by promoting the creation of puppet kingdoms in Poland and Ukraine, with Karl Stefan and Wilhelm von Habsburg as regents, but this plan never succeeded. Karl Stefan died in his Galician castle, while Wilhelm von Habsburg was killed in a Soviet military camp in 1948.[7] Increasingly, the Habsburgs had come to excel at another sort of renown: the celebrity of imperial decline. As I want to suggest, the deeper reasons for this celebrity lay not in their real achievements, not in the actual promises that their persons held for their empires, but in the symbolic significance that their figures had both internally and abroad. As Europe's oldest elites, they were also figures of public identification in the age before democratic representation. Their existence gave persons of different social, ethnic, and religious status to sense some commonality. This sense of a common background became even more important when the empires that these Habsburgs had ruled declined.

Commodifying Habsburg deaths

The property of being *célèbre*, a secularized form of sanctity, precedes the emergence of the 'celebrity' as a noun describing a type of person. This status is achieved when the name of the person itself gives the public the illusion of knowing the person behind the name, even if they know very little about the person, and independently of the person's actual deeds and

---

[7] Timothy Snyder, *The Red Prince. The Fall of a Dynasty and the Rise of Modern Europe* (London: Vintage, 2009).

actions.[8] Modern theorists of celebrity tend to explain this phenomenon as the result of the separation of particular individuals from the rest of society through a mass-mediated worship of some of their attributes.[9] According to this view, celebrities are a quintessentially modern phenomenon, born with the age of the modern revolutions; they come about as a result of the confluence between democratization, rationalization, and commodification.[10]

However, the quality of being known in virtue of being known applies particularly directly to Europe's princely dynasties and other noble families.[11] We have an illusion of being familiar with people bearing noble names, as Georg Simmel pointed out, because we recognize the names from history, not because we recognize them as persons. They have practised a careful art of self-fashioning, and other factions in their environment were historically interested in contributing to the fashioning of aristocratic identity in their own interests as well.[12] Their *devises* and coats of arms are not unlike modern brands. Moreover, the greatest majority of family members with illustrious names spent their life doing very little in the spheres of politics, science, or art, being engaged in purely representational activities, or just living their lives. Most societies know them primarily through the image they associate with their name, supplemented with personal attributes.

Celebrity is the last remnant of charismatic forms of grace; the 'King's touch' is still visible to us through the gaze of the celebrity. The origin of the term 'celebrity' is not accidentally connected to the sphere of the sacred, such as the celebration of mass. Weber had taken the theological concept of charisma to describe a particularly premodern and 'pre-rational' form of granting someone authority. Modernity is the period in which celebrity is not only a mass spectacle but the spectacle also has multiple, and seemingly impersonal, organizers. The increased intensity of economic

---

[8] Antoine Lilti, 'Reconnaissance et célébrité: Jean-Jacques Rousseau et la politique du nom propre', in *Orages, Littérature et culture*, n 9, mars 2010, 77–94; Lilti, *Figures publiques. L'invention de la célébrité 1750–1850* (Paris: Fayard, 2014).

[9] Chris Rojek, *Celebrity* (London: Reaktion, 2001), 105.

[10] Rojek, *Celebrity*, 13; P. David Marshall, *Celebrity and Power: Fame in Contemporary Culture* (Minneapolis: University of Minnesota Press, 1997), 8.

[11] This capacious definition belongs to Daniel J. Boorstin, *The Image: A Guide to Pseudo-Events in America* (New York: Atheneum, 1961).

[12] Georg Simmel, 'Exkurs über den Adel', in Simmel, *Soziologie. Untersuchungen über die Formen der Vergesellschaftung* (Leipzig: Duncker & Humblot, 1908), 732–746; Ronald G. Asch, 'Aristocracy and Gentry', entry in *Europe 1450–1789: Encyclopedia of the Early Modern World*, ed. Jonathan Dewald, 6 vols. (New York: Scribner, 2004), 96–102; Eckart Conze, *Kleines Lexikon des Adels. Titel, Throne, Traditionen* (Munich: Beck, 2005).

and cultural exchange means that the persons holding celebrity status have less control over their image than before. The difference between premodern and modern forms of celebrity, or rather between celebrity in early capitalist and advanced capitalist society, is not in the quality of the celebrity's authority over a public, which remains magical; rather, the change affects the forms in which the celebrity's image is socially mediated.

The key question for the historian is at which moment the mechanism of celebrity construction kicks in. In the case of Franz Ferdinand and the Habsburgs generally, these moments are the points in time at which their particular achievements and position come to be perceived as being representative of something far larger than they are. For Franz Ferdinand, this 'larger than his life' effect had to do with his activities as a patron of culture.

Upon his return, Franz Ferdinand began to take his duties as a curator of imperial culture as seriously as his uncle. Travelling to remote parts of the Habsburg Empire, he promoted the development of regional folk arts; he also continued collecting and expanding the family's ethnographic collection for the now-established museum. Seen through the eyes of the Habsburg Archdukes, Europeanness can be grasped through two concepts of detachment: the social detachment of the nobility, particularly of the ruling houses, from their 'ethnically other' subjects; and the ethnic distinction between Europeans (as white Christians) and non-Europeans. Members of dynastic families played the role of identity builders, not only as politicians, but also in the sphere of symbolic power, as collectors, as patrons of allegorical self-representation, and as the first dilettante ethnographers.

Celebrities did not emerge at the same time as the circulation of print and the mass market; rather, what changed in the modern period was that their image became much more widely commodified, and that as commodities, they were in competition with others. As commodities, they could not 'go to market and make exchanges of their own account', as Marx had put it in *Capital*, the first volume of which was published in 1867.[13]

In order to understand the symbolic significance of dynastic death – a peculiar kind of celebrity – in modern Europe, we need to place it in

---

[13] Karl Marx, *Das Kapital. Kritik der Politischen Ökonomie*, vol. I, ch. 2 (Hamburg: Otto Meissner, 1867), cited after the translation by David McClelland, in Karl Marx, *An Abridged Edition*, ed. David McClelland (Oxford: Oxford University Press, 1995), 52.

comparative perspective. Between 1881 and 1914, there were more assassination attempts against members of European ruling families than had ever before occurred in a comparable time span of recorded European history. Even non-ruling or minor members of a ruling family, as well as vice-regents coming from non-dynastic aristocratic families, became victims of political assaults. This is surprising not least because dynastic legitimacy was an old and carefully constructed system of beliefs; the ruling families, which had controlled much of the cultural production in their realms, sustained it by encouraging displays of their special genealogy, which secured a selective memory of their ancestors. Many groups and factions of European society maintained or at least passively accepted the image of ruling dynasties as symbolic sources of their common identity.[14] Thus even though rituals like the King's touch, which had previously affirmed the widespread belief in royalty's special powers of healing, had disappeared by the modern period, in many other respects, dynastic charisma remained intact.[15] The fact that more Europeans were ready to assassinate members of their royal families was not necessarily a sign of their decline in authority; on the contrary, it could equally be interpreted as an act of affirmation that these old rulers continued to embody a political order, albeit one whose decline many considered overdue.

Publicly mediated news of assassinated royals and their voluntary or involuntary abdication allowed contemporaries to conceptualize imperial decline through the notion of death, which was both metaphorical and literal. But this picture of imperial decline, captured in the figure of the deposed or assassinated monarch, would remain incomplete if we did not consider other ways in which imperial decline was represented allegorically.

The celebrated late-Victorian anthropologist James Frazer had remarked that assassinating a monarch used to be one of the fundamental taboos of primitive societies, more significant than the taboo of murder.[16] Yet the increased frequency of royal assassinations, together with the abolition of the nobility, might suggest that in modern times the taboo had been broken too often and in too many places at once to still merit the

---

[14] Marie Tanner, *The Last Descendant of Aeneas: The Hapsburgs and the Mythic Image of the Emperor* (New Haven: Yale University Press, 1993), 146ff.

[15] Ernst Kantorowicz, *The King's Two Bodies: A Study in Medieval Political Theology* (Princeton: Princeton University Press, 1957); for more recent treatments of the theme, see Emmanuel Levinas, *Otherwise than Being: or, Beyond Essence*, transl. Alphonso Lengis (Pittsburgh: Duquesne University Press, 2005).

[16] James Frazer, *The Golden Bough: A Study in Magic and Religion* (New York: Macmillan, 1925), see esp. Preface from 1922; and Frazer, 'The Killing of the Khazar Kings', in *Folk-lore*, xviii (1917), 382–407.

name. But even if this is the case, the widespread tendencies to break with the old imperial order must still be explained in terms of their impact and their social function. The legal and cultural forms taken by these abolitions contributed significantly to the shaping of post-imperial societies in Europe, from national democracies to authoritarian dictatorships.

As violence against the ruling dynasties took on cultural as well as political forms, these families themselves responded to the acts of terror by enacting policies of commemoration. Monuments were built in a historicist style, recalling a bygone era of greatness, whether neo-Gothic neo-classical, or neo-Mughal. Throughout Europe, an unprecedented number of monuments to living and recently deceased members of ruling families were erected in the decades between the Franco-Prussian War and the First World War. This also coincided with historicist painting coming into fashion, presenting newly made nations with the illustrated history of their rulers.

When they prepared to succeed in power, the representatives of the old empires in Europe were aware of the precariousness of imperial rule. Monuments were erected both in the centres and at the fringes of the empires. The Habsburgs built the neo-Gothic *Votivkirche* at the heart of their empire in Vienna; completed in 1879, it commemorated both Franz Josef's survival of a failed knife attack by a Hungarian nationalist in 1853 and the death by firing squad of Emperor Maximilian of Mexico. Similarly, in 1907, the Romanoffs commemorated the death of Alexander II both at the centre and the periphery; the Cathedral of *Spas na krovi* (literally: 'Savior on the Blood'), built on the spot in St. Petersburg where Emperor Alexander II had been assassinated in 1881, looks like a smaller copy of the St. Basil's Cathedral in Moscow. Like the Habsburgs, the Romanoffs also made sure to build monuments to the assassinated emperor at the more contested fringes of their empire, such as the city of Kazan itself, where a monument was erected in 1895. Beyond Europe, Lord Curzon's calls to build monuments in India to the deceased Queen Victoria resulted in construction not only in the former colonial centre of Calcutta but also at the periphery, in Lucknow, where the famous Sepoy rebellion had strongly shaken her rule in 1857.[17] At the same time, Lucknow became a tourist sight attracting global interest in imperial decline.

The symbolic commemoration of violence gave dynastic rulers a special kind of charisma. Control over the representation of this threat

---

[17] Thomas R. Metcalf, *Ideologies of the Raj* (Cambridge: Cambridge University Press, 1997); Veena T. Oldenburg, *Colonial Lucknow, 1856–1877* (Oxford: Oxford University Press, 1990).

did not remain under the control of the ruling families for long, however. Throughout the territories of former imperial control, the very places where monuments had been erected became loci of resistance. The most famous images of toppling hegemony came from revolutionary Russia.

Another example of self-promotion projects with unintended consequences was the historical archive initiated by the Habsburgs. In 1868, the Habsburg family agreed to open its archives to the public, starting a long process of collecting documents and building a representative edifice for their presentation. The Hohenzollerns, too, opened a museum for the public at this time. But just as in the case of the Hohenzollern museum, the completion of the Habsburgs' Court and state archive in 1918 would eventually coincide with the demise of the dynasty and its empire.[18] Throughout Europe, aristocratic archives, which the dynasties and minor nobility presented as documents of shared imperial history, had become instruments of their disintegration.

The increased circulation of images of destruction in the international press, books, and films meant that the power of these images transcended the borders of the former empires that the dynasties had represented. Destruction in one location was visible in several locations at once. Images of the decline of dynasties acquired a double meaning as symbols of decline. The dynastic families who had been the makers of identity became objects of an almost ethnographic interest in the past, a European self-ethnography.

The Archdukes as collectors: civilizing Europe with barbarian art

The noble courts and the imperial families that controlled them, in a variety of ways, gave Europeans their first idea of themselves.[19] For ruling families like the Habsburgs and their chief political rivals, the Protestant Hohenzollerns, the history and culture of their families were inseparable

---

[18] Eva Giloi, *Monarchy, Myth, and Material Culture in Germany, 1750–1950* (Cambridge: Cambridge University Press, 2011).

[19] Norbert Elias, *Court Society* (Oxford: Blackwell, 1983); Tim Blanning, *The Power of Culture and the Culture of Power* (Oxford: Oxford University Press, 2002); Edward Berenson and Eva Giloi (eds.), *Constructing Charisma: Celebrity, Fame, and Power in Nineteenth-Century Europe* (Oxford: Berghahn, 2010); Dominic Lieven, *The Aristocracy in Europe, 1815–1914* (New York: Columbia University Press, 1993). *Erzherzog Franz Ferdinand. Unser Thronfolger. Zum 50. Geburtstag*, eds. Leopold Freiherr von Chlumetzky, Theodor v. Sosnosky et al., *Illustriertes Sonderheft der Oesterreichischen Rundschau* (Vienna and Leipzig: K.u.K. Hofdruckerei, 1913), 9–11, 9.

from those of their empires.[20] At a time when the Habsburg Empire was threatened by national secessionist movements, the imperial family strove to embody, if not to represent, all its subjects in the figure of the emperor.[21] For instance, followers of Franz Ferdinand celebrated the fact that his 2,047 ancestors belonged to all the nations of the empire. His personal art collection, they indicated, comprised portraits of famous ancestors from across Europe, from Poland in the east to Spain in the west.[22]

European dynasties became figures of 'integration' for their subjects not only by discussing European history but also by familiarizing Europeans with non-European cultures. In doing so, they laid the foundations for comparative thinking in which class affinities with non-Europeans trumped racial separation between Europeans and non-Europeans.[23] The old dynasties were not only strange, special lineages governing a bunch of alien subjects; they had also introduced them to other types of strangeness, the 'inferior' strangeness of non-Christian folk culture. The work of collecting cultural artefacts, promoting imperial culture at home and abroad, and maintaining their family's prestige was traditionally undertaken by non-ruling family members who were next in line to the throne, and the fact that both Maximilian and Franz Ferdinand were Archdukes made heritage maintenance a central activity for them.

The title of Archduke is itself, in a sense, an early testament to European 'identity politics'. It reflects the shrewd way in which this family, whose origins can be traced to a small castle in Switzerland first recorded in the twelfth century, secured its power over the centuries, not only by military conquests and marital alliances but also by careful cultivation of the family's public image. The title derives from a fourteenth-century incident when a Habsburg, Rudolf IV, wanted to obtain the privilege of electing the emperor. To this end, he commissioned a forged document, the *Privilegium Maius*, which claimed that Austria, now the family's chief seat, was an 'Archduchy'.[24] The Holy Roman Empire technically recognized only Duchies and Grand Duchies, but the claim went through. This

[20] Ibid., Georg Graf Wycielski, 'Erzherzog Franz Ferdinand als Kunstfreund', Chlumetzky et al., *Unser Thronfolger*, 55–85.

[21] *Ahnen-Tafel seiner kaiserlichen Hoheit des durchlauchtigsten Herrn Erzherzogs Franz Ferdinands von Oesterreich-Este, bearbeitet von Otto Forst* (Vienna, 1910). Cited after Theodor von Sosnosky, 'Erzherzog Franz Ferdinand', in Erzherzog Franz Ferdinand. Unser Thronfolger. Zum 50. Geburtstag, 9–11, 9.

[22] Wycielski, 'Erzherzog Franz Ferdinand als Kunstfreund', 55–85.

[23] David Cannadine, *Ornamentalism: How the British Saw Their Empire* (London: Allen Lane, 2001).

[24] AT-OeStA/HHStA UR AUR 187 Privilegium Maius, 1156.09.17, at www.archivinformationssystem.at/detail.aspx?ID=29082.

retroactive change of status meant that the Habsburg dukes had the same status as the prince-electors of the Holy Roman Empire, increasing their chances of becoming rulers of the empire for generations to come. Francesco Petrarca proved the document to be a forgery not long after its production, but his discovery of the forgery never undermined the now widely asserted power of the ruling family.[25] Even after the forgery was rediscovered again in a nineteenth-century journal, the title had become so much a part of the identity of its imperial family that the publication made no difference. The title persisted for more than a hundred years beyond the lifetime of the Holy Empire itself and, interestingly, even Otto von Habsburg bore the title of Archduke when he died in 2011.

While the symbolic power of the title had waned since the fourteenth century, its economic significance only waxed in importance in the eighteenth. Archdukes, that is, the male members of the immediate imperial family, could now enjoy the privileges of the familial fund (Allerhöchster Familienversorgungsfond), which Maria Theresia had instituted to provide for the imperial family. Although neither Ferdinand Maximilian, as the future emperor Maximilian had been known, nor Franz Ferdinand was born in the direct line of succession to the throne, news of their new position reached them at the age of 16 and 26, respectively. Ferdinand Maximilian's uncle, who had a neurological disorder, was urged to resign in 1848; when his father also resigned, this left his brother Franz Josef in charge.

After their uncle stepped down in the wake of the revolutions of 1848, Ferdinand Maximilian's elder brother Franz Josef served as the head of the House of Habsburg, Emperor of Austria, King of a large part of central Europe and parts of the Middle East, including Jerusalem, and at this point was still President of the German Confederation. By contrast, Ferdinand Maximilian as a young man believed that he could be 'himself' because he was free from the burden of rule. He was one of the first promoters of early photography and developed a habit of writing his travel journal in verse. Despite his military education, Maximilian preferred the arts and sciences to his brother's politics. The main focus of Maximilian's interest was on

---

[25] On Petrarca's letter, see Francesco Petrarca, letter to Karl IV of Habsburg, in Francesco Petrarca, *Lettere senili*, ed. G. Fracassetti, 2 vols., vol. 2 (Florence: Le Monnier, 1870), 490–497. On the history of the forgery, see Eva Schlotheuber, 'Das Privilegium maius – eine habsburgische Fälschung im Ringen um Rang und Einfluss', in *Die Geburt Österreichs. 850 Jahre Privilegium minus* (Regensburg: Schnell and Schnell, 2007), 143–165. Wilhelm Wattenbach, 'Die österreichischen Freiheitsbriefe. Prüfung ihrer Echtheit und Forschungen über ihre Entstehung', in *Archiv für Kunde Österreichischer Geschichtsquellen*, 8 (1852), 77–119.

collecting artefacts and natural objects from around the world, for which he equipped his personal frigate, the SMS *Novara*. Supplied with the intellectual support of Alexander von Humboldt, whose own explorations dated back to the beginning of the nineteenth century, the frigate travelled to Asia, South America, and Australia, collecting specimens of the culture, flora, and fauna of each.[26] Among its anthropological findings was a collection of Aztec and Mexican folk art known as *Mexikanische Kostbarkeiten*.[27]

'I am myself' [Ich bin ich] – that was his motto of choice for writing about the jungle during a trip to Brazil as a young man in 1859–60.[28] 'Such expeditions are geared towards the individual, and for their duration, caste and estate mean nothing'. In the jungle of Bahia, he believed, the mutual dependence needed to survive against the forces of nature appeared to trump social status. In one poem about the jungle of Bahia, written in January 1860, Maximilian conjured up a mysterious sound coming from the forest, a 'ghostly army that begs for revenge against the white people – its children's butchers'. Another poem called *The Dethroned Prince* described a strange scene: in an Indian settlement in the jungle, an old man sits alone on a stone. He is the 'Prince of the Camacan', who was once the lord of his people and the forests. Now, defeated by a rival tribe, the old man 'cries about his own decline [Untergang]'; this man who had ruled all his life is now seen with his 'thin legs shaking tiredly'. In the city of Petropolis, Maximilian turns to a critique of urban life typical for Europeans of his generation, describing the appearance of a railway in the jungle. Its shrill sounds, its monstrosity, is set against the 'holy jungle' which has been violated like a virgin (geschändet); 'the Indian flees westwards in astonishment/ away from his father's place of a thousand years,/ For where the white man moves, his forest dries up,/ and his woman and child will be engulfed by a chain of sin'.[29]

Echoing the European Romantics, these fantasies of savage cultures appeared as Europe's critical bad conscience. As Heinrich Heine put it in

---

[26] Karl Scherzer (ed.), *Reise der österreichischen Fregatte Novara um die Erde*, 3 vols. (Vienna: Carl Gerold, 1861–76).

[27] On Freud's interpretations of these, see Rubén Gallo, *Freud's Mexico. Into the Wilds of Psychoanalysis* (Cambridge, Mass.: MIT University Press, 2010).

[28] Kaiser von Mexiko Maximilian, *Reiseskizzen, Aphorismen, Gedichte*, vol. 7, *Reiseskizzen XII, Aphorismen, Gedichte* (Leipzig: Duncker und Humblot, 1867), 18.

[29] Erzherzog Maximilian, *Gedichte*, vol. 1 (Vienna: Aus der kaiserlich-königlichen Hof- und Staatsdruckerei, 1863), 'Geisterstimmen im Urwald', 51; 'Der entthronte Fürst', 52–56; 'Eisenbahn im Urwald', 70–71. All written in 1860.

his 1851 poem 'Vitzliputzli', the Aztec god of war would eventually take revenge for the murder of Montezuma, the last Aztec, ruler who had been one of his priests. As Heine put it: 'This uncivilised,/ Pagan, blinded by superstition/ still believed in loyalty and honour/ and in the sanctity of hospitality'. Montezuma's gift of a crown of feathers to his future Spanish murderers at the Habsburg court left a material memory for its future heirs. It was integrated into their collection of global artefacts at Castle Ambras and, after the collapse of Habsburg rule, remained the property of the Museum für Völkerkunde. Heine thought that Vitzliputzli, the blood-thirsty God of war, evoked both fear and laughter. His appearance was so 'kooky/ it's so squiggly and so childish/ That despite an inner terror/ He still tingles us to laughter'.[30] The last word in Heine's poem belonged not to a European, but to Vitzliputzli himself who wants to 'flee to the home country of my enemies' to 'start a new career' as the Devil, Beelzebub, and the snake Lilith, to 'avenge my beloved Mexico'.

Between the French Revolution and the end of the Napoleonic era, authors like Johann Gottfried Herder, August von Kotzebue, and Heinrich von Kleist produced works in which they expressed sympathy for the oppressed native peoples and the slaves of the new world. As Susanne Zantop and others have argued, the idealization of the native 'others' was formative for these German authors' own conceptualization of national identity as a form of resistance against empire.[31] The fear and sympathy with the 'black rebellions' of the new world had been inspired by real events, the 1791 slave uprising of Saint-Domingue. French troops then worked with international, including German, mercenaries to crush the rebellion. National historians like Jules Michelet subsequently found it difficult to reconcile the French army defending the French Revolution at home against the international royalist counter-insurgency but imprisoning the black leader of the slave rebellion of Saint-Domingue, Toussaint L'Ouverture, and leaving him to die in a French prison.[32]

---

[30] *Dieser unzivilisierte,/ Abergläubisch blinde Heide/ Glaubte noch an Treu und Ehre/ Und an Heiligkeit des Gastrechts. [. . .]* Dort auf seinem Thronaltar/ Sitzt der große Vitzliputzli,/ Mexikos blutdürst´ger Kriegsgott./ Ist ein böses Ungetüm,// Doch sein Äußres ist so putzig,/ So verschnörkelt und so kindisch,/ Daß er trotz des innern Grausens/ *Dennoch unsre Lachlust kitzelt.* Heinrich Heine, 'Vitzliputzli' (1851), in Heine, *Werke und Briefe in zehn Bänden,* vol. 2 (Berlin and Weimar: Aufbauch, 1972).

[31] Susanne Zantop, *Colonial Fantasies: Conquest, Family, and Nation in Precolonial Germany, 1770–1870* (Durham, N.C.: Duke University Press, 1997), 145.

[32] Zantop, *Colonial Fantasies,* 141ff.; see also Paul Ricoeur, *Oneself as Another,* transl. Katherine Blamey (Chicago: University of Chicago Press, 1992).

Celebrity of decline before Franz Ferdinand: the case of Maximilian

The case of Maximilian of Habsburg, or Ferdinand Max, as he was known in his earlier life, is the most prominent example of a royal celebrity of decline, whose commodification went beyond the control of the royal family. Before the First World War, narratives of Maximilian's life had been based mostly on accounts of the last three years of his life, which are but a short episode in the international history of Europe and the United States. Interpreters defined his life variously as a symbol of the struggle between republicanism and imperialism, Europe and the new world, or Romanticism and realpolitik. A brief account of these three years shall suffice here. In the 1860s, French emperor Napoleon III, nephew of his greater namesake, decided to use a weakened United States in order to bring Mexico under French control. This he deemed necessary for reasons of state, as emergent republican forces in Mexico had declared themselves bankrupt, which affected French creditors. Moreover, it was a fortunate moment for an intervention because these republicans, who generally enjoyed support from the United States against the more conservative clerical faction of the country, were left briefly to their own devices since the United States were themselves involved in a civil war.

Napoleon's idea was to invade on the pretences of reclaiming an old right. One of the former rulers of Mexico was the Habsburg family, who had named a province their own after their European possession in Spain Nueva Galicia. The question was this: which member of the Habsburg family is to be cast in the role of prospective emperor. Napoleon's choice fell on Archduke Maximilian, the brother of his only recently defeated enemy, Emperor Franz Josef. As contemporary critics such as the journalist Karl Marx anticipated in an article for the *New York Daily Tribune* published in 1861, it was 'one of the most monstrous enterprises ever chronicled in the annals of international history'.[33]

Only a few decades prior to that, a similar venture by the Spanish Itúrbide family had failed. The childless Maximilian and his Belgian wife Charlotte forcefully adopted their son in order to have a future heir. But all was in vain: six years and one more failed empire later, Marx could have well concluded that the story was one of those to be written into those annals in 'letters of blood and fire'. This plan, which came to be known as

---

[33] Karl Marx, 'The Intervention in Mexico', *The New York Daily Tribune*, 23 November 1861. Accessed 5 March 2012 at www.marxists.org/archive/marx/works/1861/11/23.htm.

the Mexican Intervention or the story of the 'cactus throne', united Britain and France in their desire to establish control over Mexican territory in competition with the United States, at a time when Mexico's emergent governing elite was split between a liberal and a clerical faction. The blood to be shed was that of many people: Mexican insurgents, French officers, Mexican supporters of the empire, and others. But it was the 'blue' blood of the Habsburg protagonist, and the actions of a firing squad loyal to Oaxacan republican Benito Juárez, which in 1867 became the symbol of Europe's waning role as an imperial force in the Americas. Napoleon's plan was to ship Maximilian to Mexico and install him there as a new Emperor, which he did. In 1864, Maximilian arrived on his own frigate *Novara*, a boat he had originally destined for scientific explorations around the world.

From the beginning, this was more than just a French intervention, even though it served the interests of primarily French financiers. But the agents involved were international.[34] Not only were many of Maximilian's immediate supporters subjects of different states, including the Habsburg monarchy, Prussia, Saxony, France, and, not least, Mexico, whose status was to be determined; but several of his officers, including Maximilian's aide-de-camp, Prussian Prince Felix zu Salm-Salm, and another officer, Maximilian Baron von Alvensleben, who came from Saxon nobility, had both just served in the army of the American Unionists in the Civil War.[35] Because the financial support for the intervention came primarily from France, this meant that the campaign faltered soon after French support had become increasingly costly, while resistance to European rule in Mexico gained in strength. On top of that, in 1865, the American Civil War had ended, thus increasing the capacity of Americans to support the Mexican republic. Maximilian's officers had joined him for Romantic reasons: they wanted to support his enlightened monarchy in Mexico against what they thought would be a reactionary republic. But a few months later, the Europeans' Mexican adventure was over; all European parties involved – the Habsburgs in Austria, the Bonapartes in France, and the Saxe-Coburg-Gothas with their parliamentary government in Britain, as well as financial investors in the campaign throughout Europe – had lost spectacularly. In 1867, the mercenary officers, such as Salm-Salm, who would serve (and die) on the Prussian side in the Franco-Prussian War three

---

[34] Catherine Irvine Gavin, *The Cactus and the Crown* (New York: Doubleday, 1962).

[35] Felix zu Salm-Salm, *Queretaro: Blätter aus meinem Tagebuch in Mexico: nebst einem Auszuge aus dem Tagebuche der Prinzessin Agnes zu Salm-Salm* (Leipzig: Körner, 1868); Maximilian Baron von Alvensleben, *With Maximilian in Mexico* (London: Longmans, Green, & Co., 1867).

years later, returned to their home regiments in Europe; meanwhile, Maximilian and two Mexican officers loyal to him were publicly court-martialled.

Franz Josef tried to keep the scandal of Maximilian's death under control. Charlotte, his widow, had, in the meantime, lost her mind and lived secluded in one of her father's castles in Belgium. Maximilian's former aide-de-camp, Prince Salm-Salm, who had been instructed to gain access to Maximilian's documents at his residence in Miramar and other locations, complained in his memoirs that the family did not allow him to access the papers he needed to fulfil the promise he had made to Maximilian before he died. The royal court tried to acknowledge the tragedy in its own way. The *Votivkirche* in Vienna, whose original construction had been Maximilian's personal project, was rededicated in his memory. Franz Josef also dutifully assembled the artefacts which Maximilian's boat the frigate *Novara* had brought from Mexico in a public display in the Hofmuseum's permanent ethnographic collection. He even prohibited the song 'La Paloma', which had become the unofficial anthem of the Mexican republic, to be played in the empire, a rule that still applies in the Austrian navy. The tune 'La Paloma' originally had nothing to do with the Habsburgs. Sébastien Yradier, a Basque composer, wrote it in Cuba. The singer who sang it first, Concepcion (Conchita) Mendez, became a royal artist at the theatre recently reinstated by Charlotte at Mexico City. However, as the republican forces gained strength, they appropriated 'La Paloma', supplied it with a new title and used it to deride Charlotte of Belgium as 'Mama Carlota' on her departure from Mexico. In 1867, as Charlotte was leaving Mexico to seek support for her husband from European monarchs, Conchita Mendez was asked by the crowds to perform the song in the theatre under the new, republican, title. The news that she refused to do so reached Emperor Franz Josef, who praised Conchita's loyalty in a birthday note in 1901.[36] The subsequent story of 'La Paloma', which became one of the world's most popular tunes, only testifies the extent to which the House of Habsburg had lost control over its own media image.[37]

Above all, Franz Josef could not prevent the fame of Maximilian as a sympathizer with the revolutionary cause, and a puppet in the power politics of Napoleon III, from reaching a wider public. News of Maximilian's

---

[36] 'Emperor to Aged Singer. Francis Joseph Grateful to Woman Who Would Not Deride Carlota', *New York Times*, 29 July 1901.

[37] Sigrid Faltin and Andreas Schäfler, *La Paloma – Das Lied* (Hamburg: Mare, 2008).

execution reached Europe by telegram at the worst possible moment, when Napoleon III of France was about to open the Great Exhibition of 1867 in Paris. It could only be withheld from the public by one day. In the decade that followed, numerous memoirs, plays, and historical accounts were published and translated into a variety of languages, including French, Spanish, English, Hungarian, Czech and Slovak, Russian, Portuguese, and others.[38] The public image of Maximilian acquired more and more dramatic texture after his death, following more publications of eyewitness reports, such as that of his Mexican secretary.[39] What appealed to these audiences was primarily the drama of Maximilian's death, the negative light it shed on the much disliked regime of Napoleon III, and the fact that he emerged as a puppet figure in a struggle between an old civilization and its new rivals. 'What has become of the eager competition with which the most warlike Monarchy in the Old World and the most self-asserting Republic in the New seemed bent upon disputing the supremacy and high protectorate over so vast a part of the Western Continent?' – asked the *Times* in January 1867.[40]

In the year after his death, Maximilian's memoirs of his life and thoughts before 1864 were published at Duncker & Humblot, a publishing house with eminent predecessors to Maximilian, such as Schegel, E.T.A. Hoffmann, and Georg Wilhelm Friedrich Hegel.[41] Despite a very limited

---

[38] Maximilian Freiherr von Alvensleben, *With Maximilian in Mexico: From the Notebook of a Mexican Officer* (London: Longmans, Green & Co., 1867); Anonymous, Enthüllungen über die letzten Lebenstage und die Hinrichtung des Kaisers Maximilian I. von Mexico: nebst den nach seiner Gefangennahme gefundenen geheimen, nicht handschriftlichen papieren und correspondenzen (London: Fillmore & Cooper, 1867); in French as Maximilien, Empereur du Mexique. Sa vie, sa mort, sou procès. Détails intimes at inédits (Paris: Lebigré-Duquesne, 1867). See also Anonymous, 'Maximilian', in *The Peoples Magazine*, 1 (1867), 683–684; Anonymous, *Maximilian: A Tragedy* [in three acts and in verse] (Dublin: George Herbert, 1868). Anonymous, Kaiser Maximilians Erhebung und Fall; Originalcorrespondenzen und Documente in geschichtlichem Zusammenhange dargestellt (Leipzig: Duncker und Humblot, 1867); transl. into French as L'élevation et la chute de l'empereur Maximilien (Paris: Librairie Internationale, 1868); into Spanish, as Elevacion y caida del emperador Maximiliano. Intervencion francesa en México. 1861–1867 (México: Impr. el comercio, de N. Chavez, 1870); in Czech, as Maxmilianuv podvraceny Trun v Mexiku. Zevrubne vypsani bournych I krvavych udalosti Mexickych (Prague: Styblo, 1867). Contemporaries' memoirs: Gräfin Kollonitz, Eine Reise nach Mexico im Jahre 1864 (Vienna: C. Gerold's Sohn, 1867). Franz Liszt, Marche funèbre: pour piano. Années de pélerinage VI. Marche funèbre. En mémoire de Maximilian I, Empereur du Mexique, [mort] 19 juin 1867. 'In magis et voluisse sat est.' Grove 163, no. 6, Les fils de B.Schott; Schott & Comp.; Maison Schott; Schott frères.

[39] José Luis Blasio, *Maximilian. Emperor of Mexico. Memoirs of His Private Secretary*, transl. Robert Hammond Murray, Introduction Carleton Beals (New Haven: Yale University Press, 1934), first published as *Maximiliano intimo: El emperador Maximiliano y su corte: memorias de un secretario particular* (Paris and Mexico: G. Bouret, 1905).

[40] Anonymous, 'Who bids for Mexico?', *The Times*, 9 January 1867, 7.

[41] Kaiser von Mexiko Maximilian, *Mein erster Ausflug. Wanderungen in Griechenland* (Duncker & Humblot, Leipzig, 1868).

circulation size of 5,000 copies, it was soon translated into French and English in the same year. Maximilian's notes revealed a republican spirit. In 1859, while Franz Josef was struggling against France in the battle of Solferino, Maximilian at the nearby castle Miramar celebrated Lucca, where 'Libertas had flourished in times of a long and true peace, because it was satisfied with the small and never strove for the big.'[42] Influenced by the German Romantics who had also inspired the revolutionaries of 1848, Maximilian had been in constant search of his own identity.

After the First World War, more works on Maximilian appeared when the collapse of the Habsburg Empire left scholars free to access hitherto private family papers at the Haus-, Hof- und Staatsarchiv in the Hofburg.[43] Using this resource, as well as the published memoirs of some of Maximilian's entourage, in 1923, Viennese historian Count Corti published the first scholarly biography of Maximilian, insisting that of 'all the tragedies in history there is scarce one which has so deeply excited the sympathy of the world as that of the ill-fated Emperor and Empress of Mexico'.[44] As 'New-World Republicanism' had its 'most satisfying triumph over the Old-World Courts', Maximilian became a tragic figure whose last words kept being reiterated by biographers: 'I forgive everyone, and I pray that everyone may forgive me. May my blood, now to be shed, be shed for the good of Mexico.'[45] This was the line that had been printed on the *cartes de visite* of his execution by the studio of Adrien Cordiglia in 1867.

Corti's and other biographies had given a shape to Maximilian's figure, which made him ready for the republican causes of the twentieth century. The circumstances of Maximilian's death gave Europeans one more, albeit negative, source of identity. As the British Empire faced what became the last decade of rule in India, historian Daniel Dawson described how, at the time of Maximilian, the 'scorching sun of a Mexican summer shone on an Empire in dissolution'.[46] Maximilian became Europe's first inter-imperial and transatlantic celebrity of decline since Christopher Columbus's accidental discovery of America. Both were Habsburg enterprises, but only Maximilian obtained the peculiar status of a celebrity in virtue of his failure.

---

[42] Ibid., 126 (on Lucca) and 145 (on England). Lucca (1851). See also commentary, 136.
[43] Egon Caesar Count Corti, *Maximilian and Charlotte of Mexico*, transl. Catherine Alison Phillips, 2 vols. (New York and London: Knopf, 1928); Daniel Dawson, *The Mexican Adventure* (London: G. Bell & Sons, 1935).
[44] Corti, *Maximilian and Charlotte*, vol. 1, vii.   [45] Ibid., 410.
[46] Dawson, *The Mexican Adventure*, 396, 407.

Maximilian had become the stuff of a growing culture industry, which began with the photographic depiction of his execution. It had multiple centres of distribution: photographic studios in Mexico City and in Paris; newspaper bureaus; later, local tourism organizations based in locations associated with his life and death, including Castle Miramar near Trieste, and Querétaro, his place of death, where by the 1890s, a more formal monument to Maximilian was erected that was reproduced as one of the sights of Mexico by contemporary photographers and even marketed abroad in places such as the American magazine *Harper's. A Journal of Civilization.*

In Europe, a painting by Édouard Manet showing the execution of Maximilian was first banned from public view under Napoleon III. The impoverished Manet had cut up the painting, to be sold in parts. But his friend Edgar Degas later purchased the fragments and reassembled them. The subsequent success of this nearly complete painting eventually popularized the story of Maximilian along with Manet's own in the twentieth century.

Manet had never been to Mexico but used photographs, accounts circulating in the French press, as well as an image by Goya of the Spanish resistance against Napoleon, as a basis. He was not trying to get as close to reality as possible; but he wanted to capture the true spirit of the event. As contemporaries like Emile Zola duly noted, in one of the versions, even though it was publicly known that Maximilian's executors were Mexican nationalists led by Benito Juárez, he depicted them wearing French uniforms with their characteristic kepis. Immediately interpreted as an open critique of Napoleon III, the painting and even its lithographic reproductions were banned in France.[47] As a result, even after Napoleon's death, the painting was shown only in Boston and not displayed in France until after Manet's death.[48]

As acclaimed art historian Julius Meier-Graefe put it: 'Art changes, just as houses and dresses, morals and ideals change, and one and the same artwork changes, as if it was still being worked upon, even after it had been hanging behind a glass frame.'[49] In Paris in 1884, nobody wanted to buy Manet's painting, *The Execution of Maximilian*, probably for political reasons, since all other paintings offered at a Vente found buyers. But by 1898, French collector of impressionist art Paul Durand-Ruel purchased it

---

[47] Manet, *La Chronique des Arts et de la curiosité*, www.moma.org/interactives/exhibitions/2006/Manet/detail_litograph_oilsketch.htm.
[48] Ibid., 316.   [49] Julius Meier-Graefe, *Edouard Manet* (Munich: Piper, 1912), 7.

from Manet's wife for 8,000 francs. It was then sold on to another French buyer for 12,000. By 1908, German buyer Bernheim found that it was worth 60,000 francs. By 1910, the Mannheim art gallery bought the painting for the equivalent of 90,000 francs.[50]

In 1918, the National Gallery acquired a fourth version of Manet's *Execution of Maximilian* from the private collection of Degas, who had just died in Paris. The purchase was facilitated from a government grant by a special permission of John Maynard Keynes and Lord Curzon, who were being advised by Roger Fry. One of the economic consequences of the war was a rapid depreciation of art. Keynes and Curzon formed an ad hoc committee from the National Gallery and travelled to Paris, just as Germany was bombing the city, to acquire the painting at an auction. It was a bargain: 25,052 francs or 945 pounds sterling, which would be the equivalent of £50,000 in 2015.[51]

At the turn of the century, the Habsburgs turned from collectors to collectibles, from owners of curiosity into objects of curiosity. The Paris art salon had established a tradition for depicting decapitated and deposed monarchs, but prior to Manet, they focused mostly on France and Britain. It was particularly a contemporary of Eugène Delacroix, the great allegorist of liberty, who excelled at depicting the deaths of crowned subjects. Paul Delaroche was so drawn to depicting subjects such as the executions of Marie Antoinette and Charles I Stuart that Heinrich Heine was prompted to remark: 'Mr Delaroche is the court painter of all decapitated majesties.'[52] What gave the spectacle of their death a hue of universal tragic symbolism, even, and especially, in cases like Maximilian and Franz Ferdinand, who had barely held any political power in their lifetime? Some factors are specific to each case. Maximilian's brief rise and decline was, as we have seen, entangled with several aspects of European and transatlantic politics, making the affair an international event. Franz Ferdinand's imminent succession to the throne gave his activities more weight. Besides, both shared the familial charisma of the Habsburgs, which still carried some weight. But I believe that the most

[50] Ibid., 316.
[51] National Gallery archives, NG3294, details of sale and publications. See also Richard Shone, 'Keynes' Economies of Sale', *The Guardian*, 11 May 1996.
[52] Heinrich Heine, *Lutetia*, xxxviii (1841), in Heine, *Historisch-Kritische Gesamtausgabe*, vol. 13:1, ed. Manfred Windfuhr (Düsseldorf: Hoffmann und Campe, 1988), 145. More on Delacroix and Delaroche in Hans-Werner Schmidt and Jan Nicolaisen (eds.), *Eugène Delacroix & Paul Delaroche*, Leipzig, Museum der bildenden Künste (Petersberg: Michael Imhof Verlag, 2015).

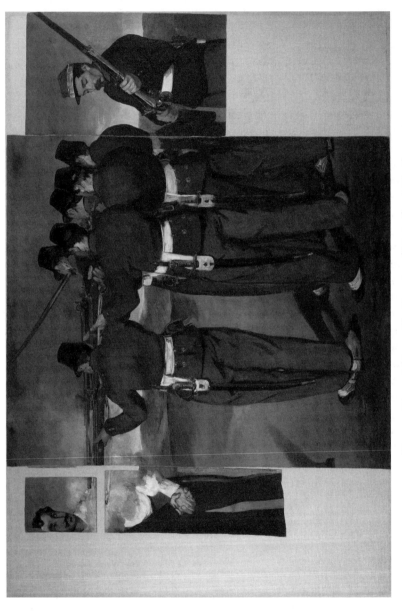

Figure 4 Edouard Manet, *The Execution of Maximilian* (1867–8). National Gallery, NG3294

significant factor, and one which helps explain the symbolic importance of all three assassinated Habsburgs, but particularly Maximilian and Franz Ferdinand, was that they made their subjects' own identity: their families', their subjects', and that of Europe at large. As scholars have argued, through institutions such as the collection of ethnographic objects, museums, and other forms of cultural heritage, the Habsburgs gave their subject shared and divided forms of identity. In their absence, the character of this identity was put into question.

Interpreters made much of the symbolism that it was the same boat, the frigate *Novara*, which on Maximilian's orders had introduced the Viennese to Mexican culture that returned to Trieste with his dead body in 1867.[53] As Rubén Gallo argued, the confluence of these symbols gave impressionable Habsburg subjects like Sigmund Freud nightmares of their very own death. Even before Franz Ferdinand was assassinated, Sigmund Freud observed that his patients had obsessive dreams that were based on their repressed fears of *agents provocateurs*.[54] Throughout Europe, terrorist plots and individual attempts against ruling families and some non-dynastic rulers were indicating the fragility of the political order.[55] Photographic documentation could not capture the moment of destruction but documented the absent body as graphically as possible, as, for example, in a police photograph of the assassinated Grand Duke Sergius in Moscow in 1905. In lectures held at the University of Vienna in 1917, he argued that mourning could be the effect of the 'loss of a beloved person or an abstraction that came to take its place such as the fatherland, freedom, an ideal, etc.'[56] The loss of a fatherland or an empire is insofar akin to the loss of a love, he suggested, as it is not caused by the mere absence of a physical body in the world, but in the disturbance of an imaginary, spiritual relationship between oneself and that other, abstract or real, person. Freud's own dreams, as Rubén Gallo surmises, reflected the history

---

[53] 'Embarkation of the Body of the Late Emperor Maximilian at Vera Cruz, Mexico', *The Illustrated London News*, 11 January 1868, 32.
[54] Sigmund Freud, 'Case Histories ("Little Hans" and the "Rat Man")' (1909), in James Strachey (ed.), *The Standard Edition of the Complete Psychological Works of Sigmund Freud*, transl. James Strachey, in collaboration with Anna Freud, assisted by Alix Strachey and Alan Tyson, vol. 10 (London: The Hogarth Press, 1955), 212, 261.
[55] See the map of political assassinations reproduced in Benedict Anderson, *Under Three Flags. Anarchism and the Anti-Colonial Imagination* (London: Verso, 2005), 76, and discussion, 69–88.
[56] Sigmund Freud, 'Trauer und Melancholie', in *Internationale Zeitschrift für Ärztliche Psychoanalyse*, 4:6 (1917), 288–301; Sigmund Freud, from Fliess papers, Manuscript G: Melancholie (no date, probably 1895), in James Starchey ed., vol. 1, *Pre-psycho-analytic publications and unpublished drafts (1886–1899)*, 200–206.

of Maximilian's own death, which Freud had also contemplated as a tourist at Maximilian's Italian castle Miramar, looking at the allegory of Maximilian ruling the new world.

It was fantastical writings like Heine's that inspired Maximilian to widen his Grand Tours beyond the confines of Europe. But, understandably, Maximilian's attitude towards the nobleness of the natives and his own European heritage was more ambivalent than that of the Romantics. He empathized with an indigenous prince, and yet also admired the idea of empire. He brought Mexican antiquities to Europe, but when he took up residence in Chapultepec Castle, an eighteenth-century palace erected for the Spanish viceroys on the tip of a sacred Aztec site, he had it redesigned in the style of Neuschwanstein – the epitome of neo-Gothic Europeanism.[57] Maximilian praised Lucca, but he also praised England for having created the *Leviathan* and the Crystal Palace. As between these two achievements of imperial power, he preferred the Crystal Palace to the Leviathan. When, in Granada, the cathedral's Quasimodo handed him the regalia of his ancestors for a few moments, Maximilian wanted to purchase them. 'Proudly and yet sadly I took in my hand the golden ring and the once powerful sword. Would it not be a brilliant dream to draw the latter in order to win the former?'[58] In Europe especially, he felt a right to control territory that used to belong to his ancestors; across the Atlantic, he felt acutely as a representative of illegitimate white power with no ancient claims to the land. Back in Europe, Maximilian was critical upon seeing the sale of women in a market in Constantinople.[59]

Representatives of other dynasties, the Hohenzollerns, Wittelsbachs, Romanoffs, and Saxe-Coburg Gothas, also sent their incumbents to the throne on global journeys between the 1880s and the 1910s. The Bavarian prince Rupprecht and the Prussian crown prince Wilhelm travelled to the Orient using the services of the North German Lloyd in 1898 and 1911, respectively. Wilhelm's documentation of his trip, which followed the same route as Franz Ferdinand's, was published in 1911 in two versions, a book and a limited-edition portfolio, while Rupprecht's appeared much later, in 1922. As Queen Victoria's great-grandson, on this occasion he became colonel-in-chief of a British regiment, the Prince Albert's Hussars, an event that was also documented photographically. In the photographs,

---

[57] Aichelburg, *Der Thronfolger und die Architektur*, 13.
[58] Maximilian I, Emperor of Mexico, *Recollections of my Life*, transl. anonymous., vol. 1 (London: Richard Bentley, 1868), 257.
[59] Egon Caesar Count Corti, *Maximilian and Charlotte of Mexico*, transl. Catherine Alison Phillips, 2 vols., vol. 1 (1924, New York and London: Knopf, 1928), plate facing page 46.

he is shown parading with an English sentry and with dragoons in various locations in India.

The Hohenzollern prince, like Franz Ferdinand, focused on his hunting of tigers and leopards in Mirzapur and Hyderabad, with one of the coloured plates showing two leopards shot by the prince on 23 January 1911. Back in Europe, Franz Ferdinand's photos of his prey, displayed by a group of seven Indians surrounding the Archduke, had been similarly retouched at the photographic studio of Carl Pietzner, who left only his highness and the tiger, surrounded by oriental wilderness, in the frame.[60] A later republication of the photograph put the Indians back in the picture.[61]

Breaking taboos

Noble families of old lineage used to be, as Norbert Elias argued in 1939, the main authors of Europe's civilizing process; but as the world public witnessed with awe and mixed feelings, the very civilization they had shaped was turning against them.[62] The ethnographic collections they had assembled were used to give authority to the autonomy of individual Habsburg ethnicities; the photographers, painters, composers, and writers who were once employed by the courts to write hagiographies and eulogies to the dynastic families now testified to the waning of their authority. In the Habsburg Empire, the commemoration of the fiftieth anniversary of Franz Josef's rule in 1898 coincided with the fiftieth anniversary of the revolutions against the Habsburg family.[63] Similarly, in Britain the celebration of European culture at home – in Grand Expositions, museums, and such like – coincided with the nascent anti-colonial rebellions in the rest of the world. They were, in the satirical language of Robert Musil, 'parallel actions' (*Parallelaktion*). In this process, the old dynasties acquired a new property – that of a celebrity of decline – suggesting that what seemed to be parallel developments were in fact crossroads of imperial disintegration.

[60] Ferdinand, *Tagebuch meiner Reise um die Erde*, vol. 1, 20.

[61] Höfer (ed.), *Imperial Sightseeing, Die Indienreise von Erzherzog von Franz Ferdinand von Österreich-Este*, 82–84. On posing and photography on sites of colonial violence, see Sean Willcock, 'Aesthetic Bodies: Posing on Sites of Violence in India, 1857–1900', in *History of Photography*, 39:2 (2015), 142–159.

[62] Norbert Elias, *Der Prozess der Zivilisation* (Basel: zum Falken, 1939).

[63] For the 1848 revolutions in transnational perspective, see Axel Körner, *1848: A European Revolution? International Ideas and National Memories of 1848*, 2nd revised ed. (Basingstoke, N.Y.: Palgrave Macmillan, 2004).

A peculiar reversal had occurred. As early as the 1850s, royal courts like those of the Habsburgs and the Bonapartes had employed court photographers. Those same photographers also produced typological ethnographic images of their subjects, both in Europe – producing exotic-looking images of various Slavic peoples – and beyond, such as a series of images of non-Europeans.[64] Court painters and photographers accompanied royal parties on grand tours where they documented acts that now appear inhuman, like the sale of women in a Constantinople market. But only a few decades later, those same photographers documented the executions of members of royal families, and some of them also became the chief authors of critical depictions of European imperial rule.

Imperial dynasties historically had a high level of control not only over their own image, but also over the cultural memory of actions carried out in their name. This was a form of cultural power or charisma at which the Habsburgs excelled even above the other families. As patrons of artists in the fifteenth and sixteenth centuries, Habsburg rulers supported such masters as Arcimboldo, Diego Velàzquez, Albrecht Dürer, and Albrecht Altdorfer, who had created memorable allegories of individual rulers and dynastic lines. In the seventeenth and eighteenth centuries, other princely houses throughout Europe commissioned artists such as Giambattista Tiepolo to represent them in allegorical frescoes of empire. What theorist of culture Guy Debord once said of the premodern Chinese emperors applies equally to Europe's dynasties: they were the private owners of history and the immortality of the soul, as each family sought to be the monopolist of Europe's cultural memory.[65] In architecture, too, the courts of major and minor princes left a fashionably neo-classical imprint on the architecture of not only the metropoles but also that of the colonies.

However, in the modern era, these tools of representation increasingly escaped the control of the royal courts.[66] During the French Revolution, the Jacobins managed to recruit the nation's leading painters, such as Jacques-Louis David, to draw allegories of rebellion against the old order. This kind of change in control over art and culture made it possible

---

[64] Pieter Judson, 'Inventing Germans: Class, Nationality, and Colonial Fantasy at the Margins of the Hapsburg Monarchy', in *Nations, Colonies, and Metropoles*, ed. Daniel A. Segal and Richard Handler, special issue of *Social Analysis*, 33 (2007), 47–67; on colonial readings of the Habsburgs, see also Ulrich Bach, 'Sacher-Masoch's Utopian Peripheries', in *The German Quarterly*, 80.2 (Spring 2007), 201–219.

[65] Ibid., 132, 97.

[66] Leo Braudy, *The Frenzy of Renown* (New York: Vintage, 1997). See also Braudy, 'Secular Anointings: Fame, Celebrity, and Charisma in the First Century of Mass Culture', in Berenson and Giloi (eds.), *Constructing Charisma*, 165–183.

for Jean-Paul Marat, a comparatively short-lived political figure with no dynastic power, to obtain a greater celebrity upon his death than the publicly executed Habsburg queen, Marie Antoinette.[67] Likewise, after the French occupation of Spain under Napoleon, a former painter at the court of Napoleon's brother Joseph, Francisco de Goya, produced a later famous allegorical image of Spanish resistance, using an anonymous man as his chief protagonist.[68] Subverting the royal minting of coins, Europeans saw the production of so-called 'medals of dishonour', where the imprint of a ruler in decline, Napoleon, was used to ridicule and mock rather than to celebrate and extol.[69] The palaces of governors and viceroys in their prime were as imposing as their destruction was dramatic, as attested to by the widely mediated picture of the destroyed palace at Lucknow after the Indian rebellion of 1857, for example. Similarly, during the Russian Revolution artists such as Boris Kustodiev, who had painted one of the last portraitists to represent Tsar Nicholas II in 1915, became enlisted as the revolution's first 'court' painters.

The revolutionaries in France were also the first to open the king's private art collection to the public. By the end of the nineteenth century, many of Europe's ruling dynasties followed suit by creating public cultural institutions themselves, but they were too late – the art market was becoming more international, and independent institutions were founded with private capital that did not depend on dynastic authority. In Europe and North America, world fairs and great exhibitions encouraged the display of paintings from several countries in what historians have described as an age of 'cultural internationalism'.[70] Imperial governments tried to control all of these institutions, but the scope was unmanageable. What Tim Blanning described as the 'power of culture' could also be used against those who had originally commissioned it.[71]

The loss of control over their own image was not a problem only for the old dynasties. Governments of every kind, including the Republican government of the United States, found it difficult to control the dissemination of visual information that could serve to critique their policies.

[67] T.J. Clark, 'Painting in the Year Two', in *Representations*, 47, Special Issue: National Cultures before Nationalism (Summer 1994), 13–63.

[68] Kenneth Clark, *Looking at Pictures* (Boston: Beacon Press, 1968), ch. on Goya.

[69] Philipp Attwood and Felicity Powell (eds.), *Medals of Dishonour* (London: The British Museum, 2009).

[70] Grace Brockington (ed.), *Internationalism and the Arts in Britain and Europe at the Fin de Siècle* (Oxford: Peter Lang, 2009).

[71] Blanning, *The Culture of Power and the Power of Culture*.

The political impact of this opening up of visual exchange was first felt in the sphere of war documentation. While governments preferred what would now be called embedded painters to depict scenes of war, or commissioned works from trusted artists after the fact, they found it increasingly difficult to prevent critical images from reaching a wider public. For example, the famous Russian battle painter Vasili Vereshchagin, who had been originally hired by the imperial army to depict heroic battle scenes, eventually became a critic of imperialism and sympathized with anarchists and socialists.[72] His depictions of the horrors of war, drawn from life and infused with biblical themes, offered a critique of wars regardless of whether they were fought by imperial Russia in Central Asia and Turkey, by the American army in the Philippines, or by the British in India. The international art market allowed him to remain independent from the payments he could have enjoyed from any of these armies. His paintings were displayed in London, Paris, St. Petersburg, Munich, Chicago, and New York, and he also sold paintings internationally. One image showing a dying Russian soldier was banned from a St. Petersburg art salon in 1873, but went on display in art salons in Chicago and Paris; conversely, his painting of British violence against Indians, *Blowing from Guns*, which revived the memory of the violent crushing of the Sepoy rebellion in 1857, was not displayed in London but was presented in St. Petersburg.[73] Such prohibitions, each of which was limited to one state, only increased his popularity. In addition to realist painting, photography was on its way to becoming an effective way to apply political pressure on governments. For instance, the celebrated French photographer Félix Nadar, who was known for his portraiture of some of Europe's leading monarchs, poets, and celebrities, in 1859 decided to fly over the battle of Solferino in a hot-air balloon to document Habsburg atrocities against the Italians.

Originally, like images of battlefields, pictures of dynastic leaders had served the purpose of what Guy Debord called a 'total justification' for the entire social system of empire.[74] Royal and noble courts mediated the way dynasties were represented, but also promoted carefully chosen representations of their own subjects, for example by organizing and documenting

---

[72] Vassili Vereshchagin, *Souvenirs. Enfance – Voyage – Guerre* (Paris: Albert Savine, 1888).

[73] Vasili Vereshchagin, *Second Appendix to Catalogue of the Verestchagin Exhibition: Realism* (Chicago: The Art Institute, 1889).

[74] Guy Debord, *The Society of the Spectacle*, transl. Black & Red (Cambridge, Mass.: MIT Press, 2010), points 6 and 4, 12–13.

parades of its subjects according to social and ethnic groups, or providing heroic images of war. Photography itself did not change this tradition. On the contrary, when Maximilian of Habsburg held court in Mexico, for instance, he took with him his court photographer, the Frenchman François Aubert, who produced extensive coverage of courtly life in Mexico City between 1864 and 1867.[75] However, changes to the way images were mediated nationally and internationally, together with the reproducibility of the photograph, meant that noble families in the modern era found it increasingly difficult to stop painters, then photographers, and later film-makers from displaying, reproducing, and distributing images on the world market. Walter Benjamin's claim that the mechanical reproducibility of art reduced the courts' ability to retain control over the production of art could thus be extended much further: dynasties could no longer exercise control over their own image.[76] Images of dynastic rulers were increasingly used as icons of their own decline in a way that differed from the fixed, static symbols of assassinations, such as the monuments and memorials which had dominated aristocratic iconography. Of the dozens of ruling houses in Europe that lost power in the twentieth-century European revolutions, two in particular became repeated targets of political assassinations: the Habsburgs and the Romanoffs, both of which lost several family members in only three generations.

The practice of photography had initially allowed dynasties to modernize their own image; members of Europe's ruling princely houses were among the first buyers of *camerae obscurae*, daguerreotypes, and other cameras. The new technologies of representation favoured displays of personal, unique, and unrepeatable characteristics, which initially allowed their aristocratic owners to continue the old hagiographic tradition.[77] However, as uses of photography spread socially, the photograph acquired a different documentary value of public significance. People used small postcard-sized photographs as *cartes de visite* through a process of reproduction invented and patented in Paris in the 1850s. The cards were pocket-sized images, usually of royal families in Europe and of political

---

[75] For Aubert's coverage of courtly life and Mexican ethnography, see *Photographs of Mexico from the mid-19th century to the early 20th century from the special collections of the Getty Research Institute* (2000, updated 2010), http://www.getty.edu/research/tools/guides_bibliographies/photography_mexico/. Accessed 1 July 2014.

[76] Walter Benjamin, 'L'œuvre d'art à l'époque de sa reproduction mécanisée', transl. Pierre Klossowski, in *Zeitschrift für Sozialforschung*, 5:1 (1936), 40–66.

[77] Roland Barthes, *Camera Lucida: Reflections on Photography* (New York: Farrar, Straus and Giroux, 1981); see also his notes for lectures at the Collège de France on Nadar's photographs of Proust's circle.

leaders in the Americas, that came in three sizes: 'cabinet', 'boudoir', and 'imperial'.[78] The new printing technique used in their production meant that these small photographs were available for a much cheaper price than the more exclusive daguerreotypes.

Public knowledge of royal assassinations far exceeded the boundaries of their empires. With new technologies improving their availability, photographs were increasingly appreciated for their documentary value; they were no longer merely hagiographic in purpose. As photographs became more easily producible and reproducible, they reached an audience that was widening in terms of both social class and geography. Within a span of twenty years, photographers originally trained in Vienna and Paris had opened offices in Berlin, St. Petersburg, Moscow, New York, Mexico City, Buenos Aires, the states of Pernambuco and Bahia, and many other locations, and the press increasingly adopted the medium as documentation of events.[79] François Aubert, who had spent time at Emperor Maximilian's court in Mexico, taking the first ethnographic photographs of Mexicans, was also the one to produce the first images of Maximilian's body and clothes riddled with bullets after his execution. Another photographer, though he probably did not witness the moment itself, used a montage to recreate the execution of Habsburg emperor Maximilian of Mexico in 1867.[80] Likewise, a 1905 daguerreotype of an open carriage in Moscow documented the assassination of Grand Duke Sergius, an uncle of Emperor Nicholas II, by means of nitrogen bomb. Revolutions against the German Barons of the Baltic provinces in Russia left vivid images of demolished country estates, which could be used both to condemn and to sympathize with the revolutionaries.

Of course, not all assassinations were documented in as much detail as that of Maximilian. In the absence of photographs showing the Romanoff family being killed, photographs taken four years prior to their execution in 1918 were scrutinized in the illustrated press and popular biographies to conjure up a feeling of immediacy. Commenting on the photograph of the Romanoff family taken a week before their execution, one article emphasized 'some of the matchless pearls afterwards stolen from their dead bodies

---

[78] Helmut Gernsheim, *A Concise History of Photography*, 3rd ed. (Toronto: Courier Dover Publications, 1986), 55ff.

[79] Armgard Schiffer-Ekhart, *Sebastianutti & Benque – Fünf Fotografen. Vier Generationen. Drei Kontinente* (Graz: Steiermärkisches Landesmuseum Joanneum, 1997).

[80] See *Le Figaro*, 11 August 1867; cf. also Juliet Wilson-Bareau, *Manet, the Execution of Maximilian: Painting, Politics and Censorship* (London: National Gallery, 1992).

by the murderers' seen around Alix von Hessen-Darmstadt's neck.[81] Instead of showing the execution of the dynastic family, Soviet filmmaker Sergei Eisenstein resorted to metonymic images: a white horse hanging from a Petersburg bridge, symbolizing the destruction of an aristocratic culture, and statues and palaces being demolished in the name of the revolution. This gave viewers a *punctum* of tragic experience, to borrow a concept from Roland Barthes's analysis of modern mythmaking. In the twentieth century, the Habsburgs and the Romanoffs shared what historian Boris Kolonitskii describes as the 'tragic eroticism' of dynastic families in decline: the irrational appeal of the royal family even and especially at the time of its greatest weakness.[82]

The Grand Tour in global circulation

If it had not been for the Habsburg's famous death, the young Prussian count Kessler would have never set foot on the colonial city of Querétaro, in north-central Mexico, which lay outside his travel route when he came to Mexico as part of his Grand Tour in 1896. As a student, Kessler had attended lectures by Wilhelm Wundt, whose multivolume comparative study on global 'folk psychology' captured the imagination of many students at the time, including Sigmund Freud.[83] As Kessler remarked in his *Notes on Mexico* of 1898, '[o]urs is possibly the last time when you can still travel; we are already hardly able to escape our civilisation; the image remains surprisingly the same from one part of the world to the other'.[84] One of the world's first users of a Kodak-2, and a great admirer of modern French art, Kessler dedicated most of his trip, a modern Grand Tour, to ethnographic exploration, documenting the Aztec ruins of the Yucatán peninsula. While in Mexico, he was a guest at the Jockey Club of Mexico

---

[81] Robert Wilton, *The Last Days of the Romanoffs* (London: Thornton Butterworth Ltd., 1920), Frontispiece; Anonymous, *The Fall of the Romanoffs. How the Ex-Empress and Rasputine Caused the Russian Revolution* (London: Henry Jenkins Limited, 1918; New York: E. P. Dutton & Co.); H. McD. S., Review of *Exeunt the Romanoffs*, *The Lotus Magazine*, 9:5 (February 1918): 231–233, 235–236. Joseph McCabe, *The Romance of the Romanoffs* (New York: Dodd, Mead and Company, 1917); Princess Cantacuzène, *Revolutionary Days. Recollections of Romanoffs and Bolsheviki, 1914–17* (Boston: Small, Maynard and Company, 1919).

[82] Boris Kolonitskii, *Tragicheskaya erotika. Obrazy imperatorskoi sem'i v gody Pervoi mirovoi voiny* (Moscow: Novoe Literaturnoe Obozrenie, 2010).

[83] Wilhelm Wundt, *Völkerpsychologie: Eine Untersuchung der Entwicklungsgesetze von Sprache, Mythus, und Sitte*, 10 vols. (Leipzig: Engelmann, 1900–20). For the context of Wundt's work, see Egbert Klautke, *The Mind of the Nation: Völkerpsychologie in Germany, 1851–1955* (New York and Oxford: Berghahn Books, 2013).

[84] Harry Graf Kessler, *Notizen über Mexiko* (Frankfurt: Insel, 1998), 59. First ed. 1898 (Berlin: Fontane).

City, the place where members of high society mingled, just as they did in Vienna and Prague. One General O. (Ochoa) he knew apparently owned the Popocatepetl. This trip resulted in an 'anthropology of decadence', as biographer Laird Easton put it; Kessler would stop at palaces and haciendas belonging to the influential local elite with professional ties to his father.[85]

Querétaro and the Yucatán ruins marked for Kessler the boundaries of European civilization and the image of a savage other. Born a year after Maximilian's execution, Kessler was the son of a Prussian banker, who had been ennobled by Wilhelm I, and an actress of Anglo-Irish nobility, whose father and grandfather were British imperial civil servants in Baghdad and in India. He had attended St. George's school in Ascot and was acquainted with the English admirers of modernist art, such as the Bloomsbury group and Roger Fry especially. In later years, on his travels along the Italian coast, he passed Maximilian's castle of Miramar and observed that 'the last Habsburgs knew how to die in beauty; Maximilian of Mexico, the Empress Elizabeth, the Archduke Rudolf, here, the Archduke Ludwig Salvator, even the humble grave of the last emperor in the small village church on Madeira, evoke aesthetic respect'. By contrast, 'the last Hohenzollerns are a slap in the face of any aesthetics, even any human respect with their rawness, fickleness, wildness and lack of taste; the last Habsburgs end their days as gentlemen, the last Hohenzollerns like carters'.[86] Worse still, at this point former German emperor Wilhelm II, whom Kessler hated, was still alive, exiled in Doorn, in the Netherlands.

The tourism industry around the Habsburgs had begun with the court itself licensing specific photographers to disseminate images of their estates to a wider public. Thus the copyright licence for distributing images of Miramar as well as monuments to Maximilian belonged to the Trieste-born photographer Guglielmo Sebastianutti. But the industry far outlived the family's own power. In the context of a blooming cultural production on the theme of crisis and decline characteristic of this period, publications on Maximilian picked up. The composer Franz Liszt wrote several works dedicated to Maximilian. Vienna State Opera commissioned the modernist composer Ernst Krenek to write a stage work on the Habsburg emperor Karl V, the reluctant emperor who agreed to have his empire reduced by half and lost the Spanish part to the Bourbons in the sixteenth century, with references to Maximilian. Outside Austria, the resonance was equally great. In Paris, Darius Milhaud wrote several musical works on the

---

[85] Laird M. Easton, *Der rote Graf. Harry Graf Kessler und seine Zeit* (Stuttgart: Klett-Cotta, 2005), 105.
[86] Kessler, 26 April 1926, in Kessler, *Diaries*, vol. 8.

subject.[87] In Mexico City, the journalist Carleton Beales, who formed part of a circle of modernist Bohemians that comprised the photographer Tina Modotti, rediscovered a forgotten memoir of Maximilian's private secretary, and edited its English translation for Yale University Press.[88]

In Germany, Maximilian was a topic of discussion among the new government elites, especially since the famous director Max Reinhardt staged Franz Werfel's play *Maximilian und Juarez*. Count Kessler's diary tells us about a conversation about it that involved the director of the Reichsbank and member of the German Democratic Party, Hjalmar Schacht; the French ambassador Roland de Margerie; the academic Otto Hoetzsch; and the president of the Reichstag, Paul Löbe.[89]

By 1938, Manet's painting and Werfel's play served as the basis for a film made in Hollywood by German expatriate Wilhelm (William) Dieterle, which extolled the new world republicanism of Mexican revolutionary Benito Juárez against the evil character of Napoleon III, who represented 'Old Europe'. By this point, in addition to Manet's Spanish source for the painting, Goya's allegory of Spanish resistance, Dieterle had one more Spanish reference to consider. Photographer Robert Capa had produced the world's first image of a man being shot dead, printed for the French magazine *Vu* and the American journal *Life*, and later discussed in his book *Death in the Making*.[90] It showed a republican soldier in the Spanish Civil War being shot by Franco's troops.[91] Dieterle, a German who belonged to the 'left' scene in Hollywood's expat community, effectively merged the two images into one, reviving the icon for the screen. The mediated production of this and other Habsburg tragedies, encouraged by the opening of the archives, turned the tragic story of one Habsburg prince into a foil, a 'transitional object' for various narratives of European decline.[92] Dieterle worked more in the tradition of a Goya than a Jacques-Louis David, making allegories of revolutionaries, rather than deceased rulers. His first published image had been a portrait

---

[87] Darius Milhaud, *Maximilien: opéra historique en trois actes et neuf tableaux* (Vienna: Universal-Edition, 1931); and Milhaud, *Suite Maximilian* (Westminster, New York, 1950, sound recsording, 33 1/3 rpm, 12 in.); Princess Marthe Bibesco, *Charlotte et Maximilien: Les Amants Chimériques* (Paris: Gallimard, 1937); George Delamare, *L'empire oublié; 1861 – l'aventure mexicaine – 1867* (Paris: Hachette, 1935); Franz Werfel, *Juárez und Maximilian dramatische historie in 3 Phasen und 13 Bildern* (Vienna: Paul Zsolnay Verlag, 1924).

[88] Blasio, *Maximilian*.   [89] Kessler, *Diary*, 12 February 1926.

[90] Robert Capa and Gerda Taro, *Death in the Making* (New York: Covici Friede, 1938).

[91] Richard Whelan, 'Proving that Robert Capa's "Falling Soldier" is Genuine: A Detective Story' (2002). The reference is to Robert Capa, 'Loyalist militiaman at the Moment of Death, Cerro Muriano, September 5, 1936', in 'Comme ils sont tombés', *Vu*, 445 (23 September 1936), 1106.

[92] Donald Winnicott, *Playing and Reality* (London: Routledge, 1971).

of Leon Trotsky in 1932.[93] In a sense, both Juárez and Maximilian are two faces of revolution; while the old European powers and the United States are forces of empire.

Many of the hagiographic films of Habsburg decline were produced by actors, directors, and composers, who, although they had been subjects of the Romanoff and Habsburg dynasties, were no particular admirers of the family: actors and directors Joseph von Sternberg and Alexander Korda, for example, or the composer Erich Wolfgang Korngold. For them, the stories of dynastic decline served as a way of rethinking their own loss of identity.[94] The deaths of these monarchs, in many cases, were 'pseudo-events' in the age of mass culture not because they never happened but because the meaning that was attributed to them stood in for many other dimensions of imperial decline. In the same way, few people beyond the borders of the Austro-Hungarian Empire had even heard of Franz Ferdinand when he was shot in 1914. Instead, interpreters focused on the 'doubly symbolic' name of his assassin, Gavrilo Prinzip, who they saw as a modern Archangel Gabriel sent to earth to let loose a 'world-cataclysm'.[95]

The growing film industry allowed a much wider audience to share in the experience of decline. The world's leading film production companies, based in the Soviet Union and in Hollywood, reproduced the memory of dynastic decline and its symbols for a much wider audience and an increasingly global market. These films included Sergei Eisenstein's film *October* (1928), for example, which documents the Revolution of 1917, or Esfir' Shub's *Padenie dinastii Romanovykh* (The Fall of the Romanoff Dynasty) (1927), a documentary. Other films on the subject include works by film-makers based in Germany – for example, Alexander Korda with his *Tragödie im Hause Habsburg* (Tragedy in the House of Habsburg) (1924), and Rudolf Raffé with the film *Das Schicksal derer von Habsburg – die Tragödie eines Kaiserreiches* (The Fate of the von Habsburgs – the Tragedy of an Empire) (1928), which featured the young Leni Riefenstahl as an actress and was filmed on location at Schönbrunn Palace in Vienna. In Hollywood, there were Erich von Stroheim's *The Wedding March* (1928), one of the last silent movies; Sidney Franklin's *Reunion in Vienna* (1933), about romance and

---

[93] http://bostonreview.net/BR30.2/linfield.php.

[94] See Leo Löwenthal, 'German Popular Biographies: Culture's Bargain Counter', in *The Critical Spirit. Essays in Honor of Herbert Marcuse*, ed. Barrington Moore, Jr., and Kurt H. Wolff (Boston: Beacon Press, 1967), 267–287, originally in *Radio Research, 1942–1943*, ed. Paul L. Lazarsfeld and Frank Stanton (New York: Arno Press, 1944).

[95] Ludwig, *Wilhelm Hohenzollern. The Last of the Kaisers*, 433–434.

social crisis in the aftermath of the First World War; *The King Steps Out* (1936), about Franz Josef's romance with Elizabeth, directed by Joseph von Sternberg; *The Great Waltz* (1938), a film about Johann Strauss junior's ambivalent relationship to the European revolutionaries of 1848; *Juárez* (1939) the story of Emperor Maximilian of Mexico, produced by Wilhelm Dieterle; and in the 1950s, a revival of the image of Sisi in Hollywood and Austrian films.[96]

As a form of voluntary homelessness, globetrotting first became an activity for the affluent, and typically male, members of the modern world. Private and corporate organizers profited from the availability of new travel routes, backed by the military power of European imperial governments. The Suez Canal, which opened in 1869, allowed direct passage from the Mediterranean to the Red and Arabian seas as well as the Indian Ocean.[97] Thomas Cook's company alone claimed to have organized tours for over two million people, including not only Europe's aristocracy but also its cultural celebrities like Robert Louis Stevenson.[98] Following Emperor Franz Josef's presence at the opening of the Suez Canal in 1869 in his capacity as King of Jerusalem, his family members also discovered the Orient as a travel destination.[99] The visit of Crown Prince Rudolf to the area in 1881 was a state occasion.[100] About a hundred years later, the Suez Canal became the symbol of decolonization.[101]

The travel notes to exotic countries that the Habsburgs left behind echoed those of other princes of their generation, such as the Saxe-Coburg Gothas, and the Hohenzollerns. They show princes shooting rare animals such as leopards and lions, which were circulated in the European press. Yet at the end of the European civil wars around the First World War, such noble celebrities themselves became victims of

---

[96] Alice Freifeld, 'Empress Elisabeth as Hungarian Queen: The Uses of Celebrity Monarchism', in *The Limits of Loyalty: Imperial Symbolism, Popular Allegiances, and State Patriotism in the Late Habsburg Monarchy*, ed. Laurence Cole and Daniel L. Unowsky (Oxford: Berghahn, 2005), 138–162.

[97] On the cultural significance of the Suez Canal as a transimperial contact zone, see Valeska Huber, *Channelling Mobilities: Migration and Globalisation in the Suez Canal Region and Beyond, 1869–1914* (Cambridge: Cambridge University Press, 2013); for the importance of the Suez Canal for European integration and the Suez crisis in 1956, see Peo Hansen and Stefan Jonsson, *Eurafrica: The Untold History of European Integration and Colonialism* (London: Bloomsbury, 2014).

[98] F. Robert Hunter, 'Tourism and Empire: The Thomas Cook & Son Enterprise on the Nile, 1868–1914', in *Middle Eastern Studies*, 40:5 (September 2004), 28–54, 31.

[99] Rudolph von Oesterreich, *Eine Orientreise vom Jahre 1881* (Vienna: Kaiserl.-Königl. Hof- u. Staatsdr., 1885).

[100] Robert-Tarek Fischer, *Österreich im Nahen Osten: die Grossmachtpolitik der Habsburgermonarchie im Arabischen Orient, 1633–1918* (Vienna, Cologne, Weimar: Böhlau, 2006).

[101] On the Suez crisis in 1956 and 1957 and Nasser's demand to nationalize the Suez Canal, see Hansen and Jonsson, *Eurafrica*, 214ff.

assassinations. The exotic cultures that they used to collect, such as the 'savage' cultures of the Aztec, instead became the starting point for a new type of modern imagination. Court publishers promoted work of 'ethnographies' not only of non-European savages, but increasingly also of their own subjects, particularly the Southern Slavs.[102] However, the Habsburgs soon became objects of touristic and ethnographic interest. The Austrian museum of ethnography has displayed the Habsburg collections of Aztec memorabilia, such as the Penacho, the alleged feather crown of Montezuma, as part of its national heritage ever since the Habsburgs had acquired the crown.[103] But in the twentieth century, even that crown has become an object of dispute between the Austrian state and Mexico. The old rulers had introduced European publics to the "savage" mind; and inspired by these images, this public now rediscovered the power of transgressing a taboo. Heine had been right: Vitzliputzli, the Aztec god of anti-colonial resistance, had finally reached Europe.

[102] Carl von Czoernig, *Ethnographische Karte der österreichischen Monarchie* (Gotha: Justus Perthes, no year).
[103] More on the fascinating history of the Penacho, see Khadija von Zinnenburg Carroll, *Fragile Crown: Empire, Collection, Repatriation* (Chicago: Chicago University Press, forthcoming).

CHAPTER 2

Shared horizons
The sentimental elite in the Great War

One day in early August 1914, Count Robert Keyserlingk-Cammerau, Prussian governor of Königsberg, was unpleasantly surprised by a knock on his door. His cousin Alfred, imperial administrator of *Tsarskoe selo*, Tsar Nicholas II's summer residence near St. Petersburg, was seeking his hospitality for the night. Under normal circumstances, the cousins would have been delighted to meet. This time, however, their meeting created an ethical dilemma. War had broken out in Europe only a few days earlier, a conflict in which the states whose imperial families they served were on opposing sides. Robert, a German imperial civil servant, was obliged to follow orders of his government, which was to arrest any Russian subject found in Königsberg. Alfred had been surprised by the war while travelling in Germany on personal business. He knew that his male staff, some 250 people, were about to be conscripted into the army, leaving the administration of the estates in his hands; he had to get back to St. Petersburg urgently. Finally, he managed to secure a makeshift seat in the toilet cabin of the last, overcrowded train leaving Berlin for Russia, but then got stuck in East Prussia, near the Russian border where, allegedly, Cossacks had disrupted trains passing to Russia. The guards on the train were instructed to take into custody and bring back to Germany all Russian subjects. Alfred narrowly escaped and made his way to Königsberg's *Altes Schloss*, where he knew his cousin was resident.[1]

For one night only, familial ties trumped political allegiance. Before sunrise Alfred departed in his cousin's official car, past the Prussian guards, to the train station. Having to seek an indirect route back to Russia, he returned to Berlin and took the train to Hamburg, then boarded a boat to Sweden. Personal connections to two famous Petersburgians, the Swedish petroleum magnate Alfred Nobel and the Petersburg delicatessen merchant

---

[1] William M. Salter, 'The Russian Revolution', in *International Journal of Ethics*, 17:3 (April 1907), 301–316, 303, citing Wolf von Schierbrand, 'Russia: Her Strength and Her Weakness' (1904).

Grigory Yelisseev, allowed him to board their private steamer, one of the few still operating on the route back to Petersburg. However, only a few days after his arrival there, he was arrested once again – this time, by the Russian gendarmes – and was taken to the Peter and Paul fortress on charges of espionage for Germany. During the ensuing Russian Revolution and Civil War, Alfred joined Kolchak's 'white' army in Siberia, which eventually lost to the Bolsheviks. Robert Keyserlingk became the German Commissioner for Lithuania and the 'eastern territories' before taking a post in St. Petersburg, now called Petrograd, as a military attaché, where he sought to promote German interests in Russian monarchist circles.[2] Moving to Berlin after the failure of this campaign, he eventually completed his political career in the Federal German Republic as a member of the Prussian Council of State and German agricultural policy advisor at the new World Economic Forum in Geneva.

Such foreign connections could be a curse and a blessing at the same time. For example, Alfred Keyserling, in addition to being a Russian subject and civil administrator of the *Tsarskoe selo* district, as well as a member of the Courland nobility, was also the founding co-owner of Baltic Lloyd, a commercial navigation agency originally co-financed by Bremer Lloyd and serving the ports of Libau, Emden, and Bremen.[3] By the twentieth century, the sort of internationalism that Keyserling and his cousins practised professionally and socially appeared to some, especially to Russians and Germans, like acts of treason.

Today, historians speak of the Great War in an increasingly cosmopolitan sense. The parties that went to war in 1914 were half conscious 'sleepwalkers', a reader learns in 2013, and the imperial or national interests they represented were at least one level of scrutiny removed.[4] The very idea

---

[2] Arved Freiherr von Taube, 'Die baltisch-deutsche Führungsschicht und die Loslösung Livlands und Estlands von Russland 1916–1918', in *Von den Baltischen Provinzen zu den Baltischen Staaten. Beiträge zur Entstehungsgeschichte der Republiken Estland und Lettland 1917–1918*, ed. Jürgen von Hehn et al. (Marburg/Lahn: Herder-Institut, 1971), 97–217, 105. See his 'Militärpolitische Berichte' from 21 December 1917 to 1 February 1918 from Petrograd, in Winfried Baumgart, 'Die militärpolitischen Berichte des Freiherrn von Keyserlingk aus Petersburg Januar-Februar 1918', in *Vierteljahreshefte für Zeitgeschichte*, 15 (1967), 87–104.

[3] Heide W. Whelan, *Adapting to Modernity: Family, Caste and Capitalism among the Baltic German Nobility* (Cologne: Böhlau, 1999); Eduard von Dellingshausen, *Die Entstehung, Entwicklung und Aufbauende Tätigkeit der Baltischen Ritterschaften* (Langensalza: H. Beyer, 1928).

[4] Christopher Clark, *The Sleepwalkers: How Europe Went to War in 1914* (London: Allen Lane, 2013); Paul Fussell, *Wartime: Understanding and Behavior in the Second World War* (Oxford: Oxford University Press, 1989); Paul Fussell, *The Great War and Modern Memory* (Oxford: Oxford University Press, 2005); Mary L. Dudziak, *War Time: An Idea, Its History, Its Consequences* (Oxford: Oxford University Press, 2012).

of war has become broader, comprising the home front and the economic and cultural aspects of life in wartime.

But at the time of the First World War, having a cosmopolitan perspective on the theatre of war was the prerogative of the imperial elites. These included aristocratic families like the Keyserlings, whose familiarity with the administration and economic structure of more than one empire gave them multiple perspectives. Privileges were also incorporated in the institutional fabric of military careers in imperial Europe. Officers of the imperial armies had a shared cultural code and even exchanged institutions of honours. Members of the affluent middle classes could also fall back on experiences of cultural consumption and personal friendships, which could be rekindled after the war. Those among them who produced written accounts of their experience were among the first generation of writers of the First World War who continued seeing the war from the point of view of 'civil society'. Some of these authors did so while recognizing that their own armies had turned into perpetrators against civilians. In this sense human sympathy, patriotism, and cosmopolitanism were entangled in the writing of officer-intellectuals in ways that were quite different from the twenty-first-century historiography of the conflict.[5]

Selfie with a periscope: the experience of imperial horizons

In one of his wartime photographs, we can see Count Kessler gazing at the horizon through a periscope.[6] This emblematic image of elite vision in the war might, anachronistically, be called a 'selfie with a periscope'. It is a curious photograph because, in a real situation of danger, an observer would not be standing in an open field. It is the reflexive character of the photograph that is of interest here: this is not a photograph of an officer in action, but one of an officer in narcissistic contemplation. The photograph simulates contemplation as a form of military action, since he is engaged in strategic analysis of the horizon. Yet the ultimate objective of this work is to provide a flattering portrait of the seer, not to communicate what he can see. In the background, the newly entrenched frontiers between the German, the Russian, and the Austro-Hungarian empires, blend into a common horizon of uncertain expectations. But for Kessler, the military frontier becomes a horizon, as he stages himself in

---

[5] Cf. Jay Winter (ed.), *The Cambridge History of the First World War*, vol. III Civil Society (Cambridge: Cambridge University Press, 2014).

[6] I am grateful to Günter Riederer for drawing my attention to this photograph in his introduction to Kessler's war diaries. In Kessler, *Diaries*, vol. 6.

Figure 5 Count Harry Kessler with a periscope on the eastern front.
Deutsches Literaturarchiv Marbach, HKN

Romantic pose. This perspective was familiar to his European contemporaries from such works as Caspar David Friedrich's *Monk by the Sea* (1808–10), which a French admirer had once praised for its capacity to convey tragedy in landscapes.[7] Like in Friedrich's famous painting, in this wartime portrait, a monotonous landscape produces a mood and an expression, which traditional portraiture would have projected onto the face of the portrayed. Aside from inverting the relationship between the figure and the landscape, the portrait also deceives the viewers, who cannot see what the figure can see and are thus forced to think and imagine their perception in their own heads. Even more than Friedrich's monk, Kessler enjoys the privilege of looking through a technical device onto a detail that remains unknown to the viewer of the photograph.

As Kessler noted in his war diary from the eastern front, the periscope view revealed an odd image of Galicia:

> a farmer's house, some three or four meters in front of it a trench occupied by the Austrians, and some thirty kilometres on the left [. . .] a Russian shelter, from which Russians were walking in and out. On the adjacent field between the Austrian trench and the Russians, some forty meters wide, a small girl was grazing a herd of sheep. As we watched, one of our grenades hit the ground near the shelter, and we could see the Russians rushing out quickly.[8]

The cold, cinematographic description of his own army's destruction of military targets along with civilian lives was the very opposite of the kind of 'flesh-witnessing', which is so characteristic of the soldier experience in the Great War, including authors such as Ernst Jünger.[9] The meaning of the experience derives from detachment, not involvement. Moreover, the tragedy of this experience is not a national one, or associated with any one empire. Before the war, Kessler, who had served as director of the influential German Artists' Union, promoted an idea of style in which there was

---

[7] The phrase belongs to the French sculptor David D'Angers, cited in André Bruel (ed.), *Les Carnets inédits de Pierre-Jean David d'Angers*, vol. I (1828–37) (Paris: Plon, 1958), 337. On Caspar David Friedrich and his reception among modernists in France and Germany, see Françoise Forster-Hahn, 'Text and Display: Julius Meier-Graefe, the 1906 White Centennial in Berlin, and the Canon of Modern Art', in *Art History*, 38:1 (February 2015), 138–169, and Pierre Wat, *Naissance de l'art romantique: peinture et théorie de l'imitation en Allemagne et en Angleterre* (Paris: Flammarion, 1999). On Friedrich and landscapes, see Joseph Leo Koerner, *Caspar David Friedrich and the Subject of Landscape*, 2nd ed. (London: Berghahn, 2009), 143ff.

[8] Kessler, 18 February 1915, in Kessler, *Diaries*, vol. 5.

[9] Cf. Yuval Noah Harari, *The Ultimate Experience. Battlefield Revelations and the Making of Modern War Culture, 1450–2000* (Basingstoke: Palgrave Macmillan, 2008).

no contrast between being a 'good German' and a 'good European'.[10] This photograph revealed a new dimension to this statement, transposing it from the realm of conflicts over styles to the realm of military conflicts between the European societies.

It was the desire to capture a complex reality devoid of meaning that prompted another officer who found himself in Galicia, Viktor Shklovsky, to reach further into the reservoirs of European literary history for a narrative model. Like Kessler, Shklovsky had begun his military service in an imperial army – of Russia, in his case – but gradually developed doubts about the logic of empire, without, however, ever fully endorsing the logic of revolution.[11] Shklovsky narrated his entire experience of war on the Galician front in the tone of his favourite English-speaking author, Laurence Sterne. His path through the eastern front was a *Sentimental Journey* with echoes of Sterne's celebrated Grand Tour to France and the continent. It was meaningless if goals were defined in terms of geographic horizons; in telling about his life, he was merely 'turning himself into a prepared substance for the heirs'. Yet, this experience of the imperial periphery also reminded him that in literature, it was the peripheral genres that had made breakthroughs in literature: 'New forms in art are created by the canonization of peripheral forms', he argued, just as Pushkin had developed the genre of the private album into an art form, as the novel had developed from horror stories like Bram Stoker's *Dracula*, and as modernist poetry drew inspiration from gypsy ballads.[12] In the same way, he hoped, the travelogue – particularly, *his* travelogue of a meaningless war on the periphery – would contribute to a new literary form, and a new way of thinking about literature. It did: it created the theory, which he described as *ostranenie*, or detachment.

[10]   Harry Graf Kessler, 'Nationalität', in *Die Zukunft*, 14:27 (1906), 17–27. Reprinted in *Harry Graf Kessler: Künstler und Nationen, Aufsätze und Reden 1899–1933. Gesammelte Schriften in drei Bänden*, ed., Cornelia Blasberg and Gerhard Schuster, vol. 2 (Frankfurt am Main: Insel, 1988), 117–130. More on Kessler's conception of the nation and the influence of Wundt on his ideas in Laird Easton, *The Red Count. The Life and Times of Kessler, Harry* (Berkeley, Los Angeles, and London: University of California Press, 2002), 162–163.

[11]   On estrangement as a device, see Viktor Shklovsky, *Iskusstvo kak priem (1919)*, in Viktor Shklovsky, *O teorii prozy* (Moscow: Krug, 1925); on sentimentalism as a literary style and a mode of narrating wartime experience, see James Chandler, *An Archaeology of Sympathy. The Sentimental Mode in Literature and Cinema* (Chicago and London: University of Chicago Press, 2013), and Mikhail Bakhtin, "The Problem of Sentimentalism", in Bakhtin, *Sobranie sochinenii v semi tomakh*, ed. S.G. Bocharev, vol. 3 (Moscow: Russkie slovari, 1996), 304–305.

[12]   Viktor Shklovsky, *A Sentimental Journey. Memoirs, 1917–1922*, transl. Richard Sheldon (Ithaca, N.Y.: Cornell University Press, 1970), 233.

To this day, historians refer to those parts of Europe which border on the eastern front and the nation states that flickered into and out of existence during the twentieth century as 'borderlands', as the locations of 'vanished kingdoms', as 'half-forgotten Europe', as 'invented' places, or even as 'no-place'.[13] In fact, in all of its history, the geography, if not necessarily the languages and cultures of eastern Europe, has probably never been as well known as in the mid-twentieth century. The image of the East as a great unknown remained a shibboleth of the post-Enlightenment *philosophes*, a geographic metaphor for the separation between civilization and barbarism, between power and weakness, and, more recently, between primitive national freedom and the imperial domination of modern civilization.

Kessler had experienced the eastern front in the First World War in an ethnographic light that might also be familiar from accounts such as Winston Churchill's *Unknown War*.[14] By contrast to the western front, the eastern and middle-eastern fronts required the use of more traditional elements in the organization of the army. Large distances had to be covered on uneven terrain, which required extensive uses of cavalry. In his letters, Kessler speculated about whether the former Pale of Settlement could be turned into a vassal empire of the Germans, to be ruled by a Jewish dynasty such as the Rothschild family.[15] The search for Europe's internally colonized peoples, like the Jews and other eastern Europeans who looked exotic, drew artists and anthropologists to the area.[16] 'Tomorrow I am going to the front to examine the battleground and collect details. I suggested sending Vogeler to accompany me so that he could make sketches', Kessler remarked in his diary.[17] The painter Heinrich Vogeler (1872–1942) eventually emigrated to Soviet Russia in 1931, where he died in a labour camp because he was suspected of being a German 'enemy'.[18]

---

[13] Norman Davies, *Vanished Kingdoms: The History of Half-Forgotten Europe [US Subtitle: The Rise and Fall of States and Nations]* (London: Penguin, 2012); Larry Wolff, *Inventing Eastern Europe. The Map of Civilization on the Mind of the Enlightenment* (Palo Alto: Stanford University Press, 1994).

[14] Winston Churchill, *The Unknown War* (New York: Scribner's Sons, 1931).

[15] *New York Times*, 22 December 1918.

[16] See Natalya Goncharova's ethnographic depictions of Jews in Southern Russia, in the exhibition catalogue *Natal'ia Goncharova. Mezhdu vostokom i zapadom* (Moscow: Tret'iakovskaia galereia, 2013).

[17] Kessler, 21 October 1915, in Kessler, *Diaries*, vol. 5.

[18] After the operation 'Barbarossa' in 1941, Vogeler was deported to Kazakhstan as an enemy alien and died there in 1942.

War ethnographies and travel literature were modes of thinking about military violence that had developed greatly on the basis of experiences of the eastern front. In the west, tear gas and shelling were the most prominent instruments of war; in the east, where large distances had to be covered and the ground was insecure, cavalry continued to be important, even though contemporaries also report aerial attacks using Zeppelins being a constant danger. Being on the eastern front required a much deeper sort of military intelligence. Confusion was everywhere: Czech nationalists with German names, Poles who thought of themselves as Lithuanians but were socialists at heart, and so on.[19] This was still true in the Second World War. During his service for British intelligence, acclaimed historian Hugh Seton-Watson remarked that people in Britain were 'aware of the existence of Zulus and Malays, Maoris and Afridis', but eastern Europe with its 'unpronounceable names' remained uncharted territory, 'another world', full of wild plains and forests.[20]

At the same time, not all of the encounters on the eastern front were confusing. Particularly officers could rely on having a shared cultural code with others of the same status. As Robert Liddell, a war journalist for the prestigious illustrated journal *Sphere*, who had just recently moved from the western to the eastern front, recalled, '[o]fficers of good family almost invariably could speak French. So could almost every Pole I met, and almost every lady doctor. [...] and certainly the soldiers from the Baltic Provinces spoke German as well as they spoke Russian; many, indeed spoke better'.[21] He recalled being greatly amused by the following anachronistic words of one Russian general Bielaiev: 'My boot', said the general, 'was filled with the gore of my steed'. General Bielaiev, who had Scottish ancestors, had learnt most of his English by reading Sir Walter Scott. For the purposes of the job, the journalist Liddell served as an officer of the Russian army, travelling along the front line with the Red Cross trains. Even though English was rarely spoken in the Russian army, he could get by on the eastern front despite his relatively poor Russian: the Russian general even called Liddell his fellow countryman, referring to his own Scottish ancestry. The half-mystical eastern Europe, some of whose local cultures, such as that of the Carpathian mountains, were hardly known to western Europeans, became one of the topoi of the 'war

[19] Vejas Gabriel Liulevicius, *War Land on the Eastern Front: Culture, National Identity, and German Occupation in World War* (New York: Cambridge University Press, 2000).

[20] Hugh Seton-Watson, *Eastern Europe between the Wars: 1918–1941* (Cambridge: Cambridge University Press, 1945), xiii.

[21] Robert Scotland Liddell, *Actions and Reactions in Russia* (New York: Dutton & Company, 1918), 16.

experience' for German audiences at home, as for instance in the liberal *Vossische Zeitung.*[22]

Social scientists also became interested in analysing and representing the various European ethnicities of the eastern front, as in the work of the anthropologist Sven Hedin, *Eastwards! (Nach Osten!).*[23] Hedin, who collected ethnographic observations of the peoples of Europe, was another civilian assigned to Kessler on the eastern front. Kessler, himself once a tourist in search of the exotic, followed Hedin's activities as he was taking pictures of local churches. The last person to study the wooden architecture of Galicia had been Franz Ferdinand himself.[24] Work of ethnography in the eastern front was also produced by German and Russian writers and artists. Arnold Zweig, who worked in German propaganda, provided illustrations of the eastern European Jews. The modernist artists Natalya Goncharova and Marc Chagall also made exotic-looking 'Jewish types' the main protagonists of their paintings.[25] In German prisoner-of-war camps, the anthropologist Leo Frobenius and a team of linguists 'worked' with interned Indians, Caucasians, Central Asians, and Africans from the British, Russian, and French armies to compare their intellectual faculties with those of Europeans.[26] Just as embedded photographers have become the order of the day in present-day wars, during the First World War, what might be called 'embedded war tourism' attracted a number of journalists and other intellectuals to war zones.

The officer's role provided opportunities for sentimental detachment thanks to privileged access to such devices as periscopes. Traditionally, the officer class had the advantage of riding on horseback. During the Great War, the horse, the earliest 'technique' of aristocratic detachment, was gradually replaced by the airship. Other devices of this kind included special weaponry as well as periscopes and cameras. The mechanisms of detachment were only available to the higher army ranks. They were not limited to technologies but included such practices as the use of embedded artists and journalists assigned to officers. All this enabled members of the

---

[22] 'Die deutschen Truppen in den Karpathen', in *Vossische Zeitung*, Nr. 112, Abend-Ausgabe, 2 March 1915, 3. See aslo Charlotte Heymel, *Touristen an der Front. Das Kriegserlebnis 1914–1918 als Reiseerfahrung in zeitgenössischen Reiseberichten* (Münster: LIT, 2007).

[23] Sven Hedin, *Nach Osten!* (Leipzig: Brockhaus, 1916).   [24] Kessler, *Diaries*, 29 April 1915.

[25] On Goncharova's ethnographic paintings of the Jews, see Cheryl Kramer, 'Natalia Goncharova. Her Depiction of Jews in Tsarist Russia', in *Woman's Art Journal*, 23:1 (Spring–Summer, 2002), 17–23.

[26] Leo Frobenius, *Der Völkerzirkus unserer Feinde* (Berlin: Eckart, 1916); on Frobenius and embedded ethnography with non-European prisoners of war, see Gerhard Höpp, *Muslime in der Mark: als Kriegsgefangene und Internierte In Wünsdorf und Zossen, 1914 – 1924* (Berlin: das Arabische Buch, 1999).

officer class to remove themselves from the theatre of war itself, both psychologically and physically. Detachment was an institutionalized privilege.[27] Zeppelin airships not only opened up the privilege of being removed from the ground but also offered the freedom to transgress political borders. For the first two decades, flights were almost exclusively a privilege of the few.

One of the first Zeppelin fleets was founded in a Saxon royal regiment. The Saxon nobleman Baron hans Hasso von Veltheim served during the war as a reconnaissance photographer. Veltheim was one of the first German enthusiasts of competitive hot-air ballooning, having joined the Fédération Aéronautique Internationale in 1905. Like the first British air minister, Sir Samuel Hoare, he was among the first generation of European elites to cross international borders by air.[28] He noted in his war diary that once he had flown as far as the imperial palace of Peterhof.[29] Before being deployed as First Officer of a Zeppelin airship, he had been responsible for photography on the Belgian front, for which he used unmanned tethered balloons as well as airplanes. Veltheim's panorama shots of the Belgian theatre of war, which he kept in his personal archive, are visual testimonies of this European apocalypse [Fig. 6].

The writing of stylized war diaries like Shklovsky's, the production of wartime self-portraits and the aesthetics of destruction in reconnaissance photography shot from the air: all these were forms of experiencing and representing horizons which invited reflections on conceptual frontiers. The meta-historical concepts of 'experience' and 'expectation', which the historian Reinhart Koselleck ascribed to the realm of theoretical reflections

---

[27] Guillaume de Syon, *Zeppelin! Germany and the Airship, 1900–1939* (Baltimore: Johns Hopkins University Press, 2002).

[28] Hans-Hasso von Veltheim, *Meine handschriftlichen Original-Reiseberichte aus Indien 1935/36*, in LHASA, MD, H 173, II Nr. 103, 1–119. See also typescript, *Bericht meiner zweiten Indienreise 1937/38*, ULB Halle, 1–832; published versions under *Tagebücher aus Asien. Erster Teil. Bombay. Kaljutta. Kashmir. Afghanistan. Die Himalayas. Nepal. Benares. 1935–1939* (Cologne: Greveb, 1951); *Der Atem Indiens. Tagebücher aus Asien. Neue Folge. Ceylon und Südindien* (Hamburg: Claassen, 1954); *Götter und Menschen zwischen Indien und China. Tagebücher aus Asien. Dritter Teil. Birma. Thailand. Kambodscha. Malaya. Java und Bali*. Unter Mitwirkung von Maria Stephan (Hamburg: Claassen, 1858). Thanks to John Palatini and Georg Rosentreter for introducing me to these materials, and for their edited collection *Alter Adel, neuer Geist. Studien zur Biographie und zum Werk Hans-Hasso von Veltheims* (Halle: Mitteldeutscher Verlag, 2012). On the history of the air force, see Viscount Templewood [Sir Samuel Hoare], *Empire of the Air. The Advent of the Air Age 1922–29* (London: Collins, 1957).

[29] Hans-Hasso von Veltheim, diary entry for 6 August 1916, Kriegstagebücher in LHASA, Mappe I, Lebensdokumente, 22.

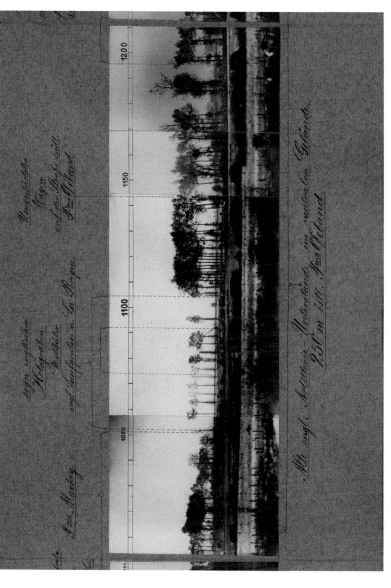

Figure 6 Panorama of Chateau Wieltje, western front. Lt. von Veltheim. Feld – Luft. Abtlg. 1. 30. October 1915. Veltheim Archive, Ostrau. Depositum Veltheim at the Universitäts- und Landesbibliothek Sachsen-Anhalt, Halle (Saale)

on horizons, were rooted in the immediate experiences of imperial horizons.[30]

The cosmopolitans in the German Society of 1914

As John Maynard Keynes and George Curzon, two lovers of post-impressionist art, arrived in Paris in late March 1918 to bid at an auction of post-impressionist art, the German army was bombing Paris. Count Kessler, German attaché in Bern and another collector of post-impressionism, wrote in his diary: 'War is a tough thing.'[31] He feared the lack of precision in bombing would damage not only Notre Dame and the Bibliothèque Nationale, which were key sites of his intellectual formation, but also the cemetery of Père Lachaise, where his father and his grand-parents lay buried.

Kessler's father had made a fortune in banking, connected to the railway business in Europe and Canada. The German emperor Wilhelm I ennobled him, according to family legend, as a sign of deference to the beauty of his Anglo-Irish wife, Alice Blosse-Lynch. The connection to Paris came from Kessler's mother, who chose to be based there. It was her side of the family, of Anglo-Irish nobility, with a home in Partrey House in County Mayo, which also made Kessler aware of British imperial history of the British Empire. His grandfather had been a British minister in Baghdad during Mehmet Ali's rule.[32] In March 1925, Kessler met distant Irish relatives in Paris who reported about the effects of the revolution in County Mayo; in the afternoon of the same day, he was engaged in debates of Count Richard Coudenhove's plans for a pan-European federation with the German ambassador in France.[33] Kessler used his connections to British and French contemporaries to foster greater understanding between what he called his three 'Fatherlands'. His autobiographic cosmo-politanism, his 'English, German blood, English, German, French cultural heritage' became a foundation for a particular form of internationalism.[34]

Returning home after the war, he could barely recognize his own former self: that man from the Belle Epoque, who had commissioned from his French friend Aristide Maillol the sculpture of a cyclist, that furniture

---

[30] Reinhart Koselleck, '"Space of Experience" and "Horizon of Expectation": Two Historical Categories', in Koselleck, *Futures Past. On the Semantics of Historical Time*, transl. Keith Tribe (New York: Columbia University Press, 2004), 255–277.

[31] Kessler, 24 March 1918, in Kessler, *Diaries*, vol. 6.   [32] Laird Easton, *The Red Count*, 1–6.

[33] Kessler, 30 March 1925, in Kessler, *Diaries*, vol. 8.

[34] Harry Graf Kessler, 'Erlebnis mit Nietzsche', in *Die Neue Rundschau* (April 1935), 391–507, 407, 402.

designed by Henry van de Velde, a Belgian, and commissioned the British artist Edward Gordon Craig to design illustrations for an edition of Shakespeare's Hamlet – it was as if this man could no longer exist. In the aftermath of the war, Kessler began to view his background as a unique form of cultural capital. Before the war, friends called him the member of an anti-Wilhelmine 'Fronde' of good taste and anti-moralism.[35] As his views later radicalized, he earned himself the nickname of 'Red Count'.

War was a traumatic experience for him. He had witnessed it on the western front, where he saw the German actions against civilians in Belgium first-hand, before being transferred east, which had shocked him no less. Kessler kept a diary, wrote letters, and engaged in discussions to cope with the traumatic experience of war. With his bibliophile Cranach press, which he had founded in 1913, inspired by William Morris's Arts and Crafts movement, Kessler turned from a Prussian patriot into a patron of doubt.[36] He began to publish poetry from the trenches, including by communist poets – 'Sulamith' by Wieland Herzfelde and 'Eroberung' ('Conquest') by the expressionist poet Johannes R. Becher, the latter, in collaboration with the communist publisher Malik.[37] Kessler's press was indeed 'cosmopolitan'.[38] But he also sponsored communist artists like George Grosz and John Heartfield to do the design, often in collaboration with established German presses such as the Insel publishing house.[39] In 1921, he published in German *War and Collapse. Select Letters from the Front* on paper handcrafted with his old French friend Aristide Maillol, with a cover by Georg Grosz.[40]

---

[35] Kessler, *Diaries*, 5 December 1931. William Shakespeare, *The Tragedie of Hamlet Prince of Denmarke*, ed. J. Dover Wilson, ill. Edward Gordon Craig and Eric Gill, printed by Harry Graf Kessler (Weimar: Cranachpresse, 1930).

[36] On Kessler's press in the context of interwar internationalism, see Dina Gusejnova, 'Die russophile Fronde. Mit Kessler zur bibliographischen Internationale', in Roland Kamzelak (ed.), *Kessler, der Osten und die Literatur* (Münster: Mentis, 2015), 41–67.

[37] Karl Kraus, 'Notizen: Was es in Berlin noch gibt', in *Die Fackel*, xxix (9 October 1917), 89. Kraus referred to Harry Kessler (ed.), Virgil, *Eclogae & Georgica, Latine et Germanice. Volumen prius: Eclogae* (Vimariae: Impressit H. Comes de Kessler in aedibus suis Cranachpresse, 1914); Wieland Herzfelde, *Sulamith* (Berlin: Barger, 1917), Salomo and Eric Gill, *Das Hohe Lied: [Auf d. Handpressen d. Cranachpresse in 3 Farben gedr.]* (Leipzig: Insel-Verl., 1931).

[38] Brinks, *Das Buch als Kunstwerk: die Cranach Presse des Grafen Harry Kessler* (Laubach: Triton Verlag, 2003).

[39] Henry van de Velde and Finanzamt Weimar, 1922, AZ RKW 27 A, in Bundesarchiv, R 32/90, 1920–27.

[40] For details of this publication, see Felix Brusberg and Sabine Carbon (eds.), *Krieg und Zusammenbruch von 1914–18. Aus den Feldpostbriefen von Harry Graf Kessler* (Berlin: Edition K., 2014). I thank Sabine Carbon and the Kessler-Gesellschaft for this image.

Figure 7 Frontispiece of Harry Graf Kessler (ed.), *Krieg und Zusammenbruch 1914–1918: aus Feldpostbriefen* (Weimar: Cranachpresse, 1921).
Image courtesy of Sabine Carbon

The war had blurred boundaries between nations and empires even more: 'politics and cabaret', 'trenches, storming regiments, the dying, U-boats, Zeppelins', 'victories', 'pacifists', and the 'wild newspaper people', Germany and its capital were surrounded by the least European of enemies, 'Cossacks, Gurkhas, Chasseurs d' Afrique, Bersaglieris, Cowboys'. If revolution did break out in this 'complex organism', Kessler thought it would be like the Day of Judgement. After all that the German troops had 'lived through, carried out in Luttich, Brussels, Warsaw, Bucharest' – Kessler referred to what is known in English as the 'German outrages' – these traumatic memories made it difficult to imagine a future for Germany.[41]

In Germany, Kessler belonged to a network of German elites who came together to discuss policy. Founded just after the outbreak of the war, the German Society of 1914 was a political club that had been initiated by prominent figures in German public life. Among its members were people such as the diplomat Wilhelm Solf, the landowner and industrialist Guido Henckel von Donnersmarck, the writer Richard Dehmel, the industrialist Robert Bosch, the painter Lovis Corinth, the theatre director Max Reinhardt, and the notorious Pomeranian professor of Classics Ulrich von Wilamowitz-Möllendorff. The club represented German society as it had crystallized since the Franco-Prussian War and the founding of the German Reich in 1871, displaying the mutual influence between the feudal, the industrial, and the creative elites of German public life under the banner of German patriotism. Most of the German Society's key members remained committed to German politics throughout their life. Walther Rathenau, the liberal technocrat, served as Prussia's war supplies director, advocating the London air raids, which were carried out from Zeppelin airships, and later became foreign minister until his assassination by a right-wing paramilitary group in 1922; Hjalmar Schacht, the banker, directed German economic policy under the Weimar Republic and the Nazis up to 1937; the painters Liebermann and Corinth came to shape the public image of the German landscape with their plein-air paintings of Brandenburg and Pomeranian lakes; the publishers Samuel Fischer and Anton Kipppenberg became representatives of the classics of German literature as such. Among the club's youngest members was the liberal Theodor Heuss, who would live to become the first German president of the Federal Republic after the Second World War.

But not all Germans in this society were patriots or defenders of its military strategy in the war. The philosopher Hermann Keyserling was

---

[41] Kessler, 18 November 1917, in Kessler, *Diaries*, vol. 6.

another person Kessler met there on a regular basis. One of his first political publications was an article published in English titled 'A Philosopher's View of the War'. There, he criticized the nationalist sentiments fuelling the war from both a Christian and a universalist perspective.[42] Keyserling protested against the war as '*Russian* citizen' and a pacifist.[43] He published this work in the journal associated with the British Hibbert Trust.[44] Founded in the previous century by Robert Hibbert, a wealthy Bloomsbury aristocrat who made his money in the Jamaican slave trade, it represented the ecumenical and largely pacifist values of the Unitarian Church. It regularly invited contributions on general topics discussed from a spiritual point of view. Among its contributors were the French historian Ernest Renan, the Bengali poet Rabindranath Tagore, and the German doctor and intellectual Albert Schweitzer.

When his friend, the sociologist Georg Simmel, heard about this, he warned Keyserling that he may have to cease their friendship if rumours about Keyserling's anti-German sentiments turned out to be true.[45] A subject of the Russian Empire, Keyserling had not been drafted into the army due to an earlier duel injury. By the end of the war, he was caught by the revolution on his estate in Russia's province of Courland. He spent this time working on an essay he titled *Bolshevism or the Aristocracy of the Future*. Between 1918 and 1920, he later remarked, 'centuries had passed'.[46] He had seen previous revolutions, like the one in 1905, when his estate was burnt, and he also witnessed a revolution in China and elsewhere. But unlike then, he saw that the old empires could now no longer hold on to their prestige. Among the voices heard at Brest-Litovsk, Keyserling remarked, it was not that of the old Prussian or Austrian diplomats but that of the Bolshevik Leon Trotsky that won the game. Much to the

---

[42] Keyserling, 'On the *Meaning* of the War', *The Hibbert Journal*, 3 April 1915, 533–546; 'Graf Hermann Keyserling als Urheber und Verbreiter der Kriegsschuldlüge entlarvt!', *Der Hammer*, Leipzig, September 1932, 725–726. HKN, folder 'Pressehetze', for example article 'Die Wahrheit über den Grafen Keyserling' by Keyserling's former publisher Otto Reichl, 18 December 1933.

[43] HKN, Pressehetze 1933ff., 'n eigener Sache' vom Grafen Hermann Keyserling', notice to be circulated to various newspapers. Precise date unknown.

[44] Hermann Keyserling, 'A Philosopher's View of the War', *The Hibbert Journal*, 3 April 1915. See HKN, 'Pressehetze', for example article 'Die Wahrheit über den Grafen Keyserling' by Keyserling's former publisher Otto Reichl, 18 December 1933, newspaper unknown but article contains a stamp from the German embassy, 'Deutsche Botschaft, eingeg. 18 Dec 1933'. See also note 'Graf Hermann Keyserling als Urheber und Verbreiter der Kriegsschuldlüge entlarvt!' Der Hammer, Nr- 725–726, Leipzig, September 1932.

[45] Georg Simmel, *Briefe 1912–18*, ed. Klaus Christian Köhnke, in *Gesamtausgabe*, 23 vols., vol. 23 (Frankfurt: Suhrkamp, 2005), Simmel to Keyserling, 18 May 1918.

[46] Hermann Keyserling, *Das Spektrum Europas* (Heidelberg: Niels Kampmann, 1928), 369–370.

confusion of his contemporaries, particularly of similar social background, he thought that listening to Trotsky was necessary in order to make room for a new, truly European aristocracy of the future.[47]

Defending himself against charges of anti-German propaganda during the First World War, Keyserling thought that idea of Germany could only survive as a 'supranational' idea: 'in the interrelated and correlated Europe of tomorrow, the spiritual root of that which once blossomed forth in the form of the Holy Roman Empire of German nationality – the supranational European idea – will once again become the determinant factor of history, in a greater, more expansive form, conforming to the spirit of the time'.[48]

The other sealed train: chivalry in the Polish revolution

In early November 1918, the German government appointed Kessler as a German envoy. His task was to release the leader of the Polish legion, Jozef Piłsudski, from Magdeburg fortress, where he was held prisoner during the war. Pilsudski had been granted the right to lead a Polish legion within the Habsburg army, but as a Polish nationalist, he had been unwelcome to the Austrians. Now that it was clear that Austria-Hungary would not be resurrected, Germany had other ways of making use of this prisoner. At the end of the war, the legion became the nucleus of a Polish nation state.[49] As early as 1915, German officers had approached Piłsudski in Volhynia, soliciting his opinions on the future of eastern and central Europe.[50] At this point, Piłsudski's Polish Legion formed part of the multinational Habsburg army. At the same time, it was increasingly taking up the powers and duties of a future Polish state; as a representative of the future Polish nation, Piłsudski refused to give an oath of allegiance to the central powers and was therefore taken prisoner by the German imperial army.[51]

Railway networks had been crucial elements of European imperial growth as well as inter-imperial financial networks in the nineteenth century. While such projects as the Baghdad railway line brought together

---

[47] Hermann Keyserling, *Das Reisetagebch eines Philosophen*, 2 Vols., vol. 2 (Darmstadt: Otto Reichl, 1920), 727, 603, 757, 850–854.

[48] Keyserling, *Europa*, 150.

[49] Harry Graf Kessler, 'Aus den Anfängen der Novemberrevolution. Pilsudskis Befreiung', *Frankfurter Zeitung*, 7 October 1928 (Zweites Morgenblatt), 1–2; and Harry Graf Kessler, 'Pilsudski. Eine Erinnerung', in *Die Neue Rundschau*, 46 (Berlin, 1935), 605–612.

[50] Kessler, *Diaries*, 18 October 1918.

[51] Kessler, *Diaries*, 14 November 1918 and 28 December 1918.

private investors across different European states and beyond, they remained publicly associated with the imperial Great Game between the European nations.[52] But in the course of the war, trains also gained a key role in Europe's post-imperial transformation. During the war, members of the German diplomatic staff worked together with Swiss politicians to facilitate the arrival of Lenin and his entourage in Russia to promote revolution there in April 1917.[53] Immediately after the war, Kessler was involved in a similar, if more modest, undertaking. It paralleled Lenin's German-sponsored passage to Russia (the preparation of which Kessler also witnessed in Bern) insofar as the German executive powers had asked Kessler personally to escort Piłsudski from Magdeburg to Warsaw in a special sealed train.[54]

Kessler described this episode in one of several small memoirs that he would publish to great acclaim in the liberal German journal *Die Neue Rundschau*. The lens through which he chose to interpret this situation was the persistence of chivalric values at a time of revolution. When Kessler personally met Piłsudski upon his release from Magdeburg prison, he handed him his sword. Together, they travelled back to Warsaw on a luxurious personal train, which took off from Bahnhof Friedrichstraße and was equipped to the standards of an 'American billionaire'. Both the aristocratic and the oligarchic elements in this handover of power contrasted markedly with the executive powers that had entrusted Kessler with this task as the fate of the revolutionaries in Germany itself was far from clear.[55]

In December 1918, Kessler oversaw the withdrawal of German troops from Poland, and Poland established a nationalist government with closer ties to France than to Germany.[56] Kessler later recalled that the Polish leader gave him 'an oral declaration in the form of a word of honour because I had refused to demand a written declaration from him' that he would not claim

---

[52] On the railway and globalization, see Jürgen Osterhammel and Niels P. Petersson, *Globalization: A Short History*, transl. Dona Geyer (Princeton: Princeton University Press, 2012), 85–86.

[53] The passage was described by the Swiss communist Fritz Platten, *Die Reise Lenins durch Deutschland im plombierten Wagen* (Berlin: Neuer Deutscher Verlag, 1924), but later popularized by Stefan Zweig in his miniature 'The sealed train' (1927), in Stefan Zweig, *Decisive Moments in History. Twelve Historical Miniatures, trans. by Lowell A. Bangerter* (Riverside: Ariadne Press, 1999).

[54] Kessler, *Diaries*, 19 November 1918. Kessler, 'Aus den Anfängen der Novemberrevolution. Pilsudskis Befreiung', 1–2, Kessler, 'Pilsudski. Eine Erinnerung' 605–612; Rom Landau, *Pilsudski and Poland* (New York: Dial Press, 1929). 'De breuk tuschen Polen en Deutschland', *Het Centrum*, 19 December 1918.

[55] Kessler, *Diaries*, 19 November 1918.

[56] Cf. Hoover Institution Archives, Poland Ambasada Papers (correspondence with French government from the 1920s).

German territory.[57] Piłsudski and Kessler probably shared certain characteristics, such as their background from lower nobility, the 'Prussian' sense of military honour, and a Mazzinian cosmopolitan nationalism.[58] Kessler saw it as the duty of persons of higher standing, such as Piłsudski and himself, 'to lead our nations *out of their old animosity into a new friendship*'.[59] In the Polish, German, Dutch, British, and American press, rumours were circulating in December 1918 that Kessler was providing support for a 'Bolshevik' uprising in Poland using government money.[60] In fact, however, Piłsudski assured him that he was pursuing a policy of social democracy aimed at steering clear of Bolshevism. Indeed, Kessler dismissed all allegations of 'Bolshevism' as ridiculous, even though he indeed had sympathy for the revolutionary councils in Germany and Poland (Lodz) and the Caesarist social democracy of Piłsudski.[61]

Like many others in his position, Kessler had suffered a nervous breakdown in the course of his service on the eastern front. He was allowed to retire from active service and was given a unique position: to head the department for Cultural Propaganda in secret, in Switzerland. At this point, Kessler could deploy his expertise in the cultural internationalism of the pre-war era to serve a more concrete goal. As he put it:

> Now I have finally reached the actual project of my life: to forge Europe together practically at the highest level. Before the war, I had tried it on the much too thin and fragile level of culture; now we can turn to the foundations. May it be a good omen that my appointment occurs on a day when perhaps through Germany's acceptance, a new era of peace will start.[62]

Before the war, Kessler's exposure to debates about national styles and tragic landscapes had been restricted to the realm of aesthetic contemplation. As a result of his wartime position, Kessler obtained a new perspective on these conceptual frontiers, a transformation that was facilitated not least because he was empowered to cross established frontlines. His experience of the German and the Polish post-imperial transformation made these revolutions appear like personal affairs, in which the populations of these states became mere secondary agents on the historical stage. The eastern European horizon became a visual concept that was highly suited for expressing his ambivalent position. Like others in his circle, Kessler

[57] Ibid.   [58] 'Ousted Envoy Tells of Warsaw Mobs', *New York Times*, 22 December 1918.
[59] Kessler's emphasis. *Diaries*, 21 November 1918.
[60] See reports in *Het Centrum*, 17 and 18 December 1918.
[61] Julie Fedor, *Russia and the Cult of State Security: The Chekist Tradition, from Lenin to Putin* (London: Routledge, 2013).
[62] Kessler, 29 August 1924, in Kessler, *Diaries*, vol. 8.

recognized his complicity with German military violence in Belgium and in eastern Europe, but stopped short of endorsing the more radical form of the revolutions in Germany and Europe. Instead, he refashioned his long-standing, initially purely aesthetic critique of national chauvinism in Germany's imperial past into a new, liberal form of internationalism.[63]

Imperial regiments after empire

With his transformation from a loyal officer of one of Prussia's elite army units into a sceptical and self-doubting witness of a European civil war, Kessler's voice was in the minority, but far from singular amidst a growing sound of disenchanted Europeans. To understand the genealogy of this disenchantment, we need to take into account the psychological effects of war trauma on the self-perception of the military elites in the war. As already discussed, members of elite officer corps were well positioned to understand the theatre of war not least due to having access to privileged forms of experience, such as airplanes. Being *cavalier* about war, and having a horse in wartime, are related not just linguistically. According to one historian, the cavalry was a 'cosmopolitan institution, and based upon the same general principles throughout Europe'. As a British historian commissioned by the Russian Tsar Alexander II to write a history of chivalry had put it, the privilege of service with the horse, or chivalry, 'was without doubt one of the most important causes of the elevation of society from barbarism to civilisation'.[64] In most European imperial armies of the late nineteenth and early twentieth century, officers generally came from aristocratic families and were educated at corresponding institutions, including the French Cadets schools, which emerged in the seventeenth century; the Cadet schools and the Theresianum academy in Vienna; Lichterfelde in Potsdam; and Sandhurst in Britain.

Historically, the imperial armies remained connected with each other through mutual partnerships. For instance, the European royal guards had a tradition of conferring honorary leadership to monarchs ruling a different state. For instance, the first West Prussian Ulan Guard regiment was formally under the leadership of three Romanoffs between 1859 and 1901,

---

[63] Thus Kessler republished, with few changes, his old essay on Nationality in the new context of the pacifist journal *Die weißen Blätter*. Harry Graf Kessler, 'Nationalität', in *Die Weißen Blätter. Eine Monatsschrift*, 6:12 (1919), 531–546.

[64] Lieut.-Col. George T. Denison, *A History of Cavalry from the Earliest Times. With Lessons for the Future* (London: Macmillan, 1877), 116, 114.

even though the commanding officers were Prussian and not Russian subjects. The regiment was even named 'Kaiser Alexander III von Russland', after the Russian tsar. From 1896 to the outbreak of the First World War, Habsburg emperor Franz Josef was the formal commander-in-chief of a British regiment, the 1st King's Dragoon Guards. The Austrian Radetzky March is still its official song. In the eighteenth and nineteenth centuries, some British regiments consisted entirely of German auxiliaries, including both officers and soldiers.[65] The French army had foreign regiments (not to be confused with the Foreign Legion) serving under its banners from the *ancien régime* to Napoleonic times. Before the revolution, there were Swiss, German (particularly, from Saxony-Anhalt and Nassau), Irish and Scottish, and Wallonian regiments serving under the French king. The practice of renting out mercenaries to foreign armies, which came to be associated mostly with the Swiss mercenaries and with several German principalities, included non-European troops – the Napoleonic army had Circassian and Egyptian ('Mameluk') regiments, and subsequent French armies had troops from Senegal.[66]

Cross-imperial connections among the elites transcended the boundaries of Europe. One of the last cavalry regiments of the British army, which was deployed in the capture of Jerusalem during the First World War, had been co-founded by a former maharajah who had been dispossessed under the Raj as a child. Prince Duleep-Singh had briefly occupied the throne in one of India's richest states, the Punjab, when an uprising against the British Raj began. The uprising was put down, but with the insurgents, the British army removed the maharajah himself. Installed in Norfolk with a generous pension but no power, the young former maharajah began to live the life of an English gentleman. He assembled, among other things, a collection of portraits of East Anglian dignitaries in Thetford Forest. The Norfolk Yeomanry, which he co-founded, was a volunteer cavalry, which fought for the British war effort at Gallipoli, and later participated in the conquest of Jerusalem before finishing the war on the western front.[67]

---

[65] Stephen Conway, *The British Isles and the War of American Independence* (Oxford: Oxford University Press, 2000), 30.

[66] Eugène Fieffé, *Histoire des Troupes étrangères au service de France depuis leur origine jusq 'à nos jours et de tous les régiments levés dans les pays conquis sous la première république et l'empire*, 2 vols. (Paris: Librairie militaire, 1854).

[67] Prince Frederick Victor Duleep-Singh. See his collection of East Anglia portraits in E. Farrer (ed.), *Portraits in Norfolk Houses*, 2 vols. (Norwich: Jarrold & Sons, 1929). On Singh, see also Obituary in *The Times*, 16 August 1926. On the Norfolk Yeomanry, see Samuel Hoare, *The Fourth Seal and the End of a Russian Chapter* (London: Heinemann, 1930). On Jerusalem and the dreams of a new

The dismantling of the imperial armies of Austria-Hungary and Germany under the Versailles treaty called into question the special hierarchical privileges of officers, which formed the very heart of the old armies.[68] The Habsburg Empire's officer corps was almost a caste, even though it had gradually become more permeable in the last decades of its existence.[69] The same can be said of the other German officer corps, above all, that of Prussia.[70] Even though changes in legislation following the reforms of the 1820s meant that new ennoblements created new military nobilities in all these states, access to officer posts had been strictly regulated and limited to specific trusted families. Those who trained with the cadet school were subject to harsh discipline, as described in some of the classical works of Austrian literature in which the cadet features prominently.

Whilst being strictly hierarchical by class, the ranks of the Habsburg imperial army effectively moderated the political impact factor of their subjects' ethnic and regional identities. Looked at horizontally, the Habsburg army especially was a thoroughly multilingual and, though to a lesser extent, also a multi-ethnic community. By contrast, the German imperial army, which had emerged, like the German empire, in 1870/71, after the Franco-Prussian War, gave Prussia de facto a leading role among the formally equal units of the German princes.[71] This difference was crucial for the structure of post-imperial conversion among the post-imperial officers.

In Austria, as Istvan Deák has emphasized, the disappearance of the Emperor as a unifying figure encouraged former career officers to seek a career in the national successor-states of the old empire.[72] For officers of the Polish and Czechoslovak legions, there was no contradiction between

chivalry, see G.K. Chesterton, *The New Jerusalem* (New York: George Doran, 1921). On the complex evolution of military identities under the British Raj, see Chris Bayly and Tim Harper, *Forgotten Armies: Britain's Asian Empire and the War with Japan* (London: Penguin, 2004), and Gajendra Singh, *The Testimonies of Indian Soldiers and the Two World Wars* (London: Bloomsbury Academic, 2014).

[68] For a comparative analysis of the social impact of the war on Germany and Austria-Hungary, see Alexander Watson, *Ring of Steel: Germany and Austria-Hungary at War, 1914–1918* (London: Penguin, 2015).

[69] István Deák, *Beyond Nationalism. A Social and Political History of the Habsburg Officer Corps, 1848–1918* (Oxford and New York: Oxford University Press, 1990).

[70] Wencke Meteling, 'Adel im preussisch-deutschen Weltkriegsoffizierkorps', in *Aristokratismus und Moderne. Adel als politisches und kulturelles Konzept, 1890–1945*, ed. Eckart Conze et al. (Weimar, Cologne and Vienna: Boehlau, 2013), 215–239.

[71] Cf. Hermann Cron, *Die Organisation des deutschen Heeres im Weltkriege* (Berlin: Mittler & Sohn, 1923).

[72] Istvan Deák, 'The Habsburg Empire', in Karen Barkey and Mark von Hagen (eds.), *After Empire: Multiethnic Societies and Nation-Building: The Soviet Union and the Russian, Ottoman and Habsburg Empires* (Boulder, CO: Westview Press, 1997), 129–141,134–135.

endorsing revolution in Austria, which gave their nations a long-sought form of sovereignty, and joining anti-Bolshevik military campaigns in the Russian Civil War and elsewhere in eastern Europe. By contrast, for the armies of the German states, the idea of a greater Germany continued to provide a source of aspirations for the future. Moreover, anti-Habsburg German nationalists like Adolf Hitler, who had already served in the Bavarian instead of the Habsburg armies in the war, now saw Germany and not Austria as their primary cadre of reference.[73]

Former officers had to adjust to an uncertain future in Germany, too: its army was now severely reduced in size after the Versailles peace settlement. But unlike Austria, Germany lost not more than one-seventh of its territory in the war, and thus remained a significant force in Europe. As critics of institutions such as the Prussian cadet training at Lichterfelde have suggested, such institutions produced forms of obedience to authority, which were inimical to a society of equals.[74] It has been a long-standing belief particularly among émigrés from Nazi Germany and Austria that radicalization among the disenchanted soldiers and officers had been one of the root causes of Germany's path to Nazism. The sociologist Norbert Elias provided the most succinct portrait of the army as a key case study for the decline of honour in German society and its descent into dehumanization.[75] Yet more recently, historians have highlighted that traumatic war experience and the abolition of privilege also produced less reactionary forms of doubt, and even served as the foundation for pro-republican beliefs.[76] A former officer of the Bavarian army, Franz Carl Endres, turned into a sociologist and remarked in the journal *Archiv für Sozialwissenschaften und Sozialpolitik* that the Prussian army had always been in the service of the Hohenzollern dynasty more than it had served the German people.[77] He thought that a future army

---

[73] On Hitler as a case study of post-war conversion, see Thomas Weber, *Hitler's First War: Adolf Hitler, the Men of the List Regiment, and the First World War* (Oxford: Oxford University Press, 2011).

[74] Erich Fromm, Max Horkheimer, and Ludwig Marcuse (eds.), *Studien über Autorität und Familie* (Paris: Alcan, 1936).

[75] Norbert Elias, *Studien über die Deutschen. Machtkämpfe und Habitusentwicklung im 19. und 20. Jahrhundert* (Frankfurt/M.: Suhrkamp, 1992).

[76] Benjamin Ziemann, *Contested Commemorations: Republican War Veterans and Weimar Political Culture* (Cambridge: Cambridge University Press, 2009). For a critique of Elias in the light of the First World War, see Mark Hewitson, 'Violence and Civilization. Transgression in Modern Wars', in Mary Fulbrook (ed.), *Un-Civilizing Processes?: Excess and Transgression in German Society and Culture: Perspectives Debating with Norbert Elias* (Amsterdam: Rodopi, 2007), 117–157.

[77] Franz Carl Endres, 'Soziologische Struktur und ihr entsprechende Ideologien des deutschen Offizierkorps vor dem Weltkriege', in *Archiv für Sozialwissenschaft und Sozialpolitik*, 58:1 (1927), 282–319.

had to develop other forms of commitment. The left-leaning magazine *Die Weltbühne* even had a regular column appearing throughout the year 1917, entitled 'From a field officer', which supplied ironic remarks on the deconstruction of the officer.[78]

Adjustment to the post-war world saw the former officers take on a variety of social roles, particularly in the wake of social unrest in Germany during the winter of 1918/19. What is most widely known now is the emergence of paramilitary groups, the so-called *Freikorps*, which took it upon themselves to fight against revolutionary movements in the German cities. This was not only done out of conviction but sometimes for pecuniary considerations as well. Baron Veltheim, for instance, after his service for the Saxon royal army, claimed that he joined a freecorps unit in Berlin to fight the 'red' revolutions there in January 1918 because he was short of money. In this way, the war continued, after only a brief intermission, in the form of a civil war on the streets of Berlin, including 'Alexanderplatz, the police prefecture, Reichstag, Brandenburger Tor' and other locations. The fighting parties, which he called the 'white and the red', were equally repulsive to him. But he was particularly shocked by the refusal of his comrades to have sympathy for the 'wishes, feelings, and thoughts' of the 'revolutionary workers'. Whenever he tried to prevent what he called 'excessive violence' against them, he was suspected of being a 'spy of the revolution'.[79]

Another example of a freecorps officer with more conviction for the cause of fighting the revolution was the Prussian officer Ernst von Salomon. He was convicted of murdering the German foreign minister Walther Rathenau and served a prison sentence in the Weimar Republic, during which he wrote a book about the times.[80] It is a fictionalized autobiography, in which his authorial self asks, 'Was it worthwhile to attack these people? No, it was not. We had become superfluous [. . .]. All over! *Finis – exeunt omnes*. The world wanted time in which to rot comfortably.'[81]

---

[78] Cf. Bernhard von Bülow and Graf Max Montgelas (eds.), *Kommentar zu den Deutschen Dokumenten zum Kriegsausbruch*, 5 vols. (Berlin: Deutsche Verlagsgesellschaft für Politik und Geschichte, 1919).

[79] Veltheim, postscript to his war diary (1921–32) on the events of January 1918, with a quotation from a letter to his wife of 25 January 1919. In LHASA, Mappe I, Kriegstagebuch.

[80] Ernst von Salomon, *Die Geächteten* (Berlin: Rowohlt, 1931); see also ibid., *Der Fragebogen* (Hamburg: Rowohlt, 1951).

[81] Ernst von Salomon, *The Outlaws* (London: Arktos, 2013), 301.

It is noteworthy that the paramilitary officers of the former armies turned to writing to make sense of their conversion as much as those who became pacifists or critics of military culture. The writer Fritz von Unruh came from a long lineage of Prussian officers. Around the turn of the century, his father had been the commander of Königsberg Castle in East Prussia. In his autobiographical novels and plays, however, he usually adopted the perspective either of plain cadets or of civilians: one of his protagonists is the poet Kaspar Friedrich Uhle.[82] Unruh consciously established an intellectual affinity between himself and an earlier Romantic disenchanted with Prussian military traditions, Heinrich von Kleist, whose *Prince of Homburg* was a modern-day Hamlet who consciously refused to exercise his duty as a Prussian officer. Unruh's relative Joseph von Unruh (or Józef Unrug, as he was known in Poland) served as an officer of a Prussian regiment in the First World War, but joined the newly formed Polish legion after the war, and in the Nazi era was an agent for the Polish government in exile in Britain.

Other former career officers became so radicalized that they abandoned their aristocratic identity altogether. The most familiar examples of such conversions belong to the history of the Third Reich. Prior to the abolition of the republican constitution in Germany, the SA, one of the paramilitary organizations which was initially in conflict with the Nazi party, had been particularly successful in recruiting former officers. The historian Karl-Dietrich Bracher called them déclassé, yet, at the time when this generation of officers served in the armies, the German aristocracy was no longer a class but merely a social configuration. In terms of class, they had long merged with the bourgeoisie.[83] By the time of the Second World War, a number of the old German officers in the post-imperial successor states also gravitated to the Wehrmacht, particularly in eastern Europe.[84]

Yes, this sort of aristocratic conversion at a time of institutional disorientation was also a phenomenon for the political left in interwar Germany. A particularly spectacular case was that of a Saxon aristocrat

---

[82] Fritz Unruh, *Die Offiziere* (Berlin: Reiss, 1911).

[83] For a classic analysis of this process, see Karl-Dietrich Bracher, Wolfgang Sauer, and Gerhard Schulz, *Die nationalsozialistische Machtergreifung. Studien zur Errichtung des totalitären Herrschaftssystems in Deutschland*, 2nd ed. (Wiesbaden: Springer, 1962), 829–855.

[84] Isvtan Deák, 'The Habsburg Empire', 135. Karina Urbach, *Go-Betweens for Hitler* (Oxford: Oxford University Press, 2015). On the cooperation of the old elites in the colonization of the East, see Shelley Baranowski, *Nazi Empire. German Colonialism and Imperialism from Bismarck to Hitler* (Cambridge: Cambridge University Press, 2011).

who first adopted a fictional alter ego and a pseudonym, and then turned his pseudonym into his new proper name. The officer Arnold Vieth von Golßenau had served in a regiment of the Saxon Royal Guards during the war. Yet his own fictionalized account of the Great War, an interwar bestseller that was translated into English and French, was written from the perspective of an infantry man because, as he later recalled, it was 'not the officer who had impressed me with his actions on the front, but the nameless soldier'.[85] Writing the novel, which quickly became a bestseller rivalling Remarque's *All Quiet on the Western Front* in popularity, he increasingly identified with the protagonist of the experiences he had himself created. He became the protagonist, Ludwig Renn. As he later recalled, he himself 'lived through this time as an officer, a man with many traditions'.[86] After the war, Ludwig Renn, as the former aristocrat now officially called himself, joined the communist party, became a leading member of the republican troops in the Spanish Civil War, emigrated to Mexico with the anti-Nazi Committee for a Free Germany. After the end of the Second World War and the division of Germany, he eventually returned to what was now the GDR to become a professor of anthropology in Jena. This is perhaps the starkest example of the capacity for detachment particularly prevalent among the officer intellectuals of the First World War.[87] Yet Renn's case was far from singular. Other examples of elite officers who became active on the international Left between the wars and in the Second World War included Count Rolf Reventlow, the son of a famous Munich Bohémienne, who was a journalist in the Munich republic and later joined the international brigades in Spain.[88]

In the light of the scholarship on Germany in the Third Reich, it is easy to overlook that in the interwar period, the German aristocratic officer could impersonate the idea of international reconciliation through the solidarity of elites, as it did in Jean Renoir's now classic film of 1937, *The Grand Illusion*. Its title derives from a book by Norman Angell, a British economist, on the futility of war, called *The Great Illusion*, dating back to 1910, for which the author won the Nobel Peace Prize in 1933.[89] The book centres on the futility of the Anglo-German arms race and has no special interest in the military

---

[85] Ludwig Renn, *Krieg* (Frankfurt: Societätsverlag, 1929), 519–20.   [86] Ibid., 520.

[87] Hubertus F. Jahn, *Patriotic Culture in Russia during World War I* (Ithaca, N.Y.: Cornell University Press, 1995).

[88] For details on Rolf Reventlow, see the Rolf Reventlow papers at the Friedrich Ebert Stiftung, Bonn. For Reventlow's role in the Spanish Civil War, see Arthur Koestler, *Spanish Testament* (London: Gollancz, 1937), 183–184.

[89] Norman Angell, *The Great Illusion* (London: William Heinemann, 1910).

elites, instead focusing on the idea of friendship between societies. But in the film, this abstract notion of friendship is made literal through the link between aristocratic aviators from France, which enables the viewer to draw Angell's conclusion emotionally. When the aristocrats in the film voice their own feeling of futility, they present a kind of first-person view of imperial decline. But Renoir did not invent this new social role for them. The officers-turned-intellectuals had already prepared it.[90]

For officers and members of internationally connected aristocratic families, war was not merely a sphere of extreme physical violence but also a field of symbolic interaction. The right of these officers to use horses and later airships in battle, literally and figuratively elevating their perspective, facilitated detachment from the experience of war as a struggle between nations or empires.

The invention of tragic landscapes

In 1923, Kessler was enjoying a picnic in the Berkshire Hills of Massachusetts. He was invited there to speak of Germany's place in Europe, and the constitutional changes which had occurred under the republic.[91] His hosts, men and women who had served in the First World War either as officers or as nurses, shared their memories of this still recent time. The beauty of nature reminded them of the Carpathian Mountains on the eastern front, while the 'moral indifference' of nature itself brought to mind the 'human atrocities' they had witnessed. Kessler remarked that there was a great feeling of mutually shared 'humanity' in these conversations.[92] Prior to the war, Kessler had been trained to believe, with Wilhelm Wundt, that landscapes evoked above all national sentiments and attachments. He now grew convinced that the 'meaning' of landscape was either tragic universalism or utter indifference to human identities. There was no ethical link between the shape or the beauty of a landscape and the actions and sentiments of the people taking root in it. For people of Kessler's circle, it was possible to think of the western front in terms of an affective geography, as a '"tragic region" to be turned into a holy site for Europe as a whole and not

---

[90] Jean Renoir, *La Grande Illusion* (1937). I am grateful to Eckart Conze for organizing the screening of this film in the context of a conference on aristocracy and modernity in Marburg in September 2009.

[91] Cf. the lectures in Williams Town, Massachusetts, were published almost immediately, as Count Harry Kessler, *Germany and Europe* (New Haven: Yale University Press, 1923).

[92] Easton, *Der rote Graf,* 407. Kessler to Schubert, 14 August 1923. PA Dept III USA vols. 4 and 5.

for any one nation in particular, to draw pilgrimages each year from all parts of the Earth to condemn war and to sanctify peace, to show their devotion in front of this great, wounded cathedral!'[93]

Publications like Michelin's *Guides to Postwar Europe*, published between 1919 and 1922, used images of war ruins on the western front in order to create a new type of mass tourism, which still exists today. As the introduction to the 1919 edition put it, 'ruins are more impressive when coupled with a knowledge of their origin and destruction'.[94] Yet until Franco-German cooperation developed joint commemoration events for the Great War in the 1980s, public memory of these sites remained tinted with national colours.

The idea of perceiving an entire landscape of war as 'tragic' required a cosmopolitan perspective. In the 1920s, psychiatrists dealing with cases of war trauma observed that certain cases of what today would be called post-traumatic stress disorder were much more likely to occur among the higher ranks. Some even ventured to suggest, as Robert Graves did, that officers had a 'more nervous' time than men, confirming some findings of new approaches to the sociology of war based on statistics from the Franco-Prussian War as well as the Great War.[95] He recalled a time when, before the war, he had been visiting his German relatives, the Rankes; at their house, presciently called 'Begone, anger', 'there was a store for corn, apples, and other farm produce; and up here

[93] Kessler, *Diaries*, 24 August 1928.
[94] *Michelin Guide to the Battlefields of the World War* (Milltown, N.J.: Michelin, 1919), 7.
[95] General Nikolai Golovin, *Nauka o voine: o sotsiologicheskom izuchenii voiny* (Paris: Signal, 1938), with thanks to Pitirim Sorokin of the Harvard Committee for Research in the Social Sciences. On the greater danger of war for officers than soldiers based on statistics from the Franco-Prussian War of 1870/71, see page 15ff; Ardant du Pie, *Etudes sur le combat* (Paris: Hachette et Dumaine, 1880); Hans Delbrück, *Geschichte der Kriegskunst im Rahmen der politischen Geschichte* (Berlin: Georg Stielke, 1922–27); Jean Norton Cru, *Essai d'analyse et de critique des souvenirs des combattants édités en français de 1915 à 1928* (Paris: Ed. Etincelles, 1929); and materials from the congress 'Sociologie de la guerre et de la paix', in *Les annals de l'Institut International de Sociologie*, xvi, ed. Marcel Giard (Paris, 1932), based on a conference in Geneva in 1930. On elites and the sociology of war, see Vilfredo Pareto, *The Mind and Society*, transl. Andrew Bongiorno and Arthur Livingston, 2 vols. (New York: Harcourt and Brace, 1935). On psychiatric treatment of shellshock and war neuroses in Austria-Hungary, see the case of von Mattanovich and others in Hans-Georg Hofer, *Nervenschwäche und Krieg. Modernitätskritik und Krisenbewältigung in der österreichischen Psychiatrie* (1880–1920) (Cologne, Vienna, Weimar: Böhlau, 2004), 366ff.; on nervousness and officers, see John T. MacCurdy, *War Neuroses* (Cambridge: Cambridge University Press, 1918), 123; on war shock, see M.D. Eder, *War-Shock. The Psycho-Neuroses in War Psychology and Treatment* (London: Heinemann, 1917); see also Ernst Hanisch, *Männlichkeiten. Eine andere Geschichte des 20. Jahrhunderts* (Vienna, Cologne and Weimar: Böhlau, 2005); see also studies by the Psychoanalytic association, S. Ferenczi, Karl Abraham, Ernst Simmel, and Ernest Jones, with an introduction by Sigmund Freud, *Psychoanalysis and War Neuroses* (London, Vienna and New York: The International Psycho-Analytical Press, 1921).

my cousin Wilhelm – later shot down in an air battle by a school-fellow of mine – used to lie for hours picking off mice with an air-gun'.[96]

Having access to education and technology gave elite participants in the war more devices through which to gain a more distant view of the war process. They could also rekindle their social connections after the war was over. It was easier for those who previously had social experiences in common. In the mid-1930s, Kessler and Graves became neighbours in exile on the Balearic island of Mallorca. Graves's exile from Britain was voluntary: he spent this time to rewrite his version of the Greek myths. Kessler, by then a refugee from Nazi Germany, wrote his memoirs on the island, which allow us to contextualize in social perspective how former German elites contributed to a new transnational sensibility after the war.

---

[96] Robert Graves, *Goodbye to All That* (London: Jonathan Cape, 1929) (London: Penguin, 1957).

PART II

The power of prestige

The subject of the following three chapters is the role of aristocratic intellectuals in shaping political discourse and social institutions in inter-war Germany, Austria, as well as Europe at large. When constitutional changes in central Europe and revolutions in Russia announced that old elites, such as the aristocratic families, would lose power in a new society of equals, some representatives of these social groups curiously became highly sought-after public speakers. In the age when aristocratic families were imbued with a sense of 'group disgrace', the aristocratic intellectuals became strangely appealing as global authorities on all things related to European identity at large.

Part of this perception came from the celebrity of particular intellectuals who became Europe's self-proclaimed ambassadors in encounters with non-Europeans. One contemporary called them 'Germany's new prophets'.[1] The photograph of one of these aristocratic celebrities, Count Hermann Keyserling, whom we last came across as a critic of the German war effort, shows him in such a role.

Characteristically, he is not in the centre of this image. The main protagonist is the Indian poet Rabindranath Tagore, whose global popularity in the 1920s had much to do with the appeal of his verdict that Europe was in need of revival.[2] To the left of Tagore is Keyserling's wife, Goedela Bismarck, the German Iron Chancellor's granddaughter. The image represents not just a meeting of different worlds, but a joining of two kinds of continental celebrity: the Indian sage and the former Baltic Baron both speak of Europe's future from the vantage point of aristocratic outsiders.

---

[1] Norbert Elias, 'Group Charisma and Group Disgrace', in Elias, *Essays III. On Sociology and the Humanities* (Dublin: University College Dublin Press, 2009), 73–82; Henry de Man, 'Germany's New Prophets', in *Yale Review*, 13:4 (July 1924), 665–683.

[2] On Rabindranath Tagore's global appeal, see Michael Collins, *Empire, Nationalism and the Postcolonial World. Rabindranath Tagore's Writings on History, Politics and Society* (London: Routledge, 2011).

Figure 8 Hermann Keyserling with Rabindranath Tagore and Goedela Keyserling
(b. Bismarck).
HKN, ULB Darmstadt

Tagore, a Brahmin, observed Europe from an Indian perspective, while Keyserling, a Baltic aristocrat, considered himself above all nationalities due to his family's relationship to more than one empire. He represented the kind of conversion of elites with inspiration from the Orient, which Max Weber had spoken about in his lecture of 1919. Keyserling's celebrity in interwar high society, not only in Germany but, like Tagore's, also in Britain and in Argentina, was the product of a particular kind of prestige, which was connected to the idea of European decline. This prestige of 'former people' is also the context in which the next chapter places Count Coudenhove-Kalergi's initiative of a Pan-European federation.

CHAPTER 3

Soft power
Pan-Europeanism after the Habsburgs

'My father dreamt of a Slavic kingdom under the reign of the Habsburgs. He dreamt of a monarchy of Austrians, Hungarians, and Slavs. [. . .] In his will, I was named heir to his ideas. It was not for nothing that I had been christened Franz Ferdinand'.[1] These were the words of the protagonist of Joseph Roth's novel, *Capuchin Vault*. It continued the story of the Trotta family, familiar to readers from Roth's bestselling *Radetzkymarsch* in which the decline of Habsburg glory was explored from the perspective of three generations of a Slovenian family whose ennoblement dated back to one ancestor's accidental role in saving the life of Franz Josef of Habsburg at the Battle of Solferino. In the sequel, written in the Netherlands during Roth's exile from Vienna after the annexation of Austria by Nazi Germany, Roth follows the decline of the von Trottas to the next two generations. Witnesses to the end of the Habsburg Empire in the revolution of 1918, Roth's characters capture the atmosphere of loss that many former Habsburg subjects felt after the disintegration of the empire.

Returning from Siberia after having been taken prisoner on the eastern front, Franz Ferdinand von Trotta finds the Habsburg Empire in ruins. The horses in the Prater are dying of old age, as all the others 'had been slaughtered, and people made sausages of them'. The back yards of the old army are filled with 'parts of broken carriages', which had previously served to transport such eminent personages as the 'Tchirskys, the Pallavicinis, the Sternbergs, the Esterhazys, the Dietrichsteins, and the Trauttmannsdorffs'.[2] These old families were now threatened by entrepreneurial new elites from the Prussian North and the Baltic lands, represented by the character of Kurt von Stettenheim, 'a mix between an international tennis star and a territorially fixed manor house owner, with a slight touch of Ocean Lloyd'.[3]

---

[1] Joseph Roth, *Die Kapuzinergruft* (1939), in *Die Kapuzinergruft. Romane aus der Exilzeit* (Berlin: Aufbau, 1990), 439–577, 441.
[2] Ibid., 544.   [3] Ibid., 545.

Roth's protagonist, Franz Ferdinand, gradually loses all he had: his wife, who runs off with a female artist; his mother, who dies on the day the revolution breaks out in Vienna in 1918; his money, lost to a Brandenburg entrepreneur; and, above all, 'his' monarchy. The proclamation of the idea of popular (self-)government, a *Volksregierung*, sounds to him like words of 'a beloved woman' telling him that 'she did not need me in the least and could just sleep with herself'.[4] He still has his son, but chooses to send him off to live with a friend in Paris. Even though the line of the von Trottas survives for the time being, their lives appear to be meaningless in the absence of the Habsburgs. Alone, Franz Ferdinand von Trotta has only one consolation: he goes to the Capuchin Vault to pay tribute to the Habsburg emperors. But his mourning is troubled by the fact that his own father had been what he calls a 'loyal deserter', a critic of Emperor Franz Josef, the Habsburgs' last successful emperor before the short final reign of Karl I, from 1916 to 1918. Observing a guard marching up and down in front of the vault, von Trotta, the 'heir', asks himself: 'What is left here to guard? The sarcophagi? The memory? The history?'[5]

These questions were Joseph Roth's own; he drank himself to death only one year after the publication of this work. Another Habsburg author and a friend of Roth's from Vienna, Stefan Zweig, followed suit in 1942, committing double suicide with his wife in Brazil, a country he had praised as the land of the future. The city where he died, Petropolis, was the place that, less than one hundred years earlier, had inspired Habsburg Archduke Maximilian to write one of his travel poems lamenting modernity: 'For where the white man moves, his forest dries up,/ and his woman and child will be engulfed by a chain of sin'.[6] Like Roth, Zweig had contributed to the charisma of declining monarchs during his exile. One of his bestsellers was the biography of Marie Antoinette; her assassination in the wake of the French Revolution had provided an example of how to end the Old Regime, but also an inspiration to critics of revolutionary radicalism like Edmund Burke.[7] Like Roth, Zweig saw Prussia, Britain, and Russia as threats to the Habsburg Empire. As two Catholic dynasties, the Habsburgs and the Bourbons, were fighting their last battles against the 'heretic people' of an England 'reaching for empire', against the 'Protestant Markgraviate of Brandenburg' seeking an all-mighty kingdom, and 'half-pagan Russia,

---

[4] Ibid., 575.   [5] Ibid., 520.
[6] Erzherzog Maximilian, 'Eisenbahn im Urwald' (1860), in Maximilian, *Gedichte*, vol. 1 (Vienna: Aus der kaiserlich-königlichen Hof- und Staatsdruckerei, 1863), 70–71.
[7] Stefan Zweig, *Marie Antoinette: The Potrait of an Average Woman* (New York: Garden City Publishing Co., 1933).

preparing to stretch its sphere of power immeasurably', they, who used to control most of Europe, grew 'tired and weary'.[8] The symbolic victim who, for Zweig, stands in for the sympathetic view of the Old Regime is Marie Antoinette, married off in accordance with a practice that used to work for Europe's old dynasties. Austria was still marrying, as the old proverb had it, but it was no longer happy. Marie Antoinette, Zweig claimed, was actually a woman of average character. There was neither anything heroic nor contemptible about her; she became heroic by virtue of dying a martyr's death at the hands of the revolution. In fact, as émigrés like Zweig and Roth saw it, the Habsburg Empire as a whole, after 1918, had suffered the fate of Marie Antoinette. Another contemporary, Robert Musil, painted the empire's most lasting satirical image as Kakania, an eminently average empire, tucked between Britain's overseas dominions and Russia's internal model of colonization.

Roth's protagonist calls his father 'Franz Josef's loyal deserter'; he is the descendant of a man who deserted an imperial dynasty whose empire no longer exists. His inheritance was a utopian ideal of reform for an empire that was no longer recoverable. When the Social Democrats came to power in Austria in 1918, outlawing the Habsburgs and all noble titles, the reform ideas of a generation of Habsburg elites were marooned in a past world whose preservation was no longer politically viable. To understand the ideals of these 1920s and 1930s idealists, it is important to know, just as with Franz Ferdinand von Trotta, the ideas they had inherited.

In the interwar years, Vienna became the capital of the Pan-European movement, a supra-party lobbying group associated with Count Richard Coudenhove-Kalergi.[9] A graduate of the prestigious Theresianum school in Vienna where Austria's imperial elite used to be trained, Richard Coudenhove-Kalergi found no empire to serve as a diplomat, which would have been his father's natural choice for him. Instead, in 1922, he presented a suggestion for a Pan-European Union with Austria at its heart.[10] The proposed federation endorsed Europe's economic unity, multicultural diversity, and the use of Africa as a resource colony. He was opposed both to the idea of a German–Austrian Union and to the idea of an accommodation of German nobles within the existing post-Versailles boundaries. Instead, he wanted a multi-ethnic empire under Austrian leadership, whose political form was not necessarily monarchical. In the

---

[8] Ibid., 1–4.
[9] Coudenhove-Kalergi, *Paneuropa ABC* (Leipzig and Vienna: Paneuropa, 1931), 24–25.
[10] Richard Coudenhove-Kalergi, 'Paneuropa. Ein Vorschlag', *Neue Freie Presse*, 17 November 1922.

Austrian, German, and Czech press, Coudenhove-Kalergi criticized both Austrian-German parochialism in Bohemia and Austria, and Czech nationalism.

Franz Josef's loyal deserters and their heirs

The assassination of Franz Ferdinand and the collapse of the Habsburg Empire four years later created options for counterfactual thinking based on a dramatic break from a past whose continuity had been provided by the Habsburg dynasty. The heritage collection assembled by successive generations of Habsburgs, and the newly institutionalized form of the multinational museum created by Franz Ferdinand and his entourage, now themselves became specimen about the Habsburgs Habsburg artefacts as much as about their purported objects.

Among the ideological debris left behind were the utopian reform plans for a multinational empire. Utopic thinking is usually associated with progressivist historical epochs such as the Enlightenment. But, as we see here, utopic and Enlightenment thinking also have their place in the context of an otherwise melancholic discourse of decline. As Karl Popper put it, 'the breakdown of the Austrian Empire and the aftermath of the First World War [. . .] destroyed the world in which I had grown up', making restoration and reform the two central tasks of his generation.[11] Imperialism imposed by an educated elite was seen by these liberal internationalists as a lesser evil than narrow-minded tribalism.[12]

Like Roth's Franz Ferdinand von Trotta, Richard Coudenhove-Kalergi was in many respects heir to his father's ideas. He was critical of the conservative elements among the Habsburg aristocracy. The core conceit of the Paneuropa idea was the prospect of a United States of Europe to occupy a position of geopolitical balance with Asia, the Soviet Union, 'Pan-America' and the British Empire. It was a 'programme of foreign policy' which invited 'leaders from all European parties', ranging from conservatives to socialists, democrats, and liberals. Questions of the internal constitutions of states, he argued, were secondary to the overall goal of European unity, and thus Paneuropa welcomed 'monarchies and republics, democracies and

---

[11] Karl Popper, *Unended Quest: An Intellectual Autobiography* (La Salle, Ill.: Open Court, 1982), 32.
[12] On Popper's critique of 'tribalism', see his discussion of Hegel in Karl Popper, *The Open Society*, 2 vols. (London and New York: Routledge, 2002), 30–38.

dictatorships'. It excluded only the 'extreme nationalists' and the 'communists', who were the 'natural and irreconcilable enemies of the Paneuropa movement'.

Austria-Hungary provided many intellectual resources for rethinking social roles.[13] As diverse as any social network in that empire, the entourage of potential reformers around Franz Ferdinand, though most of them were elite administrators of high nobility, did not subscribe to any one ideology. Yet, in terms of the overall spectrum of political opinions in the empire, they shared a common interest – to promote the stability of a centrally organized empire rooted in loyalty to the Habsburg family. Preparing for his succession, Franz Ferdinand had surrounded himself with a circle that was to provide the foundation for his future reign. Many of these, he met during his world tour, and many had their main residence outside of the Austrian crown lands, especially in Bohemia (where Franz Ferdinand himself resided), Poland, Hungary, or Croatia. In the narrower circle of Franz Ferdinand's supporters, we find such intellectuals as the moderate Baron Johann Heinrich von Chlumetzky, who, as a minister for agriculture in the imperial council in 1906, was instrumental in introducing such reforms as free elections with secret ballots.[14] Other supporters included the Romanian-born Baron Alfred von Koudelka, an admiral who had published travel notes on his journeys to America, the Croatian-born Emil Woinovich von Belobreska, and the Polish nobleman Theodor von Sosnosky, a historian.[15] Most of the aristocratic supporters had graduated from the Theresianum academy.

---

[13] For links between ethnic and sexual relations, see Kai Kauffmann, 'Slawische Exotik und Habsburger Mythos: Leopold von Sacher Masochs Galizische Erzählungen', *Germanisch-Romanische Monatsschrift*, 52.1 (2002), 175–190. Albrecht Koschorke, *Leopold von Sacher-Masoch: Die Inszenierungeiner Perversion* (Munich: Piper, 1988); Joseph Metz, 'Austrian Inner Colonialism and the Visibility of Difference in Stifter 's "Die Narrenburg"', in *Proceedings of the Modern Languages Association*, 121:5 (October 2006), 1475–1492; Barbara Hyams, 'The Whip and the Lamp: Leopold von Sacher-Masoch, the Woman Question, and the Jewish Question', *Women in German Yearbook*, 13 (1997), 67–79.

[14] *Erzherzog Franz Ferdinand. Unser Thronfolger. Zum 50. Geburtstag*, ed. Leopold Freiherr von Chlumetzky et al. (Vienna and Leipzig: Illustriertes Sonderheft der Oesterreichischen Rundschau, 1913), 9–11, 9. Georg Graf Wycielski, 'Erzherzog Franz Ferdinand als Kunstfreund', in Chlumetzky et al. (eds.), *Erzherzog Franz Ferdinand*, 55–85.

[15] Alfred Freiherr von Koudelka, *Aus der weiten Welt* (1900); Emil Woinovich-von Belobreska, *Aus der Werkstatt des Krieges. Ein Rundblick über die organisatorische und soziale Kriegsarbeit 1914/15 in Österreich-Ungarn*. Manz, Wien 1915; *Helden des Roten Kreuzes. Aus den Akten des k. u. k. Generalinspektorates der freiwilligen Sanitätspflege*. Manz, Wien 1915; Theodor von Sosnosky, *Die Politik im Habsburgerreiche. Randglossen zur Zeitgeschichte*, 1912; *Der Traum vom Dreibund*, 1915; *Franz Ferdinand, der Erzherzog-Thronfolger. Ein Lebensbild*, 1929; *Die rote Dreifaltigkeit. Freiheit, Gleichheit, Brüderlichkeit*, 1931.

Among the non-noble reformers who put their hopes in Franz Ferdinand and were in turn supported by him was the Romanian scholar Aurel Popovici (1863–1917), who, in 1906, had published a proposal for the *United States of Greater Austria* in Leipzig.[16] In his model, the different ethno-cultural components of the Austro-Hungarian empire would be given greater national autonomy in matters of culture and education; in exchange, they would remain bound to Greater Austria by means of a federal union. In total, this union would comprise fifteen quasi-independent units defined by language. Each of the fifteen states in the union would receive votes in the legislative chamber of the imperial government.

Popovici's theory was influenced by three models: Swiss federalism, as defended by the legal theorist Johann Caspar Bluntschli; the constitutional model of the United States; and Habsburg imperialism.[17] His explicit motivation in writing the work, aside from being a call to reject Magyarization, was to ensure the 'future of the Habsburg empire'.[18] His book also exhibited an outspoken anti-Semitism, opening with a call to resist what he called the 'Jewish liberal press' represented by Viennese newspapers such as *Neue Freie Presse* and *Die Zeit*, but also provincial papers like the *Bukowinaer Post*. He demanded a new idea of a 'greater Austrian state', deliberately using the words 'union' and 'empire' interchangeably. While his anti-Magyar position, underlining pragmatic uses of nationalism for the sake of strengthening the central power of the Habsburg dynasty, was characteristic of Franz Fredinand's entourage. Popovici combined his defence of multinational imperial reform with an anti-Semitic critique on the Jewish press of the Habsburg Empire.

By contrast, Coudenhove-Kalergi's father, the Orientalist scholar and diplomat Heinrich Coudenhove-Kalergi, also a believer in Franz Ferdinand's reforms, sought to deconstruct the foundations of Habsburg anti-Semitism. What anti-Semites call the 'Jewish press' he argued, was in

---

[16] Aurel Popovici, *Die Vereinigten Staaten von Groß-Österreich. Politische Studien zur Lösung der nationalen Fragen und staatrechtlichen Krisen in Österreich-Ungarn* (Leipzig: B. Elisch, 1906); Aurel Popovici, *La Question Rumaine en Transylvanie et en Hongrie* (Lausanne and Paris: Payot, 1918).

[17] He cites extensively from J.C. Bluntschli, *Allgemeine Staatslehre* (Stuttgart: Cotta, 1886), as well as Bluntschli, *Die nationale Staatenbildung und der moderne deutsche Staat* (Berlin: Habel, 1881). See also Bertrand Auerbach, *Les races et les nationalités en Autriche-Hongrie* (Paris: Alcan, 1898); L. Gumplowicz, *Das Recht der Nationalitäten und Sprachen in Österreich-Ungarn* (Innsbruck: Wagner, 1879). Other citations are of Disraeli's novel Coningsby, to Carlyle and Macaulay, and to J.C.L. Sismondi, *Etudes sur les Constitutions des peuples libres* (Bruxelles: Société, 1839).

[18] Popovici, 1906, Dedication to the reader.

fact the empire's national press; the Jewish press, by contrast, remained largely unknown to the general reader. As a speaker of Hebrew, among allegedly eighteen other languages, Coudenhove was familiar with such publications as *Esperanza* (published in Smyrna), *Haam*, published in Kolomea, *Habazaleth* in Jerusalem, *Hasaron* in Lemberg, the *Corriere Israelito* from Trieste, and *El progreso*, published in Hebrew in Vienna. In mentioning these newspapers, Coudenhove reminded his readers that the project of Europe was rooted in a commitment to the Enlightenment, which had always built on a series of micro-Enlightenments in each community for itself, one of which was the Jewish Haskalah movement. Coudenhove was drawing on an already established discourse of multicultural patriotism in the Habsburg lands, represented by a writer one generation younger, the novelist Leopold Sacher-Masoch. In *Don Juan of Colomea* (1866), he 'recovers' a link between the distant frontier town of Colomea with the Roman Empire by claiming that the word was related to 'Colonia' and that the small town had grown 'on the soil of a Roman plantation settlement'.[19] Coudenhove-Kalergi senior shared Sacher-Masoch's philo-Semitism and philo-Slavism, as well as the desire to preserve the peculiarity of the multicultural empire against the opposing, nationalizing tendencies coming from Prussia.[20] Aside from promoting reform within the old nobility, one of the Enlightenments he was particularly interested in was the Jewish one, which began with the reforms initiated by Joseph II. The supporters of Franz Ferdinand were military men of conservative views but they were also proponents of a vernacular sort of internationalism,

Another activity associated with Franz Ferdinand was a renewed interest in heritage preservation. In 1906, the Archduke had become the official head of the empire's military department, which was also responsible for the maintenance of buildings and works of art. He personally invested much into maintaining the regional peculiarities of 'his' lands, such as the wooden churches of Galicia, for example, which residents themselves were quite willing to replace with more durable stone buildings, but which he placed under national protection.[21] He also considerably expanded the state's art collection, not least through his world travels, during which he

[19] Leopold von Sacher-Masoch, 'Don Juan von Kolomea', in *Westermann's Illustrirte Deutsche Monatshefte*, 121:25 (October 1866), 1–26.
[20] On Sacher-Masoch's politics, see his periodical *Gartenlaube für Österreich*, in Ulrich Bach, Sacher-Masoch's Utopian Peripheries'.
[21] Theodor Brückler, 'Thronfolger Franz Ferdinand als Denkmalpfleger', in *Die 'Kunstakten' der Militärkanzlei im Österreichischen Staatsarchiv (Kriegsarchiv)* (Cologne, Weimar and Vienna: Böhlau, 2009).

collected specimens of art and natural history from various cultures, creating one of the first ethnographic museums. The purpose of these activities was to maintain control over the existing cultural diversity of the empire so that the dynasty and its cultural institutions could retain a monopoly over the overarching unity bridging the diverse cultures. Franz Ferdinand, in other words, prepared the institutions that would enable the Habsburg dynasty to give a form of identity for a multitude of people who had previously thought of themselves merely as Franz Josef's 'peoples'.[22]

The company of travellers who had accompanied Franz Ferdinand on his grand tour went on to witness further developments in Europe on the various fronts. Carl Pietzner became the Habsburg court photographer in 1914, in time to document the war on the eastern front.[23] Prince Kinsky served in the Austro-Hungarian army on the Russian front, but died of a nervous disorder shortly upon his return in 1919. Count Pronáy lived to see the rise of Béla Kún's communist regime in Hungary that year and joined the White Guards under Miklós Horthy who, in turn, had accompanied Franz Ferdinand's uncle, Emperor Franz Josef, on his world tour as a young man, eventually falling during the Soviet siege of Budapest in 1944.

Lessons in internal colonization from Russia, Britain, and Japan

Despite their conservatism in terms of cultural values and their critical attitudes towards rival empires such as Russia and Britain, Franz Ferdinand and his circle were also influenced by their experience of Russian, British, and non-European government reforms. On his world tour, for example, Franz Ferdinand met the Austro-Hungarian consul Heinrich Coudenhove-Kalergi, a linguist of Dutch-Cretan origin, in Japan. Fluent in Japanese, among eighteen other, mostly Asiatic, languages, he had impressed Franz Ferdinand by translating a toast by Prince Arisugawa, a highly placed member of the imperial staff, honouring the Emperor.[24] Consul Coudenhove had been in Japan for two years by this

---

[22] Contrast this with a different sense of "multitude" in Michael Hardt and Antonio Negri, *Multitude. War and Democracy in the Age of Empire* (London: Penguin, 2005), v.

[23] Anton Holzer (ed.), *Die andere Front: Fotografie und Propaganda im Ersten Weltkrieg: mit unveröffentlichten Originalaufnahmen aus dem Bildarchiv der Österreichischen Nationalbibliothek* (Vienna: Primus, 2007).

[24] Franz Ferdinand, *Tagebuch meiner Reise um die Erde*, vol. 2 (Vienna: Alfred Hölder, 1895), 392–393; Marius B. Jansen, *The Making of Modern Japan* (Cambridge, Mass.: Harvard University Press, 2000).

point and, in 1893, married the young daughter of a well-to-do merchant, Mitsuko Aoyama.

Like some of Emperor Meiji's consultants, Coudenhove was an advocate of reform; back in Austria, he had published a critical pamphlet suggesting that the nobility abandon its old practice of duelling, and had defended his doctoral dissertation with a critique of anti-Semitism.[25] The impact of his experience with the Meiji reforms and their abolition of the Samurai privileges found an unlikely interpretation in the context of Austrian society.[26] Coudenhove used his knowledge of the abolition of the Samurai practice of *seppuku* when in Japan to advocate the reform of duelling rights in Europe.

This was the third decade of the period now known as the Meiji Restoration, when a section of Japan's governing elite actively sought to integrate Japan into world politics. In 1872–73, a Japanese committee of scientists and civil servants led by Prince Iwakura Tomomi inspected the practices of government and education in North America, Britain, France, Belgium, Germany, Austria, Switzerland, Russia, Sweden, and Italy.[27] The committee's historian, Kume Kunitake, marvelled at the technological progress Europe had made in the forty years since he had last seen it, with its railways, telegraphs, and completely new fashions. Of the German states, however, it was Prussia and not Austria-Hungary that most impressed the delegation.[28]

In taking up his father's vision for an internal reform of the nobility by arguing for the foundation of a new aristocracy – a kind of composite elite – to be formed by mixing tradition and new talent, a 'serendipitous aristocracy', Richard Coudenhove-Kalergi belonged to a minority in his generation. This was even more striking considering that, as he added, the vehicle for this form of social eugenics would be 'socialism, the movement

---

[25] Ian Hill Nish, *The Iwakura Mission in America and Europe: A New Assessment*; Regine Mathias, *Deutschland-Japan in der Zwischenkriegszeit* (Bonn: Bouvier, 1990).

[26] Henrich Graf Coudenhove-Kalergi, *Der Minotaur der 'Ehre': Studie zur Antiduellbewegung und Duelllüge* (Berlin: S. Calvary & Co., 1902).

[27] Christian W. Spang and Rolf-Harald Wippich, *Japanese-German Relations, 1895–1945: War, Diplomacy and Public Opinion* (New York: Routledge, 2006). In 1929, of 251 Japanese government-funded scholars, 151 studied in Germany. Ibid., article by Kato Tetsuro, 'Personal Contacts in Japanese-German Cultural Relations during the 1920s and the Early 1930s', 119–139, 124. Physics, engineering, and literature were the most popular subjects.

[28] *Die Iwakura-Mission: das Logbuch des Kume Kunitake über den Besuch der japanischen Sondergesandtschaft in Deutschland, Österreich und der Schweiz im Jahre 1873*. By 1892 Kume was dismissed for his critique of Shintoism as a 'primitive naturalism'. See John S. Brownlee, *Japanese Historians and the National Myths, 1600–1945: The Age of the Gods* (Tokyo: University of Tokyo Press, 1999), 92.

which started with the abolition of the nobility, the levelling of humanity', but would culminate in the 'cultivation of the nobility, the differentiation of humanity'. From the 'ruins of pseudo-aristocracy' humanity will create a 'real, new nobility'.[29] In the 1920s, he wanted a multi-ethnic empire under Austrian leadership, whose political form was not necessarily monarchical. In the Austrian, German, and Czech press, Coudenhove criticized both Austrian-German parochialism in Bohemia and Austria, and Czech nationalism.

The Paneuropa project, with branches throughout central and western Europe, and sponsorship from Europe's best-known banks and industries, went through stages in which it was called an *association* and a *movement* and, from 1932 onwards, a European *party* in a non-existent European parliament. From the start, the Austrian government had offered Coudenhove a representative space for his lobbying office in the Vienna Hofburg, so that the movement was registered under the illustrious address of 'Paneuropa, Hofburg, Wien' until the annexation of Austria by Germany in 1938.[30]

The Paneuropa congresses were decorated by large portraits of great Europeans: Kant, Nietzsche, Mazzini, Napoleon, Dante, and others.[31] In one publication covering the event, a photograph of this pantheon was placed next to the portrait of Krishnamurthi, a living sage who was very popular in Germany at the time [Fig. 9].[32]

The Pan-Europeanists' architecture of public memory formed part of a quixotic palace of European memory.[33] It would be futile to attempt to reinsert some inherent logic according to which these very different intellectuals and their ideas of politics form a coherent montage of a European ideal. What we need is to understand how the invocation of these memory portraits on the walls of public buildings and private homes functioned in the social fabric of those who did 'European civilization talk' between the world wars, before it became 'European civilization' talk.

Coudenhove had shared and discussed his vision at London's Chatham House, a foreign policy think tank, from as early as 1931, the year that the

---

[29] Richard Coudenhove-Kalergi, *Adel-Technik-Pazifismus* (Vienna: *Paneuropa*, 1925), 56–57.

[30] Richard Coudenhove-Kalergi, *Ein Leben für Europa. Meine Lebenserinnerungen* (Cologne: Kiepenheuer & Witsch, 1966), 223–224.

[31] Ignaz Seipel opening the first Paneuropa Congress of 1926, Fond 554.7.470.343–416, Coudenhove-Kalergi papers, RGVA, Moscow.

[32] Photograph by Fritz Cesanek. Published in *Österreichische Illustrierte Zeitung*, 36:41 (10 October 1926) 1080.

[33] Cf. Frances Yates, *The Art of Memory* (1966, London and New York: Routledge, 1999); eadem, *Astraea. The Imperial Theme in the Sixteenth Century* (London: Routledge, 1975).

Der in Wiener Großen Konzerthaussaal tagende erste Paneuropakongreß. Allbundeskanzler
Dr. Seipel hält die Eröffnungsansprache.
phot. Cesanek

Krischnamurti wurde in Madras zum neuen
Messias ausgerufen.

Figure 9 Opening session of Paneuropa Congress in Vienna, 1926.
Photograph by Fritz Cesanek. Published in *Österreichische Illustrierte Zeitung*, 36:41 (10 October 1926), 1080

first Indian Congress met in India.[34] As the British Empire was gradually transforming itself into a commonwealth, Coudenhove and his Pan-European followers tried to make sense of continental Europe, whose empires had already begun to crumble. In place of imperial nostalgia, he presented to the world a rebranded idea of empire. His was not just a disenchanted, rational international order, as Wilson's Presbyterian-influenced League of Nations had it. He proposed an emotional European patriotism with echoes of a Catholic and a Dantean ideal of a universal monarchy, with a pinch of Habsburg nostalgia.[35]

Coudenhove fluctuated between a weaker notion of a federation of states (*Staatenbund*), as reflected in various wartime alliances like the Entente, and a stronger notion of a *Bundesstaat*, eventually preferring the latter.[36] Formally speaking, the Union was considered to be the natural successor of the Holy Roman Empire after the Napoleonic Wars; it was supposed to become a strengthened version of the Confederation of States established under the Congress of Vienna regulations of 1815. In the twentieth century, on the stage of international politics, the idea of a Union was juxtaposed with other supranational political organizations, such as the Soviet Union (which soon revealed its foreign political face as a revised Russian Empire), the 'Pan-American' Empire, and the British Empire and Commonwealth. Paneuropa was to be a macro-regional organization with world influence.

Its map presented this Pan-European territory as already existing. National boundaries within Europe, with the exception of Turkey, which was marked with a question mark, were not visually represented. In 1924, the Paneuropa programme demanded a 'systematic exploration of the European economic colony of West Africa (French Africa, Libya, the Congo, Angola) as a European resource'.[37] Coudenhove's aim, as he put it in 1934, was to turn Europe into a community of values, constituted by 'Greek philosophy, Roman law, Christian religion, the lifestyle of a true gentleman and the declaration of human rights'.[38] The question mark on Turkey was due to some of its territory belonging to Europe

---

[34] Richard Coudenhove-Kalergi, 'The Pan-European Outlook', in *International Affairs (Royal Institute of International Affairs 1931–1939)*, 10:5 (September 1931), 638–651.

[35] Ibid., 645. Dante Alighieri, *De Monarchia* (1318–21), first published in Andrea Alciati (ed.), *De formula romani imperii libellus* (Basel: Oporinus, 1559), 53–179.

[36] See Reinhart Koselleck, entry on 'Bund, Bündnis, Föderalismus, Bundesstaat', in *Geschichtliche Grundbegriffe: historisches Lexikon zur politisch-sozialen Sprache in Deutschland*, ed. Otto Brunner, Reinhart Koselleck, and Werner Conze, vol. 1 (Stuttgart: Klett-Cotta, 1972–97), 631–632.

[37] Richard Coudenhove-Kalergi, 'Das Pan-Europa-Programm', in *Paneuropa*, 2 (1924), 4.

[38] Richard Coudenhove-Kalergi, 'Antworten auf eine Rundfrage I', in *Paneuropa*, 1:3 (1925), 55–62.

'despite' its Muslim heritage, a conceptual problem for Coudenhove's Christian conception of European identity.

Coudenhove believed that 'Nietzsche's Will to Power is where the foundational thoughts of fascist and Paneuropean politics stand side by side'.[39] Kant's presence in his pantheon of Europeanists, along with that of Hugo Grotius as well as the 18th-century balance of power theorists (Mirabeau, Abbé de St. Pierre), was due to their endorsement of European unity as an abstract goal, though this in many ways fits uncomfortably both with Nietzsche's 'aristocratic radicalism' and with the discourse of national sovereignty signalled by the presence of Giuseppe Mazzini on Paneuropa's symbolic map.

Drawing on Giuseppe Mazzini's *Europe: Its Conditions and Prospects*, Coudenhove picked up on the traditions of the Young Europe movement, which bridged nationalism and cosmopolitanism. The combination between the two principles was also the motivation behind including the Bohemian humanist Comenius. Coudenhove's journal, *Paneuropa*, devoted a great deal of attention to publishing seminal texts in which European identity was discussed. Nietzsche's *Will to Power* manuscripts[40] were part of a reading list Coudenhove-Kalergi set for future Pan-Europeans, which also included Napoleon's *Political Testament*,[41] as well as about a dozen or so other works by Dante, Comenius, Grotius, Kant, and Mazzini.[42] At the opening of the first Pan-European Congress in 1924, Coudenhove's wife Ida Roland recited Victor Hugo's speech on European unification 'in the service of propaganda for the Paneuropean idea'.[43]

The symbol of the Paneuropa movement, a red cross against the yellow sun of Hellenic Greece, reveals the intellectual legacies to which

---

[39] Coudenhove-Kalergi, 'Antieuropa', in *Paneuropa*, 3 (1930), 92. On Coudenhove's relationship to fascism, see Anita Ziegerhofer-Prettenthaler, *Botschafter Europas: Richard Nikolaus Coudenhove-Kalergi und die Paneuropa-Bewegung in den zwanziger und dreissiger Jahren* (Vienna: Böhlau, 2004), 397–399.

[40] Coudenhove-Kalergi (ed.), 'Nietzsche als Paneuropäer' (excerpts from Nietzsche), in *Paneuropa*, 3 (1930), 95–101.

[41] Reprinted in *Paneuropa*, 5 (1929), 18–22.

[42] See, for instance, Abbé Saint-Pierre, *A Project for Settling an Everlasting Peace in Europe. First Proposed by Henry IV of France, and Approved by Queen Elizabeth, and Most of the Then Princes of Europe, and Now Discussed at Large, and Made Particable by the Abbot St. Pierre, of the French Academy* (London: J. Watts, 1714); François Fénelon, 'Sentiments on the Ballance of Europe', in *Two Essays on the Balance of Europe* (London: n.p., 1720).

[43] Victor Hugo, 'United States of Europe', speech held at the Paris Peace Congress of 1849. Victor Hugo, 'Discours d'ouverture aux Congrès de la Paix à Paris', in Victor Hugo, *Actes et Paroles. Avant l'éxil*, 1849–51, ed. Charles Sarolea (Paris: Nelson, 1875), 423–433. Ida Roland recited it at the Paneuropa Congress in Berlin in 1930. Mentioned in 'Wiederauftreten Ida Rolands in Wien', *Neue Freie Presse*, 7 June 1933.

Coudenhove imagined himself heir: what could be called the Christian tradition of geopolitical integration, historically framed from the Crusades, to the European unification models of Abbé St. Pierre, and to the Christian socialism of the late nineteenth and early twentieth century. Within this tradition, Freemasonry was an important sub-group; and indeed, Coudenhove himself regarded Enlightenment projects which themselves criticized Christian traditions as falling within the Christian trajectory. The intellectual background of masonic eclecticism merged neo-Hellenic ideals with Kantian rationalism as well as the German ideal of *Bildung*, the ideal of culture and education, together with more recent calls for German cultural unity and an imperial discourse. These strands of thought were invoked at Coudenhove's first international Paneuropa Congress.

This genealogy of European unity as Coudenhove presented it was thus composed of several sometimes contradictory traditions: ideas of a Christian empire and monarchy; ideas of national liberation which were based on resistance to large dynasties; ideas of a balance of power and contrary ideas of economic integration by its critics; and the emphasis on charismatic political leadership and technology as features of modern political systems, against the neo-medievalism of some of his other beliefs. Coudenhove's Christian–Hellenic baggage did not prevent him from speaking of Vienna as 'the Mecca of the Paneuropean Union'.[44] In establishing this account of Paneuropa's pedigree, Coudenhove not only marketed the noble ancestry of his own idea, but also sought to borrow authorities from other political movements. He reclaimed Kant and Grotius from Wilson and the liberal internationalists; Mazzini from the European nationalists such as Masaryk; and Victor Hugo from the social democrats. In drawing on a variety of authors, Coudenhove emphasized the inherently cosmopolitan background of the European ideal. The masonic eclecticism of his ideal of Europe was, interestingly, strongly reminiscent of the *City of the Sun* narrative by Tommaso de Campanella, whose depiction of this ideal city included references to Egyptian and Roman polytheism just as to Christianity, Islam, and fiction.

Britain, Coudenhove argued, had to be excluded for reasons of a global balance of power, while Paneuropa was to be modelled after what Coudenhove called 'Pan-America' both in its federal structure and its attitude to colonial resource. Coudenhove called for a revision of the Versailles agreement, especially with regard to the question of German

---

[44] In Richard Coudenhove-Kalergi, *Der Kampf um Europa. Aus meinem Leben* (Zurich: *Paneuropa*, 1949).

(and Austrian) war guilt; a perpetual peace between all the European states; doing away with any customs and other economic borders and bringing about a unified currency; a joint army and fleet; a European *limes* on its eastern border and erosion of all inner European borders; a true guarantee of minority rights and the introduction of punishment for any propaganda of hate in the press; a Europeanization of education at schools; and a Pan-European constitution.[45] Paneuropa was thus based on an essentialist perspective on European identity, and yet demanded policies of identity construction through education and infrastructure.

This vision had particular appeal among the non-British subjects of the Commonwealth present at gatherings such as the meeting at Chatham House. One of them was Abdullah Yusuf Ali, a Muslim British Indian and Qu'ran scholar who had been instrumental in securing Indian support for the allied war effort in the First World War. What Churchill, Coudenhove, and Yusuf Ali had in common was the belief that empires had to be reformed but not destroyed, that it was possible to decolonize without losing the sense of empire. The making of this memory was a complex social process, which was driven by the intellectual communities of interwar Europe.[46]

Coudenhove thought of the Paneuropa movement as supra-political and was happy to invite fascists and corporatists such as Benito Mussolini in Italy and Kurt Schuschnigg and Engelbert Dollfuß in Austria to patronize it. Despite this, he resisted the Nazis on account of their racial ideology and their pan-German treatment of Austria, and was in turn blacklisted by the Nazi party in 1933. The night of the Dollfuß murder, the Coudenhoves fled together with Dollfuß's wife via Hungary and Switzerland to Italy, where Coudenhove-Kalergi notified 'Mussolini through an Italian envoy' that they would be 'passing through Italy with Mrs Dollfuss and her children'. When Coudenhove looked back at his life up to this point, he concluded: 'The world in which I had grown up has disappeared. The dynasty [the Habsburgs] which my ancestors had followed from Holland to Belgium, and from Belgium to Austria, was overthrown and disempowered. The influence of the nobility was broken. The new world was democratic, republican, socialist and pacifist'.[47] After the annexation of Austria by Germany in 1938,

[45] Richard Coudenhove-Kalergi, '*Paneuropa*. Ein Vorschlag', *Neue Freie Presse*, 17 November 1922, 3–4, in http://anno.onb.ac.at/cgi-content/anno?apm=0&aid=nfp&datum=19221117&zoom=2, accessed 1 November 2008.

[46] Geofff Eley, 'Imperial Imaginary, Colonial Effect: Writing the Colony and the Metropole Together', in Catherine Hall and Keith McClelland (eds.), *Race, Nation and Empire. Making Histories, 1750 to the Present* (Manchester: Manchester University Press, November 2010).

[47] Coudenhove-Kalergi, *Ein Leben für Europa. Meine Lebenserinnerungen*, 93.

when Coudenhove was forced to flee Austria, the movement's central idea of reviving a European multi-ethnic empire based in Vienna had evidently failed. In 1940, the Coudenhoves left Europe for New York.

While Joseph Roth's hero Franz Ferdinand went to the Capuchin vault to mourn, Coudenhove chose a different path, first becoming a professor of history at New York's Columbia University and then an activist advocate for Paneuropa, in Switzerland, where the Habsburgs' history had begun. Obtaining a teaching position in history and politics at New York University, supported by the Carnegie Foundation, Coudenhove revived Paneuropa in exile by founding a Research Centre for European Reconstruction which hosted a Pan-European congress there in 1943, inviting other exiles from Europe.[48] Here, in 1977, Otto von Habsburg unveiled a monument commemorating Aurel Popovici's (and Franz Ferdinand's) work.

Personified cosmopolitanism

Coudenhove's movement was characterized by a tendency to relate the more abstract genealogy of European unity to concrete historical personalities, as well as to a performance of his own cosmopolitan history. Richard Coudenhove-Kalergi's mother, Mitsuko Aoyama, came from a Japanese Buddhist family and had converted to Catholicism.[49] She was one of the first Japanese women of her status to marry a western man. Coudenhove's wife, who became a lifelong champion of his ideas and co-manager of the project, was the Austrian Jewish actress Ida Roland.[50] Having to choose a country of citizenship after the revolution of 1918, he opted for a Czechoslovakian passport based on his place of residence, arguing that he was 'a citizen of the Republic of Czechoslovakia without feeling a commonality of sentiment with this state, apart from my personal admiration for its president Masaryk. Because I belong to German Bohemia and grew up there, I do not [even] have command of my country's official language'.[51]

---

[48] Coudenhove-Kalergi, 'The Pan-European Outlook', 638–651. See also 'One Europe', *Time*, 26 March 1945.

[49] Mitsu Coudenhove-Kalergi, *Memoirs*, section 9 ('Audienz Papst Leo XIII'), 136–137.

[50] See Heinrich Coudenhove-Kalergi, *Das Wesen des Antisemitismus* (Berlin: Calvary, 1901).

[51] Ziegerhofer-Prettenthaler, *Botschafter Europas*, 67. Coudenhove-Kalergi-Kalergy got to know Tomáš Garrigue Masaryk through the Masonic Lodge *Humanitas*. Both of them were Freemasons, and Coudenhove-Kalergi's use of the Masonic networks for promoting his cause will be discussed in more detail at the end of the chapter. See Richard Coudenhove-Kalergi, 'Czechen und Deutsche', *Die Zukunft*, Nr. 52, 24 September 1921, S. 342–350.

The Enlightenment roots of his father's ideas were still visible in the junior Coudenhove's plans. His letter of application to the *Humanitas* lodge, of which his father was already a member, shows the importance of his multi-continental heritage for Coudenhove's political ideas: 'Being children of a European and an Asian, thought in terms not of nations but of continents. [. . .] Thus in our eyes Europe was always evidently unified – it was the land of our father'.[52] He saw himself as a 'half Japanese child' whose projects culminated in the 'first successes of the work on European unification'.[53] 'My father', Coudenhove-Kalergi wrote in this motivational letter, was 'a European with Flemish, Greek, Russian, Polish, German, and Norwegian noble blood', whilst his mother was of 'bourgeois Japanese' origin. It was as 'a consequence of this background' that Coudenhove therefore lacked 'any exclusive belonging to a nation [Volk], to a race'. He considered himself to belong to the 'European cultural community and, in a narrower sense, to the German one, but not in the sense of some sort of nationalism'. For these reasons, Coudenhove could only describe his political identity as cosmopo-litan and his social circles as stretching across all 'social spheres and professions'.[54]

Coudenhove's first individual publications bore close resemblance to the moral ideals behind the political activity of the Freemasons, which, for the first time, had gained formal legal acceptance in the Austrian republic. His book *Ethik und Hyperethik* (1922) was reviewed favourably in the *Wiener Freimaurer-Zeitung* (1/3, 1922), a new organ that had begun operating since the legalization of Freemasonry. By mid-1925, the master of the Viennese lodge, Richard Schlesinger, sent a circular to the masters of the great lodges of the world asking them to support Coudenhove-Kalergi's political projects.[55]

A number of Coudenhove-Kalergi's contacts also shared a background in Masonic thought. Coudenhove-Kalergi's application to join the Viennese Freemasons was supported, among others, by the engineer and social philosopher Josef Popper-Lynkaeus and the legal theorist, and future Schmitt opponent, Hugo Heller.[56] Although Coudenhove was admitted to

---

[52] Richard Coudenhove-Kalergi, *Crusade for Pan-Europe. Autobiography of a Man and a Movement* (New York and London: G.P. Putnam's and Sons, 1943), 37–38.

[53] Richard Coudenhove-Kalergi, *Ein Leben für Europa* (Berlin and Cologne: Kiepenheuer & Witsch, 1966), Introduction.

[54] Coudenhove-Kalergi, Letter to Humanitas, 3 September 1921. Freimaurerlogen, 1412.1.2092, in OA.

[55] Circular by Dr. Richard Schlesinger, Grossmeister der Grosslogen, 1925. Freimaurerlogen, 1412.1.244, in OA.

[56] Originating from the Ghetto of Kolin, Lynkaeus belonged to the same circle of enlightened critics of anti-Semitism as Coudenhove-Kalergi's father, and also wrote a programmatic text on food manage-ment in modern societies.

the lodge, his notion of propaganda and open publicity of political ideals did not fit comfortably with the historically subtle influence of Masonic thought in Europe. Even though the Freemasons themselves expanded their modes of influencing the public after 1918 by founding a newspaper, Coudenhove's use of publicity was not welcome. After 1926, Coudenhove had grown disenchanted with the Masons. Nonetheless, he probably owed his positive connection with Masaryk and Beneš – with whom he disagreed on almost all matters of policy, from the debate over the customs union between Austria and Germany in 1931, which he endorsed and they dreaded, to the status of Germans in Czechoslovakia – to their shared Masonic heritage adding to their perspectives a touch of cosmopolitan elitism.

Coudenhove-Kalergi also shared his father's critique of anti-Semitism, which he had edited prior to its publication.[57] His wife, the actress Ida Roland, was Jewish. Rather than socializing at the salons of high nobility, he instead joined his wife's more socially mixed circles of writers, artists, and publishers, such as the salon of the Zsolnay family, a Jewish family whose regular visitors included writers like Arthur Schnitzler and Max Brod. Coudenhove's cosmopolitan elitism was more in tune with the views of a cosmopolitan elite based in Vienna. The notion of 'Heimat', or home country, was seen in this circle as parochial, petit-bourgeois, primitive, anti-urban and anti-enlightenment, worthy only of the sharpest criticism.[58]

Paneuropa was one of many geopolitical concepts of European power politics developed between the end of the nineteenth century and the 1920s. This territorial perspective on identity was encompassed by the emerging discipline of geopolitics, which was founded, in the wake of the work of nineteenth-century German liberals such as Alexander von Humboldt, by conservative political theorists in Sweden and Germany, including Johan Rudolf Kjellén, Friedrich Ratzel, and Karl Haushofer.[59] But Paneuropa was also responding to radical alternatives on the political

---

[57] Coudenhove-Kalergi (ed.), *Antisemitismus nach dem Weltkrieg*, Introduction to Heinrich Coudenhove-Kalergi, *Das Wesen des Antisemitismus* (Leipzig and Vienna: *Paneuropa*, 1932).

[58] On parochialism versus cosmopolitanism in German thought, see Celia Applegate, *A Nation of Provincials: The German Idea of Heimat* (Berkeley: University of California Press, 1990); Karl Popper, 'Zur Philosophie des Heimatgedankens', in *Die Quelle* 77 (1927), 899–908.

[59] On German geopolitical thought after the First World War, see Rudolf Kjellén, *Studien zur Weltkrise* (Munich: H. Bruckmann, 1917); Rudolf Kjellén, Karl Haushofer, Hugo Hassinger, Otto Maull, and Erich Obst, *Die Grossmächte vor und nach dem Weltkriege* (Leipzig und Berlin: B.G. Teubner, 1930). See also Mark Bassin, *Horizons géographiques* (Rosny-sous-Bois: Bréal, 2004), and Michael J. Heffernan, *Meaning of Europe: Geography and Geopolitics* (London and New York: Oxford University Press, 1998).

Left. In June 1923, Leon Trotsky called for a European Socialist Federation under the name of 'The United States of Europe', which he saw as a way out of the fragments of the old empires and towards a future worker-led global order. As he put it then, 'the moment British capitalism is overthrown the British Isles will enter as a welcome member into the European Federation'.[60] Working against the Soviet paradigm of the European Union as an instrument for a permanent world revolution, but also competing with the idea of a devolved British Commonwealth, Coudenhove-Kalergi selectively appropriated some elements of both rival projects of Pan-European influence. He took the pathos and rhetoric from Trotsky, but rested the economic and ideological foundations of his organizations on the capitalist and imperialist principles of the Commonwealth. His archive of designs for the Paneuropa Congress contains examples of a set of newspapers from the Soviet Union with their characteristic modernist aesthetic as models for Paneuropa, alongside models of stamps coming from a more traditional empire, the British [Fig. 10]. This particular newspaper featured headings such as the need for 'mass organisations' of the future, an idea which also appealed to Coudenhove.

The aristocrat as a social mediator

'This book is designed to awaken a great political movement slumbering within all peoples of Europe', Coudenhove pronounced in the first edition of his Pan-European project.[61] He sent several thousand free copies of his first Paneuropa manifesto to politicians around the world. It was translated into English in 1926, French in 1927, then Czech, Croatian, Spanish, Hungarian, Lithuanian, and Greek, but never into Russian or Italian.[62]

Coudenhove-Kalergi's strategy of influence was a more insistent and efficient propaganda effort than those of most of his contemporary theorists on European unity. It comprised a fee-paying and listed *membership* in his Paneuropa association; the publication of programmatic articles and opinion surveys in different press formats; the foundation of the journal *Paneuropa*, which was explicitly devoted to propaganda and hence did not publish any critical articles of itself; and his own private correspondence and communication network, to which he and his wife devoted considerable time. Coudenhove also organized a number of international

---

[60] Leon Trotsky, 'Is the Time Ripe for the Slogan: "The United States of Europe?"', in *Pravda* (30 June 1923). Transl. cited after www.marxists.org/archive/trotsky/1923/06/europe.htm.
[61] Coudenhove-Kalergi, *Ein Leben für Europa*, 122.
[62] Ziegerhofer-Prettenthaler, *Botschafter Europas*, 85.

Figure 10 Soviet models for Paneuropa. Newspaper *Upakovshchik* ['The Packer'].
In RNCK, Photo archive

congresses, typically held in one of the European capitals' large hotels,
bringing together politicians and industrialists.[63]

---

[63] For instance, influential politicians like Gustav Stresemann, Ignaz Seipel, Jean-Paul Boncour,
Elemér Hantos, Francis Delaisi (1942), Willy Hellpach (1928, 1944), and Mihail Manoilescu
(1936, 1939, 1941, 1944) published in both journals. On Briand's idea of a European Union, see
Aristide Briand, *Memorandum sur l'organisation d'un régime d'union fédérale européenne*, proposal at
the annual meeting of the League of Nations general assembly (1929), in *Documents relatifs à
l'organisation d'un régime d'union fédérale européenne*, League of Nations Archives, United
Nations Office, Geneva.

Coudenhove kept in touch with a diversity of what could be described as leader personalities from the spheres of politics, art and literature, and industry, and he put considerable effort into putting them in touch with each other. Many of the politicians and other activists Coudenhove worked with were also proponents of an eclectic blend of political views. This model of Europe as an imperial power was supported particularly by intellectuals. Interestingly, while *Paneuropa* attracted mostly reconstructed conservative thinkers like German Chancellor, and later Foreign Minister Gustav Stresemann, in France and in central Europe, it proved attractive to socialists, such as French President Aristide Briand, and the former Dreyfusards, such as radical socialist French Foreign Minister Edouard Herriot and economic theorist Francis Delaisi.[64]

In Britain, a new, non-governmental think tank which emerged after the First World War, Chatham House, was an important semi-public site where the imperial and colonial elites tested their ideas of imperial devolution in Europe and the world of the European empires. Coudenhove was invited as a guest from the Continent, and his ideas were widely received.[65] Here, Coudenhove was in dialogue with Muslim representatives of the Indian Congress and other intellectuals. In Britain, this strand of thought led to the emerging discipline of International Relations in Aberystwyth.[66] At the same time, among his followers in central and eastern Europe,

---

[64] In the French reception, Czech and Slovak theorists played a particularly important role. See Edvard Beneš, *Problémy nové Evropy a zahraničný politika československá: projevy a úvahy z r. 1919–1924* (Praha: Melantrich, 1924); Edvard Beneš, 'The New Order in Europe,' in *The Nineteenth Century and after* (September 1941), 141; Edouard Herriot, *La France dans le monde* (Paris: Hachette, 1933).

[65] On the British reception of *Paneuropa*, Quincy Wright, review of *Pan-Europe* by Richard N. Coudenhove-Kalergi, in *Political Science Quarterly* (December 1927), 42:4, 633–636; Arthur Deerin Call, review of *Pan-Europe* by Richard N. Coudenhove-Kalergi, in *The American Journal of International Law*, 21: 2 (April 1927), 384–385. See also Arnold Toynbee, 'Historical Parallels to Current International Problems', in *International Affairs* (Royal Institute of International Affairs, 1931–39), 10:4 (July 1931), 477–492; Inderjeet Parmar, 'Anglo-American Elites in the Interwar Years: Idealism and Power in the Intellectual Roots of Chatham House and the Council on Foreign Relations', in *International Relations*, 16:1 (2002), 53–75. See also Lucian M. Ashworth, 'Did the Realist-Idealist Great Debate Ever Happen? A Revisionist History of International Relations', in *International Relations*, 16:1 (2002), 33–53; Paul Rich, 'Reinventing Peace: David Davies, Alfred Zimmern and Liberal Internationalism in Interwar Britain', in *International Relations*, 16:1 (2002), 117–133; Michael Pugh, 'Policing the World: Lord Davies and the Quest for Order in the 1930s', in *International Relations*, 16:1 (2002), 97–115. See also Brian Porter, 'Lord Davies, E.H. Carr and the Spirit Ironic: A Comedy of Errors', in *International Relations*, 16:1 (2002), 77–97.

[66] On Christian internationalism in Britain, see William Harbutt Dawson, 'The Pan-European Movement', in *The Economic Journal*, 37:145 (March 1927), 62–67. As Michael Pugh emphasizes, this movement was radically different from the postcolonial New Commonwealth movement of the 1970s.

Coudenhove gained prominence not only through his connections to Masaryk and the Polish Foreign Minister Zaleski but also through his lecture tours, including a trip to Warsaw in 1925.[67] Among the statesmen most influenced by the Pan-European project were Aristide Briand – whose collaboration with Coudenhove culminated in his announcement of a European federation in 1930 – Edvard Beneš, Gustav Stresemann, and Tomas Masaryk.

In its initial stages, Richard Coudenhove-Kalergi's Paneuropa project was financed wholly from his private sources.[68] He quickly attracted enough attention to bring in other funding, mostly through elite circles of bankers, industrialists, and aristocrats. These comprised the Czech entrepreneur (and owner of the famous shoe production chain), Tomas Bata; the German industrialists Paul Silverberg, Carl Siemens, Adam Opel, Edmund Stinnes, Richard Gütermann, and Hermann Bücher (of the AEG, the German General Electricity Company); Carl Duisberg (of the Bayer corporation); a group of private German bankers; the Dutch industrialist N.V. Philips; and the Austrian Otto Böhler.[69] The US-American Carnegie Foundation for Peace, headed by Nicholas Murray Butler – who published a book on Paneuropa six years before Coudenhove's first publication on the subject – also supported the project.[70] All of these figures, along with the governments of several European states, donated money in support of Pan-European's activities.[71] In the later 1920s, the founders of the summer conference at Pontigny in France and the Mayrisch circle in Colpach, Luxembourg, were among Coudenhove's social contacts.[72] These events were occasions for members of the industrial elites, especially of France, Belgium, Luxemburg, Germany, and Austria, to meet and discuss concerns as well as to invite writers and poets for entertainment

---

[67] On the reception of Coudenhove-Kalergi in Poland, see Adam Barabasz, 'Poland's Attitude to the Conception of European Integration in the Years 1918–1939', in *Western Review*, 2 (2007), 229–251; see also K. Fiedor, *Niemieckie plany integracji Europy na tle zachodnioeuropejskich doktryn zjednoczeniowych 1918–1945* (Wrocław: Panstwowe Wydawn Nauk, 1999).

[68] Coudenhove-Kalergi, *Ein Leben für Europa.*

[69] See Coudenhove to Louis Loucheur, 3 February 1928, 3 May 1928, telegram of 10 December 1928, and 19 January 1929, in Stanford, Hoover Institution Archives (HA), Loucheur Papers.

[70] Ziegerhofer-Prettenthaler, *Botschafter Europas*, 112–113.

[71] As the account books show, however, most of the income was used up by Coudenhove-Kalergi himself with his extensive travel. Ziegerhofer-Prettenthaler, *Botschafter Europas*, 115–116.

[72] On French-German elite sociability, see Gaby Sonnabend, *Pierre Viénot (1897–1944): ein Intellektueller in der Politik* (Munich: R. Oldenbourg, 2005); Uwe Puschner, *Die völkische Bewegung im wilhelminischen Kaiserreich: Sprache-Rasse-Religion* (Darmstadt: WBG, Wissenschaftliche Buchgesellschaft, 2001), Michel Grunewald, Uwe Puschner and Hans Manfred Bock (eds.), *Le milieu intellectuel conservateur en Allemagne, sa presse et ses réseaux (1890–1960)* (Bern: P. Lang, 2003).

and what could be described as public relations purposes. Coudenhove played a role as a mediator on these occasions. The nature of his connection with bankers and industrialists can be illustrated by taking a more detailed look at Coudenhove's relationship with three of them: the Hamburg-based banker Max Warburg, heir to the European branch of the private bank M.M. Warburg & CO; the Stuttgart-based industrialist Robert Bosch; and the Luxemburg-based Emile Mayrisch.

Banker Max Warburg heard about Coudenhove's enterprise through Baron Louis Rothschild and offered to support the project with 60,000 gold marks. In 1926, Warburg also sponsored the travel costs and royalties for speakers attending the Paneuropa Congress in Vienna.[73] Warburg was simultaneously financially supporting other similar movements, ranging from *Die Deutsche Nation* to the Nietzsche Archive, his brother's Warburg Institute, and a number of other projects, seeking always to maximize his reach and influence. By the end of the 1920s, Warburg's support for Paneuropa subsided, since, as he put it to Coudenhove, his concern was that the movement was not sufficiently pragmatic.

Bosch's support came thanks to the mediation of another sponsor of Paneuropa, Richard Heilner (head of a German linoleum company in Wuerttemberg), who in 1927 recommended Coudenhove-Kalergi to Bosch.[74] Like Warburg, Robert Bosch was also investing in a number of rival political movements, including Karl Anton Rohan's *Kulturbund*, but expressly demanded not to be listed as a public supporter. In fact, Bosch, who was a good friend of the British internationalist David Davies, was at first critical of Coudenhove-Kalergi's exclusion of Britain from his proposed union, but was ultimately convinced and provided a link between Coudenhove-Kalergi and a number of British internationalists of the period. Bosch promised to contribute an annual sum of 2,500 Reichsmarks beginning in 1928, but in fact contributed even more until 1933. In 1930, he encouraged Coudenhove to found the 'Society for the Promotion of the Paneuropean Cause' (*Pan-Europ äische Förderungsgesellschaft*) and took a seat on its directorial board. But Bosch withdrew his support immediately when the Nazi government officially blacklisted Paneuropa, significantly undermining Pan-European activities in Germany.

In addition to prominent figures representing individual banks and industry, like Warburg and Bosch, one of Coudenhove's most successful

---

[73] Coudenhove-Kalergi, *Ein Leben für Europa*, 125.
[74] Ziegerhofer-Prettenthaler, *Botschafter Europas*, 110–111.

networking connections was with the founder of the European steel cartel, the Luxemburg industrialist Emile Mayrisch. Mayrisch was the organizer of a series of summer conferences at Colpach, which brought together politicians, industrialists, and intellectuals, especially of German, Austrian, and French origin. He was one of the interwar proponents of the idea that European integration had to begin with a union of German and French interests on the Rhine and founded the German-French Committee of Studies to discuss this form of integration. Coudenhove participated in these meetings, on the one hand as a representative of his own Paneuropa movement, and on the other hand as a representative of Czechoslovakia, whose cause he endorsed internationally by supporting the work of Masaryk and Beneš.

One of Coudenhove's chief strategies of getting prominent politicians on board was offering them honorary presidencies at Pan-European congresses, which he organized at regular intervals. The most important politicians to back Paneuropa in this way were Tomáš Masaryk, Edvard Beneš, Gustav Stresemann, Aristide Briand, Leo Amery, Zaleski, and Winston Churchill. Like Coudenhove, Beneš, and Masaryk, Zaleski joined the Freemasons during the First World War; he was a lecturer in Polish language and literature in London at the time, and was foreign minister of Poland between 1926 and 1932.[75]

Apart from Briand, socialists such as Karl Renner were typically reluctant if not entirely negative towards Paneuropa. Nationalists such as Masaryk and Beneš, on the other hand, supported Coudenhove's work as an international political mediator and themselves encouraged other politicians to join his movement.

In connection with the organization of a Pan-European economic forum in the late 1920s, Coudenhove corresponded with, among other prominent politicians with a background in industry, the French Minister of Labour, Louis Loucheur.[76] He was put in touch with Loucheur through his friend and Paneuropa supporter, Edvard Beneš.[77] Beneš wrote a note to

[75] See also August Zaleski papers, 1919–81, in HA, especially the letter by Mieczyslaw Wolfke to Zaleski on the 'Groupe du Travail Pacifiste Pratique de la Ligue Internationale des Francs-Maçons', 22 February 1932.

[76] Louis Loucheur Papers, Box 4, Folder 12, in HA.

[77] Edvard Beneš to Louis Loucheur, Prague, 1 March 1925, in Loucheur Papers, Box 4, Folder 12, in HA. As historians have pointed out, many of the advocates of European economic integration were technocrats. Thus Loucheur and Coudenhove-Kalergi were also supporters of Le Corbusier's urban modernization projects. This technocratic perspective united conservatives like Loucheur with socialists like Paul Otlet. Another important figure was the socialist Francis Delaisi. See Richard F. Kuisel and Ernest Mercier, *French Technocrat* (Berkeley: University of California

the French conservative politician and technocrat Louis Loucheur (1872–1931), then the French finance minister, in which he offered to bring Coudenhove to his first meeting with Loucheur in 1925: 'Dear Sir, the bearer of this letter is Mr Coudenhove-Kalergi, whose writings on Pan-Europe you surely know. I ask you to give him a favourable welcome and to provide him with the opportunity to lay out his pacifist ideals.'[78] This encounter then led to a series of meetings Coudenhove encouraged between German industrialists and Loucheur.[79] In the course of Coudenhove's correspondence with Loucheur, Coudenhove brought the Luxemburg industrialist Emile Mayrisch (January 1928), Bücher (of the AEG, February 1928), figures from Rhenish industry, Karl von Siemens, the director of the Warburg Bank, Karl Melchior, Caro of the Stickstoffwerke, Richard Heilner of the Linoleum factories, and Count Kanitz, German food minister (May 1928), together in a series of meetings.

The year when Germany joined the League of Nations, 1926, was also fortuitous for the Pan-European union. By 1927, Briand had become the honorary president of the union, and Coudenhove's activities in this regard contributed significantly to the success of the Young plan, which was effectively a revision of the Versailles treaty, brought about following talks between Briand and Stresemann in 1929. In the spirit of international agreement following Locarno and the Kellogg-Briand pact stabilizing especially German–French relations, symbolized by the constructive policies of Stresemann and Briand, Briand produced a 'Sketch for a Paneuropean pact', officially presented in public in May 1930.[80] Indeed, in 1930, which perhaps was the culmination of Coudenhove's activities for a Pan-European Union, Briand announced his plan to work on a European Union of twenty-six states based on Coudenhove's model.[81] However, most European governments gave this publication a cool reception at best.

Press, 1967), 73. On the concept of French Taylorism, see Judith A. Merkle, *Management and Ideology. The Legacy of the International Scientific Management Movement* (Berkeley: University of California Press, 1980), 137.

[78] Edvard Beneš to Louis Loucheur, Prague, 1 March 1925, Loucheur Papers.
[79] Coudenhove-Kalergi to Loucheur letters, especially 3 February 1928, 3 May 1928, telegram of 10 December 1928, and 19 January 1929, in HA.
[80] 'Entwurf für einen paneuropäischen Pakt. Eine Anregung Coudenhove-Kalergis', *Tagblatt*, 30 April 1930.
[81] On the emergence of the German–French alliance as a paradigm for European unification, see Jacques Bariéty (ed.), *Aristide Briand, la Société des Nations et l'Europe, 1919–1932* (Strasbourg: Presses Universitaires, 2007). On the main authors of German-French Europe, see Aristide Briand, *Frankreich und Deutschland* (Dresden: Reissner, 1928); Briand, *Dans la voie de la paix. Discours de 1929* (Paris: Stock, 1929); Edouard Herriot, *The United States of Europe* (London: George Harrap, 1931); Tomáš G. Masaryk, *Das neue Europa* (Berlin: Volk und Welt, 1922); Edvard Beneš, *La France et la nouvelle Europe* (Paris: Nouvelle Revue Française, 1932).

Coudenhove was also seeking to win over liberal internationalists, particularly German and Austrian liberals and social democrats, French socialists, and British liberal internationalists, especially proponents of a Christian empire espoused by figures such as Winston Churchill, David Davies, and Alfred Zimmern. From its inception, Coudenhove sought to involve Austrian, German, and French socialists in his Paneuropa movement – at least, those who sought no connection with Moscow. His move to contact the Briand government in 1925, after the defeat of the conservative Poincare, was motivated by the desire to engage the 'new leftist government' at a moment in time when they were 'searching for a new slogan to replace the nationalistic sentiments of revenge and resentment'.[82] With the same intentions, Coudenhove published a questionnaire to be sent to politicians of different European countries, but especially to internationalists like socialists or liberals, asking their opinion of a Pan-European Union. He then published their responses in his journal. The social democrat Karl Renner responded to the questionnaire by saying that the union was indeed 'an economic and cultural necessity'.[83] However, a year later, Renner distanced himself from the movement due to its express anti-Bolshevism.[84]

Similarly, in 1918, Coudenhove associated himself with the socialist Kurt Hiller, whose 'Political Council of Spiritual Workers' (*Politischer Rat geistiger Arbeiter*), founded in November 1918 in Munich, attracted people who were socialist but felt uncomfortable in a socialist party. What attracted Coudenhove to this project was neither its advocated pacifism nor its idea of council democracy, but rather the *intellectual* elitism that was reflected in Hiller's programme of a 'global intellectual logocracy'.[85] Hiller, like Renner, later abandoned the connection due to Coudenhove's explicit anti-Bolshevism.[86]

Among Coudenhove's least successful attempts to influence government members was his attempt at a solution of the Polish corridor problem, which, being an outcome of the Versailles settlement, separated two parts of Prussia from each other.[87] Realizing that Poland found it unacceptable to renounce its only access to its main port, Gdynia, whilst Germany could

[82] Coudenhove-Kalergi, *Crusade for Pan-Europe. Autobiography of a Man and a Movement*, 96.
[83] Coudenhove-Kalergi, Rundfrage Teil I, in *Paneuropa*, 1:3 (1925), 39.
[84] Karl Renner to Coudenhove-Kalergi, Vienna, 24 July 1926, in RNCK 554.1.132, 65.
[85] Thus the title of a book promoted by Kurt Wolff's publishing house. Kurt Hiller, *Logokratie oder* ein Weltbund des Geistes (Leipzig: Der Neue Geist, 1921). On their falling out, see also Coudenhove-Kalergi, 'Zwei offene Briefe: Kurt Hiller contra Coudenhove', in *Paneuropa*, 7 (1929), 14–21.
[86] 'Kurt Hiller contra Coudenhove-Kalergi', in *Paneuropa*, 7 (1929), 19.
[87] Coudenhove-Kalergi to Reichskanzler, in BA, R 43 I/125, 364–377.

not accept East Prussia being separated, Coudenhove proposed building a special corridor comprising a double railway line and an automobile route, which would connect Danzig viz. East Prussia with the rest of the 'Reich territory'. This line could not be maintained without infringing on Polish transportation within the corridor, 'it will have to pass subterraneously through a tunnel. A commission consisting of a representative of the German and the Polish government will coordinate all the conflicts resulting from this technical-juridical construction'.[88]

One of the reasons for Coudenhove's project coming to a halt around 1931 was that, within a short time span, a number of influential politicians and industrialists who had been supporting Coudenhove had died: Emile Mayrisch died in 1928, Gustav Stresemann in 1929, Louis Loucheur in 1931, and Aristide Briand in 1932.

From Paneuropa to the Cold War

Beyond Germany, Austria, and central Europe, Paneuropa had a lasting legacy in the Christian conservative circles of the Anglo-American elite. These included Leo Amery who, like Coudenhove-Kalergi, had an ethnically mixed and cosmopolitan background; his mother was of Hungarian-Jewish background, and he grew up in India. A co-author of the Balfour Declaration in 1917, Amery supported Paneuropa in the 1930s and also corresponded with Coudenhove concerning other matters, such as the problem of Europe's Jewish population, which Coudenhove proposed to settle in Rhodesia.

But the most prominent British politician to have been influenced by Coudenhove was Winston Churchill, who in his speech on Europe's need to unite praised the 'work [. . .] done upon this task by the exertions of the Pan-European Union which owes so much to Count Coudenhove-Kalergi and which commended the services of the famous French patriot and statesman, Aristide Briand'. Just like Coudenhove, who presented the union of Swiss cantons as an example for Europe, Churchill concluded his call for European unification by declaring that Europe should be 'as free and happy as Switzerland is today'. This was far from Max Weber's demand for national greatness to avoid succumbing to Swissification.[89]

---

[88] Ibid., 364–377, Attachment, 12.

[89] Winston Churchill, Speech delivered at the University of Zurich, 19 September 1946, in Randolph S. Churchill, *The Sinews of Peace: Post-War Speeches of Winston S. Churchill* (London: Cassell, 1948), 199–201. At the same time, as far as his own nation was concerned, Churchill indicated that alongside this European Switzerland there was still room for a British Empire which was associated but not integrated in the European Union of states.

Figure 11 Coudenhove with Robert Schuman in 1956.
IMAGNO/Austrian archives

But Coudenhove's propaganda efforts eventually were absorbed in the Franco-British plans for European integration. One of the images of Coudenhove after the Second World War shows him seated next to Robert Schuman in the European parliament.

In the last decades of the Cold War, political theorists in the United States began to use the term 'transnational' to speak of social connections beyond the control of states, as well as to call 'soft power' the ability to get people to do what you want without coercing them through weapons.[90] Unlike the 'hard', institutional power of states, soft power achieves influence through gradual projects in culture and education. But these terms also apply remarkably well to the remains of Austria-Hungary, a multinational empire that had no overseas possessions but rather a multicultural, internal space of influence. In addition to regular forms of coercion, Austria-Hungary was notable for centuries for the cultural

[90] Robert Keohane and Joseph Nye, 'Transgovernmental Relations and International Organizations', in *World Politics*, 27:1 (October 1974), 39–62; Joseph Nye, 'Soft Power', in *Foreign Policy*, 80 (Autumn 1990), 153–171.

prowess of its dynasty, the Habsburgs. After the revolution, aristocratic privilege in Austria was abolished and the Habsburgs sent into exile; however, many elements of their established practice of 'soft power' and of social connections across the borders of their empire's component states survived. It was on the foundations of these traditions, I submit, that a number of Viennese intellectuals began to develop new projects for European unity. In the absence of the 'hard' power of an imperial army, which in the course of the Great War had fragmented into its national components, they embraced the 'soft' power of culture and informal networking between intellectuals, bankers, and industrialists.[91]

---

[91] Blanning, *The Culture of Power and the Power of Culture.*

CHAPTER 4

The German princes
An aristocratic fraction in the democratic age

'German Princes and Nobility Rush Funds to Neutral Lands', the Geneva correspondent of the *New York Times* noted in October 1918. Citing a Swiss banker, he observed that a 'large proportion of the depositors bringing their money from Germany and Austria belong to the princely families, posing under assumed names'.[1] The work of a newsmaker in Europe between 1917 and 1920 must have been exciting and hopeless at once. From the Urals to the Alps, with each deposed monarch, with each exiled prince, European society was becoming increasingly unfamiliar. Many people inhabiting this large territory felt compelled to reinvent themselves under new banners: national democracies, classless societies, people without land. One of the tasks for the relatively new craft of world news reporting was to give readers a provisional image of this continent's new appearance when its former faces had become mere phantoms. A focus on the German princes allowed grasping imperial decline of the Hohenzollern, Romanoff, Habsburg, and Osman dynasties at once, and in historical perspective. As a shorthand identity, 'German princes and nobility' reveals a slice of imperial decline of more than one empire.[2]

At the same time, in Germany itself, even liberals were unsure whether a revolution had actually occurred. Not only did some Germans resent living in times 'without emperors',[3] contemporaries of liberal and even socialist leanings also expressed doubts about the viability of the German revolutions, which seemed feeble and theatrical compared to the images

---

[1] NN, 'German Princes and Nobility Rush Funds to Neutral Lands', *New York Times*, 22 October 1918, 1. http://query.nytimes.com/gst/abstract.html?res=9407E7DA1539E13ABC4A51DF B6678383609EDE, accessed 1 November 2008.

[2] On mechanisms for ascribing identity, see Rogers Brubaker, *Ethnicity Without Groups* (Cambridge, Mass.: Harvard University Press, 2004).

[3] From the prefatory note to Ernst Kantorowicz, *Kaiser Friedrich der Zweite* (Berlin: Bondi, 1927), as analysed in Martin A. Ruehl, '"In This Time Without Emperors": The Politics of Ernst Kantorowicz's Kaiser Friedrich der Zweite Reconsidered', *Journal of the Warburg and Courtauld Institutes*, 63 (2000), 187–242.

Revolutionstage in Berlin:
Die große Massenkundgebung am Bismarckdenkmal am 10. November.
Phot. Häckel.

Figure 12 Voss Zeitbilder, 17 November 1918, 1

from Russia.[4] Somebody who is accustomed to images of the October Revolution – many of which, incidentally, were only produced retrospectively, in 1927 – would look in vain for an iconic equivalent from Germany.

In November 1918, the pro-republican *Vossische Zeitung* featured a confusing photograph of crowds gathered in Berlin on its front page, with a backward-facing Bismarck statue instead of the proclamation of the republic [Fig. 12].

It took the newspaper several days to change its name from 'Royal Berlin newspaper for political and intellectual affairs' to 'Berlin newspaper for political and intellectual affairs'. Even on the five-year anniversary of the revolution, its weekend supplement showed no photographs from November 1918. Instead of images of crowds, the editors placed a large map of the world on the front page, which advertised the need for radio networks in post-war Germany, featuring the Atlantic Ocean more prominently than the continent of Europe [Fig. 13].[5]

There was a debate whether to blow up the statues of Prussian kings adorning the Alley of Victory ('Siegesallee'), an unpopular project initiated by Wilhelm II to commemorate the defeat of France in the Franco-Prussian War of 1870–71 and derisively called 'Alley of Puppets' in Berlin. It had only been completed in 1901 and included a genealogical parade of German rulers from Albrecht of Prussia, the last grand master of the Teutonic Order, to the Prussian King Wilhelm I. The satirist Kurt Tucholsky asked himself: 'What will come of the Siegesallee? Will they drive it out of the city towards the New Lake because it is too royalist, too autocratic and too monarchist? [. . .] Will they maintain the statues but place new heads on the same necks? [. . .] And was all that learning of their names for my exams in vain?'[6] In the end they remained in place until Albert Speer's grand plan to make Berlin fit for the Nazi empire forcibly removed them to a new location in 1938, where they were partially destroyed by allied bombs, then demolished under the auspices of the British and Soviet occupation, the remaining figures buried in the ground, only to be restored and reconstructed in 2009.[7]

Hans-Hasso von Veltheim, the officer who had served in the reconnaissance photography department of the Saxon royal army in the First World

---

[4] Klemperer, *Revolutionstagebuch 1919*.
[5] 'Zeitbilder', *Beilage zur Vossischen Zeitung*, 17 November 1918, featuring crowds gathered on 10 November under the Bismarck memorial, with the Siegessäule in the background, and *Die Voss*, 45 (10 November 1923), front page.
[6] Theobald Tiger, aka Kurt Tucholsky, 'Bruch', in *Ulk*, 13.12.1918, Nr. 50.
[7] Christopher Clark, *Iron Kingdom: The Rise and Downfall of Prussia, 1600–1947* (London: Penguin, 2006), 679.

Figure 13 *Die Voss, Auslands-Ausgabe*, 45 (10 November 1923), 1

War, confessed that he experienced the European revolutions as a 'purifying and revitalising' force that may yet 'constitute a large step forward'.[8] This did not prevent him from serving as a volunteer officer in a dismantled Cavalry Division of the imperial guard in Berlin in 1919. Under the leadership of Waldemar Pabst and Reichswehr minister Gustav Noske, this division was chiefly responsible for crushing the socialist rebellions in Berlin in early January 1919. But when the Spartakists Karl Liebknecht and Rosa Luxemburg were assassinated in the same month, Pabst himself was suspected of masterminding the murder. Veltheim chose to attend their funeral in civil attire. He confessed to his wife that he was 'deeply moved' by the 'composure of this immeasurable, enormous crowd'. Deputies from 'Switzerland, Holland, Denmark, Sweden, Norway, Petersburg, Moscow, Kiev, Warsaw, Vienna, Sophia' were among the mourners, and the 'funeral procession of a Kaiser could not have been more ornate, dignified and moving'. One of the 'proletariat', as he described it, even offered him a sandwich, although 'the man knew' that he was 'Oberleutnant and Dr. phil'.[9] Choosing Munich as his base for the next years, Veltheim sympathetically witnessed the socialist revolution there. He corresponded with the anarchist Gustav Klingelhöfer, who was imprisoned for treason for joining the revolutionaries of the Munich Council Republic, particularly the Red Army group led by Ernst Toller.

While individual aristocrats, like the representatives of other social groups, aligned with a variety of social forces during the revolution, aristocratic families remained objects of critique in central Europe. These ruling families saw themselves as the descendants of families who, for generations, had acquired distinction in ruling over Europe's vernacular populations of Slavs, Anglo-Saxons, various Germanic tribes, Celts, Galls, Roma, Jews, and other groups. In popular culture, the traits associated with most of these folk groups – visual features, professional affiliations, and such like – usually appeared as marks of stigma or inferiority; but for nobles, their special qualities were always marks of distinction. If in many traditional cultures, unusual physical traits are associated with some kind of evil – one need only to think of the image of the hunchback, or the witch, in the case of nobles, some traits of this kind, such as the Habsburgs' protruding lip, were used to mark a special kind of familial charisma.[10]

---

[8] In LHASA, Rep. H. Ostrau II, Nr. 188, cited in Karl Klaus Walther, *Hans Hasso von Veltheim. eine Biographie* (Halle: Mitteldeutscher Verlag, 2004), 75.

[9] Ibid., 77–78.

[10] Georg Simmel, 'Zur Soziologie des Adels'. The philosophical system of which this is a part is Simmel's theory of value, in Simmel, *Philosophie des Geldes* [Philosophy of Money] (Leipzig: Duncker & Humblot, 1900).

Figure 14 'Herrenhäuser', from *Simplicissimus* 16, 17 July 1911, 267. The caption reads: 'Let them cremate you, papa, then you won't have to keep turning so much later on'

Figure 15 'Not a penny for the princes!' Election poster from Germany, 1926. 'Den Fürsten keinen Pfennig! Sie haben genug! -rettet dem Volk 2 Milliarden Den Notleidenden soll es zugute kommen!' [Not a penny for the Princes! They have enough! – save 2 billion for the people/It should benefit those in need!] Election propaganda car (1926); Aktuelle-Bilder-Centrale, Georg Pahl.
Source: Bundesarchiv, Image 102–00685

In the early twentieth century, German aristocrats had become objects of satire in Germany and in the Habsburg lands. The Munich-based satirical magazine *Simplicissimus* ridiculed the Ostelbian Barons as symbols of the old world. 'Let them cremate you, papa, then you won't have to turn so much later on,' reads the caption on one caricature dating from 1906 [Fig. 14].

After the First World War, such jokes became more serious. Election posters made the expropriation of former princes into one of the key rallying cries for voters.

In Czechoslovakia, National Democratic Party member Bohumil Němec argued that 'nationally foreign [. . .] and rapacious noble families' had been causing harm to the Czech nation throughout history.[11] Ironically, his own Slavic surname, which means 'German', hints at the

---

[11] Eagle Glassheim, *Noble Nationalists. The Transformation of the Bohemian Aristocracy* (London and Cambridge, Mass.: Harvard University Press, 2005), 65.

history of ethnic relations in his place of origin. The imperial nobility, previously backed by the ancient power of the Habsburgs in the region, became merely another ethnic German minority, which the new governments viewed as being on a par with others, such as the Sudeten Germans.[12] In both Russia and Czechoslovakia, German nobles were granted citizenship in the new states but were effectively barred from participating in politics and exercising traditional feudal privileges like holding court.

In other states, aristocrats were mistrusted due to the disproportionate privilege they had enjoyed under the imperial governments. In fact, in Germany, for instance, already by the beginning of the twentieth century some members of the nobility had begun to organize themselves like an interest group whose interests go beyond party affiliations, such as the Agrarian Union or the Colonial Society. A number of nobles joined conservative associations of nobles such as the Deutsche Adelsgenossenschaft or the Deutscher Herrenklub, founded in 1924 by Heinrich von Gleichen; many Baltic Germans joined associations such as the Baltische Ritterschaften, which had their seat in Germany, but were active throughout western Europe in the interwar period. Other nobles from the Russian Empire joined the Union de la Noblesse Russe in France, which was founded in 1925, or aristocratic charitable organizations. Others again, particularly members of dynastic families, were active in chivalric associations, such as the Order of the Golden Fleece, the Order of St. John, and others.[13] The very idea of an aristocratic association was a modern concept, and quite unlike the medieval knighthoods known from such groups associated with the Arthurean legends as the Knights of the Round Table or the Order of the Garter. The modern associations which emerged in late imperial and republican Germany, the most prominent of which was the *Deutsche Adelsgenossenschaft*, were in fact alternatives to parties. In this way they were a reaction to growing parliamentarization, more than the

---

[12] V. Alton Moody, 'Reform Before Post-War European Constituent Assemblies', *Agricultural History*, 7 (1933), 81–95; L.E. Textor, *Land Reform in Czechoslovakiania* (London: G. Allen & Unwin Ltd., 1923).

[13] On these alignments in the interwar period, see Stephan Malinowski, *Vom König zum Führer: Sozialer Niedergang und politische Radikalisierung im deutschen Adel zwischen Kaiserreich und NS-Staat* (Berlin: Akademie-Verlag, 2003); Dimitri Obolensky, *Bread of Exile: A Russian Family*, transl. Harry Willetts (London: Harvill Press, 1999); Peter H. Johnston, *New Mecca, New Babylon: Paris and the Russian Exiles, 1920–1945* (Canada: McGill University Press, 1988); Mathias F. Müller, *Der Orden vom Goldenen Vlies und das Haus Habsburg im Heiligen Römischen Reich: ein (kultur-) geschichtlicher Rückblick* (Vienna: Gesellschaft für vergleichende Kunstforschung, 2009); Gordon Brook-Shepherd, *Uncrowned Emperor: The Life and Times of Otto Von Habsburg* (Hambledon: Continuum, 2003).

enactment of a medieval ideal. The very idea of a *Genossenschaft* of nobles is, conceptually speaking, somewhat absurd. The modern equivalent of that would an imaginary CEO solidarity network, a sort of elite cartel that borrows its language from groups socially and economically inferior to itself. As such, they became what Stefan Malinowski has called 'laboratories of aristocratic reorientation', that is, places of mutual aristocrat recognition, as much as organizations serving the purpose of making aristocrats recognized by their non-aristocratic fellow citizens.

In Germany, a communist member of the German Reichstag recalled the words of none other than Robespierre, who justified the execution of Louis XVI as 'not a decision for or against a man' but a 'measure for the public good, an act of national precaution'.[14] During the revolutionary period before the ratification of the constitution, the new governments of some former German principalities, for instance, Hessen Darmstadt, had already expropriated 'their' nobles as part of their revolutionary measures.

Although the constitutions of some smaller German states had ceased recognizing the nobility long before the revolution – for instance, the constitution of the Free City of Bremen from the period of the Kaiserreich did not acknowledge nobility as a politically privileged status – the majority of regional German constitutions had been dominated by the principles of monarchy and nobility, which only changed radically in 1918–19.[15] A government initiative for a mass expropriation of nobles, documented in photographs of election campaigns, failed to reach a quorum because only 39.3 per cent of the electorate voted [Fig. 15].[16]

Members of the Weimar government discussed at length whether it was acceptable to allow members of aristocratic associations to become members of Parliament.[17] In the end, a compromise was reached whereby the princes lost some of their real state that had representative functions but were financially compensated for this effect of the law. However, as Schmitt and other critics of this measure insisted, abrogating rights from

---

[14] '129. Sitzung des Reichstags am 2. Dezember 1925', cited in several passages in Carl Schmitt, *Unabhängigkeit der Richter, Gleichheit vor dem Gesetz und Gewährleistung des Privateigentums nach der Weimarer Verfassung. Ein Rechtsgutachten zu den Gesetzentwürfen über die Vermögensauseinandersetzung mit den früher regverenden Fürstenhäusern* (Berlin und Leipzig: de Gruyter, 1926), 13–14.

[15] For instance, the constitution of Bremen, § 17 Abs. 2, explicitly did not acknowledge noble privilege even before 1918. www.adelsrecht.de/Bibliographie/bibliographie.html, 5 October 2008.

[16] See Karl Heinrich Kaufhold, 'Fürstenabfindung oder Fürstenentschädigung? Der Kampf um das Hausvermögen der ehemals regierenden Fürstenhäuser im Jahre 1926 und die Innenpolitik der Weimarer Republik', in *Deutscher Adel im 19. und 20. Jahrhundert*, ed. Markus A. Denzel and Günther Schulz (St. Katharinen: Scriptae Mercaturae, 2004).

[17] Bundesarchiv, Berlin, R 43 II/1554, 6ff.

nobles set a precedent for future liberal legislation, which meant that under certain circumstances, states could redefine the basic principles of legitimacy in their society.

In his role as a legal counsel to the Weimar constitutional court, Carl Schmitt saw the attempts to inscribe derecognition of nobility into law as setting a dangerous precedent. Comparing the situation with the French Revolution, he argued that with the execution of a king (such as Louis XVI), both the person and the office of the monarch were simultaneously eliminated. This model of reform-by-regicide could not easily be applied to the much larger number of European aristocrats. Unless one wanted to resort to assassinations of individuals with noble names on a mass scale, as had happened in the Soviet Union, this could not be extended to an entire social class within the framework of a liberal constitution.[18] However, even when laws abolishing the nobility were effective, their effect amounted to the abrogation of the rights of an entire social group, setting a dangerous precedent for depriving other groups of rights in the future. The legal definition of nobles as a 'group of exception' who can be expropriated by the state is particularly problematic for liberal legislation which is predicated on the *a priori* equality of all of the subjects of the law.[19]

The republic was in a dilemma: the existence of aristocratic privilege threatened to derail the new ideal of political equality, but so did the possibility of expropriating nobles by law. The new constitutional assemblies ratified the abolition of the nobility by economic means, removing the prerogatives of primogeniture and title, and barring members of noble corporations from public office.[20] To give an example of popular attitudes towards the nobility in the German Republic, one K. Jannott, director of the Gothaer life insurance group, wrote to Reich Chancellor von Papen in 1932 that it would serve as 'a great example' if the noble members of government demonstratively renounced their nobility to show that they did not value the mere noble name 'and that even by name they want to be nothing else but plain civic [*bürgerlich-schlichte*] citizens'. Thus, Jannott continued, the then-current government's problems with accusations of being a 'cabinet of Junkers and Barons' could be decisively dismissed. 'Noblesse oblige!', Jannott cited the famous *bon mot* which bound nobles to serving the state and to honour their ancestors. He used it to incite

---

[18] Schmitt, *Unabhängigkeit der Richter*, 25–27.   [19] Ibid.
[20] On the abolition of titles in the Weimar Republic, see Bernhard Raschauer, *Namensrecht. Eine systematische Darstellung des geltenden österreichischen und des geltenden deutschen Rechts* (Vienna and New York: Springer 1978).

nobles to give up their nobility in favour of the new 'obligations' associated with a republican regime.[21]

Members of aristocratic families as well as those who deposed them had the spectre of Bolshevism before their eyes when they witnessed the revolutions in their regions. In Germany, where twenty-two dynastically ruled communities changed constitution between 1918 and 1921, this was particularly acute, but nowhere as immediately as in Hessen Darmstadt, since the wife of Nicholas II, who had been murdered with him by revolutionaries in Russia, was the sister of Grand Duke Ernst Ludwig. As Grand Duke Ernst Ludwig's son Georg recalled, the way in which his parents were held captive on 9 November 1918 'was a very good imitation of the pictures of the Russian Revolution which we, too, had seen in the illustrated journals, and which apparently had started quite a trend'.[22]

When Ernst Ludwig and his family found that they were not to be physically harmed by the revolutionary movement in Darmstadt but merely expropriated, the ex-Duke wished to bless the new government 'for constructive work in the best interests of our nation ["Vaterland"]'. Ernst Ludwig wished to thank the new government 'for the dignified way in which you have steered the wheel of the state under the most difficult circumstances and the often criss-crossing tendencies of the popular will, having managed a most serious transformation in the history of Hesse while avoiding all but the most necessary other hardships'. By 'other hardships', Ernst Ludwig was referring to the possibility of having been stripped not just of his status, but also of his life, as communist politicians at the time were calling for the beheading of Louis XVI. The letter was signed simply 'Ernst Ludwig', without titles.[23] In return for giving up political power and a few castles, Ernst Ludwig received financial compensation of 10 million Reichsmark.[24] However, the German hyperinflation rendered this transaction quasi meaningless.

The purposes behind abolishing the symbols of monarchy and nobility varied amongst the European states: in some cases, it was justified by the foreign heritage of formerly aristocratic families; in others, by their economic supremacy. Generally, the less radical European governments tried

---

[21] BA, 'Adel' 1925–38, R 43 II 1554–5, 38. K. Jannott to Reichskanzler von Papen, Gotha, 14 September 1932.
[22] Manfred Knodt, *Ernst Ludwig. Großherzog von Hessen und bei Rhein* (Darmstadt: H.L. Schlapp, 1978; 3rd ed. 1997), 375–376.
[23] Knodt, *Ernst Ludwig*, 375–376.
[24] Kaufhold, 'Fürstenabfindung oder Fürstenentschädigung? Der Kampf um das Hausvermögen der ehemals regierenden Fürstenhäuser im Jahre 1926 und die Innenpolitik der Weimarer Republik', 283.

to address the problem of aristocratic privilege by making it impossible to combine membership in aristocratic corporations and service to the new states. In 1929, President Stresemann's government determined that membership in the German Nobles' Union, an aristocratic corporation, was unacceptable for members of the Reichstag, the ministries, and the army. The republican government of Austria had also passed a law concerning the 'abolition [Aufhebung] of the nobility, its external privileges and titles awarded as a sign of distinction associated with civil service, profession, or a scientific or artistic capacity'. Ironically, Schmitt was right concerning the danger of the precedent, even though he himself helped bring to power the Nazi government, which went on to use the laws of the Weimar era to create its own mechanisms of derecognition. As Hannah Arent would later note, depriving Jews of citizenship in 1935 involved a multiple process of derecognition.[25] At the same time, Nazi officials could not decide whether or not the old ideal of the nobility contradicted their own ideology of the Aryan race.

In Austria, too, after 1919, nobles had become 'German-Austrian citizens', equal before the law in all respects.[26] During the parliamentary debates on the future of noble privilege in Austria, the social democrat Karl Leuthner argued that 'the glorious names of counts and princes are in fact the true pillars of shame in the history of humanity'. His Christian socialist colleague Michael Mayr described the nobility as a 'dowry of the bygone state system' and thought it was 'completely superfluous and obsolete in our democratic times'.[27] But the law itself made the difference clear: all other citizens could keep their imperial decorations, such as titles of civic or military honour. For example, the anthropologist Bronislaw Malinowski got to keep his doctoral distinction *sub auspicii imperatoriis* granted by Habsburg Emperor Franz Josef.[28] But citizens with noble names had to give up their imperial distinction and even their very names. In this sense, not all imperial

[25] Hannah Arendt, *The Origins of Totalitarianism* (Cleveland and New York: Meridian Books, 1951), 279–280.
[26] The Austrian eqivalent was called Adelsaufhebungsgesetz StGBl. Nr. 211, Vollzugsanweisung am 18 April 1919, StGBl. 237. The Austrian constitution of 1920 noted in Article 7: 'Alle Bundesbürger sind vor dem Gesetz gleich. Vorrechte der Geburt, des Geschlechtes, des Standes, der Klasse und des Bekenntnisses sind ausgeschlossen.'
[27] Hannes Stekl, *Adel und Bürgertum in der Habsburgermonarchie, 18. bis 20. Jahrhundert* (Vienna and Munich: Oldenbourg, 2004), 104.
[28] Andrzej Flis, 'Broniwslaw Malinowski's Cracow Doctorate', in *Malinowski between Two Worlds. The Polish Roots of an Anthropological Tradition*, ed. Ernest Gellner, Roy Ellen, Grazyna Kubica, and Janusz Mucha (Cambridge: Cambridge University Press, 1988), 195–200.

privileges were derecognized, but inheritable privileges associated with the German princes were.

However, perhaps paradoxically, one of the unintended effects of this policy of abolishing aristocratic privilege was the emergence of a group of derecognized nobles who turned their newly obtained 'classlessness' and social homelessness into a new source of social capital. Their heightened sense of precarity made them appealing to an international elite in search of its true self, Europeans and non-Europeans. Many of them were jointly attracted to such new ecumenical and post-Christian communities as the Theosophical Society, gurus such as Krishnamurthi and Annie Besant, and the intellectual anthroposophism of the German philosopher Rudolf Steiner.

All these were to serve as instruments for shaping a new ideal of humanity that would build bridges between the proletariat and the old aristocracy, negating the authority of the bourgeois middle class with which the policies of derecognition were mostly associated. As Joseph Schumpeter explained in 1927, much of the transition from the old imperial regime to the modern republic depended on the old elites themselves, on the way in which they embraced giving up power for personality and the degree to which they were able to endorse the ideas of the new elites.[29] The nobility itself, as he put it, became 'patrimonialized', turning into a shared heritage.

Veltheim, like a vocal minority of other aristocratic intellectuals, reflected on the future international order from a European and an internationalist point of view. Even before the revolution, Veltheim and other nobles of his circle had attached themselves to modernist literary associations, where themes of European decline and homelessness, and the search for non-European culture, were prominent. Like Veltheim, many became attached to the political Left in the course of the First World War. Historians have so far looked at cases like Veltheim's on an individual basis; and each biographer claims each of them to be singularly eccentric.[30] However, when considered together, their eccentricity appears to be a shared one; their 'redness' seems much more ambiguous; and the influence of their, however unusual, ideas happens to be much wider.

---

[29] Joseph Schumpeter, 'Die sozialen Klassen im ethnisch homogenen Milieu', in *Archiv für Sozialwissenschaft und Sozialpolitik*, 57: 1 (1927), 1–68.

[30] Cf. James Palmer, *The Bloody White Baron* (London: Faber & Faber, 2008).

Veltheim's social circle is one of the intellectual communities that was very transnational in scope.[31]

Veltheim's world: homelessness and counter-culture before and after 1918

Hans-Hasso von Veltheim-Ostrau liked to entertain. In 1927, he inherited his paternal estate of Ostrau, near Halle, and was glad finally to be able to host his friends in a location worthy of his family name. Veltheim spent the first night at the castle chiselling out the ancestral crests of his *ungeliebte* stepmother, before introducing his own, supplemented by new portraits and busts of himself and a bespoke gallery of chosen ancestors, the *Ahnengalerie*. What followed were weeks and months of replanting, redecorating, rearranging and amplifying the eroded family library. Together with the rent that he was obliged to pay his brother Herbert by the rules of primogeniture, the *Fideikommiss*, the redecoration of the house cost him a considerable sum of money.

The castle of Ostrau, surrounded by a moat and a large park, had originally been built by Charles Remy de la Fosse in the early eighteenth century, an architect of Huguenot origin who was then also employed by several predominantly south-west German noble families, such as the Grand Duke of Hesse-Darmstadt. Like the Veltheims, they wanted to introduce French style to Germany, and now, Veltheim took the opportunity to reconnect to this tradition.[32] Throughout his life, he had felt a certain sense of homelessness, which he occasionally enjoyed, since it gave him the lightness necessary for travelling. In 1908, he had copied out this poem by Friedrich von Halm in his diary: 'Without a house, without a motherland/ Without a wife, without a child/ Thus I whirl about, a straw/ In weather and wind.// Rising upwards and downwards/ Now there, and now here/ World, if you don't call me/ Why called I for you?'[33] This was not only an age where Grand Tours expanded to exotic lands; new technologies also brought explorations upwards, into the sky.

---

[31] On the idea of a group or community constituted by the memory of loss, see Maurice Halbwachs, *Les Cadres Sociaux de la Mémoire* (Paris: Alcan, 1925); see also Serguei Alex Oushakine, *The Patriotism of Despair. Nation, War, and Loss in Russia* (Ithaca, N.Y. and London: Cornell University Press, 2009).

[32] On the material culture of the aristocracy, see Tim Blanning, *The Culture of Power*, esp. ch. 2, 53–77.

[33] Cited in Walther, *Veltheim*, 36. Veltheim's diary entry of 25 March 1908. Kein Haus, keine Heimat,/ Kein Weib und kein Kind/ So wirbl´ich, ein Strohhalm,/ In Wetter und Wind.// Well auf und Well nieder,/ Bald dort und bald hier,/ Welt, fragst Du nach mir nicht,/ Was frag ich nach Dir?' In Universitäts- und Landesbibliothek Halle, Nachlass Veltheim [LHASA].

Figure 16 Veltheim's exlibris, designed by Gustav Schroeter (1918),
in Hans-Hasso von Veltheim Archive, Ostrau. Depositum Veltheim at the
Universitäts- und Landesbibliothek Sachsen-Anhalt, Halle (Saale)

Twenty years on and happily, though expensively, divorced from Hildegard née Duisburg, the heiress of Carl Duisberg, founder of IG Farben factory, Veltheim finally had found a home that could truly represent his character. Veltheim's social circle from this time offers a glimpse into the world of elite sociability in Germany and Austria between the two world wars. His guests held a wide range of political views, from a militant opposition to the new republic to international socialism, and included an array of different professions, from artists, choreographers, and publishers to officers and diplomats. His guest book features entries by prominent German politicians, such as Paul Löbe, president of the Reichstag, General Wilhelm Groener, Reichswehr minister from 1928 to 1932, and Erich Koch-Weser, leader of the German Democratic Party (DDP). But what professional politicians like these had in common with his other, more Bohemian guests, had more to do with aesthetic taste than with agreement over political matters. Most of Veltheim's guests were modernists in spirit; they experimented with new styles inspired by the 'primitive' cultures of Africa, Latin America, and the Far East. Many of them co-edited usually short-lived journals dedicated to literature, art, and political debate of a general kind, such as the character of Europe or the future of the world. Veltheim himself co-founded a publishing house, the *Dreiländerverlag*, with a base in Berlin, Zurich, and Vienna, in 1918, but was, unfortunately, forced to abandon it during the inflation.

In 1918, Veltheim had commissioned a new ex libris, designed by the Munich-based artist Gustav Schroeter, which illustrates the particular combination of modernity and esotericism in his thought.

It featured a Sphinx placed on an obelisk covered in symbolism which included a swastika. Sometimes called 'sauvastika' when facing left, as Veltheim's version did, this symbol from Hindu mythology became fashionable in nineteenth-century esoteric circles, where it was associated with the goddess Kali and signified night and destruction. Russian Empress Alexandra Fedorovna (of Hessen-Darmstadt), who was immersed in the esoteric teachings of her age, had pencilled a left-facing swastika on the walls of Ipatiev house where the family spent its last days in Siberian exile.[34] The Sphinx was likely a reference to Oscar Wilde, one of the best-represented poets in Veltheim's library, which was otherwise filled with

---

[34] On esotericism and the Romanoffs, see Greg King and Penny Wilson, *The Fate of the Romanoffs* (Hoboken, N.J.: Wiley, 2003). On Tsaritsa Alexandra's use of the swastika, see Vladimir Kozlov, Vladimir M. Khrustalëv, and Alexandra Raskina (eds.), *The Last Diary of Tsaritsa Alexandra* (New Haven: Yale University Press, 1997), 15.

works on mysticism, Orientalism, and anthroposophical writings.[35] Wilde's poem *The Sphinx*, dedicated to his friend Marcel Schwob, a contemporary French surrealist whose own passion had been Edgar Allan Poe, resonated with Veltheim's own symbolist influences: 'In a dim corner of my room for longer than my fancy thinks/ A beautiful and silent Sphinx has watched me through the shifting gloom.' Yet in the end, the Sphinx, as a fin de siècle Raven, turns out to be a deceptive guide, luring the onlooker away from his Christian faith to multiple secret passions. Veltheim's fascination with Hindu symbolism reflected influences of German Orientalism of his time alongside Victorian Orientalism. In Veltheim's ex libris, though, the Sphinx and the obelisk are merely providing a frame for another image, a view from a window onto a hot-air balloon rising up into a starry night, to reflect his passion for hot air ballooning.[36]

Just over ten years later, his residence provided the architectural equivalent to his ex libris. Along with the estate, Veltheim had inherited the patronage of the local church of Ostrau. Veltheim embraced this traditional task of aristocratic patronage, but gave it his distinctive signature. In 1932, he ordered a new design of the patron's private prayer room above the chapel, which was invisible to the congregation, with anthroposophical features. An architect who was also the designer of Rudolf Steiner's Goetheanum installed an altar here, featuring Rosicrucian symbolism. Stained-glass windows in the anthroposophical style by Maria Strakosch-Giesler, an artist who had been influenced by Vasily Kandinsky's synaesthetic theory of art, were also added. As a member of the Theosophical Society, Veltheim thereby performed a kind of hidden oecumenicism, a feature of his semi-public spiritual life, which was further augmented when he joined the Theotiskaner Order in 1935. As a proponent of cremation practices, which the Theosophical Society endorsed as a modernist cremation movement, Veltheim also commissioned the design of an urn in which his ashes were to be stored, and placed in the altar of the chapel.[37]

---

[35] On Veltheim's worldview as expressed in his library, see especially John Palatini, 'Hans-Hasso von Veltheims Bibliothek – eine Annhäherung', in *Das Erbe der Veltheims. Schloss, Park und Kirche Ostrau*, ed. John Palatini and Georg Rosentreter (Halle/Saale: Mitteldeutscher Verlag, 2014), 85–110. See also Walther, *Veltheim*.

[36] Oscar Wilde, *The Sphinx*, with decoratins by Charles Ricketts (London: E. Matthews and J. Lane, 1894). On the popularity of this poem in its time, see Nicholas Frankel, *Oscar Wilde's Decorated Books* (Ann Arbor: University of Michigan Press, 2000), 155–177.

[37] I am grateful to Georg Rosentreter for showing me the chapel itself, and to John Palatini for providing me with the intellectual context of Veltheim's beliefs: John Palatini, 'Weltanschauungsarchitektur in einer evangelischen Kirche – die Grab-Altar-Kapelle Hans-Hasso von Veltheims', in Palatini and Rosentreter, *Das Erbe der Veltheims. Schloss, Park und Kirche*, 220–260. On Theosophy and the cremation movement in the United States and Victorian

Figure 17 Hans-Hasso von Veltheim and Jiddu Krishnamurti at the sun terrace in Ostrau (April 1931) Image courtesy of John Palatini/ Schloss Ostrau e.V.

Linking global mythology and contemporary modernist movements to his personal passions was characteristic not only of Veltheim's personality, but of the particular syncretism which he actively sought in his social life. Veltheim liked to think of people he invited to his home as items in a unique collection. Unlike some of his friends of high nobility, like the Schulenburgs, he did not restrict himself to company of his social standing. He rather enjoyed the attention of people of all backgrounds, both social and geographical. This he learned from his travels around the world, which he began at a young age with the obligatory Grand Tour to Italy, and which eventually would lead him to Burma, Malaysia, India, Palestine and Egypt. From there, he not only brought artwork, Buddha statues, prints, shadow puppets and such like, but also, and more importantly, new friendships. For all his interest in foreign cultures, his steady circle of friends was mostly German-speaking. Alongside friends of high nobility such as Udo von Alvensleben, the art historian, Count Hermann Keyserling, the philosopher, and Constantin Cramer von Laue, who pursued a military career, the most significant group among his friends were poets, writers, and composers, such as the poet Rainer Maria Rilke, the existentialist novelist Hermann Kasack, the poet Thassilo von Scheffer, the artist Alastair, the Alsatian pacifist novelist Annette Kolb, the Georgian writer Grigol Robakidse, who was living in Germany since the Russian Revolution, and the composer Richard Strauß. Veltheim had met many of his friends during his studies in Munich were he attended lectures in art history. Among his favourites were Lucian Scherman's lectures on Buddha and Buddhism, and a course on Persian art by Friedrich Wilhelm von Bissung. One photograph from 1931 shows him as the host of the world's most renowned international spiritual celebrity, Jiddu Krishnamurti, at Ostrau [Fig. 17].

These were the German academics who continued the orientalist fashion that had begun in nineteenth-century German academia, with leading figures such as Indologist C.A. Lassen in Bonn or Egyptologist Heinrich Brugsch in Göttingen.[38] Those who pursued related studies in Veltheim's circle also attended courses by the ethno-psychologist Wilhelm Wundt in Leipzig and philosopher Henri Bergson in Paris. These Orientalists' influence on their students was significant in later life; it was what provided a source of cohesion even where political agreement was lacking.

Britian, see Douglas J. Davies, 'The Cremation Movement', in *Encyclopedia of Death and the Human Experience*, ed. Clifton D. Bryant and Dennis L. Peck (London: Sage, 2009), 237–240.

[38] On German Orientalism in context, see Suzanne Marchand, *German Orientalism in the Age of Empire: Religion, Race, and Scholarship* (Cambridge: Cambridge University Press, 2009), 96–97.

Figure 18 'Completed and restored', plaque on the castle of Hans-Hasso von Veltheim ('Completed and restored, 1929'), Ostrau, near Halle, Germany, photograph Andreas Vlachos

A related group of Veltheim's friends were the publishers, Anton Kippenberg, head of *Insel* publishing house; Peter Suhrkamp; and Hinrich Springer. Other friends came to Veltheim through the Theosophical Society and its German branch, the Anthroposophical Society, of which he was a member. He knew the founder, Rudolf Steiner, quite well, and another prominent anthroposophist, Elisabeth von Thadden, was a cousin. Veltheim's travels to India and China put him in touch with members of the new political elites there; he met Gandhi and in 1935, hosted one of his financiers, Seth Ambalal Sarabhai, the head of the Bank of India. The American dancers Ted Shawn and his wife Ruth St. Denis, founders of modern dance in the United States, were also among Veltheim's regulars.

When the work on his ancestral estate was finished, in 1929, Veltheim placed a plaque above the entrance to his house, which read: 'Completed and restored'. It was a paradox, of course: if it was only now completed, how could it be a restoration? The completion of the restoration came ten years after the first, radical generation of German republican politicians suggested expropriating all noble families in Germany, inspired by the Russian Revolution as a model. In this first wave of expropriations, some of Veltheim's friends, including those who had their estates in the Baltic region, and members of the former ruling princely houses in Germany, such as Ernst Ludwig, Grand Duke of Hesse-Darmstadt, lost all or significant parts of their estates. But all in all, the German land reforms of the 1920s had been minimal compared to those in some parts of eastern Europe.

Although nobles of high nobility who had inherited or were about to inherit large estates like Veltheim represented those social groups who were most threatened by the revolution, in the early 1920s they were still open to the changes these would bring to European culture. Indeed, the 1920s and early 1930s were years in which they could develop a number of projects as founders of educational and cultural institutions. Nobles who were based in Germany and Austria and who did not belong to the ruling princely families escaped the threats of expropriation that returned with Nazi legislation such as the *Reichserbhofgesetz* of 1933, with which the Nazis attempted to strengthen small-scale peasants at the expense of large landowners.

It was, indeed, not until 1945, in the Soviet part of divided Germany, that nobles who held estates in north-eastern Germany and what was now definitively Polish and Czechoslovak territory had to accept their expropriation as final. One day in October 1945, Veltheim received a call from Halle's new mayor urging him to leave his ancestral estate within an hour.

> Then I packed the barest necessities, before giving a call to the mayor to announce that I was now leaving the house – and once more, walked through my rooms and solemnly stepped down the large staircase, thinking that my great-great-grandfather Carl Christian Septimus von Veltheim (1751–1796) in 1785 [...] had also walked down this same staircase with a heavy heart, before leaving Ostrau forever and going to St. Domingo, in the West Indies.[39]

By the 1780s, Veltheim's ancestor had gone bankrupt, and to avoid prosecution by his creditors, enlisted as a cavalry officer in the British Army. Suffering a common fate of the 'Hessian' regiments – German mercenaries hired by foreign army – he died in the West Indies of a fever and was never to see his family or his house again.

Veltheim's own chosen place of exile was not the West Indies, but the northern German island of Föhr; here, he spent the remaining eleven years of his life preparing to write an autobiography, which contained numerous

---

[39] LHASA Rep H Ostrau II, Nr. 1171.

critical remarks of Europe's violent, colonial past. Meanwhile, his old estate became the site of a polytechnic high school named after Nikolai Ostrovsky, the Russian socialist realist playwright from Ukraine who is best known for his autobiographical novel *How They Forged the Steel*, published in English translation by the Hogarth Press.

After 1990, the descendants of nobles like Veltheim began a laborious process of reclaiming what remained of their properties from the German, Polish, Czech, Slovak, Lithuanian, Estonian, and Russian governments. Many estates and castles throughout Germany and eastern Europe now remain public institutions: they have been turned into universities, recreational facilities, or museums of cultural heritage that are being rented out for weddings and other ceremonies.

Veltheim's response was characteristic particularly of those nobles who by and large accepted their loss of former privileges, but saw their intellectual activities as a new source of cultural authority. The most obvious sense in which he displayed his adjustment to the loss of privileges is discernible from his production of narratives – in letters, diaries, in conversation, in memoirs, such as the letter to his mother, where he is moved when a worker treats him as an equal, despite looking like an aristocrat sounding like a 'Dr. Phil'. At the same time, his insecurity concerning his status is confirmed by the opposing tendency to reconstruct nobleness by cultivating his estate, and fulfilling his duties of supporting his younger brother associated with his status as his father's eldest son.

In addition to being allegories of old Europe and models for the genealogical and symbolic construction of identity, aristocratic intellectuals like Veltheim also developed a particular, elegiac way of thinking about their twentieth-century status as a type of homelessness. This homelessness, coupled with their earlier, poetic interests in Grand Tours and in being both detached from Europe as well as safely rooted in its deepest history, gave their cosmopolitanism a negative form. This became particularly pronounced by 1945, when nobles from East Prussia, East Germany, and the Habsburg lands had lost not only a rootedness in a particular region, which they had to give up incrementally throughout the revolutions of the earlier twentieth century, but also, the very possibility of belonging to several European regions at once. Many memoirs of nobles from this period combine the general trope of homelessness and loss with an idea of belonging to Europe as a whole and embodying its past culture. Among the most representative figures of 'noble homelessness' in German thought after 1945 was the work of the social democrat Marion Countess Dönhoff, who, after her flight (on horseback) from East Prussia, embarked on a career as one of West Germany's most prominent journalists.[40] She became the founding editor of the weekly newspaper *Die Zeit*. Another nobleman who defined himself as an expellee from eastern Europe, as 'Europe's pilgrim', was Prince Karl Anton Rohan.[41] In the 1920s and early 1930s, he was the founding editor of the journal *Europäische Revue*. In 1945, his family lost the estates in Czechoslovakia, and Rohan was forced to work on his own estate as a gardener and then to spend one and a half years as an American prisoner of war; his reflections on Europe's history, which he published in 1954, bore the title *Heimat Europa*.[42] Rohan's fellow Bohemian Alfons Clary-Aldringen published his memoirs under a similar title, *A European Past*.[43]

In the eyes of Prince Rohan and the contributors to his journal, Europe in the 1920s was facing a struggle between past and future. The European past was characterized by complexity regulated through a strict social hierarchy. In this structure, empires persisted not only thanks to formal institutions of power but also, and crucially, informally, because everyone knew in each situation how to behave appropriate to their rank or status. By contrast, in the age of modernity, those expectations were no longer clear. He could have made this point by speaking about institutional change or radical politics in the street, but his preferred example was social dance:

> There is a higher meaning in the tradition that those in power [. . .] do not dance with people, or, what is even more important, do not dance in front of people who are not of the same social standing. Today, you can see in any dance café people of high nobility, duchesses, wives of the large industrial and financial magnates, even girls of the underworld entwined in Charleston with their legs, arms, and other body parts, swinging amongst other unknown people to Negro rhythms. And at the same time, those in power in Europe attend meetings with rumpled hats and trousers. The dance of political representation has disappeared, to be replaced by the wacky body parts wobbling in Negro chaos.[44]

This passage highlights the extent to which thinking in terms of race, social status, as well as aesthetic taste became entangled in the 1920s.

[40] Mark Mazower, *Hitler's Empire. Nazi Rule in Occupied Europe* (London: Allen Lane, 2008); Marion Gräfin Dönhoff, *Namen die keiner mehr kennt* (Düsseldorf and Cologne: Eugen Diederichs, 1962, 1980), 35–37; Tatjana Dönhoff and J. Roettger, *Auf der Fluchtroute von Marion Gräfin Dönhoff* (Berlin: Nicolai-Verlag, 2004), 186–200.
[41] Karl Anton Rohan, *Heimat Europa* (Düsseldorf: Diederichs, 1954), 56.
[42] Rohan claims to have been imprisoned in six different military camps during 1945–6. Ibid., 314–316.
[43] Alfons Clary-Aldringen, *Geschichten eines alten Österreichers* (Berlin: Ullstein, 1977).
[44] Karl Anton Prinz Rohan, *Moskau* (Karlsruhe: Braun, 1927).

The threats of modernity for members of Europe's old elites such as Rohan were multiple. But this passage highlights that they were essentially reducible to two points: an erosion of hierarchy, and an erosion of identity, continental, racial, and sexual. Not all responses to these threats of modernity were pure rejections. In fact, Rohan himself was particularly attracted to aspects of a modernist aesthetic and innovations in the theatre and literature. While deeply committed to Vienna at an emotional level, after the war, Rohan had settled in Berlin and made German political circles the central sphere of his own activity as an intellectual.

The quest for new spiritual as well as new sexual identities was another prominent element in interwar aristocratic intellectual circles. Both themes, the interest in oecumenical and non-Western spirituality and the Orient, and the openness towards non-conventional sexualities, were prominent in the work of aristocratic intellectuals and the circles they supported. Just as the Habsburgs had found a way of making signs of stigma into distinction, intellectuals like Keyserling made their ironic anti-nationalism into a Brahmanic quality rather than that of a pariah.

Double Orientalism: celebrity princes in the Soviet Union and India

The aristocratic mediators like Veltheim joined a generation of new global travellers who were interested to discover alternative civilizations in India and the Soviet Union. During an extended trip to India from December 1937 until August 1938, Veltheim was in Calcutta as an informal delegate of the German Reich and official guest of the Indian government. Among his hosts was Lord Brabourne, then Viceroy of India and Governor of Bengal. A conversation between the two, which the Viceroy declared as a 'private and personal' encounter between two aristocrats and old officers', revealed that they had likely 'faced each other' at the battle of Ypres.[45] Throughout this trip, Veltheim was expected to deliver public lectures and gauge private opinion from a variety of influential personalities in India, on which he reported in extended form in typescripts that were sent back to Germany, to be read by officials, as well as a group of close friends.[46] In the typescript itself, Veltheim avoided stating his opinion on the German regime directly, however, his rendering of critical questions thrown at him on occasions such as in the immediate aftermath of

[45] Hans-Hasso von Veltheim-Ostrau, *Tagebücher aus Asien*, vol. 1 (Hamburg: Claassen, 1956), 309–310.
[46] Veltheim, typescript (1936), LHASA.

the Night of Broken Glass, 9 November 1938, makes it sufficiently plain that his own attitude to the regime was critical. This became more pronounced in the revised version of his Indian travel 'diaries', which was first published in 1954. Thus, in said conversation with Lord Brabourne, Veltheim claims to have called Hitler a dictator who would not shy away from a war. Brabourne, by contrast, emphasized Hitler's 'immediate experience of the front' as a simple soldier, unlike officers such as themselves; because of this proximity to the front line, Brabourne thought Hitler would not 'expose the German people to a war'.[47] At the same time, the typescript suggests that on other occasions, Veltheim defended the German regime from 'false' allegations, such as the assumption, which he often encountered in the company of Brahmins and Maharajahs, that the Nazi government expropriated large landowners. 'Nothing could be further from the truth', Veltheim assured his conversation partners, signalling to his readers that it was important to keep conversation with his aristocratic 'peers' in India in order to prevent them from having false views of Germany.

In addition to India, in the 1920s, many eyes turned to the Soviet Union as an alternative type of civilization: would it remain true to its radical premise and rule out traditional ranks and privileges from the army and other institutions? In 1927, Rohan went on a trip of the Soviet Union, primarily, Moscow and Leningrad, following an invitation from VOKS, the Soviet cultural organization for foreign relations. As he put it in his travelogue, he went to Russia as a Gentleman would go to the land of the Bolsheviks.[48] For people of his social circle, the Land of the Bolsheviks was another social and cultural system that posed a threat to Europe's former self.

However, the most famous project of a small court revival had been inspired by an example from India. It belonged to a philosopher from the Baltic region who initially had little to do with the smaller courts. Count Keyserling came from the Baltic region of the Russian Empire, and his wife was the granddaughter of Prussian Iron chancellor Otto von Bismarck. Yet personal connections meant that he was on good terms with the Grand Duke of Hessen Darmstadt, whose artists' colony he proceeded to reinvigorate with a new concept.

Keyserling wrote in a letter to Kessler 'strictly confidentially' that he was about to found a 'philosophical colony' with himself 'at its centre'. Its success would be 'guaranteed since the Grand Duke of Hesse presides over

[47] Veltheim, *Tagebücher*, vol. I, 310.
[48] Robert Müller, *Bolschewik und Gentleman* (Berlin: Reiss, 1920).

it'. Keyserling believed that this school would bring about 'something of importance' because 'all that was ever significant in Germany always began and will emerge only beyond the boundaries of the state'.[49] The foundation did not do entirely without political support, however, even if it was the support of a politician who had only just lost the power over his state: Grand Duke Ernst Ludwig of Hessen-Darmstadt, Queen Victoria's grandson, a cousin of Wilhelm II of Germany, and brother-in-law of the recently assassinated Nicolas II of Russia, had been deposed along with the remaining ruling princes on 9 November 1918.

In seeking to support Keyserling's project, Ernst Ludwig drew on his prior project of aesthetic education. In 1899, his knowledge of the British Arts and Crafts movement of Ruskin and Macintosh had inspired him to found an artists' colony in an area of Darmstadt called *Mathildenhöhe*, which persisted until the outbreak of the First World War. Its aim was to create a union between 'art and life, artists and the people', through a joint project of aesthetic reform through art nouveau. It eventually came to be organized in four exhibitions held between 1901 and 1914, which showcased German exponents of art nouveau. The innovative character of this colony was that it combined relatively new ideas of reform socialism, who envisaged art as a form of craft labour and introduced new concepts of living like 'garden cities' to the public imagination, with the older tradition of aristocratic patronage for artists. Ernst Ludwig's project became influential in German circles of aesthetic resistance to the bombastic masculinity of Wilhelm II.

The focus of the *School of Wisdom* was from the start less patriotic and more universalist in spirit. This expressed not only Keyserling's newly acquired knowledge of Oriental culture, but also Ernst Ludwig's more recent interest in ecumenical thought, which he displayed in his book *Easter. A Mystery* (Leipzig: Kurt Wolff, 1917), published under the pseudonym K. Ludhart. As such, it became an internationally renowned centre for cultural critics, mystics, psychoanalysts and Orientalists. By 1921 Keyserling's academy had some 600 permanent members and held three annual conferences. The rabbi and philosopher Leo Baeck, the philosopher Max Scheler, the psychoanalyst C.G. Jung, and the historian Ernst Troeltsch were among its participants. The academy functioned through membership lists and conferences, which took place regularly between 1920 and 1927, with one follow-up conference in 1930. Thereafter the academy turned into a virtual association through which members could

---

[49] Hermann Keyserling to Harry Kessler, 9 July 1919, A: Kessler, DLA Marbach.

obtain information about new books and borrow books from Keyserling's vast library collection. One of his most intensive contacts was Karl Anton Rohan, the director of the Austrian branch of the Union *Intellectuelle Française* (*Kulturbund*) in Vienna. His association sought to promote peace in Europe through publications (for example, German–French co-editions) and other cultural activities. Keyserling's early mentors included French philosopher Henri Bergson and the German philosopher (and later National Socialist ideologist) Houston Stewart Chamberlain (with whom Keyserling fell out even before the First World War). Thomas Mann's diaries abound in entries confirming his appreciation of Keyserling's works.[50]

Keyserling and his wife devoted the greatest part of their time to the management of his public appearance. Keyserling remained prolific throughout this period, publishing fourteen books between 1906 and 1945, though a number of his works are without doubt repetitive. In his thought he was strongly influenced by C.G. Jung's and other psycho-analytic theories. Together with a psychoanalyst, Erwin Rousselle, Keyserling organized meditation sessions and even experimented with occult phenomena (only so as to question them, as he argued in a book). Among such experiments he invited a miracle healer from northern Germany to test his abilities in a Darmstadt hospital.

Keyserling's school can be located within a larger circle of private educational reform associations positioned between cultural sceptics, neo-religious and reform movements of the post-First World War period, such as the Eranos group, or the anthroposophical school around Rudolf Steiner.[51] Its closest analogue in many ways was the Theosophical Society, founded by the 'clairvoyant' Helena Blavatsky and Henry Steel Olcott in New York. Like Keyserling, Helena von Hahn, or Madame Blavatsky, as she came to be known, came from Baltic German nobility as well as an old Russian lineage, the Dolgorukii family.[52] Unusually for

---

[50] Entry of 18 May 1919: 'Nachher lag ich eine Weile im Garten im Liegestuhl und las eine Schrift des Grafen H. Keyserling: "Deutschlands wahre politische Mission", deren Vortrefflichkeit mir Mut mach, mich auf sein Hauptwerk, das Reise-Tagebuch einzulassen.' In: Thomas Mann, *Tagebücher*, ed. Peter de Mendelssohn (Frankfurt: S. Fischer, 1977), 240. Mann, *Tagebücher*, entry of 21 March 1919.

[51] For this comparison, see Barbara von Reibnitz, 'Der Eranos-Kreis. Religionswissenschaft und Weltanschauung oder der Gelehrte als Laien-Prieser', in *Kreise – Gruppen – Bünde. Zur Soziologie moderner Intellektuellenassoziation*, ed. Richard Faber and Christine Holste (Würzburg: Königshausen und Neumann, 2000), 427–428.

[52] Peter Washington, *Madame Blavatsky's Baboon. Theosophy and the Emergence of the Western Guru* (London: Secker & Warburg, 1993).

a future transformation in the hand of aristocratic sages. In this sense, the School constituted, as Suzanne Marchand put it, a 'breathtaking' break from its humanist foundations, which rested on the superiority of Western civilization's Greek roots.[56] It was not just a break from humanism, but above all a radically different project from that of bourgeois intellectuals. After the over-democratised state it was in now, Keyserling concluded, the future belonged to a 'supranational European idea', which would overcome the extreme democracy of America and Russian Bolshevism.[57]

The place of Germanic culture in the genealogy of European memory

After the Second World War, the idea of two opposing German traditions of Europe, one, a benign federation of principalities, another, a malignant national empire-state, remained an influential paradigm of international thought in the twentieth century. But it was the work of individual celebrity aristocrats like Keyserling that had kept it particularly alive in the minds of the European elite in the 1930s.[58] Only a reformed aristocracy could offer such a structure.[59] Keyserling argued that Europe, which was currently in a period of historical decline and overtaken by many rival civilizations, would again reach a historic high in the future. Germany and Austria, fused in an ideal 'chord of Vienna-Potsdam-Weimar', would play the greatest role in bringing about this new constellation – not as a pan-German state, however, but as the heart of a new Holy Roman Empire. He demanded a leading role for Germany in a future European state, because the 'representatives of German culture' have displayed the least attachment to the 'idea of a nation-state'. Instead, they were more at home with the notions of a 'tribe or a party' than that of 'peoplehood', just as in the times of Arminius as Tacitus has described it.[60] The future, Keyserling argued in later works, would bring about a 'Pan-European, if not a universal Western solidarity the like of which has not existed since the Middle Ages'. As he put it in a manuscript version of a public lecture to be

---

[56] Suzanne Marchand, 'German Orientalism and the Decline of the West', in *Proceedings of the American Philosophical Society*, 145 (2001), 465–473, 472.
[57] Graf Hermann Keyserling, *Das Spektrum Europas* (Heidelberg: Niels Kampmann, 1928), 194.
[58] Keyserling, *Spektrum*, 454.
[59] HKN, in *Deutsche Allgemeine Zeitung* (1 January 1925). Keyserling, 'Eine Vision der kommenden Weltordnung', 5 January 1925, 5.
[60] Keyserling, *Spektrum*, 190.

given at the Salle Pleyel in 1937, which Nazi authorities prevented him from attending, the role of the intellectuals was to 'anticipate the best possible future on the basis of fulfilled Destiny'.[61]

As he put it in 1937, for 'the foundation of the new aristocracy of his dreams, Nietzsche hoped for a preceding era of socialist convulsions; and at this very moment we are passing through it'. In this double sense of an emotional superiority and an overcoming of bourgeois narrow-mindedness, Keyserling published an article advocating socialism as a necessary 'basis', perhaps also a necessary evil, for the transition to a future aristocratic politics.[62] In this respect, Keyserling appropriated the prominent discourse on a 'new nobility', which was common to the elite circles of German and Austrian sociability in the interwar years, albeit by infusing it with theoretical reflections on his own life.[63] Despite Keyserling's emphasis on renewal, however, his School was also an enactment of the old, pre-revolutionary order in which the Grand Duke Ernst Ludwig appeared in his function as a patron of art and culture.

A central part of Keyserling's project was his cultivation of a vast and international social network through which his project of aristocratic renewal was propagated and developed. On his international lecture tours, he was celebrated as an 'ex-hidalgo' who turned his expropriation into a new form of spirituality. Keyserling's Spanish audiences placed him at the same time on the same plane as Don Quixote and as a specifically Germanic import product. 'Antiguo hidalgo de Estonia, hoy es el conde de Keyserling un errabundo descubridor de reinos espirituales', read one of the articles covering Keyserling's visit to Spain in 1929 [Fig. 19].[64] For his English and French readers, by contrast, Keyserling becomes more a symbol of restlessness and a wandering elitism.[65]

---

[61] HKN Nr. 0093, 061.25, 10. ['Ils peuvent devancer les événement, anticiper l'avenir meilleur possible sur la base du Destin accompli. S'ils font cela, leur rôle aura été plus important que celui d'aucune élite du passé.']

[62] Hermann Keyserling, 'Der Sozialismus als allgemeine Lebensbasis' (1918), *Neue Europäische Zeitung für Staat, Kultur, Wirtschaft* (26 November 1918).

[63] Alexandra Gerstner, *Neuer Adel: aristokratische Elitekonzeptionen zwischen Jahrhundertwende und Nationalsozialismus* (Darmstadt: Wissenschaftliche Buchgesellschaft, 2008).

[64] Juan G. Olmedilla, 'Antiguo hidalgo de Estonia, hoy es el conde de Keyserling un errabundo descubridor de reinos espirituales . . .', in: *Cronica*, 11 May 1930, 2.

[65] J. de Saint-Charmant, 'Réponse à Keyserling', in *Revue Hebdomadaire*, 35:43 (2 September 1933), 349–360.

Figure 19 Juan G. Olmedilla, 'Antiguo hidalgo de Estonia, hoy es el conde de Keyserling un errabundo descubridor de reinos espirituales . . .', in: *Cronica*, 11 May 1930, 2

Following his trip to South America in 1929, he published his *South American Meditations*, which Carl Gustav Jung praised as 'a new and contemporary style of "sentimental journey"', and in another instance he characterized Keyserling as 'the mouthpiece of the *Zeitgeist*'.[66] Not least

---

[66] Aniela Jaffé (ed.), *C.G. Jung. Letters*, 2 vols., vol. 1 (London: Routledge & Kegan, 1973), 84. Jung to Keyserling on 13 August 1931. For the 'mouthpiece of the Zeitgeist', see C.G. Jung, Book review of Keyserling's *La revolution mondiale et la responsabilité de l'Esprit* (Paris: Stock, 1934), first appeared as « Ein neues Buch von Keyserling », *Basler Nachrichten*, Sonntagsblatt, xxviii:19 (13 May 1934), 78–79. Reprinted in C.G. Jung, *Civilization in Transition*, 2nd ed. (London and Henley: Routledge & Kegan Paul and Princeton University Press, 1970, reprinted in 1981), 496–501, 501.

due to the personal connections to the influential literary editor Victoria Ocampo, Keyserling's work found wide, albeit critical, reception among Spanish-speaking, particularly among Argentinian, readers such as Eduardo Mallea and Jorge Luis Borges.[67]

His *School of Wisdom*, which persisted until 1937, was partially financed through its summer conferences and membership lists, which were managed through subscriptions to two journals associated with the School: *Der Leuchter*, and *Der Weg zur Vollendung*. Informal networks were to provide an alternative to official collaborations, since Keyserling was willing to 'collaborate with all parties' who wanted to come to his 'centre of influence'. The purpose was to 'form a new human type, who is the bearer of the future'.[68] Keyserling argued that his School was designed to become a 'movement' whose 'economic substructure is the Society of Free Philosophy'.[69] It 'addresses itself not to philosophers only, but rather to men of actions, and is resorted to by such'.[70] As one reviewer commented,

> The community of Keyserling's pupils is being united by his publications. [...] From the impulse of Count Keyserling's personality – this is the firm goal of the Society for Free Philosophy – there will arise a circle of men and women in all of Germany which will smoothen the path towards the eternal goods of life for our people.[71]

The political goals of Keyserling's School were threefold: to assess the present situation of European politics as a decline into anarchy and mass culture, a period of radical and socialist ideas which had to be accepted; to emphasise the importance of aristocratic and intellectual leadership in overcoming this process of decline; and to learn from other cultures in preparing for a future transformation in the hand of aristocratic sages. In this sense, the School constituted a sharp break from its humanist foundations, which rested on the superiority of Western civilization's Greek roots. It was not just a break from humanism, but above all a radically different project from that of bourgeois intellectuals. After the over-democratized state it was in now, Keyserling concluded, the future belonged to a 'supranational European idea', which would overcome the extreme democracy of America and Russian Bolshevism.[72] His Baltic correspondence partner, the historian Otto von Taube, agreed that the

---

[67] Kaminsky, *Argentina*, esp. ch. 5: 'Victoria Ocampo and the Keyserling Effect', 70–99.
[68] Keyserling, 'Eine Ansprache an die radikale Jugend', in *Der Weg zur Vollendung* (1921), 2.
[69] HKN, Nr. 0604, folder 15 of 54, 218.15, 2.   [70] HKN, Nr. 0604, folder 1 of 54, 218.01, 8.
[71] Otto Schabbel, 'Die Schule der Weisheit', *Hamburger Nachrichten*, 1 December 1920, in 0604, Konvolut Presse zur Schule der Weisheit, folder 27, 220.03, HKN.
[72] Keyserling, *Spektrum*, 194.

princely attitude of being rooted to a region and simultaneously standing 'above nations', could serve as a model for the future of European regeneration.[73]

As Rom Landau recalled Tagore's visit in 1921, hosted by the former Grand Duke of Hesse Ernst Ludwig:

> After tea we went into the neighbouring fields, and grouped ourselves on the slope of a hill, on the top of which stood Keyserling and Tagore. [. . .] The Indian poet was wearing long silk robes, and the wind played with his white hair and his long beard. He began to recite some of his poems in English. Though the majority of the listeners hardly understood more than a few words – it was only a few years after the war, and the knowledge of English was still very limited – the flush on their cheeks showed that the presence of the poet from the East represented to them the climax of the whole week. There was music in Tagore's voice, and it was a pleasure to listen to the Eastern melody in the words. The hill and the fields, the poet, the Grand Duke and the many royal and imperial princes, Keyserling and all the philosophers and philistines were bathed in the glow of the evening sun.[74]

Keyserling's own intentions to learn from Tagore for European renewal had hit a nerve among his post-war audiences.[75] Among the most important influences on his work was the Academy at Santiniketan (today known as Visva-Bharati University), founded in 1921 by the Bengali writer and poet Rabindranath Tagore on the location of his father's *ashram*. Keyserling had first met Tagore, twelve years his senior, during the Indian part of his world tour, in 1912, when he stayed at Tagore's house in Calcutta, then again in London in 1913, and soon after the foundation of the Darmstadt School, in 1921, he invited Tagore on a lecture tour of Germany. Both men had taken similar roles upon themselves, even though Tagore's fame surpassed that of Keyserling by far after Tagore won the Nobel Prize in 1913. Both were of noble origin but also critical of the ossification of nobility; both were in some sense nationalists but at the same time considered their mission to be reaching humanity at large, and therefore travelled the world to give public lectures and, not least, receive financial backing for their educational institutions; both also took some inspiration from another Count, Leo Tolstoy, whose revolutionary peasant

---

[73] On marriage between the Balts and non-German princes, see also O. von Taube, 'Russische und litauische Fürsten an der Düna zur Zeit der deutschen Eroberung Livlands' (12. und 13. Jahrhundert), in *Jahrbücher für Kultur und Geschichte der Slawen* (1935), 3–4.

[74] Rom Landau, *God Is My Adventure. A Book on Modern Mystics, Masters and Teachers* (London: Faber and Faber, 1935), 36–37.

[75] H. Keyserling, *Politik, Wirtschaft, Weisheit* (Darmstadt: O. Reichl, 1922). Review of Hu-ming Ku, *Vox clamantis* (Leipzig: Neuer Geist Verlag, 1921), 24, in *Der Weg zur Vollendung* (1921), 2.

communities in Russia also inspired movements in South Africa. Moreover, like Keyserling, Tagore had been impressed by Victoria Ocampo's cosmopolitan cultural patronage in Argentina, where he too stayed as an honorary guest.[76]

Inspired by Tagore, Keyserling positioned himself as bridging East and West. His intention was to turn the position of Europe between the two into an advantage, and criticise the old aristocratic system without rejecting it entirely.[77] Even though he shared some premises with other elitist educational programmes of the period, Keyserling's Orientalist School differed markedly from the neo-classical background of other contemporaries. For instance, the classicist Werner Jaeger decried in 1925 that while 'in Beijing Rabindranath Tagore proclaims the reawakening of Asia's soul to the gathered crowd of yellow-skinned students, we, tired from the World War and the crisis of culture, are staring at the fashionable theory of the Decline of the West'.[78] Keyserling's School proposed an entirely different use of the comparative shift in cultural criticism by bringing Tagore to a gathering of the Darmstadt crowds and selected participants of his School at the princely palace.

Keyserling was particularly interested in proving that different cultures have always been associated with aristocracies. In his book reviews of 'oriental' cultural critics, therefore, he reserved critical positions, such as the views of Tagore himself, to footnotes, in which he commented on Tagore's remark that Indian culture had been shaped by the Kshattryas, not the Brahmins, merely as 'interesting'.[79] With regard to the more radical movement of Mahatma Gandhi, he expressly described him as a 'reactionary', because in 'sympathising with the false progressivism of modernization he denied Indian culture'.[80]

Another interest of Keyserling's in comparing his contemporary 'post-war' Europe with other cultures, was his desire to relativize the impression cultivated by many Germans that Germany had been mistreated the most by the post-war political settlements. Other countries, Keyserling argued, had suffered an even more catastrophic decline, drawing attention to Turkey. Nonetheless, as he put it, it was due to this imperial decline that countries like Turkey or Germany would be able to recreate a new

---

[76] However, Tagore was far more critical of the Indian caste system than Keyserling was of the European aristocracy.

[77] Landau, *God*, 25.   [78] W. Jaeger, *Humanistische Reden* (Berlin: de Gruyter, 1937), 104.

[79] Review of Tagore's 'Vision of Indian History', in *The Visva-Bharati Quarterly* (Calcutta, 210 Cornwallis Street), review in *Der Weg zur Vollendung* (1923), 6.

[80] Keyserling, Book review section of *Der Weg zur Vollendung* (1921), 2.

European order, as the Turkish intellectual Halidé Edib wrote in a book which she sent to Keyserling with a dedication.[81]

As one of Keyserling's followers, Prince Karl Anton Rohan wrote in his book *Europe*, first published in 1923, the old 'nobility' now had the task 'to transform the old values in a conservative way, according to its tradition, using the new impulses of the revolution'. Unlike the class struggle that motivates the Bolshevik conception of the revolution, he thought, the goal of this one was the creation of a 'unified Europe' instead of an 'ideological brotherhood of mankind'.[82] Count Keyserling, in his correspondence with Rohan, engaged in theorizing the new status of the nobility further. He described to him that he was also, 'under conditions of utmost secrecy', working on a 'vision for all the peoples of Europe'.[83]

Keyserling also promoted his School by lecturing abroad. Such lectures were paid and frequently guaranteed him his income, and they were organized by professional concert agencies.[84] He corresponded with scholars interested in his work and actively invited them to visit his School. Among those who paid attention to the project was the Flemish socialist and in later years Nazi collaborationist Hendrik de Man, who taught at Frankfurt University in the early 1920s, and became interested in Keyserling's project. He classified him as one of 'Germany's New Prophets', a generation inspired by Nietzsche's role as a philosopher lecturing to his contemporaries while also addressing a future humanity.[85] These three thinkers identified by de Man – Keyserling, Oswald Spengler, and the philosopher of fiction, Hans Vaihinger, – had also received the Nietzsche Prize of the Weimar Nietzsche Society in 1919. De Man was surprised that 'K. the aristocrat' was 'a democrat', while 'Sp. the plebeian Oberlehrer – a monarchist' and

[81] Keyserling's review of Halidé Edib, *Turkey Faces West* (New Haven: Yale University Press, 1930 and London: Humphrey Milford & Oxford University Press, 1930), in *Der Weg zur Vollendung* (1931), 19.

[82] Karl Anton Rohan, *Europa. Streiflichter* (Leipzig: Der Neue Geist Verlag, 1923). Discussed in Müller, '"Europa" als Konzept adlig-bürgerlicher Elitendiskurse', 251.

[83] Keyserling to Karl Anton Rohan, 14 July 1927, in Darmstadt, Universitäts- und Landesbibliothek, Handschriften- und Musikabteilung, Hermann-Keyserling-Nachlass (HKN), Correspondence, R-3 172.01.

[84] HKN, V-4, 205.08, Vorträge Europa – 1930, Konzertagentur Paul Neff, Inh. Walter Guttmann, Guttmann to Keyserling, 27 June 1930. See also Memoranda re Count Hermann Keyserling's visit to Harvard, Hoover Institution Archives (HA), John Davis Lodge Papers, Box 2, Folder 2–3. For Keyserling's lecture notes abroad, see HKN, V-4, Keyserling, Lecture in Rome (1925), 07.612; lecture in Vienna (1927), 076.14; lecture in Madrid (1930), 076.09; lecture in Spain (1934, 1935), various locations, 076.13; lecture in Paris (1931, Salle du Trocadéro). 076.10, and 1933, Salle Pleyel, 076.11.

[85] Henry de Man, 'Germany's New Prophets', in *Yale Review*, 13:4 (July 1924), 665–683.

a 'worshipper of aristocracy' – this to him was a 'a vindication of the psycho-analytic theory of "compensations"!'[86] For de Man's own elitist vision of socialism, Keyserling's work was of central importance.

Keyserling's influence on like-minded younger intellectuals such as Prince Karl Anton Rohan had not only intellectual, but also institutional significance. Rohan founded two institutions in the spirit of Keyserling's School: the literary and political journal *Europäische Revue*, and the *Kulturbund*, a Viennese branch of the Paris-based *Institut international de cooperation intellectuelle*. While the *Revue* eventually succumbed to Nazi propaganda efforts and eventually ceased publication during the War, the *Institut* became the institutional progenitor of UNESCO after the Second World War. Keyserling encouraged Rohan 'under conditions of utmost secrecy' to work with him on a 'vision for all the peoples of Europe'.[87] Specifically, he sought to encourage Rohan to use his private circle of 'friends' for studying the 'problem of nobility' under his 'guidance', which was supposed to contribute a chapter on 'Germany's Task in the World' to a forthcoming publication on *Germany and France* to be edited by the Prince.[88] In the proposal for an edited book on *Germany and France*, Rohan lined up not only well-known historians and legal theorists like the German nationalist historian Hermann Oncken and the constitutional theorist Carl Schmitt, but also now forgotten German and French authors who fall into the suggested category of *aristocratic writers*. They included names such as Wladimir d'Ormesson, Alfred Fabre-Luce, Henry de Montherlant, or Knight Heinrich von Srbik. Keyserling, in turn, also used Rohan's network of relatives and acquaintances among the German-speaking Habsburg nobles in Bohemia to promote his own work. In this connection, he approached Rohan's elder brother Prince Alain as well as members of the oldest Austro-Bohemian noble families like 'Count Erwein Nostitz', 'Count Karl Waldstein', 'Count Feri Kinsky, Countess Ida Schwarzenberg, Count Coudenhove', 'Senator Count Eugen Ledebur', and other, exclusively noble, families that he wanted to win over as 'donors' for his own project of a 'School of Wisdom' for the creation of future European leaders.[89]

> I was not born in Germany but in Russian Estonia. Only in 1918, when Bolshevism robbed me of all I had inherited [alles Ererbte], I moved to

---

[86] IISG Amsterdam, Hendrik de Man papers, II.88 (Spengler) and 89 (Keyserling).
[87] HKN, Correspondence, R-3 172.01, Keyserling to Karl Anton Rohan, 14 July 1927.
[88] HKN, Correspondence, R-3 172.01, Rohan to Keyserling, 16 August 1927.
[89] HKN, Correspondence, R-3 172.01, Keyserling to Rohan, 1 March 1923.

Germany and found a refuge here, a new circle of influence and a new home; . . . Since 1918 I have therefore considered it my duty of honour and obvious duty and burden to serve Germany's prestige wherever I could. [. . .] I hope to be able to contribute to Germany especially today thanks to my special constitution.[90]

The aristocrat as an anti-fascist

During a conference on the future of Europe, which the Union for Intellectual Cooperation had convened in Europe, Keyserling arrived as Germany's representative.[91] Aldous Huxley, Paul Valéry, and numerous other famous European public intellectuals were also present. Thomas Mann, who was soon to leave Germany for his first place of exile (and one that attracted most of Germany's best known writers and intellectuals) in Sanary-sur-mer, had cancelled his participation at short notice. Before travelling to Paris, Keyserling, by contrast, sent a letter to the propaganda ministry, addressed to Goebbels personally, asking for permission to travel. He secured it by promising to report on the meetings. In a letter dated 20 September 1933 and addressed to the 'Reichsminister für Volksaufklärung und Propaganda', Keyserling, on the one hand, emphasised that he participated at the congress 'only as a personality, not as a representative of Germany' [nur als Persönlichkeit, nicht als Vertreter Deutschlands]; on the other hand, he used the opportunity to assert his essentially positive attitude to National Socialism as a movement, which he dated back to the year 1918, when he belonged 'to the first who had predicted and promoted a new art of socialism as a future form of life for Germany', drawing his attention to his publication on 'Socialism as a universal foundation of life' of 26 November 1918.[92]

Keyserling held that 'politics is never the primary cause, but only the execution of popular will', regardless of whether formally the government is a 'democracy or a tyranny'. [93] Locating Europe between two 'collective primitivisms', the Russian and the American, and 'fanatic' movements – Bolshevism, Marxism, and Hitlerism – Keyserling sketched the possible future of European identity as an essentially intellectual one. It all depends on a superior type of human being, a European who is beyond the above

---

[90] HKN, Nazis 1933ff, Keyserling an Adolf Hitler, 10 April 1933.
[91] Harry Kessler, TB, Wednesday, 24 May 1933.
[92] HKN Nazis 1933ff., Keyserling an Reichsminister für Volksaufklärung und Propaganda, 20 September 1933.
[93] HKN, Nr. 0412 Vorträge Paris Salle Pleyel 1933.

Figure 20 'Enemies of the state in each other's company', in: *Die Brennessel*, 5:36 (10 September 1935). BA R 43 II 1554–5, 61ff.

movements, who has not yet been born, in short, 'un type d'Européen supérieur'. The old elites, to which Keyserling counted himself, would have to recognize their lack of worth due to the lack of applicability of their ideas. The men of the future would incorporate both ancient and modern culture and will be able to aspire for a common life disregarding the differences.

In this context, Keyserling's own position gestured towards a voluntary identification with the Jews, a posture with which he provoked his social circle. Voluntarily identifying with the Jews, or having his books translated by writers in Yiddish, as Keyserling did, was a form of 'going native' under conditions of elite precarity. In a strange way, this tendency to compare Jewish and aristocratic identity echoed the discourse on aristocracy and the Jews in Nazi propaganda. One caricature from a Nazi satirical magazine compared the Jew and the Baron in their status as enemies of the (Aryan) state [Fig. 20].

'What do you say about our times, Levi,' the nobleman asks the Jew. 'Oh, don't try to talk to me, Herr Baron. I don't want to be compromised by your company.' The image displays only one of many examples of efforts within parts of the National Socialist movement to oust nobles from the new Germany, and was sent to the Reich chancery as part of a series of complaints made by the German Nobles' Union about affronts against the status of the nobility in Nazi newspapers.[94]

One of Keyserling's relatives, another Baltic German, had become a 'Siberian and Mongolian *condottiere*'.[95] Roman Ungern-Sternberg (1886–1921) served as a self-proclaimed dictator of Mongolia during the Russian Civil War in 1921, which he entered as a member of the White Army but continued as an independent warlord. He wanted to restore not only the Khanate in Mongolia, but also the Russian monarchy, and came to fame as a ruthless anti-Semite and persecutor of communists.[96] He was tried and executed by the Red Army, however. Keyserling emphasized some positive qualities of the 'Mad Baron'. His biographers, Keyserling thought, presented him in a one-sided light. In fact, his relative was 'no Baltic reactionary, but the precursor of new Mongolian greatness, which

[94] BA R 43 II 1554–5, 61ff.
[95] Hermann Keyserling, *Creative Understanding* (New York and London: Harper and Brothers, 1929), 276.
[96] On the interwar reception of the 'bloody baron', see Ferdynand Ossendowksi, *Beasts, Men, and Gods* (New York: Dutton, 1922); Vladimir Pozner, *Bloody Baron: The Story of Ungern-Sternberg* (New York: Randomhouse, 1938), previously as *Le mort aux dents* (Paris: Les éditions Noël, 1937). Most recently in Palmer, *The Bloody White Baron*.

continues to live on in the songs and tales of the steppe.'[97] Moreover, Roman, in his eyes, was characterized by an extraordinary 'Delicadeza' – the typical softness of brutal men, which he had discerned in South American culture as the kernel for a new renaissance.[98]

These different cultural comparisons Keyserling drew on were all united by a common theme – the need for aristocratic leadership for political renewal which, Keyserling hoped, also awaited Europe. But there was one further, intellectual component to this new aristocracy, which Keyserling himself wanted to cultivate with his School.

In his role as a global thinker, Keyserling joined the anti-fascist intelligentsia which gathered in Paris in the mid-1930s and comprised mostly liberal writers and public figures. In his lecture on 'La Révolte des forces telluriques et la responsabilité de l'Esprit', delivered on 16 October 1933, Keyserling positioned himself as a fatalist.[99] These intellectuals have to show understanding for these telluric forces and they can 'preempt the event, anticipate the best possible future on the basis of a fulfilled Destiny'.[100] All the historical phenomena, which Keyserling classified as essentially telluric – Bolshevism, National Socialism, and Fascism – 'have to be accepted, for no reasoning will change them'.[101]

Only two years later, Keyserling would warn Kessler in a personal conversation that he should never return to Germany for 'anti-Semitism and the [National Socialist] movement are getting more virulent every day' and that with support from the 'majority of the population'.[102] By 1939, Keyserling was in internal exile in Germany and would only be allowed to leave Germany during the allied bomb raids thanks to the interference of his publisher Peter Diederichs.

Orientalism and cosmopolitanism

Aristocratic modernists like Veltheim and Keyserling played a key role as go-betweens between Europeans and non-Europeans. In this, they formed part of a longer tradition of German Orientalism as it had formed in the period leading up to the First World War.[103] The twentieth-century lives of

---

[97] Keyserling, book review of Frans August Larson, *Die Mongolei und mein Leben unter den Mongolen* (Berlin: Gustav Kiepenheuer Verlag, 1936), in *Der Weg zur Vollendung* (1937), 26.

[98] Hermann Graf Keyserling, *Reise durch die Zeit*, vol. 2 (Vaduz: Liechtenstein-Verlag, 1948).

[99] HKN, 0312, 070.13, 'Discours du Comte de Keyserling à la Séance d'Inauguration des Entretiens sur l'Avenir de l'Esprit Européen'. Paris 16 October 1933, 6–7.

[100] Ibid., 10.   [101] Kessler TB, 19 October 1933.

[102] DLA Marbach, A: Kessler, Keyserling to Kessler, 4 May 1935.

[103] Marchand, *German Orientalism in the Age of Empire*.

some of these Germanic Orientalists suggest a further nuance to the history of international culture between the decline of Europe's empires and the rise of National Socialism. It was their shared status as derecognized, formerly voluntarily, now involuntarily, rootless European subjects that allowed this generation of German aristocrat-intellectuals to assume an ambivalent role as forgers of a new, global elite. At the same time, the case of Keyserling also demonstrates how this ideal became increasingly compromised, as aristocratic character-builders like Keyserling came to various arrangements with the Nazi regime, or tried to associate themselves with the cultural internationalism of large interstate organizations such as the League of Nations. In this sense, the path from the princely courts into the twentieth century leads to such institutions as UNESCO, and to transnational spiritual elite communities such as the Theosophical Society.

CHAPTER 5

Crusaders of civility
The legal internationalism of the Baltic Barons

[T]hose Masters or Lords, principally to the end they might, when
they were Covered with Arms, be known by their followers; and
partly for ornament, both painted their Armor, or their Scutchion,
or Coat, with the picture of some Beast, or other thing [. . .] And this
ornament both of their Armes, and Crest, descended by inheritance
to their Children.

> Thomas Hobbes, *Leviathan*, ch. X

Around us nothing but ruins, and above our head there reigns
uncompromising fate.[1]

> Mikhail Taube, citing freely from Sophocles's *Antigone* in Baron M. de
> Taube, *La politique russe d'avant guerre et la fin de l'empire des Tsars*
> (Paris, 1928)

Sitting in his Paris apartment in December 1941, Mikhail Aleksandrovich
Taube, or Baron M. de Taube, as he was known in France, was growing
impatient. A Berlin-based history journal, specializing in eastern Europe,
had promised him a transit permit to Königsberg, but there was still no
word from them. This was an archival trip of utmost importance, as he
expected that his research would give him conclusive evidence that
Catherine the Great of Russia was in fact the illegitimate daughter of
Frederick II of Prussia. He had located a talisman ring that explained the
'Russian-Prussian alliance after the Seven-Years'-War' with this circumstance of the two powers having been related more closely than previously
assumed. Taube did not understand why it took the *Zeitschrift für
Osteuropa* so long, despite good connections in the highest offices of the
Nazi administration. From his point of view, the situation was as 'bright as
the day': He was a 'scholar of German race from the Tsarist period who is

---

[1] Michael Freiherr von Taube, *Der großen Katastrophe entgegen. Die russische Politik der Vorkriegszeit
und das Ende des Zarenreiches* (Leipzig: Koehler, 1937), 376.

honorary professor at Münster-Westphalia, who with his 72 year wants to conduct research in German libraries and archives!'[2]

In late 1941, travels to East Prussia on private business had become difficult, if not impossible, for more than merely legal reasons. In June, Germany had breached the treaty with the Soviet Union, which Molotov and Ribbentrop had signed in 1939, and opened the eastern front of the German war effort for a second time in the twentieth century. What made things more complicated for his case was that Taube, who was born in 1869 in the imperial Russian residential city of Pavlovsk, had been stateless since the October Revolution. As a holder of a Nansen passport, his intended transit called for negotiations between the Foreign Office in Berlin, the German Consulate in Paris and the Police Prefecture of a city under German occupation.

Taube's confusion was not just a bureaucratic problem of identification to external authorities. His understanding of his very self, his place in the world and his role in the past, had become uncertain. As a perpetual expatriate, Taube was one of thousands of refugees from eastern and central Europe who had come to France in the hopes of finding security. In Taube's case, the threat came more from the Soviet than from Nazi terror. In fact, his connections to Germany remained largely intact during Germany's occupation of France. But many other refugees, including people from his social circle, fled from the Nazi regime and had been active in French anti-fascist circles, at least before 1940. In the 1920s, Paris and Berlin rivalled each other as capitals of Europe's emigration, particularly from eastern Europe. By the 1930s, Paris had taken a clear lead, with streams of refugees now also coming from Europe's fascist south and centre. It was here that a number of critically minded refugees gathered for such grandiose occasions as the Anti-fascist Writers' Congresses of 1933 and 1935.[3] But paradoxically, here also, Europe's most destructive regimes, the Nazi and Soviet empires, were granted legitimacy on such occasions as the Universal Exposition of 1937.

Within this mixed demographic of refugees, Taube's case sheds light on a now forgotten elite community of imperial internationalists from the

---

[2] Mikhail Taube to Frau Dr. E. Fleischhaker-Ueberberger, 1 December 1941. MT, box 2, Folder Correspondence Jahrbücher für Geschichte Osteuropas, Columbia University Special Collections, New York.

[3] On the significance of Paris in the anti-fascist movement, see Eric J. Hobsbawm, 'Gli intellettuali e l'antifascismo', in *Storia del marxismo*, 3:2 (Turin: Einaudi, 1981), 441–490; for a transcript of the Paris anti-fascist congress, involving the Baltic philosopher Hermann Keyserling, see *Paris 1935. Erster Internationaler Schriftstellerkongreß zur Verteidigung der Kultur. Reden und Dokumente*, ed. Akademie der Wissenschaften der DDR (Berlin: Akademie-Verlag, 1982).

Baltic lands. By contrast to the role that French and Belgian scholars of the Belle Epoque played in European internationalism of the interwar period, the role of scholars from the German and Russian empires has moved out of focus.[4]

Much of this forgetting had to do with a similar kind of confusion regarding the group biography of Baltic German and other exiled elites of the Russian Empire, whose mentality has been usually reduced to the role of nostalgic or reactionary 'white émigrés'. As the case of Taube will show, the dividing line between monarchism and liberalism, however, as well as between patriotism and imperialism, was never reducible to a schematic contrast between progress and reaction, or indeed, a geographical boundary between Russia, Germany, and France. Their transnational networks connected them to contemporaries in multiple European empires, and these networks vanished neither with the October Revolution, nor with the Nazi rise to power. Instead, their commitment to the idea of pedigree made the Baltic Barons broker a strange position between compliance and dissidence under Nazi ideology as it manifested itself in Germany as well as in Paris under German occupation.

Joking relationships between class war and ethnic cleansing

What gave intellectuals from the Baltic, and some scholars of the Baltic, a deeper understanding of the relationship between municipal and state, public and private, government and international law was the fact that the region consisted of a highly complex interrelationship of porous jurisdictions.[5] Their allegiances were expressed in terms of vernacular cultures versus the culture of the overwhelmingly German literati. The Baltic region had become a sort of inter-imperial buffer zone. Part of the Hanseatic network of trade, it also attracted a wide range of mythologies from its inhabitants and visitors alike.

Intellectuals from eastern Europe living in the West, such as Bronislaw Malinowski or, later, Eugen Weber, contributed to the image of the wild East themselves. Some of them where more interested in Polynesian natives or French peasants than in the 'natives' of their own regions. Others, like Czeslaw Milosz, flirted with the idea that 'while kingdoms rose and fell

---

[4] For more details on Belgian internationalism, see the work of Daniel Laqua, *The Age of Internationalism and Belgium, 1880–1930: Peace, Progress and Prestige* (Manchester: Manchester University Press, 2013).
[5] For the difficulty in naming these ethnic groups, see Andrejs Plakans, *The Latvians: A Short History* (Stanford: Hoover Institution Press, 1995), 1–13.

along the shores of the Mediterranean', their native land was a 'virgin forest' and that the 'streets of Chicago and Los Angeles' were therefore as strange to them as the 'Incas and the Aztecs'.[6] The entire area 'from the Urals to East Prussia' was 'unpopulated' and 'filled with demons and gloomy gods'.[7] This region-transcending imperial imaginary, which projected populations in space, was characteristic of an elite perspective of this regional history.

The Baltic Barons were located in a sociocultural landscape that defied the monolingual systems of analysis that Ferdinand de Saussure in Paris and Geneva so carefully tried to establish. In fact, however, national and class identities were entangled in a complicated way in this region.[8]

Many among the Baltic Barons saw themselves as the pacifiers and civilizers in the Russian Empire. There was no unified private law, and generally, Russian legal history was highly fragmented, with many and sporadic foreign influences. A fully formed legal tradition only existed in the three Baltic provinces – Livland, Estland, and Courland – but here, too, it was deeply uneven, a kind of 'jurisdictional jockeying' that Lauren Benton has observed with regard to the peripheries of other imperial states.[9]

By contrast, the national movements, which had sprung up in the Baltic during the revolution of 1905, viewed the Baltic Barons as sources of alien oppression. One caricature from 1906 shows the mental universe of 'Count Tiesenhausen', a Baltic German: 'In Paradise, people don't live better than my workers. They walk around like Barons and drive in carriages like Lords, eat and drink well, live in magnificent houses. My life is like hell. I am working like a dog here' [Fig. 21].

Another caricature identified the Barons by their reactionary student fraternities and their joint actions against the new national revolutions [Fig. 22]. These caricatures from 1906 obtained a new meaning when, reproduced in Soviet Estonia in 1955, they were redefined as documents of

---

[6] Czeslaw Milosz, *Native Realm: A Search for Self-Definition* (Berkeley: University of California Press, 1981), 7, 263.

[7] Fritz Reck-Malleczewen, *Diary of a Man in Despair/ Tagebuch eines Verzweifelten* (New York: Macmillan, 1947, 2000), 21.

[8] On region-specific jokes, see also Wendy Bracewell (ed.), *Orientations. An Anthology of East European Travel Writing, ca. 1550–2000* (Budapest: Central European University Press, 2009); on visual jokes, see also Simon J. Bronner, 'Pictorial Jokes: A Traditional Combination of Verbal and Graphic Processes', in *Tennessee Folklore Society Bulletin*, 44 (1978), 189–196.

[9] Lauren Benton, *Law and Colonial Cultures: Legal Regimes in World History, 1400–1900* (Cambridge: Cambridge University Press, 2002), 13, 153.

Figure 21 K. Merilaid (Schnell), caricature on the Tallinn case concerning the plundering of baronial estates. From *Reinuvarder* (1906), in I.P. Solomykova, *Estonskaia demokraticheskaia grafika perioda revoliutsii 1905–1907 godov* (Tallin: Estonskoe gosudarstvennoe izdatel'stvo, 1955), 145

Figure 22 Unknown Russian artist, caricature in the Petersburg-based Estonian
revolutionary magazine *Zalp* (1906), ed. Yukhan Lilienbach, in Solomykova,
Estonskaia demokraticheskaia grafika, 115

a socialist uprising against German feudalism and not a national revolution against Russian imperialism.[10]

From the point of view of the Baltic Barons, the revolutions of 1905 and 1917 destabilized what was an essentially natural ecosystem of animosities. One of the most regrettable aspects of the late Russian Empire, in Taube's view, was the government's own propaganda against the empire's German and Jewish population, which started still under imperial rule.[11] He recalled an incident in St. Petersburg, when he received a letter from an anonymous Russian demanding to free the Russian people from the 'Germans', by which he meant both Baltic Germans like Taube himself, and the Romanoff dynasty, a family with roots in Schleswig-Holstein. The paradox was that 'our [Russia's] highest military offices, which had been so inventive in devising means of oppression against the Baltic Barons and the Polish Jews' suddenly saw itself almost incapacitated by this new nationalist force.[12]

Taube began to feel unwelcome in Russia soon after the outbreak of the First World War and even complained about it in a personal conversation with Tsar Nicholas on 29 December 1914. 'On the various military fronts', Taube argued, there are some 'twenty members of the Taube family – pure Russian, Baltic, Finnish, Polish' – fighting for the Russian cause, and yet the Russian press was full of derogatory remarks on the German menace coming from the Baltic Barons. 'I know how faithfully the representatives of families with such ancient names have served me', Tsar Nicholas replied to him, and was particularly surprised by some of Taube's fellow aristocrats trying to Russianize their German-sounding names.[13] Nicholas's own ancestors, the Holstein-Gottorps, were of German descent, albeit of much more recent nobility than most of the Baltic Barons, who could trace their genealogy to the Crusades. They were worried for good reason: in 1917, Taube's brother Boris was briefly imprisoned at Kronstadt, to be liberated thanks only to British intervention, and Tsar Nicholas would suffer a worse fate still in the following year.

Extending the metaphor of the family to an entire region, one could say that the Baltic Barons had formed what structural anthropologists call

---

[10] Cf. I.P. Solomykova, *Estonskaia demokraticheskaia grafika perioda revoliutsii 1905–1907 godov* (Tallin: Estonskoe gosudarstvennoe izdatel'stvo, 1955). I am grateful to Gert von Pistohlkors for directing me to this volume, which, as he said, he had obtained in a second-hand bookstore in Estonia in the 1990s. I had ordered my copy online from a Latvian store. For his interpretation of the caricatures, see Gert von Pistohlkors, *Baltische Länder*, in the series Deutsche Geschichte im Osten Europas (Berlin: Siedler, 1994), 421–422.

[11] Michael Freiherr von Taube, *Der großen Katastrophe entgegen. Die russische Politik der Vorkriegszeit und das Ende des Zarenreiches (1904–1917)* (Berlin and Leipzig: Georg Neuner, 1929), 355ff.

[12] Ibid., 356.   [13] Ibid., 191.

'joking relationships' with other peoples. Structural anthropologists have focused on certain types of relationships, which they call 'joking', based on the type of conversations that typically occur between these parties. As Radcliffe-Brown puts it, they are 'relationships between persons related through marriage or by kinship'. Secondly, they 'occur as social institutions in structural situations of a certain general kind in which there are two groups, the separateness of which is emphasized'. A typical example is a son-in-law and a mother-in-law. The relationship expresses and emphasizes 'both detachment (as belonging to separated groups) and attachment (through the indirect personal relation)' as well as the jokes about relationships.[14]

The term does not describe a relationship that is not serious. Rather it means the existence of a relationship in which mutual misrecognition is a sign of acknowledging within certain limits the existence of another's inalienable authority in one's own sphere of existence. This means that the Baltic Barons were, in a sense, the Russian Empire's 'mother-in-law'.

For the Baltic Barons and other old aristocratic communities, their exclusive status was not available to groups outside their own genealogical network. It was dependent on the simultaneous coexistence of other, albeit, socially inferior cultural communities. Such communities included the Jews of the Russian Pale of Settlement, a geopolitical sphere of collective inferiority that Catherine the Great had created and which persisted until the revolutions of 1918. It also included the vernacular peoples whose unwritten languages the Baltic Barons rarely cared to learn, but which they liked melodically: Estonian, Lithuanian, and Latvian. They also included, interestingly, the Russians themselves, even though the Baltic Barons also saw themselves as Russian: but their sense of being Russian, an imperial sense, was different from the vernacular sense of the Russian as a peasant.

The deconstruction of the identity of the Baltic Barons makes them archaic in an age of extreme and radical modernity and calls for an anthropologist's attention to oral practices.[15] The cultural production of this space became what Henri Lefèbvre has called a 'third' space between

---

[14] Andrew Radcliffe-Brown, 'On Joking Relationships', in *Africa: Journal of the International African Institute*, 13: 3 (July 1940), 195–210; Andrew Radcliffe-Brown, 'A Further Note on Joking Relationships', in *Africa: Journal of the International African Institute*, 19:2 (April 1949), 133–140, 136. I am grateful to Philip Wood for suggesting to look for literature in structural anthropology to get out of a theoretical impasse in this chapter.

[15] Peter Burke, 'Context in Context', in *Common Knowledge*, 8:1 (Winter 2002), 152–177.

Europe's civilized centres and its imperial peripheries.[16] What Walter Scott
had written of the Scottish borders applies very much to the Baltic lands:

> The Borderers had, in fact, little reason to regard the inland Scots as their
> fellow-subjects, or to respect the power of the Crown. [. . .] They were in
> truth, during the time of peace, a kind of outcasts, against whom the united
> powers of England and Scotland were often employed. [. . .] This strange,
> precarious, and adventurous mode of life, led by the Borderers, was not
> without its pleasures, and it seems, in all probability, hardly so disagreeable
> to us, as the monotony of regulated society must have been to those who had
> been long accustomed to a state of rapine.[17]

The Baltic also appeared in the minds of aristocratic gentlemen as
a global borderland. The Scottish gentleman Leitch Ritchie, who had
passed through Russia in 1835 as part of a Grand Tour, called the area of
sand and morass, the politically 'neutral ground' between Prussia and
Russia, a 'waste land'.[18] Another aspect that Leitch had noticed was the
region's peculiar cosmopolitanism. A chance meeting with an Englishman
revealed to him that here in the East, this English traveller had become
a peculiar 'citizen of the world', who spoke 'all languages with equal
fluency, and all equally badly; now snuffling French, now expectorating
German, and now lubricating his mouth with Italian as one greases
a coach-wheel'.[19] Up to the late eighteenth century, accounts of travellers,
who typically passed through the region between the rivers Memel, or
Nieman, in the west and Narva in the east – mostly merchants, ambassadors, and, towards the end of the eighteenth century, gentlemen on Grand
Tours – had three things to say about it: it was covered in forests, where
most of its indigenous population lived; its towns were German and
Swedish, the population was divided into 'German' and 'Ungerman'
(Unteutsche), and the non-German population was treated very harshly,
like slaves. Accounts also say that although they were Christian, they
retained many pagan rituals. Eighteenth-century maps of Livonia still
looked rather similar to eighteenth-century maps of the African cape,

---

[16] Henri Lefèbvre, *La production de l'espace* (Paris: Anthropos/Economica, 1999). See also depiction of
Livonia in Sebastian Münster's *Cosmographey oder Beschreibung aller Länder, Herrschaffienn und
fürnemesten Stetten des gantzen Erdbodens* (Basel, 1588; Munich: Kölbl, 1977).

[17] Sir Walter Scott, 'Introduction to the Minstrelsy of the Scottish Border, Consisting of Historical
and Romantic Ballads Collected in the Southern Counties of Scotland, with a Few of Modern Date,
Founded upon Local Tradition', in *The Complete Works of Sir Walter Scott*, 7 vols., vol. 1 (New York:
Conner & Cooke, 1833), 28.

[18] Leitch Ritchie, *A Journey to St. Petersburg and Moscow Through Courland and Livonia* (London:
Longman, 1836).

[19] Ibid., 43.

with the lands of the Hottentots demarcated from the territory of European civilization.

Their special family history, publicly displayed as heraldic symbols, constituted their power as much as their enormous landed wealth. To understand the nature of this symbolic power, we could turn to a number of works of anthropology and social theory from the twentieth century, most recently, that of Pierre Bourdieu and before him, the semioticians of the Tartu school such as Yuri Lotman. Yet the clearest analysis, and the most succinct, in my view, can be found in the work of Thomas Hobbes, the political philosopher who is best known for his theory of the state. Drawing on the Roman historian Cornelius Tacitus, he remarked that historically, this practice was typical for old families of Germanic origin, who would wear coats of arms principally so that 'they might, when they were Covered with Arms, be known by their followers'. The symbolism on these Coats of Arms typically contained the 'picture of some Beast, or other thing' as well as ornaments. Together, it was then 'descended by inheritance to their Children'.[20] Catalogues of appropriate animals and other attributes to be used on coats of arms were available thanks to book printing in editions such as Andrea Alciati's book of emblems.[21] According to Hobbes, the '*Value*, or Worth of a man, is of all other things, his Price; that is to say, so much as would be given for the use of his Power: and therefore is not absolute; but a thing dependant on the need and judgment of another'.[22] The idea is that symbols of universally recognizable virtues thus became connected to the name of a particular family, thus combining two kinds of recognition: one, in the sense of knowing who is being spoken about; the other, in the sense of acknowledging their particular virtues as being outstanding. By the nineteenth and

---

[20] Thomas Hobbes, *Leviathan*, ed. Richard Tuck (Cambridge: Cambridge University Press, 2001), ch. X, 68.

[21] Andrea Alciato, *Emblemata* (Venice: Gulielmus Rouillius, 1548). See also collection of photographs of early modern nobles and clergy with coats of arms, e.g. 'Männliches Bildnis mit Wappen der Bocholtz (Bischof von Paderborn), Deutschland, um 1560', Berlin, private Sammlung, Foto Marburg, Aufnahme-Nr. 65.340 (1937); 'Scheibe mit Bildnis des Herzogs Maximilian I., umgeben von den Wappen der 28 bayrischen Städte, Bayern, 1602, München, Bayerisches Nationalmuseum, Foto Marburg, Aufnahme-Nr. 110.167; Stehender Krieger mit Fahne und Wappen, Deutschland, 1501/1600, Köln, Wallraf-Richartz-Museum – Fondation Corboud, Graphische Sammlung, Inv.-Nr. Z, Rheinisches Bildarchiv Köln, Aufnahme-Nr. RBA 068 806; Bildindex der Kunst und Architektur, Bildarchiv Foto Marburg, www.bildindex.de/?+pgesamt:%27Adel%27#|1, accessed 5 November 2013. See also entries for Secular Iconography, Warburg Institute Iconographic Database, http://warburg.sas.ac.uk/vpc/VPC_search/subcats.php?cat_1=16&cat_2=260, accessed 4 April 2014.

[22] Thomas Hobbes, *Leviathan*, ed. Richard Tuck (Cambridge: Cambridge University Press, 1996), 62–63.

twentieth centuries, the art of heraldry had still been best preserved among German nobles, but particularly so among these descendants of Teutonic knights. Perhaps this is the reason why the Baltic region also produced one of the most influential schools of modern semiotics.[23]

Their coats of arms, which, as anthropologists assert, encode their identity in the form of symbols, told the story both of origin and of displacement. For example, the Keyserlings had a palm tree on their coat of arms. With a handful of other German-speaking families, the Keyserlings dominated the political and cultural life of this region for centuries, while constituting a linguistic and ethnic minority in the Baltic region. Their familial memory of this history was embodied in their familial crest, which included the image of a palm tree. Even though in the modern era, this crest was displayed in the Lutheran Cathedral of Tallinn, its symbols reflected the family's ancient service to the Popes in an attempt to conquer Jerusalem.

For centuries, this position as Europe's inner frontier provided a resource for great careers for the region's elites serving the Russian Empire.[24] They had family names with a publicly known and often distinguished family history, such as Nolde, von Maydell, von Manteuffel, von Kessenbroich, von Stackelberg, and von Dellingshausen, and were often called Alexander, Otto, or Bernhard. Even when they produced works of fiction, many of them would choose protagonists with their own family names for their heroes. By contrast, their peasants would be called Jaan, Elvine, Mats, and in many cases would not even have surnames, if they were members of the household of a German noble family. Estonian and Latvian peasants would sing vernacular folk songs at home, Protestant hymns in church, and would be free subjects of the tsar and de facto subjects of their local, German, lord of the manor. Therefore in these areas, progressive movements towards greater social equality were couched in national terms and in the terms of a national emancipation as well as social equality. Apparently, non-national or professional associations of beekeepers or study groups of vernacular cultures became points of association for political unrest, and they were monitored as such by the Russian imperial police, the Okhrana.[25]

It was traditional for noble families in the Baltic area to employ English-speaking governesses, as well as French teachers, for their children, while

[23] Alexei Losev, *Problema simvola i realisticheskoe iskusstvo*, 2nd ed. (Moscow: Iskusstvo, 1995).
[24] Henri Lefèbvre, *The Production of Space* (London: Blackwell, 1991).
[25] Arnolds Spekke, *History of Latvia. An Outline* (Stockholm: M. Goppers, 1951), 316.

the servants of lower order spoke vernacular languages, such as Latvian, Lithuanian, and Estonian. Growing up in this context was not a multicultural experience in the pluralistic sense in which it is understood today, however; on the contrary, because languages such as Estonian, Russian, German, French, and English stood in a hierarchical relationship to each other, it was the unity of this hierarchy and not the plurality of its components that stood out. French and German were languages of high culture, English was a language in which children would be educated, Russian was one of the official languages of the empire, and Estonian was for unwritten purposes. From the 1860s onwards, students seeking careers in civil administration, while still leading via German universities in Dorpat and Riga, now had to be taught Russian. Attending Russian Orthodox Church services became compulsory even for German noble lords who had their own, Lutheran, parishes to control. In other words, if Kant had lived into the reign of Alexander III, the categorical imperative would have been taught in Russian. The thought of this drove many German nobles to study in western Europe.

The generation of Baltic Barons born in the post-Napoleonic era had enough of the ruins of former civilizations that surrounded them; they wanted to manifest their links with the classical foundations of European civilization in the newest fashion. The Greek revival style, which had become fashionable throughout northern Europe and America in this period, had been brought to the Baltic area by a generation of travellers who had been inspired by the real models of ancient Greece and Rome. This style, which most people today associate with British and American public buildings such as the National Gallery in London and the Washington or Madison Capitol, was prominent in the semi-private residential architecture of landed nobility in the Baltic littoral, and in fact the Baltic nobles were among the first Europeans to develop it. One of the first archaeologists whose publications inspired the trend in Europe, Baron Otto Magnus von Stackelberg, originated from this region, and he had brought the style to his home area following excavations in Messenia, Greece. These aristocrats had reinserted themselves on the map of European high nobility architecturally as well as intellectually. They could host in style. And the way they hosted was to glorify the Eastern wilderness, the beautiful landscapes, the hunting parties, and the snow. By the beginning of the twentieth century, most Baltic Barons were Russian imperial patriots of sorts: many had converted to the Russian Orthodox Church and had acquired estates close to the summer residence of the Russian imperial family.

By the beginning of the twentieth century, and especially since the 1905 revolution, most German nobles from the Baltic responded to the Russian imperial policies of Russification by becoming more conscious of their own Germanness: consolidating ties to Baltic Germans of non-noble background, as well as the German public in the German Empire. Conversely, the population of these universities was increasingly less willing to accept the overwhelmingly German presence in its universities. Baltic scientists with their characteristic knowledge of many languages were employed in imperial expeditions of the Romanoff, Habsburg, and Hohenzollern court. In Germany they were called *Baltendeutsche*, and in Russia they were called *ostzeiskie nemtsy*, the Ostsee Germans. In the events leading up to the 1905 revolution, a group of Baltic German nobles commissioned a historian, Astaf von Transehe-Roseneck, to write a history of the Lithuanian revolution; the book, published anonymously in 1906, criticized the national revolutionaries by insisting on the civilizing force which the German nobility had been for the region.[26]

All these national interpretations of the political thought emanating from the Baltic region, however, lose sight of the basic sense of identity that most Baltic Barons had, which was not reducible to any one national narrative. As Hermann Keyserling put it, 'in the course of history, the Baltic knights formed pacts now with this, now with that regional lord and placed themselves under his suzerainty'. What allowed for that situation to serve as the foundation for a distinctive identity of the 'Balt' was their continuous base in the Baltic littoral. The loss of this basis meant a loss of identity, of the 'Balt as a type'.[27] In terms of international legal theory, they were mixed subjects or *sujets mixtes*: represented in the Prussian Herrenhaus as well as at the court of the tsar and, for those who stayed in Russia, in the Duma after 1905.[28] 'When I analyse my own self, what do I find there?' Keyserling asked himself in a book devoted to the social psychology of all European nations. 'First myself, second, myself as an aristocrat, third, as a Keyserling, fourth, as an Occidental, fifth as a European, sixth, as a Balt, seventh, as a German, eighth, as a Russian, ninth, as a Frenchman.'[29] All aristocrats, in his view, but especially the

[26] Anon., *Die lettische Revolution*, Introduction Theodor Schiemann, vol. 1 (Berlin: G. Reimer, 1906), vol. 2 (Berlin: G. Reimer, 1907).
[27] Hermann Keyserling, *Reise durch die Zeit*, 2 vols., vol. 1 (Vaduz: Liechtenstein Verlag, 1948), 33, 64.
[28] August Wilhelm Heffter, *Das europäische Völkerrecht der Gegenwart, auf den bisherigen Grundlagen* (Berlin: Schroeder, 1844), cited after 5th ed., 1867.
[29] Count Hermann Keyserling, *Europe*, transl. Maurice Samuel (New York: Harcourt, Brace and Company, 1928), 450–451.

Baltic Barons like himself, embodied in themselves the identities of all leading European cultures and were yet conscious of their detachment from them.

Perpetual Peace or Perpertual War? A Tolstoyan exile's view of the League of Nations

Among Mikhail Taube's first publications in exile from Russia was a little brochure, in Russian, called *Perpetual Peace or Perpetual War? Thoughts on the League of Nations.* Taube's *Perpetual Peace* was published by Detinets, one of the renowned Russian expatriate in Berlin. Its founder, the writer Ivan Nazhivin, gave it the name 'detinets' to allude to an older Russian political tradition. The word denotes a medieval Russian fortress, a historical predecessor of the Kremlin, known from cities such as Novgorod, which had a republican tradition. Taube's work could be considered his political manifesto. A magisterial overview of international historical alliances for peace from ancient Egypt to his present day, the book was based on the lectures Taube had given, originally in Swedish, at Uppsala University. It was given further weight by a facsimile reproduction of a letter the author had received from Leo Tolstoy in support of his project. He had previously published a much shorter version (to pass imperial censorship) in Tolstoy's publishing house Posrednik.[30]

In addition, Taube worked privately as a lawyer for the émigré nobility, including one of the surviving members of the Romanoff family, and the union of former Russian municipal governments in exile, Zemgor. He also acted as a legal advisor to the artist, mystic, and internationalist Nikolai Roerich, who was committed to fostering a language of international culture beyond the state. Roerich's 'Banner of Peace', to protect cultural monuments in times of conflict by international agreement, dated back to an idea he had during the Russian–Japanese war. 'If the Red Cross takes care of the physically wounded and sick, our Pact shields the values of the human genius, protecting spiritual health', said Roerich and his followers. Between all these activities, Taube still found the time to contribute to the small parish circular of his church, the Holy Trinity Diocese, a branch of the Russian Catholic Church in exile since the revolution.

Taube spent most of his life as a historian and theorist of international law and not as practitioner. Yet he had his moment, as a young lawyer and

---

[30] Mikhail von Taube, *Khristianstvo i mezhdunarodnyi mir*, 2nd ed. (Moscow: Posrednik, 1905).

student of the renowned Russian international legal scholar Fedor Martens, when he got sent to Paris to negotiate the crisis over the so-called Dogger Bank incident, or 'outrage', as it was better known in English. In 1904, a Russian cruiser had accidentally fired on a set of fishermen near Hull, thinking that they were Japanese military ships. In the end, some of the fishermen died, British property was damaged, and another Russian cruise ship, the *Aurora* – which would later acquire fame in the public narratives of the Russian Revolution for allegedly firing the first shot in the storm of the Winter Palace – was damaged. All participating parties were aware that this could lead to a major escalation. Thanks to benevolent mediators from France and skilled negotiation by both the Russian and British sides, however, confrontation was not only avoided, but Russia managed to broker a closer relationship with Britain than it ever had – against French interests. This incident was the closest Taube got to world historical events in his capacity of a second-order agent.

Ten years later, this success of brinkmanship that extended the peace between Europe's empires would be forever overshadowed by the unprecedented international conflict that came to be known as the Great War. It was to the understanding of this Great Catastrophe, which Taube perceived as a personal, an imperial, and a generational disaster, that his remaining life work was devoted.

Theatrical metaphors, like his image of himself in a second-tier armchair of a first-order theatre box, never left Taube's thinking about politics. In the conclusion to his book of memoirs, *Towards the Great Catastrophe*, he turned to the world of ancient Greek drama to make sense of the present. He evoked the ruined city of Thebes, which he suggested to see through the eyes of the heroine in Sophocles's drama *Antigone*, a work that experienced a particular revival in mid-twentieth-century Europe, particularly among exiles in Paris.[31] Antigone, daughter from Oedipus's incestuous union with his mother, and in love with her deceased brother, confronts Creon, the king of Thebes, who personifies the power of the state, with the wish to be loyal to her brother, who had been disloyal to the king. In the end Antigone is buried alive, but Thebes and everyone else is ruined, too.

It is perhaps peculiar to see a former member of imperial rule, albeit not an emperor but a senator, identify with Antigone and not with Creon or at

---

[31] Cf. George Steiner, *Antigones: How the Antigone Legend Has Endured in Western Literature, Art, and Thought* (New Haven: Yale University Press, 1984). For mid-twentieth-century performances, see Jean Anouilh's performance in 1944, during the Nazi occupation, and Brecht's performance in 1949.

least with the choir in this tragedy. Such a perspective is more commonly associated with theorists of revolution. Perhaps the best-known reading of *Antigone* as the plot of a revolution was that of another Paris-based exile from the Baltic, Aleksandr Kozhevnikov, who in the 1930s lectured at the Sorbonne on Hegel's philosophy of history under the name of Alexandre Kojève.[32] Kojève combined a selective interpretation of Marx's interpretation of Hegel with ideas from Russian Orthodox thought to advance a philosophy of history of his own. Marx had concentrated on one segment of Hegel's metaphysical construction in the history of mind, the 'materialist' narrative of human history. Hegel had labelled this section in his *Phenomenology of Spirit* as 'Lord and Serf' (Herr und Knecht, usually translated as 'Lord and Bondsman'). Class struggle, he said, was a '*real* historical "discussion"' that was 'different from a philosophic dialogue or discussion'. Its central agents were not 'verbal arguments', but 'clubs and swords or cannons on the one hand' and 'sickles and hammers or machines' on the other. Unlike the orthodox Marxists, Kojève believed that the agents holding these instruments were individuals and not classes. History was a process of 'bloody fights' and of 'physical work'. For Kojève, the central force of history was thus not the autonomy of mind, as in Hegel, and not a class struggle for resources, as for Marx. Instead, he argued that the motor of history was desire itself – the desire people have to be recognized by others as subjects of their own destinies. The subsequent career of Kojève's influential conceptualization of the term 'recognition' in French and American thought then shifted even further from the idea of a social struggle to that of an the intersubjective function of desire for identity.[33] However, Kojève himself developed his thoughts on revolution in an unusual direction, eventually advocating the creating of a new Latin Empire based in France after the Second World War.

What Taube had in common with other exiles in Paris, then, was an intensive preoccupation with the past, with imperial decline, and with the psychological experience of revolution. In this period of turmoil and destruction that began in 1904 and crashed in 1914–18, intellectuals like Mikhail von Taube and his circle of correspondents turned to their own

---

[32] Cf. Alexandre Kojève, *Introduction to the Reading of Hegel* (based on Sorbonne lectures from 1934 to 1939, Engl. transl., New York: Basic Books, 1969).

[33] For a critical overview, see Robert Pippin, *Hegel on Self-Consciousness: Desire and Death in the Phenomenology of Spirit* (Princeton: Princeton University Press, 2011), 11ff; Axel Honneth, *Kampf um Anerkennung. Zur moralischen Grammatik sozialer Konflikte* (Frankfurt/Main: Suhrkamp, 2003), 80–89, on Kojève's mistranslation of the term *Begierde*.

family history as a source of consolation and consolidation of their identity.[34]

Forced into emigration during the revolution, Taube and many of this class, including the distinguished minister Baron Nolde, reflected not only on Russia's history, but also on that of the Baltic elite. For Taube, doing genealogical research was one of the ways of recovering this world he had lost. He was interested in the history of international relations from the Byzantine period.[35] A loyal subject of the tsars, in the Russian Empire, Taube belonged to a circle of moderate imperial reformers: fiercely loyal to the ideology of the Russian Empire in the broad sense of its multicultural make-up officially represented by legislative and executive institutions that endorsed the Orthodox faith. He was a patriot of his empire and a liberal internationalist, the Russian equivalent of a Gladstonian. Alongside another Baltic Baron, Nolde, he was one of his generation's most distinguished scholars of international law.[36] He had taught at the University of Dorpat, now Tartu, in the province of Courland, and at the University of Kharkov in what is now Ukraine, and he believed that international relations had a history that began in the Byzantine Empire in the tenth century and would culminate in the continuation of the Holy Alliance. His greatest success as a lawyer, historian, and political advisor was the Russian initiative of the Hague agreements on maritime law, in 1907. It built on the model of universal peace brokered by the great powers that had first emerged in the post-Napoleonic era with the Holy Alliance. Both universities where Taube taught were key institutions which mediated between Western and Russian scholarship particularly in the fields of Law and Philosophy, in which Russian scholarship lagged far behind studies of international law practised in Germany, Switzerland, and increasingly, the United States. As such, they also reached an audience of students who, for personal or financial reasons, were unable to study at the more prestigious universities in Germany or France. In particular, Dorpat had been a centre for teaching of Roman law in the Russian Empire, which

---

[34] Mikhail Taube, 'K istorii gerba Romanoffykh (dogadka o proiskhozhdenii Romanoffskogo grifa)', Lecture given at the Russian Genealogical Society on the occasion of the 300th anniversary of the Romanoffs, 26 February 1913, *Gerboved* (July 1913), 109–117, http://gerboved.ru/t/july1913.html, accessed 3 April 2014.

[35] Baron M. de Taube, 'Les origines de l'arbitrage international. Antiquité et Moyen Age', in *Collected Courses of The Hague Academy of International Law*, 42 (1932). See also Baron M. de Taube, *L'apport de Byzance au développement du droit international occidental*, 67 (1939).

[36] Lauri Mälksoo, 'The History of International Legal Theory in Russia: A Civilizational Dialogue with Europe', in *The European Journal of International Law*, 19:1 (2008), 211–232.

is where liberally minded intellectuals saw a possible future for the development of a Russian system of civil law.[37]

After the revolution, Taube taught for several years at the Russian Scientific Institute, a university in exile active in Berlin between 1922 and 1932.[38] He was a regular lecturer at the Hague Academy of International Law, where a magnificent building for the International Court of Justice had been completed, ironically, in 1913, just a year before the war. He had a chair at the University of Münster in German Westphalia.[39] There were also publication opportunities on matters of international law in German, Swedish, and émigré Russian journals.

The chief outlet of the legal internationalists was the Belgian journal *Révue de droit international et de droit comparé*, which was published since 1908. After the First World War, Belgium attracted the interest of international legal thought for other reasons. Belgium's particular suffering in the war, when the German army bayonetted innocent civilians, raised international alarm in 1915. By this point, English and not French began to dominate international legal thought.[40] In 1909, the Carnegie

---

[37] Zoran Pokrovac, *Juristenausbildung in Osteuropa bis zum Ersten Weltkrieg. Rechtskulturen des modernen Osteuropa. Traditionen und Transfers* (Frankfurt: Klostermann, 2007), esp. Anton D. Rudokvas and Aleksei Kartsov, 'Der Rechtsunterricht und die juristische Ausbildung im kaiserlichen Russland', 273–317; Aleksei Kartsov, 'Das Russische Seminar für Römisches Recht an der juristischen Fakultät der Friedrich-Wilhelms-Universität zu Berlin', 317–353; Marju Luts-Sootak, 'Der lange Beginn einer geordneten Juristenausbildung an der deutschen Universität zu Dorpat (1802–1893)', 357–391.

[38] 'Delegation in Germany', in Russisches Wissenschaftliches Institut: Various Correspondence, Financial Statements, Press Cuttings, etc., 1922–1932, C1255/151/170.1, UNOG Records and Archives Unit, Nansen Fonds, Refugees Mixed Archival Group, 1919–47.

[39] Lieselotte Steveling, *Juristen in Münster: Ein Beitrag zur Geschichte der Rechts- und Staatswissenschaftlichen Fakultät der Westfälischen Wilhelms-Universität Münster/Westf*, Beiträge zur Geschichte der Soziologie, 10 (Münster: LIT-Verlag, 1999). See also O. Nippold, 'Les conférences de La Haye et la Société des Nations'. Le développement historique du droit international depuis le Congrès de Vienne, in *Collected Courses of the Hague Academy of International Law*, 2 (The Hague: Martinus Nijhoff Publishers, 1924); M. de Taube, *Études sur le développement historique du droit international dans l'Europe orientale*, in *Collected Courses of the Hague Academy of International Law*, 11 (The Hague: Martinus Nijhoff Publishers, 1926); M. de Taube, *L'inviolabilité des traités*, in *Collected Courses of the Hague Academy of International Law*, 32 (1930); M. de Taube, *Le statut juridique de la mer Baltique jusqu'au début du xixe siècle*, in *Collected Courses of the Hague Academy of International Law*, 53 (1935); M. de Taube, *L'apport de Byzance au développement du droit international occidental*, 67 (1939); M. de Taube, *La Russie et l'Europe Occidentale à travers dix siècles, Etude d'histoire internationale et de psychologie ethnique* (Bruxelles: La Lecture au Foyer, Librairie Albert Dewit, 1926).

[40] For more on this subject, see Isabel Hull, *A Scrap of Paper: Breaking and Making International Law* (Ithaca, N.Y.: Cornell University Press, 2014). Initially, the Carnegie Foundation's interest in international law was expressed in publications of the classics in their original languages. See its modern edition of Emil de Vattel's *Le droit des gens, ou Principes de la loi naturelle appliqués à la conduite et aux affaires des nations et des souverains*, Classics of International Law (Washington: Carnegie Institution, 1916).

Endowment for International Peace had already initiated a series of Classics of International Law, which began with publishing works by the forerunners of Grotius in their original languages. They began with Italian municipal law in the fourteenth century, followed by the scholarship of the Spanish Jesuits, with particular focus on the law of war in the context of early modern Italian city states on the one hand and natural law on the other.[41] The series published 352 volumes, culminating in the works of Grotius and Pufendorf.

The Hague academy attracted some of the leading international jurists of the time. Presided over by Charles Lyon-Caen, a scholar of Roman law at Paris's Science-Po and author of an influential book on international private law, it also included distinguished members from across the international legal community. One of them, Nicholas Politis, advocated making the individual, instead of the state, a legal subject of international law, personally responsible for crimes committed in political capacity.[42] Another leading member was the Italian lawyer Dionisio Anzilotti, Under-Secretary-General of the League of Nations in charge of legal affairs who was also present at the signing of the Paris Peace Treaty. A critic of the natural law tradition, he was a positivist who believed that international law had to be built up from a genealogy of European municipal law, among other sources.[43] For them, law was in existence when it was used and accepted by the communities to which it applied.[44]

A number of people from Taube's social circle were not very political men, and the subjects on which he corresponded with them largely touched upon questions such as family matters, or genealogy – a special interest for many members of Baltic nobility. Taube himself began his genealogical studies with his own family, but then also offered his services

---

[41] See, for instance, Giovanni da Legnano, *De Bello, De Represaliis et De Duello*, ed. James Brown Scott (Oxford and Washington: Oxford University Press for the Carnegie Institution, 1917).

[42] Fedor Martens, *Sovremennoe mezhdunarodnoe pravo civilisovannykh narodov* [Modern International Law of Civilized Peoples], 2 vols. (St. Petersburg: Benke, 1883). In this, Politis was in agreement with other notable lawyers such as the German Hans Kelsen and the Russian Fridrikh Martens. Politis was also instrumental in establishing the legal formulation for an 'act of aggression' in cooperation with the Soviet Union's ambassador Maxim Litvinov in 1933. On Lyon Caen, see obituary by H.C. Gutteridge in *The Cambridge Law Journal*, 6:1 (March 1936), 93–94; Nicholas Tsagourias, 'Nicholas Politis' Initiatives to Outlaw War and Define Aggression, and the Narrative of Progress in International Law', in *The European Journal of International Law*, 23:1 (2012), 255–66; see also the primary source of the documents, League of Nations treaties No. 3405 of 5 July 1933.

[43] Dionisio Anzilotti, *Teoria generale della responsabilità dello stato nel diritto internazionale* (Florence: F. Lumachi, 1902).

[44] Cf. Georg Jellinek, *Allgemeine Staatslehre* (Berlin: Haering, 1914), 337; Georg Jellinek, *System der subjektiven öffentlichen Rechte* (Freiburg: Mohr, 1892).

to others.[45] He also had links to a circle of devotees of Leo Tolstoy, who chose to go into exile after the revolution because they did not agree with the Bolshevik version of socialism that had won the day. Others were more clearly radical. For instance, the frontispiece to his memoirs, designed by fellow Balt Nils Stenbock Fermor, was a faded Russian double eagle pattern, which was sliding away to the side of the book into oblivion. Fermor, originally of Swedish extraction, was of Baltic nobility himself, but politically further to the left than Taube; in the 1920s, he also designed sets for the experimental German theatre director Erwin Piscator. His brother, Alexander, was known as a Red Count; he wrote socialist realist works under the pseudonym of Peter Lorenz. Notwithstanding their political differences, the symbolic thinking about imperial decline as the fading away of imperial insignia nonetheless united these intellectuals of Baltic background.

In 1922, the year of publication of Taube's book, at The Hague, the Permanent Court of International Justice held its inaugural meeting. If it had not been for the ruined empires that had melted in the meantime, this would have been a momentous day for internationalists like Taube who had been involved in brokering peace through international legal treaties since the Hague agreements of 1899. The court remained in operation until 1940, but in 1946, the International Court of Justice was founded in its place. Its composition reflected the structure of the League of Nations, which appointed all judges in a council decision. Most judges of this court came from states whose governments had not collapsed as a result of the war. Of these, five were professors of international law from Switzerland, Italy, and the United States; others had been judges from the Netherlands, Britain, Norway, and China.[46] Typically for European internationalism, the Hague court replaced a rival project, founded by the renowned Swiss legal theorist Johann Caspar Bluntschli at Ghent in 1873.

The forgotten Russian-German and Baltic connection in European legal internationalism of the interwar period shows how imperial memory was preserved in exile.[47] It was multilingual, multi-discursive

---

[45] M. von Taube, *Archiv des uradeligen Geschlechts Taube, sonst Tuve genannt* (Yuryev: Mattiesen, 1911); M. de Taube, 'Beiträge zur baltischen Familiengeschichte', in *Jahrbuch für Genealogie, Heraldik und Sphragistik* (1899), 143–147; 1900, 85–89; 1903, 113–115; 1904, 115–120; 1905/06, 257–262; 1907/08, 65–73; 1909/10, 13; M. de Taube., *Die von Uxkull; genealogische Geschichte des uradeligen Geschlechts der Herren, Freiherren und Grafen von Uexkull, 1229–1929* (Berlin: Julius Sittenfeld, 1930).

[46] See Ole Spierman, 'A Permanent Court of International Justice', in *Nordic Journal of International Law*, 72 (2003), 399–418.

[47] More on the imperial history of Russian legal internationalism, see Peter Holquist, 'Baron Boris Nolde. Dilemmas of a Progressive Administrator', in *Kritika: Explorations in Russian and Eurasian History*, 7:2 (Spring 2006), 241–273.

, and almost gestural in its exchange of emblematic knowledge. In this cryptic quality, it was soon forgotten and remains difficult to reconstruct. To understand these diasporic communities in exile, we need to turn to methods originally designed for spoken texts, as well as to semiotics, an approach originally conceptualized for interpreting images and emblems.

Genealogy as counter-history: a Baltic correspondence network between the world wars

The notion of 'double consciousness' has come to be associated with the colonial dimension of modernity and the attributes of Europe's oppressed ethnic 'others'.[48] However, the case of the Baltic Barons demonstrates that ambivalent social and ethnic identities constituted by colonial relations were also characteristic of Europe's oldest nobilities. In Russia itself, people still made do with a legal code that came into existence when serfdom still existed, commerce was restricted, and civil rights were only applicable to the landowning nobility.[49] A number of Russian lawyers from the Baltic region were familiar with the German school of Georg Jellinek. Thus Fedor Martens, Russia's most eminent scholar of international law, had studied with Bluntschli and reproduced some of his ideas of civilization versus barbarism in his own work. Earlier in his life, when the empire was still intact, Taube had produced and published genealogical trees of the Romanoff dynasty. Now that it was no longer in power, he turned to write about his own life and the ancestors of his Baltic peers.[50]

In his lifetime, genealogical research in general had developed new facets. From a science of empowering the ruling dynasty, the Romanoffs, it became the source of identity among displaced Baltic aristocrats in the interwar period; as an abstract genealogy of European international law, it was a mode of reading historical texts which also connected to Taube's teaching at the expatriate Russian Scientific Institute, which existed in

---

[48] W.E.B. DuBois, *The Souls of Black Folk* (Chicago: McClurg, 1904); Paul Gilroy, *The Black Atlantic: Modernity and Double Consciousness* (Cambridge, Mass.: Harvard University Press, 1993).

[49] Anomymous, 'Das römische Recht in Russland', in *Stimmen des Auslands über die Zukunft der Rechtswissenschaft*, ed. Rudolf Leonhard, series Studien zur Erläuterung des bürgerlichen Rechts, vol. 17 (Breslau: M&H Marcus, 1906), 105–106.

[50] Taube, 'K istorii gerba Romanoffykh'.

Berlin from 1923 to 1925 with three faculties: Economics, Law, and a faculty called Spiritual Culture (a variant of Divinity). By the late 1930s, genealogy had also become one of the crown sciences of the Nazi Reich, whose theory of Aryan race sent all German subjects, on a search for racial purity for fear of punishment and restrictions. But it also remained important among circles of Russian expatriates in central and western Europe.[51]

While in Paris, Taube was still maintaining his links with the descendants of the Romanoff dynasty; thus he was the family lawyer of Prince Romanovich (killed in 1918) who thought of himself as the legitimate surviving successor of the Romanoff family. In fact, one of the last letters that the tsar's wife, Alexandra, had drafted in exile in Siberia had been to Taube, who was, besides his service, a loyal friend of the family.[52] Taube's genealogical findings concerning the links between Frederick and Catherine would have changed the past in the way that he had intended to change the future as a lawyer. It was well known that the two eighteenth-century rulers of Prussia and the Russian Empire, respectively, had shared the ability to absorb, if not plagiarize, the ideas of the great Enlightenment *philosophes* on liberty and legality in such a way as to render them safe for their own rule. Frederick's *Anti-Machiavel* cast him as a lover of freedom, taking this trope from the pens of his critics. Catherine's *Nakaz* on a Constitution of Russia effectively laid out a version of Montesquieu's concept of liberty, but one that would leave her authority unchallenged. But for all their similarities in the public eye, their projects were also thought of as rival imperial endeavours, Catherine's being more suited to the wilder eastern Europe; they were two projects that produced two quite separate branches in the European genealogy of statecraft. Frederick's was the bureaucratic state that would ultimately be capable of democratization; Catherine's legacy was that of an oppressive system of internal colonization, with the infamous Pale of Settlement – a vast rural ghetto for Russia's Jews – as one of its most tangible twentieth-century legacies. If it was indeed the case that in addition to being rivals, they were also a father and daughter, this would make the case for a historically formed opposition between Germany and Russia, which was so crucially revived in 1941, much

---

[51] On the connections between the Russian expatriate universities and the old imperial elites, see the papers of Mikhail Nikolaevich de Giers, the last Russian ambassador in Rome during the First World War. Mikhail de Giers papers, Box 21, Folder 1, Hoover Institution Archives, Stanford, California. See also Robert Paul Browder and Alexander Kerensky (eds.), *The Russian Provisional Government 1917 Documents*, vol. 1 (Stanford: Stanford University Press, 1961).

[52] Kozlov et al. (eds.), *The Last Diary of Tsaritsa Alexandra*, 29.

more complicated. Taube had also proved that the Baltic Ungern family had in fact, as the name suggests, originated from Hungary, a dynastic family of semi-sovereign powers, whose records demonstrate much closer ties between pre-Christian Lithuania and Russia. The sons of Prince Igor of the Russian epos belonged to this group.

Another one of Taube's clients for genealogical research was the philosopher Hermann Keyserling, who had settled in Germany in 1919, after the new Estonian government had expropriated his estate. Having arrived on a Nansen passport, he eventually chose to claim German citizenship. By the time the so-called 'Aryan paragraph' was brought into German legislation by the Nuremberg Laws of 1935, which demanded that all German citizens were required to be of Aryan race or risked losing citizenship, Keyserling, too, was required to prove his Aryan descent. As he wrote in a letter to a friend, the irony of the law was that it was particularly harsh on noble families who could prove their descent; German families with no official knowledge of Jewish ancestry, by contrast, could simply use a physiognomic test. Indeed, the Nazis introduced their own version of the Gotha and were engaged in transferring data, once it was proven, to the Edda book, a Nazi analogue to the Gotha. The new German laws required proof of racial purity until 1800. As Keyserling wrote to his relative, the demand to prove Aryan descent to 1800 may only be the first step, and to be absolutely sure Keyserling decided to prove his family back to the fifteenth century. In this process, he encountered the greatest difficulties trying to locate the relevant documents, since the main papers which satisfied the German authorities were marriage and baptism certificates, most of which were held either in Russia or in Estonia, which were now parts of the Soviet Union, where a number of churches and parishes were being looted or destroyed.

In fact, it is highly likely that Keyserling's maternal family had Jewish roots. The German ancestors of Hermann Keyserling's maternal line, the Cancrins (Latinized from Krebs), had migrated from Hesse to Nowgorod in the fifteenth century; one of his ancestors was a famed minister of finance in the Russian Empire who was Jewish. Despite the fact that in Russia at least, the Cancrins were thought to be Jewish, Keyserling managed to procure documents from a certain Nikolai Ikonnikov, a Russian nobleman who had fled from the October Revolution and lived in Paris.

> Dear Nikolai Flegontowitsch,
>   Excuse me for writing in German and not in Russian, which I have perfect command of, but I can only dictate in German, and my handwriting is not very legible.

> For the genealogical trees of my sons, I need some detailed information
> about my ancestors the Murawioffs, and Baron Michael Taube in Münster
> writes to me that I can obtain them from you. The mother of my paternal
> grandmother, the Countess Zenaide Keyserling born Countess Cancrin,
> daughter of the Russian minister of finance Count Georg Cancrin, was born
> a Murawioff. [. . .] Now we are lacking all data on the Murawioff family.
> We only know that it was an old family from Nowgorod and that the line of
> the Murawioffs to which I am related is the one of which it was said, she does
> not hang but she gets hanged. We still possess a necessaire which belonged
> to the Decembrist Artamon Murawioff, which he woodcut in his Siberian
> exile.[53]

Nikolai Ikonnikov, who was the regional head of a nobles' association in
the Saratov province, had a brief stint as the administrator of sugar
provision in Bolshevik Russia. He had used this position to help fugitive
aristocrats escape to the west, a dangerous undertaking which he described
in memoirs of his own, published in Paris in 1933.[54] Ikonnikov was running
a business offering genealogical services, based on the rather substantial
library and documentary collections of the Russian nobility, which he had
managed to take with him on his flight to France. Against a fee, Ikonnikov
provided Keyserling with a list of his 300 ancestors of the Muraviev and
Cancrin family, and brief descriptions of anything known about them.
The fact that none of the documents mentioned the word Jew appears to
have sufficed for Keyserling's Aryan record to be approved.

Keyserling's search for his genealogical tree also took him to his native
villages in Courland, where he had to find marriage registers. These
investigations confirmed that his ancestors had many faiths – Protestant,
Catholic, Russian Orthodox – but that none had been known to be Jewish.
'Dear Aunt Jenny', Keyserling wrote on 9 July 1935 to the Baroness Jenny
Pilar von Pilchau, who was still living in Pärnu, in Estonia:

> Some serious matter today. Yesterday a highly exacerbating Aryan restric-
> tion was legislated in Germany for the admission to study, which also affects
> Germans by descent outside of the Reich, that is also your grand children.
> Only those who can prove the absence of any Jewish blood until 1700 will be
> sure to be allowed to study. [. . .] The Bismarcks had difficulties with it for
> two years. It was argued that the Whiteheads had Jewish blood, which of
> course was not the case. But it was not so easy to find the necessary

[53] Keyserling to Nikolai Ikonnikov, 16 June 1937, in HKN A-4 Ahnenforschung. Ikonnikov replied on
19 June 1937 in Russian, attaching a list of about 300 Murawioffs and their relatives and apologizing
for the incomplete information, since many documents were inaccessible to him.

[54] Nikolai Ikonnikov, 'Piatsot dnei: sekretnaia sluzhba v tylu bolshevikov, 1918–1919', in *Russkoe
Proshloe*, 7 (1996), 43–105.

certificate, because it was in Gibraltar. [...] Now, of course we are all absolutely pure Aryans. But I do not know the Pilar genealogial tree in detail.[55]

Then Keyserling asked his aunt for documents, which could help him acquire an 'Ahnenpass', a certificate of immaculate descent. All in all, this process took him nearly four years. Keyserling and his wife then had to prove that her family, the Bismarcks, was also purely Aryan. It was suspected that a relative in England, a certain Whitehead, who lived in London in the eighteenth century, may have been a rabbi.[56]

But to call genealogical research a 'private' endeavour would belie the ideological context in which issues of pedigree were discussed in Europe in the 1930s. When the Nazis introduced new laws concerning citizenship in 1935, nobles who were German citizens faced a particular problem. Unlike middle-class Germans who could not be expected to show proof of descent from centuries back and were instead expected to be examined by craniologists who measured their sculls, nobles were required to provide proof of their heritage as well as proof of the absence of Jewish blood since at least as far back as 1750. In the mid-1930s, this posed particular problems for those nobles whose family papers were held in areas where the nobility was violently abolished during the revolutions, such as the Baltic region. In lieu of legal documents, some corporate and familial associations of nobles tried to publish their own historical genealogies, in which they fervently reconstructed their history up to the thirteenth century, highlighting its German character.[57] One such history was the Book of the Keyserlings, published by Fischer in Berlin in 1937. In his introduction to a book published in 1939, the *Genealogical Table of Famous Germans*, Baltic Baron Otto Magnus von Stackelberg wrote a piece entitled 'The Ancestry of the Philosopher Count Hermann Keyserling,' in which he argued that in Hermann Keyserling's ancestry you can find most of the German and

---

[55] Keyserling to Baronin Jenny Pilar von Pilchau, Darmstadt, 9 July 1935, in HKN A-4, Ahnenforschung.

[56] Keyserling's documents contain a copy of the certificate issued by the 'Sachverständige für Rasseforschung beim Reichsministerium des Innern' on 8 November 1933, that the alleged Jewish ancestor of Bismarck, so claimed by the *Semigothasches Genealogisches Taschenbuch*, 1914, 198, was in fact an English reverend. Berlin, 8 November 1933.

[57] See, for example, Eduard von Dellingshausen, *Die Entstehung, Entwicklung und Aufbauende Tätigkeit der Baltischen Ritterschaften* (Langensalza: H. Beyer, 1928); Otto Magnus von Stackelberg, *Genealogisches Handbuch Der Estländischen Ritterschaft* (Görlitz: Verl. für Sippenforschung und Wappenkunde Starke, 1930); Oskar Stavenhagen, *Genealogisches Handbuch der Kurländischen Ritterschaft* (Görlitz: Verl. für Sippenforschung und Wappenkunde Starke, 1939).

Nordic imperial and royal dynasties.[58] As well as proving Aryan descent, in the course of his research Keyserling even proved that he was related to the Scaliger and the Visconti families.[59] By this time, the Gotha book, the aristocratic union and even the Nazi follow-up of the Gotha ceased to be acknowledged by the authorities. An article published in the *Frankfurter Zeitung* of 6 February 1935 emphasized that

> the fact of entry in the *EDDA* does *not* give a guarantee for the proof of German blood in the sense of §13 REG [Reichserbhofgesetz]. The Reich and Prussian Minister for Food Supply and Agriculture has therefore ordered that applicants who are already listed in the Iron Book of German Nobility (*EDDA*) have to submit documentary evidence on their person reaching back to 1 January 1800 ... just as *all other applicants*.[60]

Having found all the documents, the Keyserlings had to contact the department for foreign currency in order to be allowed to transfer payments for genealogical services abroad, writing letters all of which ended with 'Heil Hitler'.

When it comes to groups or individuals that lost or reconfigured their identities, such as diasporic ethnicities, political or economic refugees, we usually think of examples of inferior social status: the Jewish or African diaspora, for example; the economic or political emigration from Europe to the Americas in the nineteenth century, and such like. Few studies have focused on diasporic identities among elites, cultural or economics.[61] But diaspora is equally applicable to elites, as the case of the Barons shows.[62] Elites, too, can be seen as a 'segment of a people living

---

[58] See, for example, *Ahnentafel berühmter Deutscher*, ed. Zentralstelle für Deutsche Personen- und Familiengeschichte, 1939. Introduction by Otto Magnus Stackelberg, typescript in HKN, A-4, Ahnenerbe.

[59] Kessler, 30 January 1935, in Kessler, *Diaries*, vol. 9.

[60] 'Abstammungsnachweis für Adlige beim Erbhof- Zulassungsverfahren', Beiblatt der Frankfurter Zeitung, 6 II 1935, in HKN A-4, 194.02.

[61] For a great example of elite group cosmopolitanism, see Maurizio Isabella, *Risorgimento in Exile. Italian Émigrés and the Liberal International in the Post-Napoleonic Era* (Oxford: Oxford University Press, 2009).

[62] William Safran, 'Diasporas in Modern Societies: Myths of Homeland and Return', in *A Journal of Transnational Studies*, 1:1 (Spring, 1991), 83–99, 83–84; Orlando Patterson, *Slavery and Social Death: A Comparative Study* (Cambridge, Mass.: Harvard University Press, 1982); Gilroy, *The Black Atlantic*; Kim D. Butler, 'Defining Diaspora, Refining a Discourse', in *Diaspora: A Journal of Transnational Studies*, 10:2 (Fall 2001), 189–219; Elliott P. Skinner, 'The Dialectic between Diasporas and Homelands', in *Global Dimensions of the African Diaspora*, ed. Joseph E. Harris (Washington: Howard University Press, 1982), 17–45; Anthony D. Smith, *Theories of Nationalism* (New York: Harper, 1971); Robin Cohen, 'New Roles for Diasporas in International Relations', in *Journal of Transnational Studies*, 14:1 (Spring 2005), 179–183; Robin Cohen, *Global Diasporas, An Introduction* (London: Routledge, 1997).

outside the homeland'.[63] In the case of the Baltic knights, their point of focus for their eventual home lay not so much in their historical places of origin, as in their mythical place of destination: the grave of Jesus at the Temple of the Holy Sepulchre, which these knights' ancestors had pledged to conquer in Jerusalem. In a sense, the Baltic Barons, then, were Zionists centuries before Theodor Herzl had made Zionism into a rallying cry for eastern Europe's suffering Jews.

Post-imperial typewriters: modernity and the gender of memory

Among Taube's multilingual, multi-alphabet correspondence, one exchange with an old friend, Baron Uexküll von Gildenband, who was based in Switzerland and in Athens in the interwar period, is particularly noteworthy. Written on typewriters and by hand, in Paris, Switzerland, Germany, and Greece, Taube and Uexküll, these two friends in exile preferred to think of themselves back to Byzantine times: the dates of their letters dropped the 1 and wrote '930' instead of 1930, '932' instead of 1932, and so on. Within their letters, they exchanged jokes in Russian and typed in Latin transcription, in handwritten Russian, and in German and French. They would include Russian jokes in a German text and French jokes in a Russian text. They would wish each other Happy Easter in the Orthodox fashion ('Khristos voskrese'), even though at least one of them was Catholic. They would also parody German Nazis by writing 'Heil Hitler'. Some letters comprised sketches of genealogical trees and heraldry.

Other letters discussed the current financial crisis, the devaluation of currency, or the decline of good manners among the youth. Thus at one point, Ungern sought advice on how to address a countess. Taube recommends the title 'Reichsgräfin', even though in his day a more appropriate title would be comtesse. 'Tempora mutantur i teper kakie-to novye for-muly' [Times are changing and there are some new formulas around].[64]

---

[63] Walker Connor, 'The Impact of Homelands Upon Diasporas', in *Modern Diasporas in International Politics*, ed. Gabriel Sheffer (New York: St. Martin's, 1986), 16–46; James Casteel, 'The Politics of Diaspora: Russian German Émigré Activists in Interwar Germany', in *German Diasporic Experiences: Identity, Migration, and Loss*, ed. Mathias Schulze et al. (Waterloo: Wilfrid Laurier University Press, 2008), 117–130; Pieter Judson, 'When Is a Diaspora Not a Diaspora?', in *Heimat Abroad*, ed. Krista O'Donnell, Renate Bridenthal, and Nany Reagin (Ann Arbor: Michigan University Press, 2005), 219–247.

[64] Keyserling to Üxküll von Gildenband, 31 May 1931, Mikhail von Taube papers, Special Collections, Columbia University, New York: 'çto kasaetsia grafini U.-G., to, moe skromnoe mnenie: na konverte napischite po nemezki – Ihrer Hoch- und Wohlgeboren, Reichsgräfin etc ... W priglasitelnych na swadbu dočeri biletach Eux U.ßG napeçatal « ... Ihrer Tochter, Reichsgräfin imiarek ». W moe wremia w Wene baryschen imenovali Komtessen, a ne

As they well knew, the real ending of this idiomatic expression is different though: 'Tempura mutantur et nos mutamur in illis – times change and we change in them'. It was this conclusion that they sought to resist by means of resorting to the practice of genealogy as a way of constantly reaffirming their true self.

> Polagaiu, cto wychod v svet wtorogo toma naschei istorii ne predwiditsia w 931 godu, no moe pismo raswiashet Wam ruki et Vous pourrez faire appel à la générosité aussitôt que tous les matériels pour l'édition wtorogo toma budu druckreif. [. . .] odnim slovom ia daiu Wam carte blanche w etom otnoshenii.[65]

Mikhail Taube kept his friend updated about the progress of his genealogy, with its roots in Byzantine history, in Russian, French, and German simultaneously, with the main threat woven in Russian. 'I assume that the appearance of your second volume of our history is not to be anticipated in the year 931', he began in Latin transliteration of his Russian. Expressions of politeness were left in French, whereas technical terms relating to book production, in this case '*druckreif*' (ready to print), were left in German. In another letter, multilinguality appears to be simultaneously the expression of a tragic sentiment of decline and a critique of ideology. Says Baron Uexküll, writing from Athens, spelt in Latin script but Russian pronunciation: 'Mes tantes (89, 78 et 75 ans) évacuées à Danzig en 5 jours. Finis dominiii baltici après 7 siècles. Les Dünafürsten remplacés par Molot i serp' [My aunts (89, 78 and 75) to be evacuated to Danzig in five hours. The end of the Baltic empire after seven centuries. The Princes of the Duna replaced by Hammer and sickle] [Fig. 23].

This hyperbolic use of semiotics to describe a rapid loss of power is illuminating because it shows to what extent the Baltic elite lamented the loss of their power over the region, the empire of the 'Princes of the Duna', more than they lamented the decline of the Russian Empire. The semiotic appropriation of aristocratic emblems by the new Soviet state was all the more bitter for these masters of genealogy as the Soviet leadership had recruited artists to design their new emblems, the Hammer and Sickle, without any in-depth understanding of the practice of heraldry. Thus the

---

Reichsgräfin. Tempora mutantur i teper kakia-to nowyia formuly. Po franz. Wy, koneçno, obratilis by k grafine s « Madame ». Ia polagal by, çto obrascenie Hochgeehrte Gräfin Uxkull bylo by ssamoe prawilnoe.' See also Üxküll to Keyserling, 6 November 1939: 'Mes tantes (89, 78 et 75 ans) evacuees à Danzig en 5 jours. Finis dominie baltici après 7 siècles. Les Dünafürsten remplacés par Molot i serp. Hommages, amitiès. Votre devoué Uxkull'. G rue Patr. Joachim, 27 Afiny, Mikhail von Taube papers.
[65] Uexküll to Mikhail von Taube, 11 March 1931, Mikhail von Taube papers.

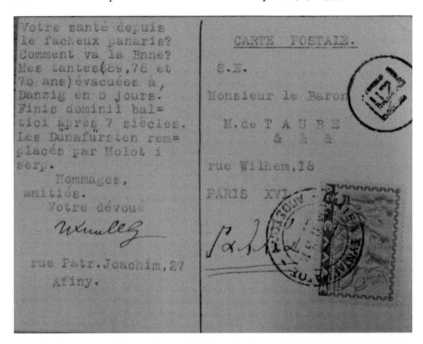

Figure 23 Baron Üxküll von Gildenband to Baron von Taube, 31 May 1931, in
Mikhail von Taube papers, Bakhmeteff Archive, Columbia University Special
Collections

hammer and sickle became a non-dialectical symbol, a brand showing the
unity of workers and peasants; by contrast, the animals and other symbols
typically shown on the emblems of old families are there because they are
symbols of the powers that had been defeated by the power bearing the
insignia.[66] The intertextual irony in the private correspondence of the
Baltic Barons was a kind of 'elite subalternism' in response to the hegemonic use of chivalric symbolism by organizations such as the VchK, the
Soviet security organization founded by another Balt, Feliks Dzerzhinsky,
and the Hammer and Sickle emblem itself. The new emblems of honour

---

[66] On the design of the hammer and sickle, see the work of Viktor Narbut, as discussed after his death
in the mid-1920s by Viktor Lukomskii and others. There was a commemorative album of his designs
of heraldic symbols for the Soviet Union, published in Kiev in 1926. *Giorgi Narbut. Posmertna
vystavka tvoriv* (Kiev, 1926), but I have not been able to locate it. For more references, see http://
sovet.geraldika.ru/print/6069, accessed 1 June 2013. For a philosophy of the symbol within and
beyond a Soviet context, see the rival views of Alexei Losev, *Znak, simvol, mif* (Moscow: Izd-tvo
moskovskogo un-ta, 1982); and Yuri Lotman, *Semiotika kul'tury i poniatie teksta* (Tallinn: University
Press, 1992).

for a proletarian class had become emblems of dishonour and uncivilization for the former elites.

The typed correspondence between these Baltic Barons was a response to two conditions with which the Barons had been confronted in the twentieth century. One was their status as stateless citizens, a dramatic fall from grace after having been close to ruling one of Europe's largest empires. The other was their status as a potential threat to the ideal of a new nobility that the Nazis were conjuring up with their theory of the Aryan race. For the Baltic Barons, this was like their worst nightmare come true. A paradigm derived from Herder and Saussure, the growing enthusiasm for vernacular cultures became a force for anti-imperial resistance. Paradoxically, in their home region, the myth of the Indo-Germanic race had thus served to undermine, rather than support the power of the oldest Germanic nobility in the region.

The social function of typewriters among this aristocratic elite suggests another sense in which culture remains a divisive feature in the age of modernity. It is also divisive in terms of gender. Keyserling's letters and works were typed by his wife Goedela and are therefore bearing an imprint of Prussian traditions: here, aristocratic ladies would increasingly take on the fashion of typing works dictated by their husbands. In fact, men would not typically learn how to type. In Britain, too, one of the first typists was Queen Victoria, for instance. Throughout his life, Keyserling depended on Goedela's skills as a typist because, as his correspondence partners frequently lamented, his handwriting was very bad. The moments when it becomes visible in the text that he did not type it himself are few and far between, but particularly noteworthy, as in the letter to Ikonnikov, which is preceded by the apology: 'Excuse me for writing in German and not in Russian, which I have perfect command of, but I can only dictate in German, and my handwriting is not very legible.'[67]

Contrary to what many theorists of modernity from Heidegger to Wiezbicka have said, this technological aspect of modernity did not lead to a greater uniformity of cultural consciousness, of 'everyone looking the same'.[68] This can even be seen in widely known documents of post-imperial transition, like the treaty of Brest-Litovsk. The text of the treaty, which was eventually signed by five parties, made more common features amidst this heterogeneity visible: the German and Hungarian signatories

---

[67] Keyserling to Nikolai Ikonnikov, 16 June 1937, HKN.
[68] Martin Heidegger, 'The Hand and the Typewriter' (1942–43), in *Gramophone, Film, Typewriter*, ed. Friedrich Kittler (Stanford: Stanford University Press, 1999).

had signed a typed text, the Ottoman section was written in classical calligraphy, and two more columns in Bulgarian and Russian were written in plain Cyrillic.[69] The dislocation of this revolutionary period affirmed differences in social position and inverted others. Thus paradoxically, in the peace treaty of Brest-Litovsk, the typewriter became an instrument of the old regimes.

Likewise, the Baltic barons' typed reconstructions of genealogical heritage reveal a gradual process of identity deconstruction. Their old sense of self as Crusaders who had become colonizers of eastern Europe was being deflated. They became a modern diaspora, stigmatized in the Baltic land for being German, in Soviet official discourse, for being aristocratic, and in western Europe, for being Russian. To contemporaries, their attempt to express themselves easily made the impression of a kind of aphasia.[70] Here, archaic features coexist with ironic commentaries on present ideologies, as the 'Heil Hitler' appears along with the more heartfelt 'Happy Easter'.[71] It demonstrates also the feature which linguists note as 'instances of deviation from the norms of either language which occurs in the speech of bilinguals as a result of their familiarity with more than one language'.[72]

The form of theorizing the international that the Baltic Barons had traditionally developed rested on the patriarchal order of Europe's imperial elites, which was in tension with dynastic power that could tolerate both male and female lines of succession. Not only were their estates passed down, whole, as patrimony of their eldest sons. Their family names, too, only encoded a male pedigree of history. In the female line, such passing on was more indirect. Daughters would lose their fathers' names and gain new names; wives would become the typists who would eventually carry the memory of the Baltic Barons to a wider market.

---

[69] Treaty of Brest-Litovsk, 3 March 1918. Facsimile at www.1000dokumente.de/index.html?c=doku ment_ru&dokument=0011_bre&l=de, accessed 5 July 2015.

[70] On heredity as a type of memory, the continuity between psychic and physical memory, and forgetting, Théodoule Ribot, *Les Maladies de la mémoire* (Paris: Alcan, 1895), 49ff, 164–165; Sigmund Freud, *Zur Auffassung der Aphasien. Eine kritische Studie* (Leipzig and Vienna: Deuticke, 1891); and Roman Jakobson, *Kindersprache, Aphasie und allgemeine Lautgesetze* (1941) (Frankfurt: Suhrkamp, 1969); on multilingualism and trauma, see Jacqueline Amati Mehler, Simona Argentieri, and Jorge Canestri (eds.), *The Babel of the Unconscious Mother Tongue and Foreign Languages in the Psychoanalytic Dimension* (Madison, Conn.: International Universities Press, 1993).

[71] Anna Wiezbicka, *Semantics, Culture and Cognition: Universal Human Concepts in Culture-Specific Configurations* (Oxford: Oxford University Press, 1992).

[72] On code-switching and language loss, see Uriel Weinreich, *Languages in Contact: Findings and Problems* (The Hague: Mouton, 1953); Steven G. Kellmann, *The Translingual Imagination* (Lincoln: University of Nebraska Press, 2000).

As a historical diaspora, the Baltic nobility, like many other noble families, had turned estrangement into a marker of distinction. Erving Goffman's theory of 'stigmatization' as a constructed entity has invited generations of social theorists to think of this kind of marking as an act of making the other inferior to oneself. But as Sofia Tchouikina and Longina Jakubowska have shown, markers of distinction follow the same logic.[73]

Reading the archive of this strange grouping of exiles is almost like listening in on a conversation among people who are speaking with an inflection and in a dialect that is no longer spoken today. In the end, Taube's hypothesis about the relationship between the two 'Greats', Catherine of Russia and Frederick II of Prussia, remained unconfirmed. Taube died in 1961 in Paris. In 2013 I was able to obtain a copy of his typescript on Catherine's genealogy via a major online second-hand bookseller from an antiquarian bookstore located in New Zealand.[74] I have been unable to verify the archival sources that Taube wanted to research; they were likely lost in the war, confiscated either by Alfred Rosenberg's department of historical research or by the Soviet Army in 1945. Another copy of the typescript can also be found at Columbia University's special collections in New York, where part of Taube's archive is now based, which Columbia had bought in the 1970s. Taube's pre-1917 archive remains in Russia.

Despite the inconclusive end to his career as a lawyer and a historian, the history of Taube's life in exile, as well as that of his archive, reflects more than just the fate of an unusual individual. What it shows is the social process by which a memory of empire was produced and shared in multiple languages, on typewriters and by hand, in private and public contexts, and in different cities such as Berlin, Uppsala, and especially Paris. Unlike most fugitives, these intellectuals projected themselves not just to their old home country, but into an entirely different epoch. The images they conjured up were images of multiple ruins of what they considered to be a lost European civilization. This is why, in this particular tragedy, like many in Paris, they felt closer to Antigone than to Creon. They traced their titles further back than the ruling dynasties or the new national governments of their day, back to the history of the Holy Roman Empire of the German

---

[73] Longina Jakubowska, *Patrons of History. Nobility, Capital and Political Transitions in Poland* (London: Ashgate, 2012); Sofia Tchouikina, Dvorianskaia pamiat': 'byvshye' v sovetskom gorode (Leningrad, 1920e–30e gody) (St. Petersburg: Izd-vo Evropeiskogo universiteta v StPb, 2006).

[74] Michael Taube, 'The Birth Secret of Catherine II and Its Political Significance', typescript marked uncorrected, my archive (acquired on abebooks.com from New Zealand bookseller), probably a translation by Nicholas Danilow.

Nation, effectively a Franco-Germanic conglomerate of states with a dominant German cultural tradition, which had ceased to exist by a whim of Napoleon's revolutionary fervour in 1806. By 1941, the Nazis were turning Germany into a Third Reich and stepping in Napoleon's footsteps on their Russian campaign. In this process, Paris itself had turned from the capital of Europe's refugees and the international struggle against fascism into a peripheral city of a republic under Nazi occupation. Against this backdrop, the Baltic Barons, descendants of the Crusaders, could do little else but idealize the internationalism of Europe's second Byzantine Empire by dropping the '1' from the years '1939–45'.

PART III

Phantom empires

In Europe in the mid-1930s, a selective memory of the imperial past shaped new mass ideologies as well as the ideas of much smaller social groups. Many Europeans, one could say, not only suffered the 'phantom pains' of imperial decline. They also tried to reassemble elements of knowledge from the historical past of Europe to build up the faces of future empires. In the final two chapters, I reconstruct how the ideas of the mostly liberal fraction of the European elites, which I discussed earlier in this book, related to both trends.

Chapter 6 focuses on the emergence of a racial memory of empire. Looking at the rise of Nazi ideology through the lens of social history foregrounds the importance of common forms of imperial memory, which facilitated the social recognition of newcomers such as Nazi ideologue Alfred Rosenberg. Rome is introduced as the capital of a transnational neo-imperial sensibility, and Munich is a site where the ideologues of National Socialism first gained prominence. The chapter is concerned with the question of how elements of aristocratic identity, such as the idea of pedigree, became absorbed in Nazi ideology.

In 1944, the Nazi propaganda journal *Signal* produced a mental map of Europe [Fig. 24]. On this map, we can see an abstract genealogical tree superimposed over a map of Europe. Its central lineage leads from ancient Greece to a generic Aryan European family in the present. Two side lineages, with notable influences from Jewish culture and Orthodoxy, point to the United States and the Soviet Union, respectively. In reconstructing the social relationships between the Nazis and the representatives of the old Germanic nobility in the 1930s, I want to establish the difference between the racial and the familial use of pedigree in Nazi ideology and in the genealogical practice of Habsburg and Baltic nobility.[1]

---

[1] Joseph Deniker, *The Races of Man: an Outline of Anthropology and Ethnography* (New York: Charles Scribner, 1913).

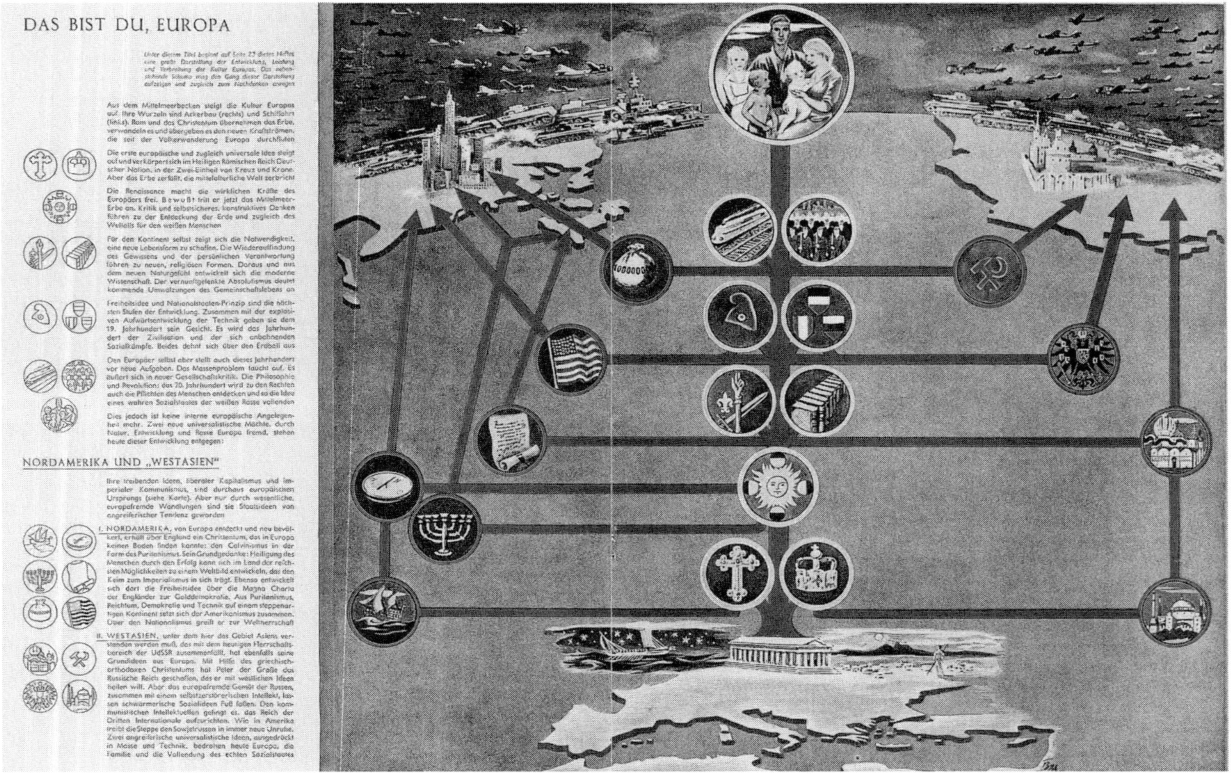

Figure 24 'Map of Europe's Cultural and Historical Development', in M. Clauss (ed.) *Signal*, 11, 1944. From Facsimile *Querschnitte durch Zeitungen und Zeitschriften*, 14 (Munich, Bern, Vienna: Scherz, 1969)

Chapter 7 looks at a very different nostalgia for empire, which was characteristic of a small transnational elite community whose cultural centres were Paris and London. At the centre of this configuration was the Bloomsbury group. Its members associated imperial sensibility with a kind of multiculturalism, which they believed was threatened not only by the rise of fascism but also by narrow-minded nationalism elsewhere in Europe. In the chapter, I hope to recover the extent to which some of the German cosmopolitans discussed earlier in the book had influenced the nature of imperial memory in these circles.

CHAPTER 6

Knights of many faces
The dream of chivalry and its dreamers

When, in November 1918, Alfred Voldemarovich Rosenberg, subject of the Russian Empire, returned to his hometown of Reval after two years in Moscow and in Crimea, the only thing that had remained unchanged was the city's architecture. The name of the city was now not Reval, but Tallinn; the state it was in was no longer the Russian Empire, but Estonia. Alfred Rosenberg was the subject of a non-existent empire. His plan to join the administration of the German army occupying Livonia, or the land 'Ober-Ost', as they called it, was futile: after the collapse of the German Empire, the German army, which had been victorious against the Russian Empire from the start of the war, was beginning to withdraw.[1] In twenty-two German states, new governments had just proclaimed a republican order, and all questions of citizenship were suspended, so that Rosenberg could not hope to obtain the citizenship of any other country either.

Rosenberg's political career began at this moment with a public speech hosted by his student fraternity in Reval about the Jewish conspiracy in the Russian revolution. It ended twenty-seven years later, with death by hanging at Nuremberg's Court for Human Rights. The scale of civilian destruction under the regime to which his ideas provided legitimacy was so unprecedented that he and the core of his fellow party members were tried under an altogether new criminal code: 'crimes against humanity'. Rosenberg, an engineer by training and historian of Europe by vocation, had contributed to a system of thought, which the international legal community deemed planetary in terms of its scale of destruction to human lives and to existing legal norms of more than one nation.

---

[1] *Das Land Ober-Ost. Deutsche Arbeit in den Verwaltungsgebieten Kurland, Litauen und Bialystok-Grodno* (Stuttgart: DVA, 1917); see also Arnold Zweig, *Einsetzung eines Königs* (Amsterdam: Querido, 1937).

One of the questions that historians have been asking themselves ever since is this: How was it possible that a political regime accorded to itself such a degree of licence in breaking norms of national and international law? Imperial decline was, if not a cause, certainly the necessary circumstance behind this radicalization, which occurred when the imperial city states lost their special status. In this period, ideas of 'special' legislative frameworks, which were opposed to the principles of equality, gained new attraction. During the Great War, the Middle Ages had become fashionable among an entire generation of disoriented Europeans. The special role of cavalry on the eastern front was one of the triggers for this return to the classic ideal of the knight. In the Baltic region, chivalric dreams had particular appeal among the educated middle classes, whose representatives identified with different parties in medieval struggles between Livonian Knights and Lithuanian Dukes, Teutonic Knights and Russian Princes, which went on from the thirteenth to the fifteenth centuries. As we have seen in the chapter on the Baltic Barons, the chivalric model of exclusivity associated with such organizations as the Teutonic Knights still persisted, as the knightly orders continued to exist until the 1930s. At the same time, the cities developed their own cult of identity, with merchant guilds rivalling the exclusivity of old Crusaders' lineages and competing with them for favours of the current ruling imperial dynasties.

During the last years of the Great War, Rosenberg had been a student at Riga's Polytechnic School, which had been evacuated to Moscow while the German army occupied Livonia. He spent the winter of 1916 and 1917 in a suburb of Moscow, reading Chamberlain, Balzac, and Dostoyevsky. Never enlisting in the army, Rosenberg nonetheless witnessed the Russian Civil War in Moscow and also in Crimea. Here, another Baltic German, Baron Wrangel, a general who had distinguished himself on Russia's Galician front against the Austrians, formed a resistance army against the Bolsheviks, the nucleus of what is now known as the 'white army'.[2]

In this time of uncertainty, Rosenberg's most stable affiliation was not with a state organization but with his university fraternity, Rubonia. The fraternities at the universities of Reval, Dorpat, and Riga were now all based in different states, and the communities that made them up aspired to different citizenships, but individual memberships had remained intact. In 1918, Rubonia was to be his first and last point of call before he

---

[2] See the biography by Ernst Piper, *Hitlers Chefideologe* (Munich: Karl Blessing, 2005).

would begin a new life in Germany. Less than ten years later, Rosenberg became the co-founder of a new Germanic order that would fulfil the dreams of the German crusaders that had been crushed at the battle of Tannenberg of 1214. In 1934, 700 years after the Livonian order had been defeated at Tannenberg and twenty years after the imperial German army under Hindenburg defeated the Russians at the same place, he and fellow members of the National Socialist party gathered at Marienburg near Gdansk to consolidate their commitment to a new German Empire under the leadership of a new Teutonic Order.[3] In Germany, in 1934, Rosenberg wrote admiringly how in the Middle Ages, 'knights were departing Germany into the wider world again and again in pursuit of their phantasy of a world empire and the conquest of Jerusalem'.[4] The motion that began during the Russian Civil War propelled Rosenberg from his intended career as a civic engineer in one of the minor, yet culturally advanced cities of the Russian Empire into the core of a political movement that for a few years would control a territory reaching from the Crimea in the south to the Baltic in the north, from Moscow in the east to Normandy in the west. It was, in other words, a journey from empire to empire.

Twenty years after his departure from Reval, Rosenberg became one of the chief ideologues of the Nazi party, which meant having one of the largest budgets for culture at his disposal available to a government minister of his generation. The Nazi project was a new 'Order State', led by a small circle of vanguard representatives devoted to a charismatic leader like the Teutonic Knights were to their grand master. Men like Rosenberg, as well as Heinrich Himmler, Martin Bormann, Josef Goebbels, and others, saw themselves as the new knights, whose shared fidelity to their leader, they believed, could outshine their mutual rivalries. They held smaller conventions in historic locations such as the ruined castle of the Livonian Knights, Marienburg Castle, when it was still in Polish hands, and in Weimar, while its recently deposed princely family was still present. These revived Teutonic Knights had recourse to the highest technologies of modern mediation. Deliberately opposing the idea of a secret order, which they associated with Freemasonry and the Jesuits, their ideas and the meaning they attached to their flag, a swastika, would soon reach the widest possible public thanks to radio and sound film.

---

[3] Alfred Rosenberg, *Der deutsche Ordensstaat: Ein neuer Abschnitt in der Entwicklung des nationalso-zialistischen Staatsgedankens* (Munich: Zentralverlag der NSDAP, Eher, 1934).
[4] Rosenberg, *Ordensstaat*, 3; G.K. Chesterton, *The New Jerusalem* (New York: G.H. Doran, 1921), 31.

The scope of his cultural activities reached from the smallest German town to the newly occupied territories of western, southern, and eastern Europe. The department named after him would be responsible for the collection and public presentation of information on Germanic heritage and that of its enemies. He was one of the organizers of the Degenerate Art and music exhibitions in Munich and Düsseldorf, alongside major historical exhibitions on European history. Under his auspices, the Nazi party sponsored local and folk culture as well. After the occupation of Paris and parts of France, Rosenberg's team organized the spoliation of artworks and archives, chiefly belonging to Jewish families who were resident or had moved to Paris. A second strand of Rosenberg's career started with the expansion towards the east, when, in 1943, Rosenberg became Minister for the Eastern Territories. He saw his life project as a restoration of the project began by the Teutonic Knights in the Middle Ages until their crushing defeat by a Polish army of 1415. The period from 1415 to 1914, in his view, was a dark time for Germanic culture, whose true home was in the Nordic Middle Ages. But the German victory against Russia at the Battle of Tannenberg in 1914 – the main victory in a war Germany had lost – began to 'right' the historical wrongs that Rosenberg identified with the entire period of European history that was associated with republicanism and the emergence of eastern Europe's small states.

The new Nazi Order was an attempt to revive a new Middle Ages against what the Nazis considered the subversion of this tradition: the Enlightenment associations they associated with the Freemasons, for instance, with their lofty ideas of human rights.[5] By 1945, of the inner circle of Nazi 'knights', about one-third would be killed by internal agreement for failing to live up to the ideal, and one-third would commit suicide. The closest to Rosenberg's heritage movement, Baron Kurt von Behr, would die from a mixture of champagne and cyanide at Castle Banz, one of the bastions of looted art. The remaining third – including Rosenberg himself – would die by hanging for a new kind of crime: crimes against humanity. The language in which the new legislation was formulated, in a desperate attempt to match the scale of human destruction masterminded by the Nazi movement, hearkened back to the French Revolution and those ideals of humanity which Rosenberg himself most deeply despised.

[5] On the debate between enlightenment anti-enlightenment concepts of the political in German *Staatsrecht* which preceded Nazi ideology, see Duncan Kelly, 'Revisiting the Rights of Man: Georg Jellinek on Rights and the State', in *Law and History Review*, 22:3 (Autumn, 2004), 493–529.

In some ways Rosenberg's ideas were not extraordinary but typical of his time, and particularly, his place of origin. In his memoirs, Rosenberg outlines the path of a middling sort of person, thrown out of his orbit by radical social and geopolitical changes of his time.[6] This should not be interpreted as saying that the sort of 'evil' to which his regime contributed was necessarily banal, as Hannah Arendt said of the lower functionaries of the Holocaust machine. Rather, what was common was the ideological make-up that these actions received. Given the fact that life in interwar eastern Europe is largely familiar to us today through the pens of Holocaust survivors or émigrés from the Baltic region occupied by the Soviet Union, it is almost shocking to see the extent to which Rosenberg's impressions of life in a Baltic city in the 1900s and 1910s echo the way these other representatives of the urban middle classes, not only of German but also of Russian, Jewish as well as of Lithuanian heritage, saw their cities.[7]

Beyond the confines of this region of eastern Europe, the new interest in 'barbarism', imagined as the opposite of feeble, civilizing spirit of the French and the Norman, was attractive to a whole generation of new Europeans. The Russian fascination with its Scythian past, the British fascination with Celtic heritage, and the emergence of neo-masculine movements such as the Boy Scouts all form part of the same tradition. Moreover, the Baltic rediscovery of its medieval heritage was closely entangled with the neo-medievalism of British and Russian intellectuals. Lithuania had one of the earliest chapters of the World Scouting organiza- tion started in Britain by Baden-Powell, and also founded on a chivalric ideal.[8] In 1932, Baden-Powell even travelled there to receive the Order of the Grand Duke Gediminas of Lithuania for his 75th birthday from the president of the short-lived republic. The honour codes of neo-chivalric youth associations like the Scouts were the predecessors not only of the SS, or Schutzstaffel, but also of the Soviet Comsomol, as well as some dissident organizations fighting against the Nazi and the Soviet regimes and main- taining identities in exile.[9]

---

[6] Rosenberg's own account of his life, which he left in prison, remained largely inaccessible to a wider public until several decades after his death. Even today, it is available only in digital form, put online by communities with Neo-Nazi leanings, which utilize the neutrality of the San Franscisco-based digitized resource archive.org for this purpose.

[7] Isaiah Berlin, 'In Conversation with Steven Lukes', in *Salmagundi*, 120 (Fall 1998), 52–134; Sergei Eisenstein, *Beyond the Stars*, 4 vols. (London: BFI, 1996).

[8] On Baden-Powell in Palanga, see http://knygynas.skautai.net/knygynas/lithscouting/sko3_.pdf, accessed 5 March 2014.

[9] Chris Manias, *Race, Science, and the Nation: Reconstructing the Ancient Past in Britain* (London: Routledge, 2013). On Baden-Powell's influence of the Soviet Comsomol, see www.zpu-journal.ru

Nearly a decade before the infamous Stalinist purges reached their apogee in 1937, it was Feliks Dzerzhinsky, a native of this region, who set in motion that machinery of purging the revolution from its internal enemies that had guaranteed him lasting fame in Soviet commemoration and the nickname 'Knight of the Revolution' from his successors.[10] Dzerzhinsky's brainchild was an organization called the 'VChK', or 'All-Russian Emergency Committee', a unit that combined intelligence and military work in identifying counter-revolutionary elements from within the ranks of the Bolshevik party as well as across Soviet society. Its symbol was an emblem: a sword crossed on a shield, covered by another emblem, the newly established hammer and sickle, as symbols of the worker and peasant. This double emblem was minted and given for the first time as a decoration of honours in 1922, the fifth anniversary of the VChK.[11]

People of their circle had grown up reading Walter Scott's adventures in the Scottish highlands. In the Russian Empire, the first translations had appeared as early as 1828 and were a common presence in a classical eighteenth-century estate library.[12] They later also became supplements to the popular journal *Vokrug sveta* [Around the World, an imitation of the Parisian *Revue du Monde*]. Closer to home, an important narrative was the story of the despicable behaviour of Russian imperialists during the uprisings of the mid-nineteenth century, chiefly embodied by Count 'Muraviov, the hangman'. This illegitimate form of hegemony was personified by the Russian governor general of Vilna, Nikolai Muraviev, who hanged over a hundred people and deported nearly a thousand to Siberia during the so-called Polish Uprising of 1863. An album, published in Polish in the Habsburg-controlled city of Lemberg on the eve of the First World War, commemorated the event in pictures.[13]

/e-zpu/2011/3/Krivoruchenko-Tsvetliuk_Juvenile-Movement/, accessed 5 March 2014. On the SS as a model for a new aristocracy, see Herbert Ziegler, *Nazi Germany's New Aristocracy: The SS Leadership, 1925–1939*, 2nd ed. (Princeton: Princeton University Press, 2014).

[10] The epithet was first used by R. Menzhinsky in two articles on Dzerzhinski, 'O Dzerzhinskom', *Pravda*, 20 July 1927, and 'Dva slova o Dzerzhinskom', *Pravda*, 20 July 1931, www.fsb.ru/fsb/history/author/single.htm!id%3D10318093@fsbPublication.html, accessed 6 April 2014.

[11] For an example of a medal for the fifth anniversary of the VChK, see www.numismat.ru/au.shtml?au=47&per=270&descr=&material=&nominal=&lottype=&ordername=&orderdirection=ASC&num=10&page=4, accessed 6 May 2014.

[12] Cf. Walter Scott, *Konnetabl' Chesterskii ili obruchennye* (St Petersburg: Smirdin, 1828). For an example of a typical country home library, see catalogue of books nationalized by the Red Army during the Civil War. Opis' knig vyvezennykh iz sela Spasskogo-Kurkina', produced during the handover to the holdings of Vologda Soviet Public Library. GAVO, fond 635, opis' 1a.d.4, 13–18; and catalogue of the Russian books of Nikolai Fedorovich Andreev, 1892', GAVO, Fond 635, opis' 1a.d., 51–77.

[13] www.wbc.poznan.pl/dlibra/doccontent?id=92148&dirids=1.

Emigrés and victims of the Cheka highlighted his ruthlessness.[14] There was, they all agreed, a logical necessity to figures such as Dzerzhinsky: people like him were radical negators of Russian imperial oppression. But resistance to Russian hegemony alone was not enough: young radicals like Dzerzhinsky were searching for an alternative community, and not all in his generation identified with national causes, which in any case were very difficult to formulate given the region's multi-ethnic and multiconfessional make-up. Originally destined for a career as a Catholic priest, Dzerzhinsky came to utilize methods of the Inquisition against the party whose catechesis he preached. Only ten years later, after his death in 1926, Dzerzhinsky would symbolize to hundreds of Russians and other peoples of the Soviet Union who had fallen out of favour with the new Bolshevik regime what Count Muraviev had symbolized to the Lithuania of his childhood: a brutal hangman. Unsurprisingly, the dismantling of a Dzerzhinsky monument on one of Moscow's prominent squares (and still the location of Federal Security headquarters) marked the symbol of Russia's de-Sovietization in the 1990s. Yet Dzerzhinsky's apologists, in the 1920s as now, emphasized the importance of the chivalric ideal for his work. Indeed, to some, the secret services agency that he helped found – the Cheka – was comparable to a secret order in which certain ideals of virtue were cultivated in the name of a higher good. The ideational arsenal for rebuilding an alternative sense of chivalry was evidently convertible into a number of different projects in the post-imperial era.

Dzerzhinsky and Rosenberg shared a desire not only to find new post-imperial orders but also to re-enchant modernity through a new look at Europe's medieval past. As a resident of Reval, Rosenberg was aware of being a citizen endowed with the privileges of the Russian Empire's most modern, Western face. Here were some of its highly capitalized and most modern factories. Coming from a moderately wealthy, middle-class background of German merchants himself, he took up the opportunity of acquiring a solid education in a promising field, civil engineering.

---

[14] For the most recent apologetic biology, see Sergei Kredov, *Dzerzhinskiy*, series Zhizn Zamechatel'nykh ludei (Moscow: Molodaia Gvardia, 2013); this biography, with no references or footnotes, relies extensively on Roman Gul', *Dzerzhinskiy (Nachalo terror)* (New York: Most, 1974), based on Anonymous, *Les Maitres de la Tcheka. Histoire de la Terreur en URSS, 1917–1938* (Paris: Les Editions de France, 1938), http://lib.ru/RUSSLIT/GUL/dzerzhinsky.txt, accessed 5 April 2014. Other documentary publications, for example on the predominant presence of Lithuanians in the VChk, see E. Pierremont, *Tche-Ka. Matériaux et documents sur la terreur bolcheviste recueillis par le bureau central du parti socialiste révolutionnaire russe* (Paris: J. Povolozky, n.d.), 191. On Dzerzhinsky, see Boris Cederholm, *In the Clutches of the Tcheka*, transl. F.H. Lyon (Boston and New York: Houghton Mifflin, 1929), 140–142.

Moreover, gruesome as it seems in hindsight, he embarked on what seemed to be a growing sphere of work in this field. His diploma project, which he finished while his university was evacuated to Moscow, was the design of a new crematorium for the city of Riga. It was a modern, even a radical project, for the Russian Empire, because the Orthodox custom did not allow it, but it was a technology of the future that had already been well developed by this point in western Europe. Rosenberg's project was never built, but Soviet Russia eventually turned cremation into a general practice from the mid-1920s onwards. The Nazi regime took the technology to a different level altogether, using it for the most unimaginable act of destruction, the mass incineration of millions of civilians murdered by the Nazis. It was only in his mature years that the contrast between medievalism and modernity reached new heights. Rosenberg and many of his social circle desired simultaneously a new age of chivalry and a new modernity, the honour code of an exclusive order and the extraordinary killing of innocents on a mass scale.

Rosenberg was a modernist whose modernism came from negating previous practice. Rosenberg's initial choice of engineering as a profession reflected the status of this profession in Riga, one of the Russian Empire's most modern and most 'European' cities. Its most representative buildings expressed all the stylistic stages of European urban history, from Romance to Renaissance to art deco. The most recent buildings were designed by a regional star architect, Petersburg-educated Mikhail Eisenstein. But the most iconic architectural land-marks of the Baltic were the medieval spires of the city's medieval silhouettes and, in the countryside, the ruined castles of the Teutonic Orders.

Likewise, the middle-class student fraternities like Rubonia looked as much forward as back to a mythical past. They had their *devises* modelled after the old Crusaders. Rubonia's was 'With Word and Deed for Honour and Right'. Urban representative buildings such as the *House of the Blackheads*, a Renaissance building dating back to the sixteenth century, had coats of arms attached to them, which were modelled after the coats of arms of aristocratic families. In the form of reliefs attached on their fronts and painted on wooden doors, they displayed ties between the Hanseatic cities of Novgorod, Bergen, Bruges, and London. Other symbols included images of a moor and St. George's cross, which demonstrated the historic origins of the association in the chivalric circle of the Knights of St. George in England, who celebrated their union with feasts in honour of King Arthur since the fourteenth century.

There were ties between student fraternities which were restricted to middle-class students only and the medieval guilds. The most famous of them, the Brotherhood of Blackheads, was an association of unmarried merchants whose chivalric and monastic ideals excluded nobles from membership. It was a tradition, however, to welcome members of high nobility, and particularly dynastic rulers, incognito, and the walls of the brotherhood's congregation halls were adorned with portraits of monarchs. Among such incognito visitors had been three Russian tsars, Peter the Great, Paul, and Alexander I, as well as German Chancellor Otto von Bismarck. Their festivities were called Artus courts. Their original patron saint was St Maurice, the Theban Moor who in the third century AD fought for the Christian faith and died a martyr's death. The organization's ties to the Dominican order went back to a period in the fourteenth century, when a group of foreign merchants helped the Dominicans establish themselves in the Baltic littoral in their defence against an uprising by the local pagan population. The first merchant associations of this kind had formed in England and then expanded to the German lands, and especially to the Hanseatic cities. From a chivalric organization for high nobility, which was modelled on the mythical memory of King Arthur, it had been transformed in the cities of the Hanseatic league into a Christian association of merchants who combined the ideals of chivalric virtue with the understanding of virtue associated with monastic life. Older members of *Rubonia* who were active in suppressing the 1905 uprisings against the Tsarist Empire included Max Erwin Ludwig Richter, who later ennobled himself by marriage to become Erwin von Scheubner-Richter, and who joined the Cossacks during the Civil War; and Otto von Kursell, an architect and caricature painter.[15]

After 1905, but even more so, after 1919, many more Germans, especially those of noble background, fled the Baltic littoral and were now settled in the successor states of the German Empire, mostly in Bavaria. In the Baltic lands, they were seen as 'Germans'. In Germany, they now defined themselves as 'Balts', *die Balten*. In the latter half of the twentieth century, the role that intellectuals of Baltic background played in the forging of Nazi ideology, particularly when it comes to the ideas of German expansion in eastern Europe, has come more into focus of historians' attention. Some scholars even speak of a streak of 'Baltic eugenics' in Nazi ideology,

[15] Michael Garleff (ed.), *Deutschbalten. Weimarer Republik und Drittes Reich*, vol. 1 (Cologne, Weimar and Vienna: Böhlau, 2001); Michael Kellogg, *The Russian Roots of Nazism: White Emigrés and the Making of National Socialism* (Cambridge: Cambridge University Press, 2005); Johannes Baur, *Die russische Kolonie in München 1900–1945* (Wiesbaden: Harassowitz, 1998).

mentioning the role of biologists like Jakob von Uexkuell and Lothar Stengel von Lutkowski alongside Alfred Rosenberg's and that of the non-Baltic race theorist Hans Günther.[16] To understand more precisely how these 'Baltic' ideas became so central to Nazi ideology, however, we need to delve more into the cultural history of post-First World War Munich.

The aristocratic ideal in Munich: rereading *Politics as a Vocation* in its social context

It was Alfred Rosenberg's wife Hilda, a dancer from Reval who had trained in Paris, who wanted to move to Munich in 1918 because of the city's reputation as one of the centres of modern dance. One of the Munich-based dance teachers was Edith von Schrenck, whom Rosenberg's wife knew from her studies at the Dalcroze Institute in St Petersburg, an institute of modern dance and eurythmics run by Prince Volkonsky, who had been educated at Hellerau near Dresden. Also in Munich, the choreographer Rudolf von Laban formulated his first ideas about dance, which laid the foundation for his work as a prominent figure in Goebbels's culture industry, before he moved to England.

Intellectuals and politicians who had passed through Munich between the 1900s and the 1920s had different social, geographic, and political trajectories. This mixture produced new political visions that reached far beyond the borders of the German Empire. A year before the revolution of 1905 in Russia, for instance, Leon Trotsky settled there to edit his revolutionary newspaper *Iskra* (Spark). Helphand, alias Parvus, an entrepreneur from Odessa who ended up organizing Lenin's passage to Russia, lived there around the same time. But most people who arrived in Munich did not choose the city for political reasons; in fact, they were all attracted by the city's promise of alternative lifestyles, particularly, in the visual arts, in theatre, and in modern dance.

The crowd that flocked to Munich in the last months of the First World War and the early years of the republic was still inspired by a search for alternative life forms, as those earlier generations had been. Munich's Suresnes Palace, an eighteenth-century residence for the Wittelsbachs,

[16] Paul J. Weindling, 'Race, Eugenics, and National Identity in the Eastern Baltic: From Racial Surveys to Racial States', in *Baltic Eugenics: Bio-Politics, Race and Nation in Interwar Estonia, Latvia and Lithuania 1918–1940*, ed. Björn M. Felder and Paul J. Weindlin (Amsterdam: Rodopi, 2013), 33–49, 41; Walter Laqueur, *Deutschland und Russland* (Berlin: Propyläen, 1965); Michael Geyer and Sheila Fitzpatrick (eds.), *Beyond Totalitarianism: Stalinism and Nazism Compared* (Cambridge: Cambridge University Press, 2009).

became available for rent as an artists' space, where Paul Klee had a studio in 1918, and where expressionist poet Ernst Toller was hiding after the failure of the Eisner government in 1919. During the war, another Wittelsbach palace, the Prince Georg Palais, had become the site of charitable activities sponsored by the Bruckmanns, publishers with wide-reaching connections, who organized a series of much-attended lectures in the series 'War relief for intellectual professions'. Lectures on poetry and on antiquity were particularly prominent. Renting an apartment at Villa Alberti, poet Rainer Maria Rilke was among those both attending and giving talks on Roman antiquity to Munich's elites, before he left the city in 1919. As Munich became of Europe's first socialist republics, along with Hungary, it attracted particularly intellectuals of the radical left, who came here from Vienna. Anarchists, revolutionaries, counter-revolutionaries, they all gathered at places such as the Café Stefanie to discuss the crisis of modern life.

Like Laban, whose family name, De la Banne, denoted a French familial origin, many of the Bohemians in Munich were men and women of high nobility who sought an escape from traditional society. A significant number of them came from the Austro-Hungarian Empire. Munich's official institutions, such as the Academy of Art and the University, were the first point of entry for many who flocked to the city for its art, but these soon found smaller and more informal circles. Munich's Fine Arts Academy around 1900 was more progressive than both Vienna's Academy and that of Berlin. But in addition to Munich's traditionalists like Franz von Lenbach, it also had a group of more radical painters whose association, the Secession, mirrored an eponymous organization in Vienna and promoted internationalism in art since the turn of the century. This tension attracted independent artists like the Slovenian painter Anton Ažbe, who would in turn draw affluent students from across Europe to the city. Thus by the beginning of the twentieth century, the city had established a charisma of its own, which distinguished it from other German cities. It was more remote from government affairs than Berlin but also less provincial than cities like Weimar or Darmstadt. The city provided something for artists and intellectuals of high society as well as lower- and middle-class representatives. In his memoirs, written shortly before his execution at Nuremberg, Rosenberg recalled arriving in Munich with a sketchbook of watercolours drafted in Reval and in Skhodnya near Moscow, which he was trying to turn into sellable pieces of work on Munich's art market,

With the end of the First World War, the period of cultural radicalism in Munich was followed by ten years of radicalism, in which the conflict of forces struggling for Germany's future was particularly palpable. On 7 November 1918, the Wittelsbach King Ludwig III, who had only reigned since 1913, fled to the Austrian castle of Anif near Salzburg, where on 13 November he typed a declaration releasing all civil and military servants of his state from their duties, without formally resigning himself. The Bavarian king was one in a small group of five German heads of state who, like the Habsburg Emperor Karl I, had refused to abdicate; the majority, seventeen monarchs and princes, resigned on behalf of themselves and their families. Like all of them, Ludwig too feared for his life; he moved between castles in Hungary and Austria before returning to Bavaria, where he died in 1921.[17] The socialist leader Kurt Eisner had already declared Bavaria a Republic on 7 November, two days before Scheidemann and Ebert would do so in Berlin. Eisner interpreted Ludwig's declaration as a form of resignation. In this period of upheaval, another intellectual to move to Munich was the Viennese philosopher of science and economist Otto Neurath, who was appointed head of the Central Planning Office of the Munich Council Republic. In May 1919, some 600 people were shot during clashes on Munich's streets, and others were imprisoned.

Among the moderate intellectuals who also settled in Munich in the years of revolution was the sociologist Max Weber. Having recently recovered from a nervous breakdown, he favoured the Bavarian capital over offers of professorial positions at universities in Vienna, Bonn, Berlin, and Frankfurt. His choice of Munich as the place to revive his academic career after a break of twenty years was informed by personal and professional connections, some of which established ties to the heart of the republican socialist government. In the winter of 1918/19, Weber published a series of programmatic works in a set of special pamphlets published by the nationally renowned *Frankfurter Zeitung* under the series title 'On the German Revolution', through which he wanted to establish the theoretical foundations for a republican order in Germany from a liberal standpoint.[18]

---

[17] Franz J. Bauer, *Die Regierung Eisner 1918/19. Ministerratsprotokolle und Dokumente*, Series Quellen yur Geschichte des Parlamentarismus und der politischen Parteien (Düsseldorf: Droste, 1987); Lothar Machtan, *Die Abdankung. Wie Deutschlands gekrönte Haeupter fielen* (Berlin: Propyläen, 2008).

[18] Max Weber, 'Deutschlands künftige Staatsform', in *Zur deutschen Revolution. Flugschriften der Frankfurter Zeitung*, 2, special edition. January 1919. More on Weber's suggestions for Germany's future constitutional design, see MWG I:15, 261–278.

Not only would the foreign powers not allow Germany to be restored in her previous, dynastic order, Weber argued; this was not in Germany's interests either. Instead, Weber advocated a solution for Greater Germany, whereby Prussian sovereignty would be crushed in favour of a federal system of nearly equal states.

Only a year after the revolution had begun, Eisner was assassinated, and Neurath, the economist Edgar Jaffé, as well as other leading members of Eisner's socialist government were put on trial for treason. Max Weber, who did not share their radicalism, nonetheless appeared as a defendant in court: although a more outspoken critic of the left, in his actions he was far more sympathetic to the socialists and anarchists than he admitted in print. He did not live to see this, having died in 1920, but it quickly became apparent that the threat of violence was at least as great, if not greater, from the right as it had been from the now declining communist left. In March 1920, Wolfgang Kapp, a leading member of the All-German Union, and General Walter von Lüttwitz, then used one of the disbanded military corps, the Marine brigade Ehrhardt, in an attempt to seize power. The putsch was thwarted by a general strike of the trade unions and a form of passive resistance by the military bureaucracy. In 1923, Adolf Hitler, who chose to settle in Bavaria having been released from the Bavarian infantry, which he had joined as a volunteer, undertook a putsch in Munich's Beer Hall, during which he proclaimed himself Reich chancellor, again with support from former generals such as Ludendorff. After it failed, one of his leading supporters, Erwin von Scheubner-Richter, was shot at the scene, while Hitler was taken prisoner for one year. This period of imprisonment not only gave him time to write his main ideological treatise, *Mein Kampf*, but it also provided him with the right status for becoming a celebrity in Munich. While in the short term unsuccessful, these Munich-based attempts at destabilizing the republican regime paved the way for the foundation of the Third Reich merely ten years later in Berlin.

Much political action in Munich occurred not only on the streets but in the private circles and salons, as well as in artistic associations that ranged from public to exclusive. While men clearly dominated radical street politics, behind the front doors, but still very much in public, women were very influential. Once again, among Munich's high-society ladies, members of high nobility were particularly prominent: salonière Elsa Bruckmann, née Princess Cantacuzène, emerged as a hostess of a series of lectures in support of the German war effort during the war and continued to bring together representatives of different political and social groups at her home in Nymphenburger Str. Other ladies of high nobility included the Prussians Else Jaffé, née von Richthofen, and Franziska 'Fanny' von Reventlow, who was a celebrity of experimental life. She lived in a prominent cooperative *Wohngemeinschaft* with the art connoisseur Bohdan von Suchocki and Franz Hessel, a novelist, in Munich's Kaulbachstrasse. Subsequently celebrated as one of the lead protagonists of the film *Jules et Jim*, based on Hessel's memoirs, her aura, just as the city's, was the birthplace of a new type of human being: the 'homme curieux'.[19] Members of these circles made the practice of experimental life forms into the content of their political message. Experimental communities with prominent Munich connections included the society of the Eranos circle, a loose group of intellectuals of high society interested in psychoanalysis, social cooperative movements, and alternative forms of spirituality, which gathered for regular conferences at Ascona's Monte Verita, a Swiss commune, between the 1900s and the 1930s. Two other circles of intellectuals, philosophers, and poets, who sought to establish a secret society or even a state within German society in transition between states, which had a base in Munich, were the *Cosmics* around writer Ludwig Klages and Bachofen, and the circle of young men around poet Stefan George. Though overwhelmingly masculine, these circles included some of the more radical attempts to revisit the sources of antiquity in search of new conceptions of masculinity and sexuality; they also shared with their more left-leaning fellow residents an interest in challenging bourgeois conceptions of marriage and such like.

It was in these circles that sociologist Max Weber observed the social types which he described as 'charismatic': a form of social power which individuals exercise, and which transcends the apparently significant differences between premodern and modern societies.[20] The themes of their gatherings were often very broad: to define European identity and to broaden cultural connections; to pursue interests in various kinds of Orientalisms; to discuss the potential threats posed to Europe by the non-European world and the Soviet Union; to discuss the differences between the 'Latin' and the 'Germanic' peoples of Europe, of Catholics and

---

[19] «L'avenir est aux curieux de profession.» (Words of Jim in the dialogue from François Truffaut's film *Jules et Jim*, 1962).

[20] S.N. Eisenstadt (ed.), *Max Weber on Charisma and Institution Building* (Chicago: Chicago University, 1968). For a critical edition on Weber's writings on charisma, see the sections 'Charismatismus', 'Umbildung des Charisma', and 'Errhalt des Charisma', in Max Weber, *Wirtschaft und Gesellschaft. Die Wirtschaft und die gesellschaftlichen Ordnungen und Mächte. Nachlass*, Teilband 4: Herrschaft, in MWG I:22–24, 460–542.

Protestants, and the place of non-Christians in Europe; to discuss the character and, in some cases, the danger of National Socialism and fascism.[21] French historians describe the activities of these social circles as 'européisme', a meta-ideology in which many otherwise conflicting parties met and mingled. What connected these societies was their shared admiration of sacred and secular medieval orders associated with chivalry and monastic knighthood. Somewhat related to these associations, albeit less socially exclusive, was the neo-medieval *Thule* society, which met at Hotel Vierjahreszeiten. *Thule* was the ancient Greek word for the northernmost known corner of Europe. Its membership was mixed; alongside some members of nobility, such as Prince Gustav von Thurn und Taxis and Rudolf von Sebottendorf, most members came from lower middle-class backgrounds. One of the authors connected to the circle was the playwright Dietrich Eckart, a Frankonian, who had moved to Munich from Berlin to become the editor of an anti-republican journal, *Auf gut Deutsch*. In 1921, he introduced Rosenberg to another outsider to Bavaria, Adolf Hitler, who, despite being a subject of the Austro-Hungarian army, volunteered to join the Bavarian army during the First World War and thereafter returned to Munich, rather than Vienna, in the hopes of resuming a more successful career than his failed attempts at art and architecture in Vienna had intimated. Both ended up working for Eckart's journal. Eckart, a failed lawyer and a somewhat more successful playwright, returned to Bavaria after a brief stint in Berlin, where he was befriended by a member of Wilhelm II entourage, Georg von Hülsen-Haeseler; his theatrical experience subsequently was used to coach Adolf Hitler in public speaking. Other members included Rudolf Hess, Heinrich Himmler, and Alfred Rosenberg. The ideological orientation of this society was not only anti-republican, but in general directed against the ideals associated with the Enlightenment.

The New Order State that Rosenberg began projecting first on paper and in public speeches during the Russian Civil War was a pastiche from the medieval history of the Baltic region, the Italian city states, and the Holy Roman Empire of the German Nation. This broad ideological structure, for which Alfred Rosenberg was one of the chief contributors, was then further supplemented by other, more modern ideas: the association of a modern, unified press, as well as the creation of one, streamlined

---

[21] On these communities, see, for instance, Michel Grunewald and Uwe Puschner (eds.) *Le milieu intellectuel conservateur en Allemagne, sa presse et ses réseaux (1890-1960)* (Bern: P. Lang, 2003).

workers' organization and the commitment to modernization and technological progress.

By studying the ideas of individuals whose actions eventually shaped an
entire generation, we can turn individual biographies into group biographies, a way of seeing the past in the shape and the scope of human lives.
But to understand more how their ideas intersected, and how exactly the
ideas of some individuals gained more traction, we also need to investigate
settings in which their speech acts are being received. One such setting is
official congresses and conferences. Other settings are private dinner
parties and reunions, insofar as they have been rendered into textual
forms in diaries and memoirs. The case study in this chapter focuses on
an international congress on the future of Europe, which the fascist
government convened in 1932. It united representatives of a wide range
of views on Europe's future in Rome.

Vanguards for a noble race? Nazi ideology in transnational context

The neo-medieval ideal as a factor in the formation of Nazi ideology has
been a recurrent theme of some of the genealogies and intellectual biographies of leading Nazis: from the esoteric readings of Hitler and some of his
followers from their early days in Vienna and Munich to the foundation of
their own new orders such as the SS.[22] Historians have recently highlighted
the seriousness with which the Nazis thought of their project not only in
terms of nationalist and socialist paradigms, but also in terms of empire
building.[23] In the choice of orientation between traditional and modern,
between restoration, reform, and revolution, the idea of chivalry appealed
as a timeless alternative: like charisma, it promised to infuse the best of the
traditional against the worst of the modern.

Munich in the period from the November Revolution until 1923 provides
a microhistory of a milieu in which National Socialism became socially
acceptable. They were also settings in which the combinations of chivalric
and modern were tried and tested, often in a way that confronted old elites
like Prince Rohan with the newcomers and outsiders like Rosenberg.
Mixed couples of high nobility and bourgeoisie, like the Bruckmanns,
were as important in creating new connections between recent migrants to
the city, as were lower middle-class figures like Dietrich Eckart, who had

---

[22] Brigitte Hamann, *Hitler's Vienna* (London: Tauris, 2010).
[23] Cf. Shelley Baranowski, *Nazi Empire: German Colonialism and Imperialism from Bismarck to Hitler*
(Cambridge: Cambridge University Press, 2011).

come to Munich from not quite so far; intellectuals like the circle of Stefan George played as important a role as the anti-intellectual Russian monarchists who had come here after the collapse of the White Army in the Russian civil war.[24] One of the things that united these people was a shared myth of a lost historical past, which many associated with an aristocratic ideal: the image of the chivalric past in eastern Europe and Russia, where organizations such as the Teutonic Order, elite merchant unions, and German colonists, all believed to raise levels of civilization in what they thought of as a backward part of Europe. While Munich was not the birthplace of Nazi ideology, it was certainly the place where its leading ideologues and supporters met and where, based on their mutual attachment, its different strands became amalgamated.

Many in the circle surrounding the publisher Hugo Bruckmann and his wife Elsa perceived the abdication of figures like the Wittelsbach King Ludwig III as a tragic event. Hugo Bruckmann, the publisher who since the beginning of the First World War began actively to promote literature of pan-Germanic ideology by H.S. Chamberlain and others, endorsed a cult of chivalry and aristocracy, as did many in their circle, such as Stefan George and his circle of followers. Elsa Bruckmann was believed to be the direct descendant of Byzantine Emperor John VI Cantacuzenus; her nephew, Norbert von Hellingrath, was a member of Stefan George's circle and an editor of the first complete works of Hölderlin, whose romantic poeticization of Germany tied it to the ancient world of the pre-Socratics. All Wagnerians, this circle also cultivated their ties to Wagner's neo-medieval estate at Bayreuth. One of the commonly seen figures in their salon was Karl Alexander Müller, the historian who became the editor of *Süddeutsche Monatshefte*, an increasingly *völkisch* magazine. From 1930 to 1936, he served as director of the Institute for the Study of the German People in the South and the South East (Institut zur Erforschung des Deutschen Volkstums im Süden und Südosten), whose aim was to establish a comprehensive analysis of the impact of German culture on European civilization. It continued the ethnographic work of Baron August von Haxthausen, paving the ground for historically founded claims of legitimacy for Nazi expansion in the East. By the time Hitler had begun composing *Mein Kampf*, in 1923, his recent acquaintance Rosenberg had already developed in a nutshell his idea about the importance of the medieval nobility in creating the ideal type of the Aryan. Both interacted

[24] More on this subject, see Kellogg, *The Russian Roots of Nazism*.

at Elsa Bruckmann's salon with its emphasis on the need for the rejuvenation on the old nobility.

Their joint project, the *Nationalsozialistische Monatshefte* [the National Socialist Monthly] was the main platform for debating the cornerstones of a new ideology. At the beginning, one of the unifying themes was a critique of the old national bourgeoisie, a point of connection for rising social groups of which Rosenberg and Hitler were representative, with old elites. In the first issue from 1930, one of the paper's 'pedigreed' contributors, Count Ernst von Reventlow, spoke of the 'nemesis' of the bourgeoisie.[25] Goebbels echoed in the same issue, speaking of the anaemic and subservient psychology of Germany's bourgeoisie.[26] By 1933, Goebbels was ready to declare that the Nazi seizure of power, and not the end of its monarchy, was Germany's real revolution, which pointed to a third way beyond Right and Left.[27]

In this process, nobles of old lineage, as well as people of lower social backgrounds and those who aspired towards nobility by adopting a noble surname – such as the ideologue Josef Lanz von Liebenfels – all played slightly different roles. Visibility, which, as social theorist Georg Simmel insisted, was one of the key sources of aristocratic privilege, was not only given through symbolic markers such as having the right particle. Nobility was traditionally also performed socially, one had to 'pass' in order to be accepted as noble.

Paying attention to the intellectual genealogy of this ideal does not provide an explanation for all the aspects of the Nazis' appeal, such as why certain groups or residents of certain regions were more likely to vote for the Nazis. But what it can explain is how the Nazis succeeded in ultimately reaching such a diverse population. In explaining Nazi appeal, scholars pay particular attention to the years from 1928, when the Nazi party only had a support base of 800,000 voters, to the Reichstag elections of 1930, when six million voted for the party.[28] Another focus of interest is the growth of the Nazi propaganda machine following the seizure of power in 1933, with its powerful synaesthetic impact through radio, film, and public exhibitions. But by this point, its influence already had a snowball

[25] Ernst Graf von Reventlow, 'Nemesis über dem Bürgertum', in *Nationalsozialistische Monatshefte*, 1 (1930), 5–11.

[26] Joseph Goebbels, 'Das patriotische Bürgertum', in *Nationalsozialistische Monatshefte*, 1 (1930), 221–229.

[27] Joseph Goebbels, 'Die deutsche Revolution', in *Nationalsozialistische Monatshefte*, 39 (June 1933), 247–248.

[28] John O'Loughlin, Colin Flint, and Luc Anselin, 'The Geography of the Nazi Vote', in *Annals of the Association of American Geographers*, 84:3 (September 1994), 351–380, 357.

effect. Far more open-ended, and therefore more interesting, is the question how the Nazis became the Nazis as the world got to know them in the first place, and for this, we need to look in more detail at the intellectual atmosphere and social circles in which the chief ideologues – Adolf Hitler, Alfred Rosenberg, Joseph Goebbels, Heinrich Himmler – mingled.

Political ideals have not only an intellectual genealogy such as the 'palingenetic myth' which underpins the idea of racial superiority in Nazi ideology. They also have a social one. The social milieus of cities in transition, like Vienna, as described by Brigitte Hamann, and Munich, described by Richard Evans, and more recently, Wolfgang Martynkewicz, provided the material that forged these disparate images together.[29] The image of declining dynasties and the ideals of a rejuvenated nobility was a dominant paradigm of discourse in these circles, one that was promoted not only by poets of bourgeois origin like Rilke but also by nobles themselves, particularly hostesses and Bohemians such as Elsa Bruckmann, Fanny von Reventlow, and the von Richthofen sisters.

One of the last issues of *Nationalsozialistische Monatshefte* before the Nazis took power in Germany was devoted to the Crisis of Europe.[30] At the heart of the paper was coverage of Alfred Rosenberg's recent visit to Rome, where he was one among many venerable speakers from different European countries. In his editorial to this issue, Adolf Hitler noted that the congress organizers had refrained from inviting leading politicians of their time, opting instead for the most noteworthy 'intellectuals', writers, and politicians who had once occupied an important role and felt a vocation to do so again in the future. This explains the combination of 'outstanding historians' with 'renowned politicians' such as Count Apponyi, Rennell Rodd, former British ambassador to Italy, and others. The aim was not to turn this into a discussion of 'diluted internationalism' of a League of Nations but to create instead a firm 'sentiment of national socialism'. In this spirit, the paper noted four attempts to create a united Europe: in the Middle Ages, through the Holy Roman Empire; in the modern era, under Napoleon; after the Great War, through the League of Nations; and in the same period, in the form of the Bolshevik revolution. All four attempts failed for different reasons, and it was the task of the gathering at the renowned Renaissance villa Farnesina to find the resources for Europe's true regeneration. It was particularly important for this endeavour, Hitler

---

[29] Richard Evans, *The Coming of the Third Reich: How the Nazis Destroyed Democracy and Seized Power in Germany* (London: Penguin, 2003), 446ff; Wolfgang Martynkewicz, *Salon Deutschland* (Berlin: Aufbau, 2009).

[30] *Nationalsozialistische Monatshefte*, 33, special issue on 'Krisis Europas' (December 1932).

emphasized, to stay away both from Bolshevism and from the Paneuropean utopianism of a Coudenhove-Kalergi.

Ten years prior to the Nazi monthly, Count Ernst von Reventlow founded the *Reichswart* [Imperial Herald], a party-independent magazine, which favoured Austro-German unity, demanded a revision of the Versailles treaty and a new colonial policy for Germany. Reventlow himself was a member of the German National People's Party (DNVP) until 1927, when he joined the Nazi party.[31] The paper retained a curious combination of being committed to a systematic and institutional anti-Semitism in Germany, whilst regularly picking up on reports of anti-Semitic purges in the Soviet Union, as early as in 1930.[32] Ernst's younger sister, Fanny von Reventlow, was, by contrast, at the heart of the Schwabing Bohemians, which included a different kind of fascination with the aristocratic and an internationalist anti-bourgeois community: the circle around artists such as the exiles of minor Russian gentry, Marianne von Werefkin and Alexej von Jawlensky, the Cosmic circle and the community that would travel regularly to Ascona's Monte Verità gatherings. This small network of associations shows the ambivalence of neo-aristocratic anti-bourgeois sentiment in post-war Munich and simultaneously the personal interconnectedness between intellectuals of quite opposing political views.

The chivalric ideal acted as an ideational glue for a very disparate community in interwar Munich. Above all, it gave general recognition to newcomers from the periphery, such as Alfred Rosenberg and Adolf Hitler, who came out of the Great War with a great sense of disorientation. Their radicalization was shared by an entire generation, but not all of its representatives felt the need to form actual alternative social and ideological networks for the rebuilding of a future empire. To the detriment of European society, of many neo-aristocratic dream projects born in Munich in the 1920s, it was their project of a Third Reich and their idea

---

[31] See *Der Reichswart*, 1:6 (6 November 1920), editorial. http://zefys.staatsbibliothek-berlin.de/dfg-view er/?set%5Bimage%5D=1&set%5Bzoom%5D=default&set%5Bdebug%5D=0&set%5Bdouble%5D=0 &set%5Bmets%5D=http%3A%2F%2Fzefys.staatsbibliothek-berlin.de%2Foai%2F%3Ftx_zefysoai_p i1%255Bidentifier%255D%3Db79dd7f8–1ee9–4a58–8775–7562c0c3b467, accessed 15 March 2014.

[32] Reventlow's work was translated into English for an American edition by George Chatterton-Hill, a philo-German Irishman who had been interned in a German camp during the First World War but subsequently received support from the German government in organizing the Sinn Fein movement in Germany and the free Irish brigades in the United States. See, for instance, *Der Reichswart*, 11:7 (14 February 1930), article on 'Wir fordern: Revision der Judengesetzgebung', 1. http://zefys .staatsbibliothek-berlin.de/dfg-viewer/?set%5Bimage%5D=2&set%5Bzoom%5D=default&set%5Bd ebug%5D=0&set%5Bdouble%5D=0&set%5Bmets%5D=http%3A%2F%2Fzefys.staatsbibliothek- berlin.de%2Foai%2F%3Ftx_zefysoai_pi1%255Bidentifier%255D%3D53ff1ff5-fe1b-4746-904f-e9 b74689f37c, accessed 5 March 2014.

of a neo-medieval order – the SS – that succeeded in the subsequent decade. Later, Rosenberg's appointment as a special Commissioner for the Eastern Territories in 1941 gave him further opportunities to put his mythology of a reformed eastern European colony governed by a Teutonic Order into practice. Alongside mass deportations of the Jews, Rosenberg was in charge of resettling the population of Baltic nobility in the formerly Polish area of the Wartheland.

As soon as 1935, Germany, unlike most other central European states with the exception of Hungary, revived the old status of nobility, even though the Nuremberg laws of 1935 required nobles of known old lineage to provide proof of racial purity until 1800. At the same time, leading members of the Nazi party sought to regain the cooperation of nobles in their project of national renewal, which was done both at the level of reintroducing new forms of rank to the army and at the level of co-opting nobles who had held possessions in what was now no longer Germany into projects of re-colonization of these territories under the Nazi aegis. As recent historians have argued, such attempts were partially successful, particularly when it came to establishing partnerships between the Nazi party and those associations of noblemen that had already moved to the political right before the Weimar Republic had been conceived. The primary organization to cooperate with the attempts by the Nazi party to reinstitute the nobility was the *Deutsche Adelsgenossenschaft*.[33] Indeed, throughout its time in power, the Nazi government in Germany redefined both its concept of nobility based on race and its policies towards organized nobles' organizations such as the DAG.[34]

The authority in the party who oversaw the reform of the existing nobility in Germany was Hans Guenther, minister of health. In some sense, Guenther sought to reverse the radicalism of Weimar constitutional attempts to remove the institution altogether.[35] Already in his time as a constitutional lawyer in the Weimar Republic, the jurist Carl Schmitt had called the movement to abolish the nobility a form of 'Jacobinism'.[36]

---

[33] Stephan Malinowski, *Vom König zum Führer*.

[34] See Bundesarchiv (BA), 'Adel' 1925–38, R 43 II 1554–5.

[35] In Germany, a similar form of legislation was ratified by its Constitutional Assembly as § 181 and § 109 of the Weimar Constitution, according to which noble privileges were abolished '129. Sitzung des Reichstags am 2. Dezember 1925', cited in several passages in Carl Schmitt, *Unabhängigkeit der Richter, Gleichheit vor dem Gesetz und Gewährleistung des Privateigentums nach der Weimarer Verfassung. Ein Rechtsgutachten zu den Gesetzentwürfen über die Vermögensauseinandersetzung mit den früher regierenden Fürstenhäusern* (Berlin und Leipzig: de Gruyter, 1926), 13–14.

[36] Schmitt, *Unabhängigkeit der Richter*, 25–27.

In Austria and Germany, the first constitutional assemblies of the new republics implemented decrees abolishing all forms of noble status in 1919. The nobility was abolished, along with 'its external privileges and titles awarded as a sign of distinction associated with civil service, profession, or a scientific or artistic capacity'. Nobles were to become 'German Austrian citizens', equal before the law in all respects.[37] In republican Germany, nobles were allowed to continue using their titles as part of their name, without the right to inherit them.[38] Nazi law partially reversed these changes.

Nobility of Blood and Soil

Another author to be inspired by Rosenberg, albeit already during the period of Nazi rule, was Walther Darré. His *Neuadel aus Blut und Boden* [New Nobility from Blood and Soil] cast the peasant as a bearer of Germanic customs in the centre of attention. Frequently referring back to the architecture and history of the Ostsee provinces, Rosenberg continuously emphasized the achievement of the Teutonic Order as a civilizing force in eastern Europe. Visiting Westphalia, Rosenberg was reminded not only of the connections between the old families of the Teutonic Orders that had moved from here to East Prussia and the Baltic but also of the entourage of Widukind, the ancient Saxon knight, whose descendants still honoured him in the form of the Seppelmeier Hof, a traditional residence of ten families or so in Westphalia and Lower Saxony who were thought of as Widukind's descendants.

The aristocratic ideals of exclusivity, military prowess, and cultural patronage were eventually divided among different offices. Alfred Rosenberg became the chief of an eponymous cultural department, which collected artworks from across Europe and established a network of museums of racial culture as well as exhibitions on the history and future of Europe across Nazi-occupied territories and the new empire's German heartlands. In the meantime, another newcomer, Heinrich Himmler, founded the neo-chivalric Schutzstaffel SS, where, likewise, ideas of 'fidelity' and 'honour' were applied to the Fuehrer.[39]

---

[37] For Austria, see Adelsaufhebungsgesetz StGBl. Nr. 211, Vollzugsanweisung am 18. April 1919, StGBl. 237.

[38] On the abolition of titles in the Weimar Republic, see Bernhard Raschauer, *Namensrecht: eine systematische Darstellung des geltenden österreichischen und des geltenden deutschen Rechts* (Vienna and New York: Springer, 1978).

[39] Heinrich Himmler, *Die Schutzstaffel als antibolschewistische Kampforganisation* (1937), https://archi ve.org/stream/Himmler-Heinrich-Die-Schutzstaffel/HimmlerHeinrich-DieSchutzstaffelAlsAntibo lschewistischeKampforganisation193717S.Text#page/n15/mode/2up, accessed 13 May 2014.

Government correspondence from the Nazi period reveals an internal debate about whether or not to acknowledge that some families had a 'higher significance for the state than other families', – the internal definition of nobility depending on other than racial purity – implying also 'higher tasks and duties' for nobles in return. 'In this connection', one minister argued, 'we will also have to determine whether we should grant such a special status exclusively to families of former nobility, or also consider admitting new families'. One means of helping to make this determination was to work with anti-Semitic groups within aristocratic organizations, resulting in a follow-up to the *Gotha Almanach* of nobility and listing all ennobled Jews in a separate edition called the *Semi-Gotha*. In its occupied territories, the Nazi government even commissioned book-length studies on how to distinguish, for instance, Polish nobility of Slavic origin from those of Jewish origin by looking at surnames.[40] The idea of the nobility as a superior group within the general population contradicted Nazi ideas about the racial superiority of the Aryan race, all members of which were supposed to be mutually equal.

The Nazi government had particular difficulties in addressing the issue of aristocratic privilege. On the one hand, the ideal of the Teutonic conqueror of eastern Europe was important for the ideology of recolonizing the East. Hitler and Nazi ideologue Alfred Rosenberg had discussed both the Teutonic Knights in East Prussia and the Baltic as a model for the Nazi takeover of eastern Europe. In *Mein Kampf*, the nobility remained a more ambivalent concept than in Rosenberg's work, in which the nobility appears first as an example of racial degeneration, based on examples of dynastic incest among families such as the Habsburgs. Hitler's distaste for the Habsburg dynasty was balanced by his acceptance of Franz Josef's authority when he was emperor, as well as an outright admiration of the Hohenzollerns. Likewise, Hitler's emphasis on the nobility's history of degeneration and racial mixture with Jews was counterweighed by his idealization of the medieval chivalric orders. Further, nobles are condemned for introducing Jews to European high society.[41] Only the Teutonic Order, which had colonized the Baltic littoral and some parts of eastern Europe beginning in the thirteenth century, receives a positive treatment from Hitler. In his so-called *Second Book*, though not published in his lifetime,

---

[40] See, for instance, a study commissioned by the German Ministry of Foreign Affairs called *Der polnische Adel jüdischer Herkunft (Szlachta polska pochodzenia zydowskiego/ The Polish nobility of Jewish birth)* by Ludwik Korwin (1935–38). In: Bundesarchiv, Berlin Lichterfelde, R/153/1915/40, see also R/153/480/40.

[41] Adolf Hitler, *Mein Kampf* (Munich: Eher, 1933).

Hitler was concerned with the National Socialist concept of a new empire in which an Aryan nobility plays a leading role.[42]

Following this logic, the Nazi government partially reinstated some noble privileges after 1935, and indeed managed to create attractive positions of power for nobles such as Gottfried von Bismarck and the von Hessen family, while also maintaining its image as a revolutionary and socialist party.[43] Thus, in keeping with republican legislation, noble titles under the Nazis continued to be seen as part of the family name. Nobles were mere 'members of families with a noble name', although the regime itself provided more exclusive opportunities for nobles than the Weimar Republic.[44] Nobles were recruited for active collaboration with the regime in connection with the conquest of eastern Europe. Following the Hitler–Stalin pact of 1939, as Hitler's chief ideologue for Eastern colonization, Rosenberg invited nobles from the Baltic region to lead the colonization of parts of Poland and Ukraine and to employ their knowledge of agricultural organization since feudal times for a new development of the region, using Polish forced labourers. For this purpose, the Nazis even briefly reinstated the Teutonic Knights. On the other hand, the ideology of the Aryan race had no room for an exclusive group within the community of Aryans.

Subsequently, western European and North American historians of modernity have constructed 'special paths' in establishing separate genealogies of Nazi and later, Soviet totalitarianism, which were quite different from the idea of a more normal, more humane modernity that led from empires to modern nation states. With greater distance and more documentary evidence at their disposal, it is only since the end of the Cold War that historians have gradually become aware how many of these representatives of different national and political regimes had come from a shared ideational and social background. Totalitarian and democratic states had the same genealogy, even though historical accounts like Hannah Arendt's *Origins* used this genealogy to draw out contrasting lineages. The phrase 'Iron Curtain', which many attributed to Winston Churchill, we now know, had been traced back to a speech by Joseph Goebbels and perhaps even further back.[45] The image of a Europe containing separate genealogies, with one leading from ancient Greece via Rome to modern Europe,

[42] Adolf Hitler, *Das zweite Buch* (Stuttgart: DVA, 1961).   [43] BA, 'Adel' 1925–38.

[44] BA, R 43 II 1554–5, 80. Berlin, 14 July 1933. Justice Minister Gürtner to Hitler, 2.

[45] Mark Mazower, *The Dark Continent: Europe's Twentieth Century* (London: Allen Lane, 1998); Fond 1488, Büro des Reichsprotektors in Böhmen und Mähren, esp. Fond 1447/1/ 504: property taken from the Czernin Palace and Konopischt to the Heydrich residence at Prague Castle, 1942–43.

and two rogue branches leading to Bolshevik Russia and the capitalist United States, was first printed in a Nazi propaganda brochure distributed in Vichy France in the 1940s.[46] Not only the Soviet Union and Nazi Germany, which signed a pact of non-aggression in 1939, but also informal representatives of western European and American societies and the Soviet Union were much more connected than the public discourses of these states conveyed. In fact, these Europeans who contributed to mass civilian destruction had a common past in the system of imperial rule, which the Habsburg, Hohenzollern, and Romanoff dynasties had overseen for many generations.

Rome as a shared capital of imperial nostalgia

'Duce, Eccelenze, Signore, Signori!' With these words, the venerable Italian inventor of the radio, Guglielmo Marconi, opened the Congress on Europe at Rome's Capitol in November 1932. In what would be his last public role, Marconi now served as honourable president of the Royal Academy, which had recently been reconstituted under Mussolini's tightening control.[47] A resurrected institution of the Enlightenment in a resurrected city, the Academia had invited a wide range of leading intellectuals and politicians to debate the future of Europe. Mussolini himself, a new Cesare Borgia or perhaps a new Caesar himself, was present at the opening, as was the king, Vittorio Emmanuele III, and other royalty. Among the list of Excellencies, only one was markedly absent: Pope Pius XI. Relations between the rising Mussolini entourage and that of the papacy had reached their lowest point around that year.

The ideal of debating Europe in its oldest capitals was at the heart of a new internationalism that struggled to find its own voice against the Catholic internationalism of the Vatican, on one side, and the Protestant internationalism of Wilson's Geneva-based League of Nations, on the other. In this project, the congress fulfilled the function of consolidating a transnational group of politicians, academics, industrialists, and writers. It combined archaic and modern, a fascination with the past and the search for modernity that was so characteristic of the political generation that formed this period. The congresses were also exclusively masculine; no

---

[46] Hans Dollinger (ed.), *Facsimile Querschnitt durch Signal* (Munich, Bern and Wien: Scherz, 1969), 180–181. The original in *Signal*, 11, 1944.

[47] Guglielmo Marconi, *Convegno 'Volta'* (Roma: Reale Adcademia d' Italia, 1932), 9.

women were invited, and those who attended were the wives, secretaries, and daughters of delegates.

The beginning of the Volta Congresses went back to the year 1925, when a group of intellectuals under Mussolini began working on a new philosophy of Europe.[48] One of them, Francesco Orestano, a Kant and Nietzsche scholar and a lawyer, had studied in Germany and belonged to the first generation of Nietzsche followers. Their plan was to use an international congress across nations and disciplines in order to discuss what the identity of Europe would be: its unity; its unique concept of civilization; the nature and causes of its current crises; the relationship between Europe and the non-European world, and particularly, the colonial question. The latter was the subject of an additional congress on Africa. The congress attracted an illustrious crowd of academics, journalists, and former diplomats. The organizers worked under the auspices of the Mussolini-controlled Roman Senate. Even the conference programme was printed at the Senate's own publishing house. The financial backing came from the Volta foundation associated with Edison Electric corporations.

The most obvious beneficiaries were the newcomers on the political scene, and those who travelled to Rome for the first time. On a group level, it was of far greater significance to representatives of those nations which either did not exist prior to the First World War or had significantly changed their constitution, such as Germany, Hungary, Czechoslovakia, and the host country itself. This was also reflected in the disproportionately declining number of participants from other countries that survived the Great War more or less intact, such as Britain. It was particularly noteworthy that one new state was conspicuously absent because it had not received an invitation: the Soviet Union.[49]

The meeting also brought together what could be called the Captains of Industry with the Captains of Science, eminent diplomats working for former empires such as Austria-Hungary, such as Count Albert Apponyi, as well as former diplomats working for still-existent empires, like the retired British ambassador to Italy, Baron Rennell Rodd. Events like these were not only a validation for Italy as the host country, and the

---

[48] AV 17.44.1–25.
[49] To qualify, the Soviet Union was invited to a specialized congress dedicated to theories and practices of theatre, also held in Rome in 1934.

Duce personally as leader of a neo-Roman Empire; it was also a validation for some of its participants.[50]

Many of the more affluent representatives of the generation that gathered here in 1932 had witnessed the first major excavations of antiquity in their childhood. From the 1880s to the 1890s, hidden ruins of the Forum in Rome and the patrician houses in Pompeii were dug up. By the mid-1920s, archaeologists also discovered residential multistorey houses in Ostia. Now, in the 1920s, a new building boom in Rome underlined the classical heritage of the city with new representative buildings in neo-classical style.[51] Rome was to be a capital of the twentieth century. Excursions to the city were an integral part of the congress on Europe. A further congress on the future and colonial administration of Africa, held in Rome in 1939, after the Italian conquest of Lybia, included a special treat: a scheduled flight for delegates to the ruins of antiquity at Tripoli.

Events like the Volta Congress on Europe, and a follow-up congress on Africa, highlighted the international connections between what seemed rather different models of imperial attachment. Of 120 participants in the Europe congress, an overwhelming majority had served in leading diplomatic or military posts by the time the Great War broke out. These included military leaders like the Duke of Abruzzi, an ex-Hungarian minister of Austria-Hungary, the president of the French diplomatic academy, former diplomatic staff of the British Empire, and members of the League of Nations staff. Among the cultural figures were established intellectuals in their fields and nations, such as the archaeologist Charles Petrie, the sociologist Alfred Weber (brother of Max), the writer and diplomat Salvador de Madariaga. But a smaller group of men were the rising stars of a new generation of politicians and intellectuals. Chief among them were new political leaders and ideologues, like Mussolini and Alfred Rosenberg.

Among the scholars and writers invited to the congresses on Europe and Africa, there were also other authors whose fame had crystallized in the 1920s out of a similar mood of European decline and quest for a new political vision: Stefan Zweig, who sent his paper but did not attend in person; the historian Christopher Dawson; Tomasi Marinetti, who attended the Africa congress; Bronislaw Malinowski, the anthropologist,

---

[50] AV 19.44.25. Topics include Principe K.A. Rohan, 'La realta europea', Stefan Zweig, 'La disintossicazione morale dell' Europa', and Wilhelm Medinger, 'La pacificazione delle minoranze nazionali'.

[51] Walter Benjamin, *Paris, Die Hauptstadt des XIX Jahrhunderts* (1935), first in Walter Benjamin, *Schriften*, 2 vols. (Frankfurt: Suhrkamp, 1955).

who at the Africa congress represented the British Anthropological Association; Prince Karl Anton Rohan, editor of *Europäische Revue*.

Moments like this congress can provide us with some insights on how different ideology-drafters mutually perceived each other's ideas of the past in the light of the future. It is significant to see these men of different social standing, a different relationship to the former empires, and varying age be located on the same page of a congress staged with such symbolic panache. Rome was everybody's capital, but many of the people who had arrived there had their own post-imperial projects on their mind. Prince Rohan attempted to recover the place of Vienna as Europe's cultural capital. Count Apponyi and other representatives of the more disenchanted elites of the Habsburg era had been seeking to widen audiences by appealing to European expatriates in the United States. The British intellectuals saw London as a new Rome. For the representatives of the Soviet Union, who were not invited to the Volta congresses on Europe and Africa but were welcome at a special congress on theatre and the arts, the Fourth Rome was Moscow.[52] The German representative, legal internationalist Mendelssohn-Bartholdy, was a proponent of a new Germany based on the neo-classical foundations in Weimar, while others favoured Munich, capital of the secessionist Bohème. Finally, and most crucially for Europe, for the Nazis, represented by Alfred Rosenberg, the real capital of a new Third Reich was Nuremberg. Instead of Berlin, Vienna, or Weimar, the Nazi party chose this city, the former seat of the imperial Diet of the Holy Roman Empire, as a symbol of its power. Architect Albert Speer soon had it redesigned for the purpose of mass public rallies, and it was here where, three years after the congress in Rome, the party would pass its most significant piece of legislation, the Nuremberg Laws of 1935.[53]

For the old elites, the congress made clear that their sense of self was still tied to the old empires. This was particularly true of the Habsburg nobility. The contrast between old and new elites became most marked in a clash over the historical roots of European identity that emerged in the speeches between Prince Rohan and Alfred Rosenberg. Rohan, who chose to publish his works in Berlin rather than in Vienna, pointing out that in Vienna 'there is no Prince Rohan any more, only Karl Anton Rohan', thought that the old 'nobility' now had the task 'to transform the old values in a conservative way, according to its tradition, using the new impulses of the

---

[52] Katerina Clark, *Moscow, the Fourth Rome. Stalinism, Cosmopolitanism, and the Evolution of Soviet Culture, 1931–1941* (Cambridge, Mass.: Harvard University Press, 2011).

[53] On Nuremberg as one of the capitals of post-imperial nostalgia, see Stephen Brockmann, *Nuremberg: The Imaginary Capital* (Woobridge: Camdenhouse, 2006).

revolution'.[54] He wanted to create 'unified Europe' instead of an 'ideological brotherhood of mankind'.[55] The new Europe, saved from Spenglerian decline, as well as the threats of Bolshevism and fascism, would be a fusion of aristocratic leadership and collective action by workers who, as he put it, were not mere 'prols' but conscious of belonging to a collective. The bourgeoisie, by contrast, 'today already rare, will probably slowly disappear altogether'.[56]

The Nazis' effectively Prussianized account of European history was at odds with Rohan's own continued espousal of the Habsburg Empire as a model of Catholic universalism, which was in a sense ironic, as the Rohan family itself had a glorious prehistory in the Protestant struggle of the Duc Henri de Rohan during the Reformation in France. In light of subsequent events, the rise of the Nazi party, another World War, and a much more significant collaboration between international parties in its aftermath, the congresses of the 1930s in Rome might seem peripheral to world politics. Yet for anyone who wants to understand the language in which an entire generation exchanged ideas about Europe before this exchange escalated in unprecedented levels of destruction, they are a rich field of study. What the congresses highlighted was the extraordinary degree of commonality that these different men shared, and the fact that those lines which divided them did not run along the political borders of Europe in their day. Instead, they were rooted in classical texts of the past, above all, Tacitus's *Germania*. The contrast between them was between multiple ideas of Europe: a Latin and a German model of Europe's greatness, modelled either after the great patrician aristocracy of the Roman past or after the 'barbarian'; and a Nordic racial ideal. This was a generation of secularized Christians in which the conflict between Protestant and Catholic Europe had been transformed into the believed opposition between races: Nordic, Latin, and Slavic. Another commonality was their shared rejection of the Soviet experiment and the Bolshevik party. In this climate, it turned out that their conversation revolved around the question what kind of aristocratic past, what kind of patrician or chivalric, Romance or Latin, Nordic or Southern, was going to win.[57]

[54] Karl Anton Rohan (ed.), *Umbruch der Zeit 1923–1930* (Berlin, Stilke, 1930), introduction by Freiherr Rochus von Rheinbaben9.

[55] Cited from Guido Müller, '"Europa" als Konzept adlig-bürgerlicher Elitendiskurse', in *Adel und Bürgertum in Deutschland*, vol. II, ed. Heinz Reif (Berlin: Akademie-Verlag, 2002), 235–268, 251.

[56] Karl Anton Rohan, *Europa* (Leipzig: Der Neue Geist-Verlag, 1924), 35.

[57] The list of proposed speakers is worth dwelling upon in some detail. The proposed list of British participants included Lloyd George, Winston Churchill, Austen Chamberlain, Rudyard Kipling, George Trevelyan, Hilaire Belloc, and John Maynard Keynes. What united these politically quite

This Volta Congress on Europe of 1932 served the purpose not only of identifying the crisis of Europe but also of giving legitimacy to a new, imperial vision of Italy that Mussolini and his circle were trying to establish. It was a moment of glory for Mussolini but also for the National Socialists, whose internal political triumph was yet to come. One of the key figures of the future, it turns out, was Alfred Rosenberg, by the beginning of the congress still a marginal figure.

Most speakers were forgers of new ideologies, of a new outlook on European identity and future, and most began their intervention with references to the crisis of the League of Nations, and the dangers of economic and political instability. One notable feature was the emphasis on an ecumenical and international project of rebuilding empire, which featured Protestant, Catholic, and, though to a much less prominent extent, Jewish intellectuals, but noticeably excluded Muslim and Russian Orthodox representatives. There were no representatives of Europe's political Left. Likewise, there was not a single female delegate; women were only welcome as secretaries, wives, or daughters of delegates. In fact in the correspondence, a special point was made in emphasizing the distinction between wives and partners. A special translation service, the office of Dr Giuseppe Milandri, was drawn upon to help during the congress, although many of the delegates spoke at least two languages.

The press reports ranged from dispassionate accounts of how Europe's dignitaries had gathered on the Tiber to angry voices arguing that 'Europe had been robbed by fascists dressed in academic uniforms'.[58] The *Journal de Genève* reported that the atmosphere in Rome that year was one of euphoria over the new regime, which celebrated its first ten-year anniversary that year.[59] 'Nothing could be less aristocratic, less conservative, than the fascist regime', the journalist signed W.M. concluded, listing the new aqueducts, railways, and other innovations introduced under Mussolini's rule. And yet, it was a noticeable feature of the Europe congress, as part of this year of festivities, that it included a noticeable number of delegates of old European nobility who had been public figures of Europe's defunct

---

different men, aside from their gender and British background, was their intellectual links to an imperial kind of internationalism, and their respective roles as public intellectuals in a set of overlapping, yet not identical, establishment circles. The German list included Alfred Hugenberg, Hjalmar Schacht, Friedrich Meinecke, Alfred Rosenberg, Albrecht Mendelssohn-Bartholdy, Willy Hellpach, Werner Sombart, Alfred Weber, and Karl Anton Rohan.

[58] 'Le congrès Volta, à Rome', *Révue de Génève*, 24 November 1932; 'Europa na rzymskim Kapitolu!', *Ilustrowany Kuryer codienny*, 18 November 1932, 320; 'Europa am Tiberstrand', *Dresdener Neueste Nachrichten*, 27 November 1932.

[59] 'Rome au lendemain des fêtes décennales', *Journal de Genève*, 25 November 1932.

continental empires. These individuals included especially families loyal to the Habsburg Empire, such as the Rohans, the Apponyis, and also Spanish and Swiss Catholic nobility. What they had in common was a particular espousal of Catholicism – the universalist, but not the socialist message – with an imperial form of internationalism. These residents of cities, no longer imperial subjects, and not yet national citizens, were now above all burghers: patricians in Rome, dandies in London, and consumers of culture in Paris.[60] They looked at these cultural capitals for guidance of the future. And yet it turned out that the most influential politicians of the twentieth century were not Romans, Parisians, or Londoners. They were men who had grown up in Europe's lesser cities, places like Reval, Linz, and Tbilisi. Here, the aristocratic and chivalric ideals and neo-imperialist aspirations had a particular, more colonial inflection.

In the European cities suspended in the 1930s between old and new empires and new nation states, such as Munich, Rome, Reval, Königsberg, Geneva, and the Vatican, ideals of chivalry were quickly turned into programmes for new types of post-imperial orders. Here, new charismatic personalities saw politics as their vocation. They presented themselves to their public in the international language of a new aristocracy of the future. Liberals like Weber had high hopes in the capacity of cities to regenerate the European bourgeoisie through the production of democratic forms of charismatic empowerment.[61] But these less established former imperial subjects were not citizens of a democratic republic. Many of these transient burghers were looking at the old elites of continental Europe for guidance on how to revive empires.

[60] See Saskia Sassen, *Territory, Authority, Rights. From Medieval to Global Assemblages* (Princeton: Princeton University Press, 2006).

[61] On Weber's notion of a charismatic city, see Max Weber, 'Probleme der Staatssoziologie', *Bericht der Neuen Freien Presse*, report on the lecture pf 25 October 1917, in MWG, 22/4, 752–756.

CHAPTER 7

Apostles of elegy
Bloomsbury's continental connections

A visitor to the National Gallery in London easily overlooks, as I have done many times, that the floor is also a space of visual display. Close to the main entrance, between the busy shops on the ground floor and the first floor's galleries, two large mosaics show allegories of the British character and allegories of modern life. One of them, labelled Courage, has Winston Churchill taming a wild monster, probably of Nazism, arising from the sea.

The artist behind the mosaic, Boris von Anrep, was a Baltic aristocrat who had escaped the Russian Revolution.[1] Between 1933 and 1952, Anrep designed two floor mosaics for the National Gallery. The latest sequence dates from 1952 and is called *Modern Virtues*. Like Anrep's earlier work, *The Awakening of the Muses* of 1928–33 [Fig. 25], it uses recognizable figures from public life, including Virginia Woolf, in place of abstract figures.

Not far from a segment titled Humour, which shows Britannia herself, along with a Union Jack, is a small segment featuring an unknown man with the line 'Here I lie' [Fig. 26]. The statement is likely an expression of English humour, linguistic pun in the style of a John Donne or Shakespeare. One of the ways in which the mosaic offers the viewer open 'lies' in displaying images of British national identity is the association of each virtue or abstraction with real historical personalities. The poets Anna Akhmatova, with whom Anrep had a love affair before the First World War, and T.S. Eliot are there, alongside the German scientist exiled in the United States, Albert Einstein.

As a group, these people never shared a pint in the same British pub. But as nodes of an imagined network of memory, they were nonetheless very influential. Like Anrep's mosaics, the creation of trans-imperial memory in interwar Europe was one of the by-products of intellectual exchange in European society of this period. This transnational mosaic of memory was

---

[1] For more details, see Lois Oliver, *Boris Anrep: The National Gallery Mosaics* (London: National Gallery Company, 2004).

Figure 25 Boris von Anrep, Clio, from his National Gallery mosaic (1928–32). ©
The National Gallery, London. Reproduced by kind permission of the estate of
Boris Anrep

significant not only because of what it contains but also because of what it left out.

Anrep's mosaic, figures of German, French, and most cultures which are not classical Greece or modern Britain and the United States, are conspicuous by their absence. The only German to be absorbed in British national memory of Europe's common past was Albert Einstein, then already an American citizen. The place of German culture in this British version of Europe has been visibly called into question, while France and other European countries as well as the United States are altogether absent.

Anrep owed this prominent commission to the influential British art critic Roger Fry, who rose to fame in 1910 as a champion of the post-impressionists after a much-acclaimed exhibition in London's Grafton Galleries. Fry had turned a series of observations on contemporary art into a visible 'character' of the modern world.[2] He had brought neo-impressionism to London, including

<hr />

[2] Roger Fry, 'Modern Mosaic and Mr. Boris Anrep', in *The Burlington Magazine for Connoisseurs*, 42:243 (June 1923), 272–278. See also J.B. Bullen, 'Byzantinism and Modernism 1900–14', in *The Burlington Magazine*, 141:1160 (November 1999), 665–675.

the purchase of the Degas collection, which was discussed earlier. But now, the group was uncertain of its visual taste and shifted its attention to literature. As Virginia Woolf, a close friend, put it in 1924, the time was suffering from an absence of a 'code of manners' in which to express ideas, since neither the code of any one nation nor of any one particular period – Victorian, Edwardian, Georgian – seemed to apply. Theirs was an age of 'failures and fragments', and yet all the plots demanded completeness and success. Just as they had done with impressionist art, Fry and Woolf agreed, their contemporaries had to learn to tolerate the 'spasmodic, the obscure, the fragmentary, the failure', mixing 'scraps of talk' with different contradictory ideas and elements of theory.[3] For this community, Anrep's mosaic was a kind of mirror.

Germany and the builders of international society

Raymond Williams has used the case of the Bloomsbury group to identify 'fractions of a class' as a social phenomenon distinct from classes or groups as such.[4] The Bloomsbury circle, a group that, as a saying goes, 'lived in squares' (an allusion to the squares of Bloomsbury in London, where they lived) and 'loved in triangles', were an association of friends from Cambridge University, as well as their siblings, partners in marriage, and lovers. Unlike the Apostles, an exclusively male secret society in Cambridge, their circle in London was conspicuous by greater intellectual as well as sexual openness, even though it remained socially exclusive. This constellation is famed for having produced a creative environment in which individual authors also achieved great distinction. People like John Maynard Keynes, Virginia and Leonard Woolf, the Strachey brothers, as well as Roger Fry were each in their own right highly successful members of the British Edwardian elite. But what Williams did not remark on in that essay is the fact that such fractions always had connections to like-minded configurations across imperial and national boundaries. In fact, in transnational perspective, such communities appeared even more significant in their role as shapers of public opinion in spheres such as literature and the arts, and increasingly, also politics. In the late nineteenth century, they had started entire fashions such as impressionism among Europe's educated elites; in the twentieth century, their interest shifted to literature. But what remains invisible is the whole of which that

---

[3] Virginia Woolf, 'Mr Bennett and Mrs Brown', in *The Hogarth Essays* (London: The Hogarth Press, 1924), 21–24.

[4] Raymond Williams, 'The Bloomsbury Fraction', in Raymond Williams (ed.), *Culture and Materialism: Selected Essays* (London: Verso, 2005), 148–170.

fraction is a part: that whole, to the extent that any society is a whole, was not national but continental.

'We were in the van of the builders of a new society.'[5] Leonard Woolf, in one of the most quoted passages of his work, thus announced what held the multi-vocal activities of the Bloomsbury circle together. Contemporaries of the aesthetic avant-gardes and of political vanguards, these builders gave themselves a different kind of nobility by indicating that their aesthetic genealogy was older.[6] They proceeded from engineering a revolution in aesthetic taste to what they hoped would be a social, political, and economic transformation. Vanity, though not a word that is obviously related to the families of vanguards, was another component of their work. Much of it involved the cultivation of different pursuits of self-representation, including bibliophile handwriting, self-portraits in front of hand-designed interiors, and publications of smaller and larger works of memoirs. This body of work has been influential both as a group and individually, especially the economic theory of 'Keynesianism'.[7]

A key element in Bloomsbury's capacity to furnish relationships, personal as well as political, were their global connections. These former Victorians were also Wagnerians, Nietzscheans, and admirers of modern impressionist art. The Bloomsbury fraction was simultaneously influenced by the cultural impulses associated with Bolshevik radicalism, the 'white émigré' culture' of people like Anrep and, indirectly, the 'internal exile' of like-minded elites like Anna Akhmatova, who occupied a former palace in the heart of Leningrad. Among these connections, however, their German network has been forgotten.

Thinking without headmasters: from the age of bad taste to a new society

One of the key figures whose life and thought allows us to reconstruct this connection was Count Harry Kessler, the Prussian count who had travelled to Mexico as a young man, then became a promoter of post-impressionist art in Germany, served as an officer in the Prussian army, and then

---

[5] Leonard Woolf, *Sowing: An Autobiography of the Years 1880–1904* (London: The Hogarth Press, 1964), 137.

[6] On Bloomsbury thought as a group, see Victoria Rosner (ed.), *The Cambridge Companion to the Bloomsbury Group* (Cambridge: Cambridge University Press, 2014), esp. introduction by Victoria Rosner, 1–15.

[7] On Keynes' rise in the 'golden age of capitalism' and calls for a return to Keynesianism in the economic crisis of 2007–09, see Robert Skidelsky, *Keynes: The Return of the Master* (London: Allen Lane, 2009).

advocated an alternative League of Nations. Like Roger Fry, Count Kessler in Germany identified 'bad taste' as a *chiffre* and perspective for his critical stance towards Wilhelm II. As Kessler admitted, the source of his irritation with the establishment of the Reich was the Kaiser's uniform 'lack of taste' in almost all spheres of life, in 'the choice of his friends and advisors, in art, in literature, in lifestyle, in politics'.[8] Wilhelm II, he argued in 1931, was in fact the very 'opposite of the German nobleman or the English gentleman' and made the German people more 'barbarian'. His interest in secessionist art movements and his open criticism of Wilhelm II himself made him susceptible to a search for political alternatives. Just like the Bloomsbury group, particularly, Leonard Woolf and John Maynard Keynes, Kessler turned his taste in art and literature, for which he was renowned in the European intellectual circles of his time, into the foundation of his political activism. For him as for them, the project of a bibliophile press combined aesthetic with political activism on an exclusive scale.

Having inherited a vast fortune from his father in 1892, Kessler became a patron for artists and writers and built an important collection of impressionist and neo-impressionist art. He was one of the first European patrons of Edvard Munch and Aristide Maillol.[9] By 1905, Kessler thought that 'no one else in Germany' enjoyed such high 'means of influence' on his contemporaries – especially in the sphere of cultural politics – as he did at that point.[10] His roles included his position on the directorial board of the German Artists' Union, co-founded by Kessler in 1903; his role as Artistic Director of the Weimar museums, a post he held since 1902; his connections with the modernist theatre of Max Reinhardt; his relations with the Nietzsche Archive, which he helped to found in 1894; his personal friendships with great artistic personalities in Europe like the Austrian poet Hugo von Hofmannsthal, with whom he collaborated on his opera *Der Rosenkavalier* and other works, and the Belgian designer Henry van de Velde, whose work he promoted in Germany; the progressive press, including *Die Zukunft* and *Die Neue Rundschau*; as well as 'Berlin society, the Harrachs, Richters, [. . .], the Regiment'; and finally, he added, his 'personal standing'.[11] Kessler sought to use this unique social position for

---

[8] Kessler, 5 December 1931, in Kessler, *Diaries*, vol. 9.

[9] On the reasons for his resignation, see Thomas Steinfeld, 'Als die Moderne nach Weimar wollte: Harry Graf Kessler, die Kunstdiplomatie und der Skandal um Auguste Rodin', in *Frankfurter Allgemeine Zeitung*, Nr. 26, 31 January 1998, as well as chapters in Grupp and Easton McLeod.

[10] Kessler, *Diaries*, 15 November 1905.

[11] Kessler was referring to his 3rd Guard Ulan Regiment and the names of prominent Berlin salonières, such as the house of Helene von Harrach, Helene von Nostitz, or the salon of Cornelie Richter, perhaps the most prominent meeting place for German intellectuals in Berlin at the time.

a 'renewal of German culture' and to become nothing less than a *princeps juventutis*.[12] Weimar's classical age was one historical model for this endeavour, Nietzsche's utopia of a revived European culture another.

Kessler, who, as we saw, worked as cultural attache for the German Foreign Office during the war, responded to the war similarly to the Bloomsbury group in other ways, too. He used German funds to sponsor the Comintern-funded Malik Publishing House, which had a very similar publishing programme in German to the Hogarth Press. One of its founders, the poet Else Lasker-Schüler, chose this name from the Hebrew term *melek*, which means King, but was also reminiscent of the *Moloch*, the false idol who demands large sacrifices.[13]

Historians of political thought have paid little attention to Kessler as a political thinker and, indeed, compared to contemporaries like Max Weber, whom he knew personally, he was hardly a significant writer. Yet, Kessler's political works – the essay on Nationality (1906, 1919, 1921), the manifesto *Guidelines for a True League of Nations* (1919–21), and the book *Germany and Europe* (1923) – represent a novel aspect of interwar German political thought.[14]

Discrediting old authorities and a commitment to a new internationalism was a key characteristic, which the Bloomsbury group shared with their wider European network, which included Kessler. For the Bloomsbury group, this idea was most clearly represented in one of the portraits of *Eminent Victorians*, the critical account of the Rugby school left by the influential Victorian Matthew Arnold.[15] This sense of dissidence towards received forms of authority was associated with a positive figure, namely, Friedrich Nietzsche. But they also shared many common influences. Among them was the work of Oscar Wilde, and the bibliophile press movement with its intellectual origins in the Victorian Arts and Crafts movement such as William Morris's Kelmscott Press.[16] Kessler belonged to the core of the first interpreters of Nietzsche who attempted to combine his aristocratic radicalism and his 'good Europeanism' into a political

[12] Kessler, *Diaries*, 15 November 1905.

[13] Wieland Herzfelde (Hg.), *Der Malik-Verlag*, Ausstellungskatalog (Berlin: Deutsche Akademie der Künste, 1967), 21.

[14] See, for example, Lothar Müller, 'Sekretдr seiner Zeit: Harry Graf Kessler', in *Merkur. Deutsche Zeitschrift für europдisches Denken*, 43 (1989), 174–181; Bernhard Zeller, *Harry Graf Kessler. Zeuge und Chronist seiner Epoche*, in *Abhandlungen der Klasse der Literatur* (Wiesbaden and Stuttgart: Franz Steiner, 1989).

[15] Lytton Strachey, *Eminent Victorians* (Letchworth: Garden City Press, 1918).

[16] On the importance of the Kelmscott Press for Bloomsbury, see Katherine Mullin, 'Victorian Bloomsbury', in Rosner (ed.), *The Cambridge Companion to the Bloomsbury Group*, 19–33.

programme.[17] But he was also intimately familiar with the world of the English schoolmasters and those who rebelled against them, having attended St George's School in Ascot as a boy.

The case of Kessler and his circle highlights the transnational significance of new cult authorities invoked to dismantle old beliefs. Kessler used the abbreviation 'Marx+Nietzsche', sometimes adding Kant, in this list.[18] This implied a middle ground between the violent political revolutionary action of the Spartakists (which they rejected) and 'formal' or 'bourgeois democracy' with its strong emphasis on the role of the state through party representatives. In addition to the more radical November Club, Kessler was also involved in the foundation of the more patriotic and centrist Union for a New Fatherland.[19]

Like Sidney and Beatrice Webb of the Fabians, and Leonard Woolf with his 1917 Club, the members of Kessler's November Club were also influenced by Saint-Simonean and Cobdean ideas of the modern as a technique of industrial as well as social organization. The emphasis of the November group on a foreign policy that emphasized national integration together with internationalist projects which involved the integration of labour and industry in Europe, and a domestic policy focusing on the social question and the nationalization of industry, marked not only the identity of the Weimar coalition. It was also a sign of the left and liberal policy that the Fabians were trying to find a kind of third way between the Comintern and the League.

From candour to new diplomacy

In 1929, Kessler was in London preparing for a radio conversation at the BBC about Germany's role in the present world, with the editor of the observer, the Irish intellectual James Louis Garvin. At this time, Virginia Woolf was engrossed in reading Kessler's biography of Walther Rathenau,

---

[17] Justus H. Ulbricht, *Klassikerstadt und Nationalsozialismus: Kultur und Politik in Weimar 1933 bis 1945* (Jena: Glaux, 2002); John A. MacCarthy, *Zensur und Kultur: zwischen Weimarer Klassik und Weimarer Republik mit einem Ausblick bis heute: From Weimar Classicism to Weimar Republic and beyond* (Tübingen: Niemeyer, 1995). Finally, Rathenau also followed Nietzsche's postulate 'to live dangerously' – a citation that had been heavily used in the British and French press during the First World War to show Nietzsche's influence on German militant spirit. Harry Graf Kessler, *Walther Rathenau*, transl. Denise Van Moppès (Paris: Grasset, 1933), 125. Nicholas Martin, '"Fighting a Philosophy": The Figure of Nietzsche in British Propaganda of the First World War', *The Modern Language Review*, 98:2 (1 April 2003), 367–380. Kessler, *Rathenau*, 75.

[18] Kessler, *Diaries*, 19 February 1919.

[19] The Union for a New Fatherland would be re-founded as an organization of exiles from Nazi Germany in 1935 as *Bund Neues Deutschland*.

the German finance minister who had been assassinated by right-wing extremists in 1922. 'You know, you have been spoiling my sleep this last week, by my husband insisting on reading to me passages of Your book', Virginia confessed to Harry over tea in her Bloomsbury home, soon after the book had been translated into English.[20] The work was an example of 'new diplomacy', an idea that captivated both the German and British disenchanted elites who saw in it a polite response to the post-imperial frankness of the Bolshevik *Red Archives* publication of formerly classified imperial documents.

The biography was written in the sprit of the Bloomsbury group's shared passion for personal memoirs. The Memoir Club gathered at the Woolfs' house regularly since the early 1920s. About sixty meetings are reported to have taken place in the forty-five years of the club's existence.[21] One occasion was particularly emblematic, when Leonard Woolf read a piece about his Ceylon civil service, E.M. Forster on difficulties with a landlord in Surrey, and Duncan Grant on the Cambridge Apostles. Woolf recalled that it was 'composed of old friends and family who were thoroughly familiar with the lives, characters and personalities of each memoirist'.[22] Kessler's *Rathenau* book and his work as a memoirist for the *Deutsche Nation* were thus not only socially but also formally complementary. They were all in search of a common phantom, the 'character' of the modern: not only their own, but also of others. Rathenau was a famously elusive and difficult character, and a model for Robert Musil's *The Man Without Qualities*. Peculiarly for this age, his murderer, Ernst von Salomon, not only outlived him but also published memoirs in later years.[23]

The new post-war memoirists made use of the interest in 'new diplomacy' as a vehicle of political communication, which included literature and literary exchange. At the same time as 'diplomacy by conference' continued a long tradition of international affairs established since the Holy Alliance, this generation of intellectuals acted as a collective 'social conscience' and a check on the politicians.[24] As Felix

---

[20] Kessler, *Diaries*, 14 November 1929.

[21] S.P. Rosenbaum, *The Bloomsbury Group Memoir Club* (London: Palgrave Macmillan, 2014), 8.

[22] Woolf, *Sowing*, 158 on Keynes' *Two Memoirs*. See also S.P. Rosenbaum and James H. Haule (eds.), *The Bloomsbury Group. A Collection of Memoirs and Commentary* (Toronto: University of Toronto Press, 1995), 5.

[23] Robert Musil, *Der Mann ohne Eigenschaften* (Hamburg: Rowohlt, 1930–43); Ernst von Salomon, *Der Fragebogen* (Hamburg: Rowohlt, 1951).

[24] Arno Mayer, *Political Origins of the New Diplomacy, 1917–1918* (New Haven, Conn.: Yale University Press, 1959); Kenneth W. Thompson, 'The New Diplomacy and the Quest for Peace', in *International Organization*, 19 (1965), 394–409; Frederick Sherwood Dunn, *The Practice and*

Gilbert remarked in 1951, repeating the experience of the United States and France in the eighteenth century, the twentieth-century idea of a 'new diplomacy' was once again developed by authors writing on behalf of states, which found themselves in an isolated position. This explains why the concept became attractive to Russia and post-war Germany.[25] The case of Kessler reflects this perspective. He wanted Germany to regain the status of a world power. He also wanted to show that out of its very defeat it generated new ideas that other states could learn from.

It had become common to speak of a new age of foreign affairs, when the old 'cabinet diplomacy' would be replaced with new forms of 'mass diplomacy'.[26] Like the League of Nations project, this notion of a 'new diplomacy' was associated with Woodrow Wilson, who proclaimed that in the future the world needed 'open covenants of peace, openly arrived at'.[27] Wilson's 'new diplomacy' responded to the Bolshevik declaration of a new diplomacy, developed around the same year. Kessler's circle, the November Club, espoused this notion programmatically.[28] Kessler considered the League of Nations to play a fundamental role in this new diplomatic turn. In an article on 'A New Method of Diplomacy', he argued that Europe and the world needed to establish institutions and regular conferences that would ensure the status of war as 'ultima ratio' in conflict.[29]

Procedure of International Conferences (Baltimore, London: The Johns Hopkins Press; H. Milford, Oxford University Press, 1929).

[25] On the 'new diplomacy' in international perspective, see Gordon Craig and Felix Gilbert, *The Diplomats: 1919–1939* (Princeton: Princeton University Press, 1953); and Hajo Holborn, *The Political Collapse of Europe* (Westport, Conn.: Greenwood Press, 1982).

[26] Kessler, *Diaries*, 20 January 1918.

[27] On the paradigm of new diplomacy, associated with Wilson and then applied to other historical periods, see Felix Gilbert, *The 'New Diplomacy' of the Eighteenth Century* (Indianapolis: Bobbs-Merrill, 1951), 1. Sidney Bell, *Righteous Conquest; Woodrow Wilson and the Evolution of the New Diplomacy* (Port Washington, N.Y.: Kennikat Press, 1972); A. L. Kennedy, *Old Diplomacy and New, 1876–1922, from Salisbury to Lloyd-George* (London: J. Murray, 1922).

[28] See *Eine neue Methode der Diplomatie*, special edition of *Der eiserne Steg* (Frankfurt/Main: Societätsdruckerei, 1925). The list of contributors comprises most members of the November Club and members of the pro-republican parties: Apart from Kessler, Friedrich Ebert, Hugo Preuss, René Schickele, Heinrich Simon, Fritz von Unruh, Alfred Fabre-Luce, Georg Bernhard, Leo Frobenius, Alfons Pauet, and some twenty other authors were among the contributors.

[29] Harry Graf Kessler, 'Eine neue Methode der Diplomatie', in *Die 5. Genfer Völkerbundtagung. Welche großen grundsätzlichen Fortschritte hat im September 1921 diese Tagung gebracht? Welche Vorteile hat Deutschland vom Völkerbund zu erwarten?* (Berlin: Deutsche Liga für Menschenrechte, 1924), 18.

Queer sexuality and political dissidence

The link between sexual openness and the Bloomsbury fraction is often presented as a unique case both within British culture and of this particular configuration. But in some respect, this feature was one of the transnational features of its mentality. According to Florence Tamagne, there was a strong connection in interwar Europe between sexual deviance, aesthetic counter-culture, and political dissidence.[30] This was also true of queer identities in Germany, Austria, and Soviet Russia.[31] At the same time, Weimar Germany and republican Austria functioned for British Edwardians like John Lehman and the wider circle of poets and intellectuals like Stephen Spender and Christopher Isherwood like the Maghreb did for André Gide: as sites where colonial and post-imperial situations of instability enabled new forms of sexual experimentation despite the nominal persistence of repressive laws.[32]

Like members of the Bloomsbury circle, Kessler was known as a prominent dandy. He not only enjoyed what we now call Weimar culture in the company of male sexual partners but also enabled new forms of gender performance in general, for instance, by sponsoring private performances of Josephine Baker. When in 1906, Maximilian Harden, the editor of the journal *Die Zukunft*, started a public scandal by arguing that the so-called Liebenberg circle of advisors for Wilhelm II formed a 'homosexual conspiracy', Kessler faced a difficult choice.[33] As a homosexual himself, he nonetheless shared much of Harden's criticism of the Wilhelmine court.[34]

Thus, the most productive period of intellectual exchange between the disenchanted elites of Wilhelmine Germany and Victorian Britain was the interwar period. A number of key members who got involved in his project

---

[30] Florence Tamagne, *A History of Homosexuality in Europe: Volume 1 & 2: Berlin, London, Paris – 1919–1939* (New York: Algora, 2006).

[31] Dan Healey, *Homosexual Desire in Revolutionary Russia. The Regulation of Sexual and Gender Dissent* (Chicago: The University of Chicago Press, 2001).

[32] Cf. John Lehman, selections from *The Whispering Gallery* (1955), in Horst and Lois Jarka (eds.), *The Others' Austria* (Riverside, Calif.: Ariadne Press, 2011), 196–205.

[33] Susanne Zur Nieden, *Homosexualität und Staatsräson: Männlichkeit, Homophobie und Politik in Deutschland 1900–1945* (Frankfurt and New York: Campus, 2005). See also Kessler, *Diaries*, 15 September 1918: 'Rantzau sei unmöglich, weil er, wie Stein aus sicherer Quelle zu wissen vorgiebt, von der Polizei in Kopenhagen "vigiliert" werde, wegen homosexueller Sachen; es existierten Polizeiprotokolle, die die Entente, wenn er Reichskanzler werde, veröffentlichen könne.'

[34] Maximilian von Harden, 'Enthüllungen', in *Die Zukunft*, 57 (3 November 1906), 169–198; Maximilian von Harden, 'Präludium', in *Die Zukunft*, 57 (17 November 1906), 251–266; 'Dies Irae. Momentaufnahmen', in *Die Zukunft*, 57 (1 December 1906), 325–341; 'Schlussvortrag', in *Die Zukunft*, 61 (9 November 1907), 179–210; See also Isabel V. Hull, *The Entourage of Kaiser Wilhelm II, 1888–1918* (Cambridge and New York: Cambridge University Press, 1982).

'Third Weimar', such as André Gide, formed part of a kind of sexual dissident elite in France who formed a network of anti-fascist intellectuals. These networks obtained existential importance when they helped each other escape the Nazis.[35] Many of this group shared Virginia Woolf's belief that rather than being a deviant minority, their more pluralistic conception of gender and sexuality signalled the changing nature of 'human character' itself which had changed in this period.[36] In searching for an adequate form for this new character, they naturally gravitated towards a new kind of poetry.

The age of new internationalism was not to be confused with the practice of foreign military conscription in imperial Europe, Then, as Bernard Shaw had written, 'the Englishman' was forced to 'fight as a pressed man for Russia, though his father was slain by the Russians at Inkerman, and at France, though his grandfather fell at Waterloo charging shoulder to shoulder with Blücher's Prussians. The German is compelled by the Prussian, whom he loathes, to die for Turkey and for the Crescent as against Anglo-Saxon Christendom.'[37] Only Germany, Shaw predicted, would come out of this victorious process of post-imperial conversion.

When the League of Nations was founded, the Fabians, just like their German analogues, did not like the form that the League eventually took. They all proposed their own ideas for a League of Peoples, a model where the nation would be far less prominent. For Leonard Woolf, the solution lay in an international organization of heavy industry as well as workers. Because trusts in industry were becoming increasingly international, they were using the opportunity to break strike by virtue of their employees' divisions.[38] The task was to create structures that, in addition to these passions, would also represent 'group interests' which are not national.[39] As Daniel Laqua, Patricia Clavin, and others have shown, the institutional landscape associated with the International Labour Organization and similar associations has in fact indeed been greater than previously thought.[40] It remains one of the unjustly forgotten innovations of the

---

[35] Wolfgang Bialas and Burkard Stenzel (eds.), *Die Weimarer Republik zwischen Metropole und Provinz. Intellektuellendiskurse zur politischen Kultur* (Weimar, Cologne and Vienna: Böhlau, 1996).

[36] Virginia Woolf, 'Mr Bennett and Mrs Brown'.

[37] Bernard Shaw, introduction to Leonard Woolf's *International Government* (New York: Brentano's, 1916), ix–x. More on Leonard Woolf's work on the League of Nations and its reforms, see documents of the Fabian Research Department, and esp. his correspondence with Sidney Webb on 'supranational reform' (1915) at The Keep, Brighton.

[38] Ibid., 349.   [39] Ibid., 356.

[40] Cf. Daniel Laqua, 'Transnational Intellectual Cooperation, the League of Nations, and the Problem of Order', in *Journal of Global History*, 6:2 (2011), 223–247; see also Patricia Clavin's joint research project into the history of the League of Nations: www.leagueofnationshistory.org/homepage.shtml, accessed 5 May 2014.

interwar period, particularly in the age when the concept of sovereignty again applies more to corporations than it does to states.

The Emperors of Elegy

In the intellectual networks of the European queer community, some texts, including Virgil's *Eclogues*, served as key nodes of cultural identification. Kessler's Cranach Press also published a bibliophile edition of this text.[41] But after 1920, these ancient poets were eclipsed by new voices. To this disenchanted fraction, T.S. Eliot's *Waste Land*, which Leonard and Virginia Woolf first published in their journal *Criterion*, conveyed most clearly the ambivalent sense of loss associated with imperial decline.[42] One of the main voices of this multilingual poem calls out in German: *Bin gar keine Russin. Stamme aus Litauen. Echt Deutsch!* This polyglot swan song of European culture gave a subjective form to what was a geopolitical crisis. Out of the territorial fragments of the Habsburg, Hohenzollern, and Romanoff empires, two generations of politicians shaped parliamentary republics or smaller kingdoms along new principles of political legitimacy, such as national self-determination and the referendum. For some groups of people who inhabited these regions, the conversion of their former imperial identities into a national form of status was less straightforward than for others, and it is those polyglot subjectivities that Eliot's stylized poem evokes most poignantly.

The woman's words in T.S. Eliot's polyphonic vision of the *Waste Land* belonged to a person who is 'not a Russian', 'from Lithuania', but 'truly German'. In his recollection of past seasons spent in Europe, 'mixing memory and desire', T.S. Eliot conjured up the memory of summers spent on Munich's Starnberg Lake.[43] Embedded in the author's memory of summer is another person's memory of a winter, recollected by a woman called Marie: 'And when we were children, staying at the archduke's,/ My cousin's, he took me out on a sled,/ And I was frightened./ He said, Marie,/ Marie, hold on tight. And down we went.'[44] The reference to Lithuania, to a family of noble background (the archduke), and the notion

[41] *Les Eclogues de Virgile*, transl. and ed. Marc Lafargue, ill. by Eric Gill (Weimar: Cranachpresse, 1926).

[42] J. Howard Woolmer, *A Checklist of the Hogarth Press, 1917–1938* (Andes and New York: Woolmer & Brotherson, 1987).

[43] T.S. Eliot, 'The Waste Land', in *The Criterion*, 1:1 (October 1922), 50–64, 50.   [44] Ibid., 50.

of a nostalgic kind of memory suggests that one of the voices in his patchwork of European decline belongs to that of German settlers from the Baltic littoral, probably of aristocratic descent.

Another poet who was extremely popular in both British and German social circles in the 1920s and 1930s was Rainer Maria Rilke. He wrote elegies that appealed to a new generation of disenchanted educated elites in continental Europe because of his evocative sense of loss. He spoke like an oracle for that in-between generation of people who no longer belonged to the past and yet did not feel at home in the present. He called them the 'disinherited', or 'those who used to be', because they had never come into their own in the post-imperial world. To behold and to lament the world that they believed has been lost forever was all they could do. As Rilke put it:

> Every time the world turns upside down it leaves some disinherited
> Those who no longer own the past and do not yet grasp what is coming
> For the nearest is too far for the people
> *We* shall not be confused by this
> may it strengthen in us the purpose to glimpse
> a flicker of that recognised form.[45]

The Adriatic castle of Duino, which elicited Rilke's elegiac lament on decline, became a glue that connected this disparate yet related community of intellectuals who had been critics of empire yet mourned its decline.[46] In actual fact, the Rilke fans were the very opposite of a 'disinherited' community. Heirs of imperial wealth, derived from projects such as Anglo-German railway construction, banking, the British sugar trade, or the benefits of abolition, which resulted in compensation payments to a number of Bloomsbury families in the mid-nineteenth century, they were a rather well-to-do community of intellectuals who had made a point of converting this financial capital into symbolic values. Their influence consisted in their distinctive elite mentality, a sense of exclusivity

---

[45] 'Jede dumpfe Umkehr der Welt hat solche Enterbte/ denen das Frühere nicht und noch nicht das Nächste gehört./ Denn auch das Nächste ist weit für die Menschen. *Uns* soll/ dies nicht verwirren; es stärke in uns die Bewahrung/ der noch erkannten Gestalt.' My translation. Rainer Maria Rilke, Seventh of the *Duino Elegies* (1912–22).

[46] The last page reads:
   Count Harry Kessler planned the format of this volume. Eric Gill designed and himself cut on wood the initials. The italic type was designed by Edward Johnston and cut by E. Prince and G.T. Friend. The paper was made by a hand process devised in joint research by Count Harry Kessler and Gaspard and Aristide Maillol. The book was printed in the spring and winter of 1931. [...] The book was printed for the Hogarth Press, 52 Tavistock Road, London W.C. 1, and both the English and the German texts were reproduced by the courtesy of the Insel-Verlag in Leipzig who are also the Agents for the book in Germany.

and anti-herd sentiment.[47] Rilke with his elegiac evocation of imperial decline as an irrevocable fact of modern life provided one of the affective bonds between these former dissidents of Wilhelmine Germany and the renegade establishment of Victorian Britain and Austria-Hungary, which formed between the 1890s and reached an apogee at the beginning of the 1930s. These links demonstrate the social and emotional genealogy of a very distinctive European internationalism that was politically neither on the Left nor on the Right. Politically, they could be called the global Fabians due to their espousal of an aristocratic form of socialism; aesthetically, their tastes evolved from post-impressionism and the visual arts towards an espousal of lyrical modernism, best represented in Rilke's work, towards Soviet and anti-colonial socialist realism. By pursuing the social network behind the literary fashion of decline, we can also reconstruct the structure and function of what was a transnational affective community. This reconstruction takes us back to the late nineteenth century, when Kessler and the Bloomsbury people alike formed the vanguard of Europe's art connoisseurs and the first collectors of artists like Manet.

Rilke himself was rather familiar with these elite contexts and enjoyed the patronage of a number of such figures in his lifetime. Often without a permanent residence, Rilke often stayed for extensive periods at the palazzos and houses of his many patrons and, more often, patronesses: owners of palaces on the Adriatic, in the Swiss Alps, apartments in Venice and in Paris. One of Rilke's most spectacular hosts was the Duchess of Thurn and Taxis, owner of the Castle of Duino at the edges of the Adriatic Coast, which was not far from Emperor Maximilian's romantic castle of Miramar. Rilke had spent time there in 1912. The Adriatic Littoral and its cosmopolitan owners shaped a cultural zone between pan-Slavic and Italian nationalism under Habsburg hegemony, which was under threat as a result of war. Heavily destroyed in 1915 after bombing from Italian dirigible balloons and clashes between Italian and the remaining Austrian imperial army, after the Great War it became part of the new Italian state.[48] Occupied by fascist leaders of the Saló Republic and later by the Gestapo, in 1945, the joint Anglo-British allied command that took control over the Adriatic after the defeat of the Axis powers would choose Duino as its headquarters.[49]

[47] Desmond MacCarthy, unfinished Bloomsbury memoir, in Rosenbaum and Haule (eds.), *The Bloomsbury Group. A Collection of Memoirs and a Commentary*, 66–67.

[48] Dominique Kirchner-Reill, *Nationalists Who Feared the Nation. Adriatic Multi-Nationalism in Habsburg Dalmatia, Trieste, and Venice* (Palo Alto: Stanford University Press, 2012).

[49] Franklin Lindsay, *Beacons in the Night: With the OSS and Tito's Partisans in Wartime Yugoslavia* (Stanford: Stanford University Press, 1993).

On 2 November 1917, the war not over yet, Rilke was having breakfast with Kessler in Berlin's fashionable Hotel Adlon. He had briefly served in Austria-Hungary's propaganda department. After abandoning this office, he was stateless out of necessity and homeless out of choice.[50] Rilke is often thought of either as a German poet, by which people primarily mean the language in which he wrote but often imply the state, or as a poet of modernity without further specification.[51] Yet in fact, both Rilke and Kessler formed part of a specific cosmopolitan community. Their way of thinking was geographical but not in a static way; they remembered the past in terms of symbolic events connected to symbolic places, experiences, and works of art that they considered canonical.

The encounter between the poet and reluctant propagandist for Austria-Hungary, and Kessler, the Maecenas, officer, and head German propaganda, was symptomatic of a particular circle of disenchanted imperial elites. Rilke admitted that the ongoing war made him confused. 'Where do I belong?' he asked. Kessler explained his sentiment with the fact that the war had undermined the 'entire foundation of his former life, of every poem that he had written'. His individual 'drive towards form', Kessler surmised, contradicted the 'force of the state', especially an Austrian state.[52] Rilke's highly stylized sonnets and hexameters were particularly suited to the German language, and yet, Kessler thought, not to a particular state. At this time, his main publisher and supporter, Anton Kippenberg of the Insel publishing house, was leading propaganda efforts on Germany's western front, in Belgium; under his aegis, the image of the Leipzig Battle of the Peoples memorial, completed as a warning for peace in 1913, became the symbol of another war as it had been turned into the design for the censorship of the German army.

Rilke had been among a close circle of people who would receive Kessler's diary-like reports on the war from the eastern front. But like Kessler, he saw the war in a Tolstoyan light, as a social universe rather than as a frontline where Russia, Germany, and Britain were on opposite sides. He praised Kessler for writing about war in the spirit of Tolstoy's *War and Peace*.[53] Rilke himself had been a Tolstoyan before the war. Rilke's lover at

---

[50] Originally, Kessler had wanted Rilke to move from Vienna to Bern in 1918, but then Rilke was able to acquire Czechoslovak citizenship by virtue of having been born in Prague and used this citizenship to continue living in Switzerland, where he died in 1926. Kessler, *Diaries*, 18 April 1918.

[51] Cf. Charles Taylor, *The Sources of the Self. The Making of Modern Identity* (Cambridge, Mass.: Harvard University Press, 1989), 501, drawing on Heidegger.

[52] Kessler, *Diaries*, 2 November 1917.

[53] Rilke to Baronin Dorothea von Ledebur, 14 November 1917, in Rainer Maria Rilke, *Briefe Zur Politik*, Hg. Joachim W. Storck. (Frankfurt/main und Leipzig: Insel, 1992), Nr. 90.

the time, Lou Andreas Salome, a former passion of Nietzsche and a student of Freud, had introduced Rilke to Tolstoy on their trip to Russia.[54] In the 1920s, he immersed himself in translations of a historical epic poem from medieval Russia, the Song of Igor, about the decline of princely power and the Time of Troubles in the thirteenth century.[55] The Bloomsbury group was also attracted to these plots.

The kind of conversation that Rilke and Kessler were having was both a product and a contribution to the process of a sentimental education. In their conversations and in writing, they developed an emotional code whose function is to reflect on the loss of a beloved object: the life of Europe in the past.[56] When in England, Kessler frequented meetings of the Fabian Society, who influenced much of his political and economic thought. He was particularly drawn to intellectual circles which promoted new artistic movements, such as impressionism and neo-impressionism, across national boundaries. As a member of the artistic union *Pan* around the art historian Julius Meier-Graefe, he had introduced impressionist and neo-impressionist art to Germany, stirring resistance from nationalist circles. In Germany, Kessler also formed part of the first generation of German youths attracted to the cult of Friedrich Nietzsche, and began to play a prominent role in these circles. He closed Nietzsche's eyes on his deathbed in August 1900.[57]

Rilke's elegiac sense of threat to this way of life, expressed in his *Duino Elegies*, a cycle of poems that he composed between 1912 and 1922, brought him world fame. It found echoes in his social circle, which comprised educated Europeans of higher social background. Most of them came from Germany, Russia, France, and Austria-Hungary. In translation, he would also become famous among English-speaking readers, but this fame would grow primarily after the Second World War.

Lovers of Rilke ranged from the Bloomsbury group in Britain to former admirers of neo-impressionist art in Germany, to a wider circle of European Nietzscheans.[58] A closer look at the transnational dimension of

---

[54] Lew Kopelew, 'Rilke in Rußland', *Die Zeit*, 21 April 1972. Cf. also Rilke to Alexei Suworin, 5 March 1902, in Rainer Maria Rilke, *Briefe in zwei Bänden*, 1. Bd. 1896 bis 1919, ed. Horst Nalewski (Frankfurt and Leipzig: Insel, 1991), Nr. 27.

[55] 'Und da, Brüder, begann eine ungute Zeit; in der Einöde lag begraben die russische Macht'. 'Die Mär von der Heerfahrt Igors', Übertragung von R. M. Rilke, in *Dichtung und Welt*, 7 (1930); Rainer Maria Rilke, 'Aus der Übertragung der altrussischen Dichtung «Das Igorlied»', *Insel-Almanach auf das Jahr 1931*.

[56] On the term 'semantic deprivation', see Andreas Lawaty and Hubert Orlowski (eds.), *Deutsche und Polen. Geschiche – Kultur – Politik* (Munich: Siedler, N6, 2003).

[57] Kessler, *Diaries*, 27 August 1900.

[58] Leonard Woolf recalls being secretary of Roger Fry's second post-impressionist exhibition at the Grafton galleries. Woolf, *Sowing*, 122.

this community of taste raises the question as to what extent we should consider them 'fractions' of their class within any one nation or empire, or if we should consider them representatives of one 'fraction' of the same class across national boundaries. I would suggest that it is at least as valid to speak of a transnational emotional community of lovers of modernist art whose taste, however, ceased to evolve in some respects after the mid-1920s. To use an expression coined by Barbara Rosenwein, these emotional communities also contributed to a political sentiment or political regime, which has very real political repercussions.[59]

After Rilke's untimely death in 1926, Count Kessler collaborated with Germany's Kippenberg publishing house, as well as Leonard and Virginia Woolf's Hogarth Press, to bring out the *Duino Elegies* in English translation.[60] The illustrations were designed by the British sculptor Eric Gill, who made woodcuts for the book, and the paper was made by the Maillol brothers; the printer was Kessler's long-time lover Max Goertz.[61] The Woolfs also published Rilke's *Notebooks*, and the Hogarth executive John Lehmann later oversaw the English translation rights for Rilke in the British Empire in negotiation with US publishers.[62] The taste for Rilke shared by this small circle of British and German intellectuals was echoed by other contemporary literary cults, such as the growing fascination with the poetry of T.S. Eliot, the prose of Marcel Proust, and, in Germany, the poetry of Stefan George.[63]

The European social network of Rilke lovers had evolved from similar roots. For people such as Kessler and the Woolfs, this path began with an aesthetic and spiritual disenchantment with the political ideology into which they were born, which was Victorian Britain and Wilhelmine Germany. It led them through a period of aesthetic innovation, during which – around the 1900s – they began promoting neo-impressionist

---

[59] Barbara Rosenwein, 'Worrying About Emotions in History', in *American Historical Review*, 107:3 (June 2002), 821–845.

[60] Rainer Maria Rilke, *Duineser Elegien. Elegies from the Castle of Duino*, transl. V. Sackville-West and Edward Sackville-West (London: The Hogarth Press, 1931); this book was printed by Harry Kessler and Max Goertz in Weimar: Cranach Press.

[61] Woolmer, *A Checklist*, 92–93.

[62] Rainer Maria Rilke, *The Notebook of Malte Laurids Brigge*, transl. John Linton (London: The Hogarth Press, 1931). See also the Woolfs' edition of Rilke's *Poems*, transl. J.B. Leishman (London: The Hogarth Press, 1934), as well as, by the same translator, *Requiem and Other Poems* (1935), *Sonnets to Orpheus* (1936), and finally, *Later Poems* (1938). For the background to this collaboration, see Ms2750/379, Archives of the Hogarth Press, Reading, for a correspondence with Cranach Press regarding the translation of Rainer Maria Rilke's *Duino Elegies*.

[63] On the Stefan George circle in the context of post-imperial mourning, see Melissa Lane and Martin Ruehl (eds.), *A Poet's Reich: Politics and Culture in the George Circle* (London: Camden House, 2011).

French art in Germany and Britain, respectively, and took on Ruskinian ideas in promoting an elite kind of socialism. Finally, politically, it culminated with a sincere attempt to contribute to a new European internationalism through the institutional framework of the League of Nations and international labour organizations.

As Heinrich Simon of the Fischer publishing house said of Count Kessler, he formed the centre of a social circle that constituted the aristocratic Fronde against the conservative milieu around Wilhelm II. It was this Fronde that eventually shaped the transition of the Kaiserreich into a 'republic'.[64] This group had long delegitimized Wihelm II and his entourage. While critical of the Versailles settlement, they nonetheless saw in Germany's peace settlement a unique opportunity for a revolution from above. The parallel with the original Fronde implied in this reference worked on two levels. Firstly, labelling them a 'Fronde' was appropriate because it referred to the seventeenth-century resistance of the French nobility against the encroachment of its liberties by a corrupt monarch and his counsellor Cardinal Mazarin; secondly, it indicated that, just as in seventeenth-century France, a civil war mounted between the nobility and the monarch eventually culminated in a European war of a much larger scale.[65]

Mixing memory and desire: in search of a post-imperial character

From questions of aesthetic modernism and the education of a public, the community of British Fabians and German republican dissidents turned easily to the subject of international order. Leonard Woolf began compiling a series of works on war and peace with significant contributions from Russia during the war, along with a memorandum on international government that was given to the British delegation in Versailles.[66] With the help of poets like T.S. Eliot and Rilke, post-imperial melancholy became an affective glue for an international community of intellectuals located on the left-liberal spectrum, whose lives span both the interwar period and Europe's second post-war.[67] Leonard Woolf's *International Government*

---

[64] Kessler, *Diaries*, 5 December 1931. Kessler's publisher Heinrich Simon used this expression to describe Kessler's career.

[65] On the Secession group, see Peter Paret, *The Berlin Secession: Modernism and its Enemies in Imperial Germany* (Cambridge, Mass.: Belknap Press of Harvard University Press, 1980); Peter Gay, *Weimar Culture: The Outsider as Insider* (London: Secker & Warburg, 1968).

[66] Leonard Woolf papers, IF9b, 'A short peace and war bibliography', University of Sussex Special Collections. On Woolf's internationalism, see also Christine Froula, 'War, Peace and Internationalism', in Rosner (ed.), *The Cambridge Companion to the Bloomsbury Group*, 93–112.

[67] Kessler, *Diary*, 6 December 1929.

(1916) was in many ways a British forerunner to Kessler's *Guidelines for a True League of Nations* (1919–21).[68] Both author-publishers significantly transformed their patronage of other people's writing in the interwar period. In Woolf's case, he began promoting anticolonial writing such as the work of C.L.R. James, while Kessler published a collection of war poems with illustrations by the communist artist George Grosz. Both were sensitive to the ambiguity of empires between cultural pluralism and economic hierarchy, they devoted a significant amount of time to the League of Nations, and particularly to drafting its reforms. Moreover, both did so by considering the possibility of a synthesis between spiritual internationalism, industrial and workers' councils, and parliamentary democracy. They also forged ties between Russian socialists and Western liberals, something Kessler was very much part of during his time in Switzerland.[69]

In the American preface to his novel about Ceylon, one of Britain's first experiments of imperial devolution in which Woolf served as a civil servant, Woolf provided an allegory of civilization and barbarism through the lens of the village and its surrounding jungle. His main fascination was with tracing 'vanished' villages in the midst of desolation. One particular village

> had strange things about it and in it. It had once many hundreds of years ago been populous, a country with powerful kings and a civilisation of its own. The ruins of great buildings and kings' palaces and temples and gigantic dagobas still stand in Tissamaharama. And in the north, buried in the jungle so deep that thirty yards away you can see no trace of them, I have come upon the remains of magnificent irrigation works, giant sluices, stone work and masonry, and the great channels which – you can still trace them – brought the water miles and miles from the Walawe River to the great tanks and reservoirs, now mere jungle. In those days all over the country which is now a wilderness there must have been villages and rice fields. Those were the days of Sinhalese kings.[70]

The effect of post-imperial mourning among this transnational fraction of an imperial elite was varied. On the one hand, it produced highly articulate accounts of international government and justifications for supranational

---

[68] See, for example, Müller, 'Sekretär seiner Zeit: Harry Graf Kessler', 174–181; Zeller, *Harry Graf Kessler. Zeuge und Chronist seiner Epoche*, in *Abhandlungen der Klasse der Literatur*.

[69] Cf. Boris Nicolaevsky Papers, Correspondence between N. Rubakin and Prof. Yaschenko (book seller in Berlin), Folder 32: 126 (17 January 1921), HA; Box 496/ 3, Letters from M.N. Pavlovski (31 October and 8 and 26 November 1962), with copies of enclosed internal German government correspondence, Akten Ru (Martel), L. 849/L. 244.000.244.046, HA.

[70] Leonard Woolf, *The Village in the Jungle* (New York: Harcourt, 1937), preface.

organizations for labour as well as producers and, in the case of Kessler's plan, of spiritual organizations. On the other hand, these circles retained some serious limitations, from being almost exclusively masculine to having their origins in secret or closed associations. They originated in student fraternities and secret societies such as the Cambridge Apostles or the Canitz fraternity in the case of Kessler. The biographical and autobiographical genres provided them with a means to express contradictory feelings of nostalgia for imperial multiculturalism and sympathy for the new revolutions.

Within this genre, they engaged in detailed phenomenologies of cosmopolitan identity in the age of empire. As Leonard Woolf put it, 'When I try to look objectively into my own mind, I detect feelings of loyalty to: my family; "race" (Jews), my country, England in particular, and the British Empire generally, places with which I have been connected, such as Kensington and London (born and bred), counties, Middlesex and Sussex, where I have lived, Ceylon, Greece; school; Trinity and Cambridge.'[71]

There is a painting by Vanessa Bell, which illustrates how memory functioned at both a personal and a social level in the Bloomsbury circle. In 1920, the group, including the Woolfs, the Bells, the Keynes, and others, started a series of gatherings they called 'The Memoir Club'. It persisted into the early 1960s. On the painting itself, from 1943, we see twelve members of the Bloomsbury circle, mostly men like Leonard Woolf and Maynard Keynes, and some women like Lydia Lopokova, Keynes's wife, surrounded by portraits of deceased members, including, by this point in time, Virginia Woolf herself.[72]

The purpose of sharing such diverse memories was to identify their place in the present in relation to a common account of the past. As Leonard Woolf put it,

> I feel that my roots are here and in the Greece of Herodotus, Thucydides, Aristophanes, and Pericles. I have always felt in my bones and brain and heart English and, more narrowly, a Londoner, but with a nostalgic love of the city and civilization of ancient Athens. Yet my genes and chromosomes are neither Anglo-Saxon nor Ionian. When my Rodmell neighbours' forefathers were herding swine on the plains of eastern Europe and the Athenians were building the Acropolis, my Semitic ancestors, with the days of their national greatness, such as it was, already behind them, were in Persia or Palestine. And they were already prisoners of war, displaced

---

[71] Woolf, *Sowing*, 212–213.   [72] Vanessa Bell, *The Memoir Club* 1943. Tate Britain.

Figure 26 Boris von Anrep, 'Here I lie'. Fragment from his National Gallery mosaic
(1952).
© The National Gallery, London. Reproduced by kind permission of the Estate of
Boris Anrep

persons, refugees, having begun that unending pilgrimage as the world's
official fugitives and scapegoats which has brought one of their descendants
to live, and probably die, Parish Clerk of Rodmell in the County of Sussex.[73]

He then gives another test to his divided identities by suggesting that in
a game or sport he is distinctly happy if one of the following wins:
St. Paul's, his school, Cambridge University, his university, followed by
England, and the British Empire, followed by Sussex and Middlesex in
county cricket. In the autobiographic remarks of this 'born and bred'
Londoner, we can sense a greater multiplicity of consciousness than in
the pages of the colonial subject C.L.R. James, who is at home in the great

[73] Woolf, *Sowing*, 15.

Figure 27 Vanessa Bell, *The Memoir Club* (ca. 1943).
© estate of Vanessa Bell. Reproduced by kind permission of Henrietta Garnett

literary genres, in the game of cricket, and in the national idea of the West Indies.

In a contribution to an earlier gathering, the Society of Heretics, in 1924, Virginia Woolf suggested that the character of the British imperial self was changing in their lifetime. She compared this process to the way an imaginary train moved from Richmond to Waterloo. The works of the age of transition are full of 'incompleteness and dissatisfaction' because they fail in the primary expectation which people have from literature, namely to turn 'phantoms' into the actual characters of an age. Imagining a classic scene of literary modernism, a conversation in a train, she thought how a Frenchman, an Englishman, and a Russian would narrate it, before concluding that great novels, 'clumsy and verbose' as well as 'rich and elastic', would betray their calling if they praised the 'glories of the British empire' or any doctrine instead of being sincere expressions of the characters of their time.[74] The challenge was that in the 1920s, imperial

---

[74] Woolf, 'Mr Bennet and Mrs Brown', 10 and passim.

dissolution itself had become manifest in the characters of particular individuals, and it is from the crisis of that character that the crisis of forms, in her view, also derived.

The international thought of this combined fraction of post-Victorians and the post-Wilhelmians could be described as the theoretical equivalent to this aesthetic search. Insofar as they acknowledged the need to disarticulate forms of privilege and geopolitics typical for empires, experimentation with genres for this community was inseparable from their experimentation with theories of social organization. The Hogarth Press was the virtual location that brought all of these strands together: alternative diasporic identities for Jewish and Caribbean intellectuals, personal memoirs and biographies, internationalist political treatise, and poetry reflecting on Europe as a wasteland. Here was the link between a form of exclusive print production in the era of print capitalism, a voluntary demodernization of an intellectual elite. The connection between decolonization and psychoanalysis, as Said perceptively noted, was not only a connection that later scholars would impose on the past. It was also rooted in the corporate history of the European presses of the interwar period, their collaborations with each other, and with their authors.

Bell's painting of the Memoir Club can be compared to another room with portraits we last encountered in the context of Pan-Europeanism. In the photograph of the opening of Coudenhove's Paneuropa Congress, we saw a very different public space. Yet, in some essential way, it is a space that is very similar to the private intimacy of the Memoir Club. The photograph of the congress of 1926 is emblematic of the enthusiasm with which European internationalists set out to build better post-imperial foundations for a new and better European Empire. The painting from 1943 – even the fact that it is a painting is significant – indicates a retreat into the private realm of introspection and memoirs. In this juxtaposition, we have the arc of development that the social history of 'European civilization' had taken from the end of the First World War until the outbreak of the Second World War.[75]

The oceanic feeling for empire

While Leonard Woolf and the Fabians primarily meant the working classes when speaking about non-national interests, there were also two more functions of the Hogarth Press that their press ended up fulfilling. They

---

[75] Williams, 'Fraction', 154 and passim.

served as a bridge for two social groups that at first sight do not have a lot in common. They were the Jewish community of refugees from Nazi Germany and Europe, who settled in London after 1933, and the community of intellectuals who came to London or other parts of Britain to study from the Caribbean. For all these communities, imperial memory provided a secular analogy to the 'oceanic feeling' that they, together with Freud, criticized among the religious fundamentalism of the Victorian 'headmasters'.[76]

An interest in reading against the grain of dominant historical narrative was another commonality of this circle. In this respect, James's interest in Toussaint L'Ouverture, the black Caribbean double to Europe's continental revolutionaries, can be compared to Freud's interest in Habsburg philosemitism and in Moses's non-European, Egyptian roots. In his essay on anti-Semitism from 1938, which he published in the émigré journal *Die Zukunft*, co-edited by Arthur Koestler and others, Freud recalled an author whose name he had forgotten, and who had written a text that celebrated the contributions of the Jews to European cultural life. He invited his readers to help: 'Perhaps one of the readers of this periodical will be able to come to my help?' But then, Freud interjected:

> A whisper has just reached my ears that what I probably had in mind was Count Heinrich Coudenhove-Kalergi's book *Das Wesen des Antisemitismus*, which contains precisely what the author I am in search of missed in the recent protests, and more besides. I know that book. It appeared first in 1901 and was re-issued by his son in 1929 with an admirable introduction. But it cannot be that. What I am thinking of is a shorter pronouncement and one of very recent date. Or am I altogether at fault? Does nothing of the kind exist? And has the work of the two Coudenhoves had no influence on our contemporaries?[77]

To those authors who mourned the Habsburg past, this mourning was often expressed with reference to the dynasty itself, or to other noble families.[78] Habsburg's decline and that of other high nobility became an allegorical narrative for the loss of a cultural system. Sigmund Freud's work provided a guide for viewing geography psychologically. His amateur studies of Roman archaeology and the multilayered archaeological

---

[76] See Freud's critique of Matthew Arnold in the introduction to *Civilization and its Discontents*.

[77] Sigmund Freud, 'A Comment on Anti-Semitism', in Freud, *Moses and Monotheism, An Outline of Psycho-Analysis and Other Works* (1937–38), vol. xxiii, ed. and transl. James Strachey (London: Vintage/The Hogarth Press, 2001), 287–301, 292–292. Originally published in *Die Zukunft: ein neues Deutschland, ein neues Europa*, 7 (25 November 1938).

[78] Freud, *Moses and Monotheism*.

memory of the city of Rome served to him and the international following of his Psychoanalytic Society as a metaphor for grasping the decline of
more than one empire. If, by a 'flight of imagination', Freud urged his
readers, we supposed that the city of Rome was a 'psychical entity with
a similarly long and copious past', what we would find would be a multilayered presence of all its epochs at once. The ruins of the city made
visible to visitors of Rome the absence of the past, which for many people
looked different. Some longed for Rome of Antiquity in the republican
period; the fascists around Mussolini, undoubtedly, looked for the
Roman Empire's expansion under the Caesars as their model. For others
again, the model of Roman greatness lay in the Renaissance, when the
city had actually shared its importance with other cultural centres, such as
Florence. The city became an object of different kinds of political
mourning, the suffering of a loss not of a 'beloved person' but of 'an
abstraction' with which one could be enamoured, such as the 'fatherland,
freedom, an ideal, etc.'[79]

The Hogarth Press not only first introduced Freud to English readers.
It also did the same for another intellectual outsider, the West Indian
aesthete C.L.R. James, who had arrived in England first to accompany
a cricketer and who ended up becoming a theorist of West Indian self-
government with the help of the Woolfs. His *Case for West Indian Self-
Government* effectively extrapolated the Wilsonian logic of nation states
devised for post-imperial Europe for the colonies of the British Empire in
the Caribbean.

At a time when other British publishers were reluctant to publish
critiques of empire, such as Eric Williams' *Capitalism and Slavery*, the
Woolfs seemed to be happy to take the risk. C.L.R. James can be rightly
counted as a belated member of the Bloomsbury group. He had even
adopted their manner of writing memoirs and biographies – the subjects of
a regular club formed by the original Bloomsbury circle – and ended up
writing further books in a much more biographical fashion. His master-
piece remains his cricket autobiography *Beyond a Boundary*, a book in
which he argued that the British art of cricket was an imperial art form.
A reluctant Trotskyist, James eventually gave up his identity as a diasporic
theorist for the case of West India in favour of a more universalist espousal
of socialist realism. Leonard Woolf was concerned with the British man-
date system and was a very active member of the League of Nations

---

[79] Sigmund Freud, 'Trauer und Melancholie', in *Internationale Zeitschrift für Ärztliche Psychoanalyse*,
4:6 (1917), 288–301.

Union.[80] These imperial elites' previous complicity in colonial violence, wrote John Strachey in 1959, gave Europeans the task to resist turning the 'sword of empire' into a 'stone of indifference' to the plight of the formerly colonized.[81]

More recently, new British history has challenged previously existing ideas of the 'national' character to which such groups contribute by extending Bloomsbury to the British Empire. But these directions of research have not yet challenged the image of the club as distinctly national, rather than internationalist, in character. In this way, Anrep's mosaics could be compared to the selected 'scraps of talk' and fragments which dropped German and other cultures from this selectively cosmopolitan memory of empire.

On 23 July 1940, three years after Kessler had passed away in exile in Lyon, the Hogarth Press was trying to locate his heirs in order to transfer payments for royalties from the book. In response, they received these words passed on from a renowned British calligrapher who knew William Rothenstein, who had gone to the same British school as the German Count: 'Kessler was a good man who lost, not only a fortune, but practically everything he valued in life.'[82]

Financial ruin, suicides, on one end, and radicalization towards the Soviet Left or fascist right on the other end were the most visible markers of this dissolution. This elite had been most at home in the opposition to imperial governments with bad taste, those associated with Wilhelm II or high Victorianism. But in the absence of these institutions, they were no longer the angriest of the angry young men. In fact, their aesthetic tastes had evolved in a rather similar direction to the international modernism which the new empires, the Nazis and the Soviet Union, demonstrated in Paris. This, as Kessler remarked, was particularly awkward as they had been used to associating good taste with ideas for a good government.

This generation of internationalists provided other Europeans and non-European contemporaries of their class with a vocabulary for grasping multiple forms of political decline and social disintegration. Between the year 1937, the year of the Great Exposition in Paris, and 1941, the year when the Blitz war destroyed large parts of Bloomsbury, this

---

[80] Leonard Woolf, 'The Mandates and the Mandated Areas (Tropical Colonies)', in Leonard Woolf papers, 3.1, Special Collections, the University of Sussex. See also Leonard Woolf, 'Perpetual Peace by Immanuel Kant 1795', and 'A short Peace and War Bibliography', ibid., section 9.

[81] John Strachey, *The End of Empire* (New York: Random House, 1959).

[82] George Milsted to the Directors of the Hogarth Press, 23 July 1940. Reading Special Collections, Hogarth archive.

group disintegrated. As Europe's imperial frontiers had moved more aggressively into Africa in the nineteenth century, terms like 'hinterland' and 'borderland' began to be used closer to home and applied metaphorically to the unconscious.[83] After the Second World War, it became particularly common to compare the internal frontiers of eastern Europe with the uncharted lands of Africa.[84]

This transnational social fraction of an old imperial elite had a significant impact on the way Europeans imagined Europe in the inter-war period and on the formation of the concept of a European civilization that was to survive even such atrocities as the Holocaust. Its impact beyond Europe was to provide a framework for thinking postcolonially. But in Europe these 'civilizers' never decolonized themselves. Even the sceptical fraction of a self-doubting European imperial class remained, to adopt the title of Leonard Woolf's book, a small village in the jungle. Its intellectual exclusivity and its narcissistic parochialism were two sides of the same coin.

[83] Mary Katharine Bradby, *Psycho-Analysis and Its Place in Life* (1919).
[84] Evelyn Waugh, *Brideshead Revisited* (Boston: Little, Brown and Company, 1945).

Epilogue

'Choose your ancestors'

Devise found on a coat of arms

The longevity of imperial mentalities in the age of mass culture and revolution appears to be a paradox, or at least an anachronism. Empires offered unequal benefits to their subjects, and in the twentieth century, people had more capacity to recognize this, thanks to the rise of global media, and the transnational connections of the revolutionary movements. Some historians have called this the puzzle of the 'persistence of the old regime', meaning the continued inequality in the national distribution of resources in European societies in the aftermath of the twentieth-century revolutions.[1] Even the most recent debates about Europe's economic future see the continuity of power associated with patrimonial private wealth as one of the principal causes for social inequality.[2]

In this book, I have taken a step away from the 'persistence' debate by looking at the transformation of imperial prestige in Europe's intellectual communities. Recovering the way in which the European intelligentsia spoke, thought, and felt about imperial decline, I hope, will invite more discussion of the question of 'how' patrimonies of empire were absorbed in transnational contexts. The European network of intellectuals discussed here recycled their sense of past empires into a new concept of Europe. Their varied experiences of imperial administration, the management of international relations between empires, were offered in response to the revolutions and civil wars in Russia, Germany, and Austria. In this context, their roots in the dissident fractions of Europe's imperial elites became part of the peculiar prestige of this group.

---

[1] Arno Mayer, *The Persistence of the Old Regime* (London: Croom Helm, 1981); Hans-Ulrich Wehler (ed.), *Europäischer Adel 1750–1950* (Göttingen: Vandenhoeck & Ruprecht, 1989).
[2] Thomas Piketty, *Le capital au XXIème siècle* (Paris: Seuil, 2013).

In addition to uncovering this broader intellectual terrain, I wished to explain the importance of a particular set of German-speaking elites in shaping cosmopolitan visions of empire. This had nothing to do with the desire to rehabilitate some aspect of Germany's national past, or that of elites more generally. Rather, I hoped to rebalance the history of post-imperial European thought in transnational perspective. In the aftermath of Germany's second defeat in 1945, the relationship between German elite culture and liberal internationalism has been understandably obscured, since historians have been focusing largely on the history of Germany's political deviance. But a more recent turn to German intellectual history in transnational and global perspective has enabled a different perspective on this past.[3]

Pan-Europe: brief history of a separation

In a speech that he gave in the aftermath of the Second World War at Zurich University, Winston Churchill contrasted the 'frightful nationalistic quarrels' of the twentieth century provoked by the 'Teutonic' nations with the image of another Europe. 'This noble continent', he argued, 'comprising on the whole the fairest and the most cultivated regions of the earth, enjoying a temperate and equable climate, is the home of all the great parent races of the western world'.[4] This noble Europe was the site of 'western civilisation', he argued, whose pedigree included the 'ancient States and Principalities' of the 'Germany of former days' but excluded the 'Teutonic nations'.[5]

With utterances of this kind, an essentially Anglo-American community of political leaders took it upon itself to save the idea of Europe after the defeat of National Socialism. Severing ideas of Germanness from notions of civility and nobility was one part of that undertaking.[6] As they buried the failed League of Nations and proclaimed the United Nations as its successor, intellectuals and policymakers of a new world order in western Europe, the Middle East, and the United States were effectively saying:

[3] Cf. Dirk A. Moses, *Empire, Colony, Genocide: Conquest, Occupation, and Subaltern Resistance in World History* (Oxford: Berghahn, 2008); Conze, *Das Europa der Deutschen*.
[4] Winston Churchill, *Europe Unite: Speeches 1947 and 1948* (London: Cassell, 1950), esp. 'A Speech at Zurich University', 19 September 1946, 197–202, and at the Albert Hall on 14 May 1947, 194–197.
[5] Ibid., 194–197.
[6] On the concept of European rehabilitation in connection with German history, see especially Charles Maier, *The Unmasterable Past: History, Holocaust, and German National Identity* (Cambridge, Mass.: Harvard University Press, 2009).

'Europe is dead. Long live Europe!'[7] The impact of this idea of Europe on European society is that it has allowed Europeans to reconstruct their good conscience, to create a continent that is largely peaceful inside its borders, even though Europeans continue to fight wars beyond Europe and justify their arbitrary frontiers with references to historical pasts. The result could be compared to the way the ideal body of the king was remembered in medieval political theology: for the sake of a stable order, it is necessary that the ideal body survives the physical death of any particular office holder in the minds of its subjects.[8] The difference was that here the physical bodies that had died were multiple and had disparate meanings for different communities: dynastic leaders in the First World War followed by millions of individual and unnamed soldiers, and populations which had become victims of ethnic cleansing.[9]

Membership in the new body of Europe, which was economically grounded in the Rome agreements of 1957, was the result of a longer process of selection and division in which historical arguments played a key part in justifying political changes. Thus in Churchill's mind, Germany's principalities became associated with the 'good Germany', while Prussia was relegated to the destructive, Teutonic side of German culture. Political considerations led others to a selective mapping of the rest of Europe as well. The recipients of the Marshall Plan, which was the economic side to this reconstruction, included Turkey but excluded Spain, which was then still under Franco's rule.[10] The other part of the plan involved saving western Europe from the Soviet Union. The leaders of Europe's post-war reconstruction of Europe used the boundary established at Brest-Litovsk as Europe's eastern frontier, and joined the Soviet leadership in dividing Germany along the same principles.[11]

---

[7] The latter phrase is taken from the humorous essay by Aleksander Wat, 'Long live Europe', in ibid., *Lucifer Unemployed* (1927) (Evanston, Ill.: Northwestern University Press, 1990), 77–81.

[8] Ernst Kantorowicz, *The King's Two Bodies: A Study in Medieval Political Theology* (Princeton: Princeton University Press, 1957); for more recent treatments of the theme, see Emmanuel Levinas, *Otherwise than Being: Or, Beyond Essence,* transl. Alphonso Lengis (Pittsburgh: Duquesne University Press, 2005). Pablo Schneider, 'Political Iconography and the Picture Act: The Execution of Charles I in 1649', in Pictorial Cultures and Political Iconographies. Approaches, Perspectives, Case Studies from Europe and America, ed. Udo J. Hebel and Christoph Wagner (Berlin: De Gruyter, 2011), 63–83. For an older treatment, see Marc Bloch, *Les Rois Thaumaturges: Etude sur le Caractere Surnaturel Attribue a la Puissance Royale Particulierement en France et en Angleterre* (Paris: Gallimard, 1925).

[9] Michael Rothberg, *Multidirectional Memory. Remembering the Holocaust in the Age of Decolonization* (Stanford: Stanford University Press, 2009).

[10] Josef L. Kunz, 'Pan Europe, the Marshall Plan Countries and the Western European Union', in *The American Journal of International Law*, 42:4 (October 1948), 868–877.

[11] On the notion of 'post-war' as a formative paradigm of European identity, see Tony Judt's *Postwar. A History of Europe since 1945* (New York: Penguin, 2005). On Nazi government in Europe as an

At the economic level, the ideas of John Maynard Keynes and others were heeded in the late 1940s and 1950s, and the isolation of West Germany was avoided. But with few exceptions, this did not apply to much historical writing. In intellectual history, too, a selective and divisive interpretation of European identity prevailed throughout the post-war and Cold War period. Thus key intellectual contributions of German as well as Russian thought of the 1920s for liberal ideas of international order have fallen out of sight.

I would compare attempts to restore the 'nobility' of European civilization by means of selective history to the way twenty-first-century management consultants proposed to restructure bankrupt banks. Such a process involves separating the good parts in the continent's credit history from the bad parts, and supplying the good part with an impeccable past and a refreshed or even a different name. This kind of salvation through restructuring is neither a miracle, nor a revolution; it is merely an attempt to preserve the status quo and the continued political functioning of society after a moment of crisis.[12] Associating the problematic heritage of European identity with essentially Germanic features, such as theories of race and the pursuit of Lebensraum, was politically an easy way forward, especially given that the Nazis had themselves prepared this kind of vision. Moreover, the catastrophe of the Holocaust indeed resists comparative perspectives not just by virtue of its scale. But more recent approaches to historical understanding of twentieth-century crises have shown that it is possible to account for the uniqueness of such excesses without forgetting their transnational entanglements.[13]

German intellectual history of this period has only recently been placed in a more global comparative context.[14] The German case evokes other instances of historical retribution in colonial and imperial

'empire', see Mark Mazower, *Hitler's Empire. Nazi Rule in Occupied Europe* (London: Penguin, 2008).

[12] Theodor W. Adorno, *Minima Moralia: Reflexionen aus dem beschädigten Leben* (Frankfurt: Suhrkamp, 1951).

[13] Kate Brown, *A Biography of No Place: From Ethnic Borderland to Soviet Heartland* (Cambridge, Mass.: Harvard University Press, 2005); Timothy Snyder, *Bloodlands: Europe between Hitler and Stalin* (New York: Basic Books, 2010); Tara Zahra, 'Imagined Noncommunities: National Indifference as a Category of Analysis', in *Slavic Review*, 69:1 (Spring 2010), 93–119.

[14] Cf. Aimé Césaire, 'Notebook of a Return to the Native Land' (1939), in *Aimé Césaire. The Collected Poetry*, ed. Clayton Eshleman and Annette Smith (Berkeley, Calif.: University of California Press, 1983), esp. p. 42; with respect to the imperial elites, see esp. Catherine Hall, *Civilising Subjects. Metropole and Colony in the English Imagination, 1830–1867* (Cambridge and Chicago: Polity and Chicago University Press, 2002), and the new collaborative research project on The Legacies of Slave-Ownership, www.ucl.ac.uk/lbs/. See also Catherine Hall and Keith McClelland (eds.), *Race, Nation and Empire. Making Histories, 1750 to the Present* (Manchester: Manchester University Press,

contexts.[15] However, the role of German intellectuals in the history of the European community remains to be recovered. As I have tried to flesh out, German intellectuals of elite background formed part of the European and transatlantic international community throughout this time. People like Coudenhove, who was once described as 'a Bohemian citizen of the world turned visiting professor of history at New York University', had deeply influenced both conservative and liberal models of Pan-Europeanism.[16] He lectured at Chatham House in London, corresponded with Churchill, spent time as an expat in New York teaching European history at Columbia, and also brought together the French and the Italian advocates for European unity after the First World War.[17] But beyond such individual personalities, the transnational networks of German-speaking dissident elites were also important in their effect as groups and networks.

'Scraps of talk': a social history of the civilizers

Is it worth reconstructing what Virginia Woolf called the 'scraps of talk' of intellectuals against this background? I hope to have provided a different kind of genealogy of Europe as an idea, one which centres on forms of speech and recorded utterances. Civilization talk formed a dominant theme in the discursive sphere of what Daniel Gorman has recently identified as 'international society'.[18] My analysis has centred on elite representatives of what I suggested to call the European intelligentsia, not because elites make history, but because their prestige was a key factor in the post-imperial culture industry. German aristocrats, in particular, became indispensable public figures even in mass culture such as Hollywood films of this period. Indeed, in America, the former counts and barons had particular appeal even though their appearance was often a cause of humorous remarks. One of Count Keyserling's hosts at Harvard, the American actor John Lodge, who later starred as Archduke Franz

November 2010); see also Keith McClelland and Sonya Rose (eds.), *At Home with the Empire. Metropolitan Culture and the Imperial World* (Cambridge: Cambridge University Press, 2006).

[15] István Deák, Jan T. Gross, and Tony Judt (eds.), *The Politics of Retribution in Europe: World War II and Its Aftermath* (Princeton: Princeton University Press, 2000).

[16] Cf. Conze, *Das Europa der Deutschen*; Anne-Isabelle Richard, 'The Limits of Solidarity. Europeanism, Anti-Colonialism and Socialism at the Congress of the Peoples of Europe, Asia and Africa at Puteaux, 1948', in *European Review of History*, 21:4 (2014), 519–537.

[17] NN, 'One Europe', *Time Magazine*, 26 March 1945, www.time.com/time/magazine/article/0,9171,803470,00.html?iid=chix-sphere, accessed 5 November 2008.

[18] Daniel Gorman; Wolfram Kaiser, Brigitte Leucht, and Morten Rasmussen (eds.), *The History of the European Union: Origins of Trans- and Supranational Polity 1950–72* (Oxford and New York: Routledge, 2009).

Ferdinand in a 1940 film by Max Ophüls, recalled that Keyserling's regular demands as a speaker included plenty of oysters and champagne and always having female company at the dinner.[19] The aristocratic intelligentsia had particular appeal to new forms of the culture industry.[20]

The figure of the declining aristocrat also appeared in the work of Russian parodists of early Soviet life Ilya Ilf and Evgeny Petrov, for instance, or, in the 1950s, the US TV comedian Sid Caesar.[21] The lady that vanishes from Alfred Hitchcock's train in 1938 was also remarkably similar to Queen Victoria, the grandmother of so many German dynasties that vanished after the war.[22] Imperial tunes of vanished empires remain audible in post-imperial Britain on such surprising occasions as the funeral of Margaret Thatcher, an occasion on which, among others, the Radetzky March was performed.

Throughout this book I suggested using the metaphor of a 'phantom' in the sense of a spectre of pain, and secondly, as a forensic phantom image. But when it comes particularly to the global and more universal reception of this afterlife of imperial imagination, a third layer of meaning becomes significant. In a perceptive book from 1927, the American publicist Walter Lippman defined the problem of modern democratic societies as the dilemma of a *Phantom Public*.[23] He argued that problems of institutional design and suffrage were secondary compared to a less obvious problem from which modern societies suffered: it was a lost sense of their own democratic constitution, an involuntary transformation of potential agency into back-row spectatorship. Absentee voters, non-voters, and voters who were voting in the dark: this was the bleak future of democratic modernity.

The mentality of the small fraction in this book explains one element behind this passive spectatorship. That fraction had a paradoxical constitution: at one level, it had a high level of self-consciousness and ability to articulate itself aesthetically and politically. At another level, these social circles of second-row, yet influential, imperial elites were also distinctly unwilling

[19] John Davis Lodge papers, box 2, folder 2–3, Memorandum regarding the visit of Count Keyserling (1928), in Hoover Institution Archives.

[20] S.N. Eisenstadt (ed.), *Max Weber on Charisma and Institution Building* (Chicago: University of Chicago Press, 1968); Edward Shils, 'Charisma, Order, and Status', in *American Sociological Review*, 30:2 (April 1965), 199–213.

[21] I am grateful to James Collins for drawing my attention to the character of Sid Caesar.

[22] Alfred Hitchcock, *The Lady Vanishes* (1938). I am very grateful to Josh White for drawing my attention to this film.

[23] Walter Lippman, *The Phantom Public* (New York: Macmillan, 1927). I am grateful to Georgios Varouxakis for drawing my attention to Lippman as Woodrow Wilson's collaborator after the First World War.

to situate themselves in the institutional landscape of democratic states. You do not need representation when you have visibility and celebrity. Culture was not only in the keeping of this intellectual minority but also in its captivity.[24]

In this sense, the non-governing elites can create a milieu in which passivity is presented as an intellectual virtue, and in which certain ways of being an intellectual are reproduced without much thought. While civilization talk was mostly the remit of men, the listeners, note-takers, typists, and partners were often women. They were the ghostwriters of their post-imperial phantom pains. The story of this matrilineal lineage of imperial memory is yet to be told. They can become the loyal keepers of their partners' and fathers' memories in another sense of uncritical and eulogistic archiving. In the archive of this aristocratic fraction, it is sometimes difficult to remember that women are not a minority. Yet thinking of women as a de facto minority in this configuration cuts across both liberal and socialist values. Likewise, thinking of majorities and minorities purely in terms of legal status ratios, such as the ratio of men to women, or people of homosexual to people of heterosexual orientation, dominant or minor ethnic groups, is only an incomplete model for recognition. These Europeanists styled themselves as queer Brahmin-samurai-pariahs, which did not prevent them from asserting the legitimacy of the economic exploitation of non-European populations by Europeans as a norm, or of associating mostly masculine forms of sexual deviance with political dissidence.

In Europe after 1945, estrangement served a constructive function because it meant solving the puzzle of how so much civilization could produce so much barbarism. Perhaps this also explains how assuming an aristocratic identity behind or on the screen, or on the pages of historical fiction, was an opportunity for actors and writers of Jewish background to overcome a traumatic alienation from European culture in the wake of the Holocaust. In retracing their steps to a seemingly more serene period of European history through its aristocrats, perhaps, Stefan Zweig and Erich von Stroheim thought, some faint sense of connection could be restored to the deranged plot line of the twentieth century at least at the level of representation.[25] The Jews, insofar as they acquired new emotional

---

[24] On culture being in the keeping of minorities, see F.R. Leavis, *Mass Civilisation and Minority Culture* (Cambridge: Minority Press, 1930), 13.

[25] On Yiddish and Jewish actors and overcoming alienation through film, see Stuart Samuels, 'The Evolutionary Image of the Jew in American film', in *Ethnic Images in American Film and Television* (Philadelphia: The Balch Institute, 1978); and Saverio Giovacchini, 'The Joys of Paradise. Reconsidering Hollywood's Exiles', in *The Dispossessed: An Anatomy of Exile*, ed. Peter I. Rose (New York: Doubleday, 2005), 281–307.

cohesion by being a community of traumatic memory after the Holocaust, were the largest European community to have suffered from a common 'category crisis'.[26] To this, the paradigmatic image of the aristocrat served as a helpful foil for reflection.

The cadres of European memory

Searching for the proper cadre that might shed light on post-imperial dissolution as a transnational process, I relied on a set of mental images, each of which enables and precludes different dimensions of understanding. A map, for instance, captures the legal and geopolitical changes in the aftermath of the First World War, but obscures the presence of phantom empires behind the boundaries of nation states, and gives fragile borders the semblance of longevity.

Even the seductive new genre of videomapping, which modern technology makes available to all of us, does not solve the limitation of maps as representations of spatial identities. People see the same map differently, and they can also connect older feelings about landscapes to new places. Moreover, in the course of the longer period charted in this book, from the 1860s to the 1950s, we have seen how common it has become for people to recognize seemingly familiar European landscapes on other continents, to see the Carpathian mountains during the First World War in the Berkshire hills of the United States or in the mountains of Northern Mexico. A retreat from politics and revolution in the present was no longer expressed through the sentimental attachment to one's own home landscape, like, for instance, the generations of English-speaking Wordsworth readers had done by assuming his feelings about *Grasmere Lake*. The children of the Victorian Wordsworth readers were appraising 'foreign' sentiments, such as Rilke's contemplative wandering between the homes of other people, or the search for new adventures in E.M. Forster's visions of India. Conversely, passionate readers of English and Scottish Romantic poetry and prose could be found in eastern and central Europe, in the United States, the Caribbean and the West Indies.[27] An exiled poet

---

[26] Cf. Marjorie Garber, *Vested Interests: Cross-dressing and Cultural Anxiety* (London: Routledge, 2011).

[27] See the discussion of 'Wordsworthiana' in Richard Bourke, *Romantic Discourse and Political Modernity. Wordsworth, the Intellectual and Cultural Critique* (New York: St. Martin's Press, 1993), 257; see also references to Derek Walcott in Ann Laura Stoler, *Imperial Debris*. On C.L.R. James and Wordsworth, see C.L.R. James, 'Bloomsbury: An Encounter with Edith Sitwell' [1932], in Anna Grimshaw (ed.), *The C.L.R. James Reader* (Oxford: Oxford University Press, 1992), 42–48. Notable translators of Wordsworth and the Lake Poets in Soviet Russia included Samuil Marshak,

and writer like Czeslaw Milosz found himself unable to speak of his native realm, Lithuania, without reference to Africa or Chicago.

I have tried in this book to learn from these poets and their readers. Political thought about imperial fragmentation does not have to be fragmentary itself, but can take the form of a mosaic of multiple utterances of the kind that the artist Boris Anrep created.[28] Maps were important acts of visual persuasion. This idea of 'mapping-in-use' is something I have tried to follow both literally and metaphorically. Places were mapped in intellectual practice when they were recoloured and reproduced in particular argumentative settings, such as was the case with the map of Paneuropa in Coudenhove-Kalergi's work, or the genealogical map of Europe in Nazi visions of the continent.

A second mode of mental image processing concerns the representation of the intellectuals who imagine European spaces themselves. Photographs and portraits, even if they are group portraits, made the faces of authors visible but risked supplanting my pursuit of reconstructing the social context of intellectual authority with a more literal reproduction of visibility. The painting by Vanessa Bell of a group of people gathered beneath a set of portraits of deceased members, or the photograph of a Pan-European congress featuring the portraits of great European intellectuals, are better at showing the social character of influence and memory than individual portraits. However, ultimately, the image I needed was once again more dynamic. It is in this sense that I would liken the evolving portrait of the European to the forensic practice of producing a hybrid phantom image from an assembly of existing sketches and photographic footage gathered as evidence.

Taking a step away from visual metaphors for the evolving sense of European identity among my protagonists, I also played with a classic conceptual tool of the historian, the timeline. This device organizes events sequentially, but often provides a false sense of safety and security in moving about past events. Some people think it is the business of historians to provide their patrons or their communities with a reliable timeline of

e.g., in Boris Kluzner (ed.), *Vosem' romansov iz angliiskoi, shotlandskoi i bel' giiskoi poezii* (Tallinn: Muzfond, 1955). On modernist postcolonial poetics and classical heritage, see references to Wagner in the work of W.E.B. du Bois, *The Souls of Black Folk* (Chicago: McClurg, 1902), in T.S. Eliot, and references to Rimbaud and Walt Whitman in Aimé Césaire, 'Cahier d'un rétour au pays natal', in *Volontés*, 20 (1939).

[28] A great inspiration in this has been Robert Crawford, *Identifying Poets. Self and Territory in Twentieth-Century Poetry* (Edinburgh: Edinburgh University Press, 1993), and, in practice, the work of Robert Chandler.

'what really happened'.[29] Yet such a way of organizing our sense of the past by degrees of complicity in acts would have led me astray from the real pursuit of this book. I wanted to explore the hypothesis that identities, ideologies, and ideas do not 'happen'; they are produced as a result of human interaction. From the point of view of explaining human motivation, that is, the question how some ideas, ideologies, and actions are grounded in memories, what matters most is the order in which people remember events, not the order in which things happen.

Rather than 'applying' a theory to a process, I wanted to make the history of social theory part of understanding the process. Situated in a social as well as an intellectual historical context, social theories such as Weber's idea of social action and the paradigms of charismatic rule, Wittgenstein's idea of meaning in use, Saussure's idea of structure, Simmel's idea of value, Cassirer's notion of symbolic forms, and Elias's idea of a civilizing process evolved together with the dissolution of social structures they had set out to explain. Ways of being in the world, such as typing on a typewriter, or travelling, are also 'structures'. As such, they can orient our reading of a past in which the things that are being written about, or the spaces which are being crisscrossed, have changing and multiple names and partly incomprehensible provenances.

Travel, voluntary and involuntary, real and imagined, in war and in peacetime, became a leitmotif of this exploration of imperial memory among the Europeans. Travel seems hardly structured, particularly in the form of an existential, soul- and world-searching pursuit of an unknown goal in which it was practised in the Belle Epoque, but equally, in the form of inhuman and involuntary displacements in wartime. Yet accounts of travel have their own rules of genre and turn out to be subtle and insightful modes for grasping transitional identities, as the examples of such influential travelogues as Viktor Shklovsky's *Sentimental Journey*, which themselves entered the canon of 'theory', suggest. In the case of my archive, the corresponding text was Hermann Keyserling's *Travel Diary of a Philosopher*, which, I would argue, supplied the equivalent of a theory to readers of European decline narratives such as Spengler's *Decline of the West*.[30] In the *longue durée*, too, movement and sociability have given shape to the idea of Europe as a type of shared experience at least since the travels

---

[29] As formulated by Leopold von Ranke, *Geschichte der romanischen und germanischen Völker* (1824), 3rd ed. (Leipzig: Duncker & Humblot, 1895), vii.
[30] Viktor Shklovsky, *A Sentimental Journey: Memoirs, 1917–22* (1923), transl. Richard Sheldon (Ithaca, N.Y.: Cornell University Press, 1970).

of the humanists and Enlightenment scholars. This became increasingly a mass phenomenon in the twentieth century.

Another structural dimension of travel is that it enables the emergence of increasingly global contact zones and yet is often restricted to particular social circles.[31] As I tried to show, some spaces in Europe, particularly the shifting frontiers of eastern Europe, reveal how photographic representations of geographic space with devices such as periscopes ground the production of seemingly abstract horizons of experience in the logic of strategic needs. Viewed in a dynamic and contextual perspective, the ground between enlightenment and intelligence is actually a liminal zone somewhere between humanistic scientific exploration and the essentially anti-human work of the secret services.

The optic of travel provides an understanding of the relationship between people, spaces, things, and time that exposes the constancy of relationships such as groups of friends or intellectual companions over the fragility of territorial units and even personal identities. As an individual, a Habsburg Archduke may have levels of self-doubt that are similar to those of any other traveller, yet even incognito, his social position frames his experience differently. Conversely, the value of a Manet painting might change over time, but what remains constant is the importance of 'Manet appreciation' for groups of friends like the Bloomsbury and the Kessler circle. The place of a memory of having been the first fans of Manet remains rooted in the emotional genealogy of these intellectuals. Based on this formula, there are at least three types of chronology that are intertwined in this book: a timeline of events, that is, the most widely accepted and shared account of the major political, economic, and constitutional changes in Europe; a timeline of situations in which the past is remembered; and a timeline of intellectual production in and through which ideas about empire and Europe could be traced.

Foregrounding travel was also a way of providing an account of my own extraction of evidence, and a personal history of 'civilization'. Indicating awareness of this process is the equivalent of the natural scientist's 'experimental report'. My first conscious encounter with the word 'civilization', or a 'civilized country', was on a journey to Soviet Estonia. In 1988, my father was invited to a conference in Tallinn. Our overnight train arrived early in the morning, when the city was only waking up, and the vision of this city with its Gothic spires and cobblestones made me think that I had been transported to one of Grimm's fairy tales. With the exception of

---

[31] Marie Luise Pratt, *Imperial Eyes: Travel Writing and Transculturation* (London: Routledge, 1992).

Leningrad, which I had never seen by this point, the Estonian capital
was the most Western and also the most 'European' city of the Soviet
empire. The cathedral had not opened to tourists yet at this hour, and I was
surprised to find that lying on the floor against its large wooden door was
a camera in a leather case, which a distracted tourist must have left behind
and which, as I imagined it, in Moscow, would have invariably been stolen
overnight. Soviet school children like myself in 1988 thought Estonia was
civilized because it had beautiful school uniforms, blue and grey, instead of
the black and brown of our own. Later, from conversations in my parents'
social circle, I got used to thinking of Tallinn and its rival, the city of Tartu,
or Dorpat, as the Germans had called it, or Yuriev, as the Russians used to
call it, as havens of dissident culture: this is where, in the 1950s, the cultural
historian Yuri Lotman had founded the school of semiotics, which had
produced numerous scholars of language and culture based on the traditions of Russian formalism. Many of their followers became active political
dissidents and left the Soviet Union. Many of them spent years in labour
camps, some never returned. The conference that occasioned our trip had
also been organized by a group of linguists from this circle, the early
formalists Shklovsky and Tynyanov, and Lotman. It was the last gathering
to take place in the capital of the Estonian Soviet Socialist Republic;
Estonia would soon be independent for the second time in its twentieth-
century history, twenty years later it would join the European Union and
begin a wave of de-Russification in its history and monuments.
Optimistically, it now turns out, some of the old Russian intellectuals
from Tartu announced in the early 1990s that they had 'ceased being
structuralists' because they looked forward to a less isolated future for
Russia in Europe.[32]

The Soviet guidebook to Tallinn, published in 1977, says that 'the
capital of the Estonian Soviet Socialist Republic is located in the North-
West of the USSR'.[33] The whitewashed walls of the city's cathedral are
covered with the familial crests of the Baltic nobility, which had only
briefly been removed by the nationalist government of Päts in the interwar
period. The guidebook is careful to point out that the German (Teutonic)
knights who built the cathedral and had colonized the area in the thirteenth century were 'greedy and rapacious usurpers', while the subsequent
'annexation' of Estonia to the Russian Empire after the Northern War of

---

[32] Boris Gasparov, 'Pochemu ia perestal byt' strukturalistom' (1989), in *Moskovsko-Tartuskaia semioticheskaia shkola. Istoria, vospominania, razmyshlenia*, ed. Sergei Nekliudov (Moscow: Shkola
'Yazyki russkoi kul'tury', 1998), 93–95.
[33] Kh. Taliste, *Tallinn. Stolitsa estonskoi SSR. Putevoditel*, 3rd ed. (Tallinn: Periodika, 1977), 6.

the early 1700s had played a 'progressive role in the history of the Estonian people'.[34] Throughout these different phases of historiographical and literary debates about the Baltics, the nobility remained one of the central subjects of contestation. The Nazis wanted to make them German; the Soviet historians focused on their social status as exploiters and usurpers; and the vernacular nationalists concentrated on their status as ethnic strangers.

Throughout my research in archives or museums reaching from Moscow, Berlin, and Děčin to Darmstadt, Dublin, Rome, Geneva, New York, and Stanford, my access to the social process of memory has itself relied on being prepared to contradict my expectations. From the futile search for a manuscript I believed lost in northern Portugal to the unexpected find of a typescript in New Zealand thanks to a simple web search, elements of adventure and risk highlighted the importance of serendipity and contingency in the historical process as well. Preparing for my trip to the state regional archives at Děčin, I left myself only very little time for researching where to stay, and eventually settled on a small and cheap hotel called 'By the Old Bridge', which I booked online. Having the Old Bridge in Prague on my mind, I imagined that this location would be both central and picturesque, and a quick look at the map suggested to me that a brisk daily walk across the bridge to the archive would provide a good start to my working day. My disappointment was rather great when upon my arrival, I realized that the 'old bridge', originally from the twelfth century, was a mere ruin, and that towering over it was a prime example of Soviet town planning: a huge highway-style edifice of a bridge, with no room for pedestrians at all. Moreover, traffic on the bridge was one way only. To get to the archive, I had to get to a different bridge and then loop back through the other side of the city. A one-way bridge with no pedestrian access in a city of 50,000: I recognized this peculiar signature of Soviet civilization. In fact, I later learnt that the castle of Děčin had been the seat of the Soviet authorities in Czechoslovakia after 1945, just as Rilke's castle of Duino had been occupied by the British and American armies. Reconstructions of all these sites of imperial memory have been an integral part of post-1989 identity making. Whether in the Czech Republic or in Dalmatia, in Saxony or in Thuringia, the recovery of heritage has been central for the cultural restitution of identity in post-socialist societies.[35]

---

[34] Taliste, *Tallinn*, 10.

[35] I have been following this process more systematically through an archive of 'aristocratic cultural memory', which my grandmother, Nadezhda Dmitrieva, has been assembling from the *Leipziger Volkszeitung* between 2009 and 2014, whose regional focus is East Germany, particularly, Saxony.

Such cultural restitution of the past was as partial as its economic restitution. It was also implicated in commercial and financial processes of European integration, which obscured origins while restoring them. Not only on the continent but also in Britain, these sites in the twentieth century often aim to recover the heydays of aristocratic culture, somewhere between the eighteenth and early nineteenth centuries, which produces postmodern effects of synchronicity: a copy of Hitler's *Mein Kampf,* for instance, forgotten on the bookshelf of the library at Castle Sychrov, which is otherwise immaculately restored in the nineteenth-century style of *empire*. This points back to the place of heritage in cultural memory, a story that still needs to be reconstructed for Europe in a way that would integrate post-imperial and post-socialist memory.[36] Throughout continental Europe, the very idea of culture as an institution still takes the form of an aristocratic heritage. The German *Schloss* and the French *Château*, the Polish *zamek*, the Russian *dvorets*, and the Italian *palazzo*, they all contain elements of estranged uses of aristocratic culture. A team of anthropologists has recently called them constructed 'places of happiness'.[37]

Resisting the Leopards

Everyone, as Hobsbawm says, 'is an historian of his or her consciously lived lifetime', and yet we may not be aware 'how much of it' – empire, that is – is 'still in us'.[38] In analysing key moments during which Europe's empires lost power, I suggested that Germanic elites played a particularly important role as authors of European identity narratives.[39] In seeking to understand how personal experiences were connected to publicly shared ideas and ideologies, one particular struggle I faced was the invasion of ready-made

---

See also Longina Jakubowska, *Patrons of History. Nobility, Capital and Political Transitions in Poland* (London: Ashgate, 2012).

[36] Cf. Astrid Swenson, *The Rise of Heritage: Preserving the Past in France, Germany and England, 1789–1914* (Cambridge: Cambridge University Press, 2013); for the history of English heritage, see Peter Mandler, *The Fall and Rise of the Stately Home* (New Haven: Yale University Press, 1999), and recent work by Margot Finn's project 'East India Company at Home', as evidenced by her Inaugural Lecture at UCL, 'The East India Company at Home: Private Fortunes, Public Histories' (11 February 2014), UCL. On the project, see http://blogs.ucl.ac.uk/eicah/, accessed 5 May 2014.

[37] Nikolai Ssorin-Chaikov (ed.), *Topografia schast'ia: etnograficheskie karty moderna* (Moscow: NLO, 2013). Jakubowska, *Patrons of History.*

[38] Eric Hobsbawm, *The Age of Empire, 1875–1914* (London: Weidenfeld and Nicholson, 1987), 5.

[39] For this critique, see Geoff Eley, 'Imperial Imaginary, Colonial Effect: Writing the Colony and the Metropole Together', in Hall and McClelland (eds.), *Race, Nation and Empire.*

images and fictional characters, which prefigured my expectations concerning the linkages between intellectuals, the idea of civilization, and the phantom image of Europe. These figures, carefully prepared by the best authors of literary fiction, were always larger than life. First and foremost among them was that grand figure of aristocratic decline, Tomasi di Lampedusa's *Leopard* (1957), whose year of birth coincides with a key date in the institutional founding of the European Union.

Listening in on the civilization talk in the interwar period, it became clear to me that the link between such melancholic or elegiac accounts and those who experienced imperial decline was best grasped in group relationships. The 'Leopards' were an emerging focal point of attention among an irreducibly transnational elite. In their role as objects of memory as well as in their subjective experiences of imperial decline and the world wars, the central figures in this book were emblematic of a particular form of elite precariousness.

As historians, we can easily be seduced by the iconic power of such narratives, which enforce viewing the history of post-imperial elites in terms of familiar plots, such as tragedy or elegy. But when this happened, I found it useful to ask myself what this tragic feeling was a tragedy of. At closer sight, it is not immediately clear why some of us identify with the narrators of such stories as Joseph Roth's *Radetzky March*. What do we mourn when we – people of the twenty-first century, women, descendants of former imperial subjects – identify with tragic or elegiac modes of thinking about political loss? In the 1930s, the British Mass Observation movement, a self-organized group consisting of social and literary scientists and a poet, decided to apply anthropological perspectives usually applied to the non-European, in a study of working-class cultures in a northern British town. Looking at such practices as drinking rituals in pubs, they were surprised to find just how many pubs were named after aristocratic figures, such as dukes and queens. Emblems of aristocratic identities, such as coats of arms, are also embedded in public buildings, bridges, and on station buildings.[40]

What the Mass Observation group had suggested back in the 1930s is that the radical disconnection of the experience of buildings associated with aristocratic figures, and the lives of these figures themselves, introduces an element of alienation to one's own life. Estrangement does not only occur when there is a dramatic gap in class background, such as when

---

[40] Mass Observation, *The Pub and the People: A Worktown Study* (London: Gollancz, 1943).

my house is not big enough to allow me to understand what it is like to live in a palace. It is a qualitatively specific experience if the name I put on my 'pub' or my experience is not actually familiar to me. At another level, the aristocrats themselves are not necessarily more familiar with the labels they carry either. Queens, dukes, and duchesses are equally 'estranged' from the places, commodities, and services to which they lend their names. Working against such hegemonic plots, one can be inspired by poets who have captured something essential and universal about processes of revolution, dissolution, and ruination. But it is equally illuminating to consider the consumption of such narrative to be as important an object of analysis as these narratives themselves.[41]

Restoring some nobility to the idea of Europe was also a kind of political cross-dressing act. It was important politically in the post-Nazi era, where Anglo-American, Franco-German, and Soviet ideas of Europe were played out in different guises during the Cold War. But assuming the aristocratic pose, even if this is done ironically, like the Beatles did in posing as colonial governors on the *Sgt. Pepper* cover of 1967, can only provide a temporary solution to the way Europeans relate to their – or our – ambiguous past.[42] As the history of the last three decades suggests, yesterday's good banks can easily become tomorrow's bad banks. If we consider the low turnout of voters for the European elections, regional economic inequality within Europe, or the fact that the European Court of Human Rights is used overwhelmingly to process the claims of non-EU citizens prosecuting their own governments, we might wonder to what extent the 'good Europeans' today are also just an estranged transnational minority which justifies rising levels of inequality through a new language of prestige. Here, historical and political judgement will have to part ways. If European identity retains elements of imperial contradictions, so do national, regional, and personal forms of organizing power and prestige. The European elites, whose affective genealogy I tried to recover, made sense of their implicated status within several waning empires by progressively retreating from political involvement. But whether their elegiac pathos concerning imperial decline should make any of us today equally estranged from the democratic process in Europe is a question not of the past but of present and future choices. Awareness of the power which imperial memory can have over us should

---

[41] Eric Santner, *The Royal Remains: The People's Two Bodies and the Endgames of Sovereignty* (Chicago: The University of Chicago Press, 2011).

[42] Peo Hansen and Stefan Jonson, *Eurafrica: The Untold History of European Integration and Colonialism* (London: Bloomsbury, 2014).

not mean submission to this power. If there is one thing one can learn from these Leopards, it is not the content of their ideas or their ambiguous concept of civilization but their intellectual technique. They not only turned transnational phantoms of empire into new *devises* for the future. As model teachers of selective memory, they also excelled at forgetting.

Archives

Accademia Nazionale Dei Lincei, Rome

17.44.1–25, 19.44.25, 33 50.1–51, 43.50.12–52

Bundesarchiv, Berlin

BA, 'Adel' 1925–38
BA, R 2 11957
BA, R 43 II 1554–5
BA, R 43 II 1554–5 Deutsche Adelsgenossenschaft to State secretary
R 32/90, 1920–27
R 43 II 1554–5
R/153/1915/40, R/153/480/40

Columbia University Libraries, Rare Books and Manuscript Library, New York

Bakhmeteff Archive, Mikhail Alexandrovich Taube papers
Carnegie Collections, 329/9, correspondence between the Foundation
  and Richard Coudenhove-Kalergi

Deutsches Literaturarchiv Marbach a. Neckar

Archive Eugen Diederichs, correspondence with Keyserling, 1913–25
Archive Harry Graf Kessler
Arthur Schnitzler archive, Schnitzler to Coudenhove-Kalergi, Letters
  1925–29, Marbach, Deutsches Literaturarchiv, folder 308
Ivan Kalaïeff, Verschiedene Fassungen, Entwürfe und Notizen des
  ersten und zweiten Aktes, 1931–33
Kessler to Elisabeth Förster-Nietzsche (1907–30), 18 letters
Keyserling to Kessler Letters, 1918–36

Goethe-und-Schiller-Archiv Weimar

72/BW 4497

Hessische Landes- und Hochschulbibliothek, Darmstadt

A-4 Ahnenforschung, correspondence with Nikolai Ikonnikov
Archive of Hermann Keyserling and the School of Wisdom
Folder Nazi 1933ff, Keyserling to Hitler, 10 April 1933
Keyserling, 'Der Bolschewismus und die Arisokratie der Zukunft' (1918, typescript), 'Eine Vision der kommenden Weltordnung', *Deutsche Allgemeine Zeitung* (1 January 1925)
R-3 172.01, Correspondence
V-4, Lectures abroad, especially in Rome (1925) 07.612, Vienna (1927), 076.14, Madrid (1930), 076.09, Spain (1934, 1935), various other locations, 076.13, Paris (1931, Salle du Trocadéro). 076.10, and 1933, Salle Pleyel, 076.11
V-4, 205.08, Lectures in Europe

Hoover Institution Archives, Stanford

Boris Nicolaevsky papers
John Davis Lodge Papers, Box 2, Folder 2–3
Louis Loucheur papers
Mikhail de Giers papers, Box 21, Folder 1

Poland Ambasada Papers
Internationaal Instituut voor Sociale Geschiedenis, Amsterdam

Hendrik de Man papers, II.88 (Spengler) and 89 (Keyserling)
Karl Kautsky Papers, correspondence with Kessler

The Keep, University of Sussex Special Collections, Brighton

Archive of the League of Nations Union
Leonard Woolf Papers, SxMs-13/1: Peace Organizations: 1914–18 War; SxMs-13/1/F/1: League of Nations Society, SxMs-13/1/F/2 League of Nations Union, SxMs-13/1/F/3 League of Nations; SxMs-13/1/L/10: International Government (1916)
'The Mandates and the Mandated Areas (Tropical Colonies)', in Leonard Woolf papers, 3.1, Special Collections, the University of Sussex. See also Leonard Woolf, 'Perpetual Peace by Immanuel Kant 1795', and 'A short Peace and War Bibliography', ibid., section 9

National Gallery Archive, London

Dossier on Manet, 'The Execution of Four Soldiers', NG3294.4
NG14/25 Acquisition: Pictures by Corot, Delacroix, Forain, Gaugain, Ingres, Manet, Rousseau and Ricard, and Drawings by Ingres, David and Delacroix, Purchased at Degas sale, 1918

Teixeira de Pascoaes Archive, Amarante, Portugal
Reading, Special Collections

Ms2750/379, 43pp. archives of the Hogarth Press, correspondence with Cranach Press regarding the translation of Rainer Maria Rilke's *Duino Elegies*

Rossiiskii gosudarstvennyi voennyi arkhiv, Moscow

554/7, 451/4, 9–12, 8, 19, 22, 23, 24, 28; 654/1, 3, 112–3; 654, 1, 210, 164, 123
Aufstellung über die im Czernin-Palais am 9. Januar 1942 abgeholten Einrichtungsgegenstände
'Dynasten', unfinished fragment, 1911–12 and unfinished manuscript, 'Zur Psychologie der Dynasten'
Fond 552 k, Paneuropean Union, Vienna
Fond 594.1.92, 55pp., Georg Bernhard archive, Paris
Fond 634, 1, 188, Walther Rathenau Archive, Manuscript, 'Zur Psychologie der'
Fond 1488-1-9, 1939–45, Confiscation of the property of the Maltese order, 'Schriftverkehr von Generalkonsul von Janson re Gobelins im Malteser-Palais', 18 August 1941

Rossiiskaia Gosudarstvennaia Biblioteka

Fond 358, Nikolai Rubakin; 358/498/28 Letters to Rubakin; Fond 358/350/4–5 Letters concerning state pension from the Soviet Union (1935–6); 358/195/33 Correspondence with pacifist Rene Schickele (1917) and 358/317/106 correspondence with Kessler, 1919–21

Štátny oblastny archiv, Dečin, Czech Republic

Alain Rohan archive, folder 987, Correspondence with relatives (1912–18); folder 989, folder 310 postcards from the front from Karl Anton Rohan Archive Clary-Aldringen, folders 906 and 1011 (relating to the Runciman mission), in DA. 993 Maltese order, Congress in Rome, 1,008 Deutsche

Liga für Völkerbund, 1,011 Lord Runciman, 1,014 various Nazi organizations

Eugen Ledebur archive, box 14, folders 194–200, 'Speech concerning interests of Sudeten Germans in Paneuropa' 'Deutsches Mitteleuropa oder Slavische Wirtschaftsentente?', folder 203, 'Memorandum für Mission Runciman, August 1938', handwritten manuscript 'Adel und Demokratie'

Karl Anton Rohan archive, folder 1034, Correspondence with Alain, folder 315, 1908–45; folder 317, 'Front correspondence'

Friedrich Thun, Diary for 1919

United Nations Archives, Geneva

Documents re Zemstvos Prince Lvoff.R 1724, Réfugiés intellectuels russe

R 1725, Petition from Baron Rausch von Trautenberg about confiscated horses from Finnish government after fall of Murman with British Foreign Office

R 1727, Letter by Baron Wolff-Hinzenburg August 1921; Baltic elites Red Cross etc

R 1738, Mme Krusenstern wants to open a hotel employing Russian refugees in Constantinople

UNOG Records and Archives Unit, Nansen Fonds, Refugees Mixed Archival Group, 1919–47, 'Delegation in Germany', in Russisches Wissenschaftliches Institut: Various Correspondence, Financial Statements, Press Cuttings, etc., 1922–32, C1255/151/170.1

Universitäts-und Landesbibliothek Sachsen-Anhalt, Halle-Saale Veltheim, Typescript (1936), LHASA

1/E c/8 Correspondence with Cousin Elisabeth von Thadden, 178 Letters. 2. 17–18

Correspondence with Munich anarchist Gustav Klingelhöfer, 1920. 11p

Erinnerungen eines Kronprinzen an dessen Reise nach Indien (Wilhelm of Hohenzollern (1911))

Mappe I, Lebensdokumente, Tagebücher. Diaries: 1895–1901: 41pp.; 1907–09: 54pp.; 1933: 208pp.; 1934: 204pp.; 1937, 1938, 1942: 200pp. each, 1944: 188pp

Mappe II, Sammlungen/Manuskripte, p. 77

Mappe III, S. 78

Notes from Anthroposophical Union, Deutscher Theotiskaner Orden

Notes on Distinction, Order of St John

Bibliography

Digital resources

www.archive.org
Alinari online: www.alinari.it
www.bild.bundesarchiv.de
Deutsches Dokumentationszentrum für Kunstgeschichte: www.fotomarburg.de/
Europeana online: www.europeana.eu/portal/
Library of Congress online: www.loc.gov/library/libarch-digital.html
Die Fackel online: http://corpus1.aac.ac.at/fackel/
Der Weg zur Vollendung online: www.schuledesrades.org/palme/schule/erbe/?Q=
     4/7/38
www.simplicissimus.info/
www.gallica.fr
www.memoryatwar.org/projects
United Nations Geneva Library
http://www.wdl.org/en/search/?institution=united-nations-office-geneva-library

Interviews and conversations

Conversation with Samuil Lur'ie (Gedroyc) (4 February 2012, St. Petersburg).
Conversations with Alec Rainey (2014–15).
Conversations with Friederike von Lukowicz (1998–2000, 2005, Bremen).
Conversations with Igor' Golomstock (2005–14, London).
Email correspondence with Gabriel Superfin (2005–14, Bremen).
Interview and email correspondence with Harald von Keyserling (July 2008, Berlin).
Interview with Natasha Wilson and David Wilson (Lord and Lady Wilson of
     Tillyorn) (12 June 2013, London, Westminster).

Published primary sources

Journals and periodicals

Das Abendland. Deutsche Monatshefte für europäische Kultur, Politik und Wirtschaft
     (1925–45).

Archiv für Sozialwissenschaften und Sozialpolitik (Tübungen, 1888–1933).

Atti dei convegni Volta, Reale Accademia d'Italia Fondazione Alessandro Volta, Convegno di scienze morali e storiche (Rome: Reale Accademia d' Italia, 1929–38).

Crisis. A Record of the Darker Races (New York, 1919–).

The Criterion (London, 1927–39).

Die Deutsche Nation (Berlin, 1919–25).

Eastern Europe (Paris, 1919–20).

Europa Year Book (London, 1930–58).

Europäische Gespräche: Hamburger Monatshefte für auswärtige Politik (Berlin-Grunewald, 1923–33).

Europäische Revue (Berlin-Leipzig, 1925–43).

Die Fackel (Vienna, 1899–1936).

The Hibbert Journal. A Quarterly Review of Religion, Theology and Philosophy (London, 1902–68).

Illustrated London News (London, 1842–2003).

L'Illustration (Paris, 1943–44).

International Affairs (London, Royal Institute of International Affairs 1931–39).

Internationale Zeitschrift für Ärztliche Psychoanalyse (Leipzig and Vienna, 1913–37, with *Imago*, London, 1939–41).

Krasnyi Arkhiv (Moscow, 1922–41).

Der Leuchter (Darmstadt, 1919–31).

Nationalsozialistische Monatshefte (1930–44).

Das neue Europa (Zürich, Berlin, Wien, 1914–34).

New Orient (New York, 1924–27).

The New Republic (New York, 1914–).

La Nouvelle Revue française (Paris, 1908–43, 1953–).

Les Nouvelles Littéraires (Paris, 1922–58).

Der Neue Orient (Vienna, 1917–43).

Die Neue Rundschau (Berlin, 1890–1944, restarted Stockholm, 1945–).

L'Ordine Nuovo (1919–22).

Rul' (Berlin, 1920–31).

Sammlung (Amsterdam, 1933–35).

Signal (Paris and other cities, 1940–45).

Simplicissimus (Munich, 1896–1944).

Sovremennye Zapiski (Paris, 1920–40).

Sozialistische Monatshefte (Berlin, 1897–33).

Sur (Buenos Aires, 1931–66).

Vossische Zeitung (Berlin, 1918–33).

Der Weg zur Vollendung (Darmstadt, 1920–42).

Zeitschrift für Geopolitik (Berlin, Heidelberg, 1925–51).

Die Zukunft. Ein neues Deutschland: ein neues Europa (Paris, 1938–40).

Publishing houses

Allert de Lange (Amsterdam)
Cranachpresse (Weimar)
Der Neue Geist (Leipzig)
Detinets (Berlin)
Duncker & Humblot (Leipzig)
Eugen Diederichs (Jena)
Feltrinelli (Milan)
Fischer (Frankfurt/Stockholm)
Gallimard (Paris)
Gollancz (London)
Harcourt & Brace (New York)
The Hogarth Press (London)
Insel (Leipzig/Frankfurt)
J. Povolotzky (Paris)
Kurt Wolff (New York)
Malik (Berlin)
Minority Press (Cambridge)
Pantheon (New York)
Posrednik (Moscow)
Querido (Amsterdam)
Rascher (Zurich)
Suhrkamp (Frankfurt)
Tovarishchestvo I.D. Sytina (Moscow)

Government publications

AT-OeStA/HHStA UR AUR 187 Privilegium Maius, 1156.09.17, at www
.archivinformationssystem.at/detail.aspx?ID=29082.
*Das deutsche Weißbuch über die Schuld am Kriege mit der Denkschrift der deutschen
Viererkommission zum Schuldbericht der Alliierten und Assoziierten Mächte*
(Charlottenburg: Deutsche Verlagsgesellschaft für Politik und Geschichte,
1919).
Briand, Aristide, *Memorandum sur l'organisation d'un régime d'union fédérale
européenne*, proposal at the annual meeting of the League of Nations general
assembly (1929), in *Documents relatifs à l'organisation d'un régime d'union fédérale
européenne* (Geneva: League of Nations Archives, United Nations Office). www
.wdl.org/en/search/?institution=united-nations-office-geneva-library.
Browder, Robert Paul and Alexander Kerensky (eds.), *The Russian Provisional
Government 1917 Documents*, vol. 1 (Stanford: Stanford University Press, 1961).
Constitutions of the German States and Austria.
Constitutions of Poland, Lithuania, Latvia, and Estonia.
*Das Land Ober-Ost, Deutsche Arbeit in den Verwaltungsgebieten Kurland, Litauen
und Bialystok-Grodno* (Stuttgart: DVA, 1917).

Decree 'On the taking down of monuments, which had been erected in honour of the tsars and their servants, and the development of projects for memorials of the Russian Socialist Revolution', by the Socialist Peoples' Committee of the Russian Federation, 14 April 1918.

Schmitt, Carl, *Unabhängigkeit der Richter, Gleichheit vor dem Gesetz und Gewährleistung des Privateigentums nach der Weimarer Verfassung. Ein Rechtsgutachten zu den Gesetzentwürfen über die Vermögensauseinandersetzung mit den früher regverenden Fürstenhäusern* (Berlin und Leipzig: de Gruyter, 1926), 13–14.

von Bülow, Bernhard and Graf Max Montgelas (eds.), *Kommentar zu den Deutschen Dokumenten zum Kriegsausbruch*, 5 vols. (Berlin: Deutsche Verlagsgesellschaft für Politik und Geschichte, 1919).

Weimar, Finanzamt, 1922, AZ RKW 27 A, in Correspondence with his lawyer regarding tax claim, Bundesarchiv, R 32/90, 1920–27, van de Velde, Bemühungen um Beilegung von Differenzen zwischen dem belgischen Architekten und früheren Leiter der Kunstgewerbeschule in Weimar, Professor Henry van de Velde, und dem.

Newspaper reports

'Anniversary of the War's Origin', in *New York Times* (27 June 1915).

Capa, Robert and Gerda Taro, *Death in the Making* (New York: Covici Friede, 1938).

'Comme ils sont tombés', in *Vu*, 445 (23 September 1936), 1106.

'Crusade for Pan-Europe', in *Time Magazine* (29 November 1943).

'Die deutschen Truppen in den Karpathen', in *Vossische Zeitung*, Nr. 112, Abend-Ausgabe (2 March 1915), 3.

Die Voss, 45 (10 November 1923), front page.

'Dva slova o Dzerzhinskom', in *Pravda* (20 July 1931).

'Embarkation of the Body of the Late Emperor Maximillian at Vera Cruz, Mexico', in *Illustrated London News* (11 January 1868).

'Emperor to Aged Singer. Francis Joseph Grateful to Woman Who Would Not Deride Carlota', in *New York Times* (29 July 1901).

'Europa am Tiberstrand', in *Dresdener Neueste Nachrichten* (27 November 1932).

'Europa na rzymskim Kapitolu!', in *Ilustrowany Kuryer codienny* 320 (18 November 1932).

'Hind Swaraj', in *Indian Opinion* (11 and 18 December 1909).

'Le congrès Volta, à Rome', in *Révue de Génève* (24 November 1932).

Marx, Karl, 'The Intervention in Mexico', in *The New-York Daily Tribune* (23 November 1861).

Weber, Max, 'Deutschlands künftige Staatsform', in *Zur deutschen Revolution. Flugschriften der Frankfurter Zeitung*, 2, special ed. (January 1919).

'Menaced with Extinction by War: European Bison in Lithuania', in *Illustrated London News* (4 September 1915), 299.

NN, 'German Princes and Nobility Rush Funds to Neutral Lands', *New York Times* (22 October 1918).

'O Dzerzhinskom', in *Pravda* (20 July 1927).
'Obituary for Duleep Singh', in *The Times* (16 August 1926).
'Rome au lendemain des fêtes décennales', in *Journal de Genève* (25 November 1932).
Theobald Tiger, aka Kurt Tucholsky, 'Bruch', in *Ulk* (13 December 1918), Nr. 50.
'Who Bids for Mexico?', in *The Times* (9 January 1867).
'Wiederauftreten Ida Rolands in Wien', in *Neue Freie Presse* (7 June 1933).

Political writings

Alighieri, Dante, *De Monarchia* (1318–21), first published in Andrea Alciati (ed.), *De formula romani imperii libellus* (Basel: Oporinus, 1559), 53–179.
Angell, Norman, *The Great Illusion* (London: William Heinemann, 1910).
Annan, Noel, 'The Intellectual Aristocracy', in John Plumb (ed.), *Studies in Social History* (London: Longmans, 1955).
Anonymous, 'Das römische Recht in Russland', in Rudolf Leonhard (ed.), *Stimmen des Auslands über die Zukunft der Rechtswissenschaft*, series Studien zur Erläuterung des bürgerlichen Rechts, vol. 17 (Breslau: M&H Marcus, 1906), 105–106.
Anonymous, 'Die Privilegien der Ostseeprovinzen Esthland, Livland und Kurland', in *Deutsches Adelsblatt*, iv (1886), 21–23.
Anonymous, 'Ritter, Mönche und Scholaren. 700 Jahre deutsch-baltische Dichtung, Teil 1', in *Deutsches Adelsblatt*, 36:1 (1934), 642ff.
Anzilotti, Dionisio, *Teoria generale della responsibilitá dello stato nel diritto internazionale* (Florence: F. Lumachi, 1902).
Arnold, Matthew, *Culture and Anarchy: An Essay in Political and Social Criticism* (London: Smith, Elder, and Co., 1896).
Atkins, Francis James, *Europe's New Map* (London: Noel Douglas, 1925).
Bariéty, Jacques (ed.), *Aristide Briand, la Société des Nations et l'Europe, 1919–1932* (Strasbourg: Presses Universitaires, 2007).
Benda, Julien, *La trahison des clercs* (Paris: Grasset, 1927).
Beneš, Edward, 'The New Order in Europe,' in *The Nineteenth Century and After* (September 1941), 141.
Beneš, Edvard, *Problémy Nové Evropy a Zahraniční Politika Československá: Projevy a Úvahy Z R. 1919–1924* (Prag: Melantrich, 1924);
Benjamin, Walter, *Paris, Die Hauptstadt des XIX Jahrhunderts* (1935), first in Walter Benjamin, *Schriften*, 2 vols. (Frankfurt: Suhrkamp, 1955).
Bernstein, Hermann (ed.), *The Willy-Nicky Correspondence. Being the Secret and Intimate Telegrams Exchanged between the Kaiser and the Tsar* (New York: Knopf, 1918), with a foreword by Theodore Roosevelt.
Bluntschli, J.C., *Allgemeine Staatslehre* (Stuttgart: Cotta, 1886).
Bluntschli, J.C., *Die nationale Staatenbildung und der moderne deutsche Staat* (Berlin: Habel, 1881).
Briantchaninoff, Aleksandr, *Le Problème de l'union fédérative européenne* (Paris: Attinger, 1930).

Brockhausen, Karl, *Europa 1914 und 1924. Bild und Gegenbild* (Wien: Wiener literarische Anstalt, 1924).

Brugmans, Henri, *L'idée européenne* (Bruges: De Tempel, 1965).

Burke, Edmund, 'Reflections on the Revolution in France' (1790), in Paul Longford (ed.), *The Writings and Speeches of Edmund Burke* (Oxford: Oxford University Press, 1981).

Butler, Nicholas Murray, *The United States of Europe* (New York: Carnegie Endowment for International Peace, 1915).

Césaire, Aimé, 'Cahier d'un rétour au pays natal', in *Volontés*, 20 (1939).

Chabod, Federico, *La storia dell'idea europea* (Bari: Laterza, 1961).

Chamberlain, Houston Stweart, *Die Grundlagen des Neunzehnten Jahrhunderts*, 2 vols. (Munich: Bruckmann, 1912).

Chesterton, G.K., *The New Jerusalem* (New York: G.H. Doran, 1921).

Churchill, Winston, *Europe Unite; Speeches 1947 and 1948* (London: Cassell, 1950).

Churchill, Winston, Speech delivered at the University of Zurich, 19 September 1946, in Randolph S. Churchill, *The Sinews of Peace: Post-War Speeches of Winston S. Churchill* (London: Cassell, 1948), 199–201.

Churchill, Winston, *The World Crisis*, part I, 1911–15 (Toronto: Macmillan, 1923).

Cole, G.D.H., *Europe, Russia, and the Future* (London: Gollancz, 1941).

Coudenhove-Kalergi, Heinrich Graf, *Der Minotaur der 'Ehre': Studie zur Antiduellbewegung und Duelllüge* (Berlin: S. Calvary &Co., 1902).

Coudenhove-Kalergi, Richard, *Adel-Technik-Pazifismus* (Vienna: Paneuropa, 1925).

Coudenhove-Kalergi, Richard, 'Antworten auf eine Rundfrage I', in *Paneuropa*, 1:3 (1925), 55–62.

Coudenhove-Kalergi, Richard, 'Das Pan-Europa-Programm', in *Paneuropa*, 2 (1924), 4.

Coudenhove-Kalergi, Richard, *Ein Leben für Europa* (Berlin and Cologne: Kiepenheuer & Witsch, 1966).

Coudenhove-Kalergi, Richard, 'The Pan-European Outlook', in *International Affairs* (Royal Institute of International Affairs 1931–1939), 10:5 (September 1931), 638–651.

Coudenhove-Kalergi, Richard, 'Paneuropa. Ein Vorschlag', in *Neue Freie Presse* (17 November 1922).

Coudenhove-Kalergi, Richard Nicolaus Graf von, *Adel* (Leipzig: Der Neue Geist, 1922) und *Paneuropa* (1922).

Cron, Hermann, *Die Organisation des deutschen Heeres im Weltkriege* (Berlin: Mittler & Sohn, 1923).

Czernin von und zu Chudenitz, Ferdinand, *Europe, Going Going Gone: A Sketchy Book Trying to Give a Rough Explanation of Europe, Its Politics, and Its State of Mind, for the Benefit Mainly of Anglo-Saxons, Politicians, and Other Folk with Uncomplicated Minds* (London: Davies, 1939).

Davies, David, *A Federated Europe* (London: Gollancz, 1940).

Dawson, Christopher, *The Making of Europe* (London: Sheed & Ward, 1932).

Dawson, Christopher, *The Modern Dilemma: The Problem of European Unity* (London: Sheed & Ward, 1932).

Dawson, William Harbutt, 'The Pan-European Movement', in *The Economic Journal*, 37:145 (March 1927), 62–67.

Dekrety sovetskoi vlasti (Moscow: Gosudarstvennoe izdatelstvo politicheskoi literatury, 1957).

Delaisi, Francis, *Les Deux Europes* (Paris: Payot, 1929).

Deniker, Joseph, *The Races of Man: An Outline of Anthropology and Ethnography* (New York: Charles Scribner, 1913).

Drieu de la Rochelle, Pierre, *L'Europe contre les patries* (Paris: Stock, 1931).

Eder, M.D., *War-Shock. The Psycho-Neuroses in War Psychology and Treatment* (London: Heinemann, 1917).

Effendi, Mehemed Emin, *Civilisation et humanité* (Paris: G. Fickler, 1920).

Elias, Norbert, *Der Prozess der Zivilisation* (Zurich: zum Falken, 1939).

Erzherzog Franz Ferdinand. Unser Thronfolger. Zum 50. Geburtstag, ed. Leopold Freiherr von Chlumetzky et al. (Vienna and Leipzig: Illustriertes Sonderheft der Oesterreichischen Rundschau, 1913), 9–11.

Fabre-Luce, Alfred, *Anthologie de la nouvelle Europe* (Paris: Plon, 1942).

Fabre-Luce, Alfred, *Histoire de la Revolution Européenne, 1919–1945* (Paris: Plon, 1954).

Febvre, Lucien, *L'Europe, genèse d'une civilisation, cours professé au Collège de France en 1944–1945*, établi, présenté et annoté par Thérèse Charmasson et Brigitte Mazon, avec la collaboration de Sarah Lidemann, préface de Marc Ferro (Paris: Perrin, 1999).

Ferenczi, Sándor, Karl Abraham, Ernst Simmel, and Ernest Jones, with an introduction by Sigmund Freud, *Psychoanalysis and War Neuroses* (London, Vienna and New York: The International Psycho-Analytical Press, 1921).

Frazer, James, *The Golden Bough: A Study in Magic and Religion* (New York: Macmillan, 1925).

Frazer, James, 'The Killing of the Khazar Kings', in *Folk-lore*, xviii (1917), 382–407.

Freud, Sigmund, 'A Comment on Anti-Semitism', in Sigmund Freud, *Moses and Monotheism, An Outline of Psycho-Analysis and Other Works (1937–38)*, vol. xxiii, ed. and transl. James Strachey (London: Vintage/The Hogarth Press, 2001), 287–301, 292–292. Originally in *Die Zukunft: ein neues Deutschland, ein neues Europa* 7 (25 November 1938).

Freud, Sigmund, *Das Unbehagen an der Kultur* (Wien: Internationaler Psychoanalytischer Verlag, 1930).

Freud, Sigmund, *Die Traumdeutung* (Leipzig and Vienna: Deuticke, 1900).

Freud, Sigmund, *Totem und Tabu. Einige Übereinstimmungen im Seelenleben der Wilden und der Neurotiker* (Leipzig and Vienna: Hugo Heller, 1913).

Freud, Sigmund, 'Trauer und Melancholie', in *Internationale Zeitschrift für Ärztliche Psychoanalyse*, 4:6 (1917), 288–301.

Fry, Roger, 'Modern Mosaic and Mr. Boris Anrep', in *The Burlington Magazine for Connoisseurs*, 42:243 (June 1923), 272–278.

Galton, Francis, *English Men of Science: Their Nature and Nurture* (London: Macmillan, 1874).

Gobineau, Comte de, *The Inequality of Human Races* (1854), transl. Adrien Collins (London: Heinemann, 1915).

Goebbels, Joseph, 'Das patriotische Bürgertum', in *Nationalsozialistische Monatshefte*, 1 (1930), 221–229.

Goebbels, Joseph, 'Die deutsche Revolution', in *Nationalsozialistische Monatshefte*, 39 (June 1933), 247–248.

Grey of Falloden, Viscount, Twenty-Five Years, 1892–1916 (New York: Stokes, 1925).

Heine, Heinrich, *Lutetia*, xxxviii (1841), in Heinrich Heine, *Historisch-Kritische Gesamtausgabe*, vol. 13:1, ed. Manfred Windfuhr (Düsseldorf: Hoffmann und Campe, 1988), 145. More on Delacroix and Delaroche in Hans-Werner Schmidt and Jan Nicolaisen (eds.), *Eugène Delacroix & Paul Delaroche*, Leipzig, Museum der bildenden Künste (Petersberg: Michael Imhof Verlag, 2015).

Herriot, Edouard, *The United States of Europe* (London: George Harrap, 1931).

Herzfelde, Wieland, *Sulamith* (Berlin: Barger, 1917).

Hitler, Adolf, *Mein Kampf* (Munich: Bruckmann, 1923).

Hoare, Samuel, *The Fourth Seal and the End of a Russian Chapter* (London: Heinemann, 1930).

Hugo, Victor, 'Discours d'ouverture aux Congrès de la Paix à Paris' (21 August 1849), in Victor Hugo, *Actes et Paroles. Avant l'éxil*, 1849–1851, ed. Charles Sarolea (Paris: Nelson, 1875), 423–433.

Ikonnikov, Nikolai, 'Piatsot dnei: sekretnaia sluzhba v tylu bolshevikov, 1918–1919', in *Russkoe Proshloe*, 7 (1996), 43–105.

Iswolsky, Aleksander, *Recollections of a Foreign Minister*, transl. from French original by Charles Louis Seeger (New York: Doubleday, 1921).

James, C.L.R., *The Case for West Indian Self-Government* (London: Hogarth Press, 1938).

James, C.L.R., 'An Encounter with Edith Sitwell' (1936), in Anna Grimshaw (ed.), *The C.L.R. James Reader* (Oxford: Blackwell, 1992).

Jouvenel, Bertrand de, *Le reveil de l'Europe* (Paris: Gallimard, 1941).

Jung, Carl Gustav, *Civilization in Transition*, 2nd ed. (London and Henley: Routledge & Kegan Paul and Princeton University Press, 1970, reprinted in 1981).

Kennan, George [Mr X.], 'The Sources of Soviet Conduct', in *Foreign Affairs* (July 1947).

Kerensky, Aleksandr, *The Prelude to Bolshevism*, transl. from Russian unknown (New York: Dodd, Mead and Company, 1919).

Kessler, Count Harry, *Germany and Europe* (New Haven: Yale University Press, 1923).

Kessler, Harry Graf, *Das Tagebuch 1880–1937*, Roland S. Kamzelak and Ulrich Ott (eds.), Veröffentlichung der Deutschen Schillergesellschaft 50, 9 vols. (Stuttgart: Klett-Cotta, 2004–09).

Kessler, Harry Graf, *Das Tagebuch 1880–1937*, Roland S. Kamzelak and Ulrich Ott (eds.), 9 vols. (Stuttgart: Klett-Cotta, 2004–10); vol. 5, 1914–16, Günter Riederer und Ulrich Ott (eds.) (Stuttgart: Klett-Cotta, 2008); vol. 6,

1916–18, Günter Riederer (ed.) (Stuttgart: Klett-Cotta, 2006); vol. 7, 1919–23, Angela Reinthal (ed.) (Stuttgart: Klett-Cotta, 2007); vol. 8, 1923–26, Angela Reinthal, Günter Riederer und Jörg Schuster (eds.); vol. 9, 1926–37, Sabine Gruber and Ulrich Ott (eds.) (Stuttgart: Klett-Cotta, 2010).

Kessler, Harry Graf, 'Erlebnis mit Nietzsche', in *Die Neue Rundschau* (April 1935), 391–507.

Kessler, Harry Graf, *Gesammelte Schriften in drei Bänden*, ed. Cornelia Blasberg and Gerhard Schuster, 3 vols. (Frankfurt/Main: Fischer, 1988).

Kessler, Harry Graf, 'Nationalität', in *Die Weißen Blätter. Eine Monatsschrift*, 6:12 (1919), 531–546.

Kessler, Harry Graf, 'Nationalität', in *Die Zukunft*, 14:27 (1906), 17–27. Reprinted in *Harry Graf Kessler: Künstler und Nationen, Aufsätze und Reden 1899–1933. Gesammelte Schriften in drei Bänden*, ed. Cornelia Blasberg and Gerhard Schuster, vol. 2 (Frankfurt am Main: Insel, 1988), 117–130.

Kessler, Harry Graf, *Walther Rathenau*, transl. Denise Van Moppès (Paris: Grasset, 1933).

Keynes, John Maynard, *The Economic Consequences of the Peace* (London: Macmillan, 1919).

Keyserling, Hermann, *Creative Understanding* (New York and London: Harper and Brothers, 1929).

Keyserling, Hermann, 'A Philosopher's View of the War', in *The Hibbert Journal* (3 April 1915).

Kraus, Karl, 'Der Adel von seiner schriftstellerischen Seite', in Die Fackel, vol. XXVII (1925), 137. Printed from http://corpus1.aac.ac.at/fackel/.

Kropotkin, Peter, *Kropotkin's Revolutionary Pamphlets*, ed. Roger Baldwin (1927) (New York: Dover, 1970).

Landau, Rom, *God Is My Adventure. A Book on Modern Mystics, Masters and Teachers* (London: Faber and Faber, 1935).

Las Cases, Emmanuel Comte de (ed.), *Mémorial de Sainte-Hélène. Journal de la vie privée et des conversations de l'Empereur Napoléon à Sainte-Helène* (London: Henri Colburn & Co., 1823).

Legnano, Giovanni da, *De Bello, De Represaliis et De Duello*, ed. James Brown Scott (Washington and Oxford: Oxford University Press for the Carnegie Institution, 1917).

Lippman, Walter, *The Cold War: A Study in US Foreign Policy* (New York: Harper, 1947).

Lippman, Walter, *The Phantom Public* (New York: Macmillan, 1927).

Loos, Adolf, 'Ornament und Verbrechen' (1908), printed in *Cahiers d'aujourd'hui*, June 1913. First German version published in *Frankfurter Zeitung* (24 October 1929).

Lyons, H.L.S., *Internationalism in Europe, 1815–1914* (Leiden, Neth.: A.W. Sijthoff, 1963).

MacCurdy, John T., *War Neuroses* (Cambridge: Cambridge University Press, 1918), 123.

Maine, Sir Henry Sumner Maine, *Lectures in the Early History of Institutions* (London: John Murray, 1905).

Martens, Fedor, *Sovremennoe mezhdunarodnoe pravo civilisovannykh narodov* [Modern International Law of Civilized Peoples], 2 vols. (St. Petersburg: Benke, 1883).

Marx, Karl, *Das Kapital. Kritik der Politischen Ökonomie*, vol. I, ch. 2 (Hamburg: Otto Meissner, 1867), cited after the transl. David McClelland, in Karl Marx, *An Abridged Edition*, ed. David McClelland (Oxford: Oxford University Press, 1995).

Masaryk, Thomas G., *The New Europe* (London: Eyre and Spottiswoode, 1918).

Maximilian, Erzherzog, *Gedichte*, vol. 1 (Vienna: Aus der kaiserlich-königlichen Hof- und Staatsdruckerei, 1863).

Maximilian, I., 'Emperor of Mexico', in *Recollections of my Life*, transl. Anonymous, vol. 1 (London: Richard Bentley, 1868).

Maximilian, Kaiser von Mexiko, *Aus meinem Leben. Reiseskizzen, Aphorismen, Gedichte* (Leipzig: Duncker und Humblot, 1867).

Maximilian, Kaiser von Mexiko, *Mein erster Ausflug. Wanderungen in Griechenland* (Leipzig: Duncker & Humblot, 1868).

Mazzini, Giuseppe, 'Europe, Its Condition and Prospects', in *Westminster Review* (April 1852), 236–250.

Mexiko, Maximilian Kaiservon, *Reiseskizzen, Aphorismen, Gedichte*, vol. 7, *Reiseskizzen XII, Aphorismen, Gedichte* (Leipzig: Duncker und Humblot, 1867).

Michels, Robert, *Zur Soziologie des Parteiwesens in der modernen Demokratie* (Leipzig: Klinkhardt, 1911).

Milosz, Czeslaw, *Native Realm: A Search for Self-Definition* (Berkeley: University of California Press, 1981).

Montgelas, Maximilian Graf, *Leitfaden zur Kriegsschuldfrage* (Berlin: De Gruyter, 1923).

Napoleon Bonaparte (attributed to), in anon. ed. and transl., *Des Kaisers Napoleons Politisches Testament, nebst hinterlassene Vermächtnisse, mit dem politischen Testamente Peters des Großen, Kaisers von Rußland*, 2nd ed. (Quedlinburg and Leipzig: Ernstsche Buchhandlung, 1829); probably edited and composed by Count Emmanuel de Las Cases.

Naumann, Friedrich, *Mitteleuropa* (Berlin: Reimer, 1915).

Neurath, Otto, *Gesellschaft und Wirtschaft. Bildstatistisches Elementarwerk. Das Gesellschafts- und Wirtschaftsmuseum in Wien zeigt in 100 farbigen Bildtafeln Produktionsformen, Gesellschaftsordnungen, Kulturstufen, Lebenshaltungen* (Leipzig: Bibliographisches Institut, 1930).

Nietzsche, Friedrich, *Jenseits von Gut und Böse. Vorspiel zu einer Philosophie der Zukunft* (Leipzig: C.G. Naumann, 1886).

Nippold, O., '"Les conférences de La Haye et la Société des Nations". Le développement historique du droit international depuis le Congrès de Vienne', in *Collected Courses of the Hague Academy of International Law*, vol. 2 (The Hague: Martinus Nijhoff Publishers, 1924).

Ortega y Gasset, José, *La rebelión de las masas* (Madrid: Revista de Occidente, 1929).

Österreich, Rudolf von, *Eine Orientreise vom Jahre 1881* (Vienna: Kaiserl.-Königl. Hof- u. Staatsdr., 1885).

Pareto, Vilfredo, *The Mind and Society*, transl. Andrew Bongiorno and Arthur Livingston, 4 vols. (New York: Harcourt and Brace, 1935).

Pareto, Vilfredo, *Trattato Di Sociologia Generale*, 4 vols. (Florence: G. Barbera, 1916).

Pierremont, E., *Tche-Ka. Matériaux et documents sur la terreur bolcheviste recueillis par le bureau central du parti socialiste révolutionnaire russe* (Paris: J. Povolozky, n.d.), 191.

Pistohlkors, Harry von, *Livlands Kampf um deutschtum und Kultur; eine Übersicht aller bedeutungsvollen Ereignisse aus der Geschichte der alten ordensgebietes Livlands* (Berlin: Puttkammer & Mühlbrecht, 1918).

Platten, Fritz, *Die Reise Lenins durch Deutschland im plombierten Wagen* (Berlin: Neuer Deutscher Verlag, 1924).

Popper-Lynkeus, Josef, *Die allgemeine Nährpflicht als lösung der sozialen Frage: eingehend bearbeitet und statistisch durchgerechnet; mit einem Uschweis der theoretischen und praktischen Wertlosigkeit der Wirtschaftslehre* (Dresden: Carl Reissner, 1912).

Popper-Lynkeus, Josef and Emmerich Tálos, *Materielle Grundsicherung: Popper-Lynkeus' Programm 'Die allgemeine Nährpflicht als Lösung der sozialen Frage'; ein auszugsweiser Reprint* ([Vienna]: Verl. d. Österr. Staatsdr., 1989).

Rathenau, Walther, *La Triple Revolution*, transl. David Roget (Paris-Basel: 1921).

Reck-Malleczewen, Fritz, *Tagebuch eines Verzweifelten* (Lorch: Bürger, 1947).

Reed, John, *Ten Days That Shook the World* (New York: Boni and Liveright, 1919).

Reisner, Larisa, *Hamburg auf den Barrikaden. Erlebtes und Erhörtes aus dem Hamburger Aufstand 1923* (Berlin: Neuer Deutscher Verlag, 1923).

Reventlow, Ernst Graf von, 'Nemesis über dem Bürgertum', in *Nationalsozialistische Monatshefte*, 1 (1930), 5–11.

Reynold, Gonzague de, *L'Europe tragique: la revolution moderne: fin d'un monde* (Paris: Spes, 1934).

Rheinbaben, Baron von, *Vers une nouvelle Europe* (Groupe Collaboration, 1941).

Rohan, Karl Anton, *Europa: Streiflichter* (Leipzig: Der Neue Geist, 1923).

Rohan, Karl Anton, *Heimat Europa* (Düsseldorf-Köln: Eugen Diederichs 1954).

Rohan, Karl Anton, *Moskau* (Karlsruhe: Braun, 1927).

Rohan, Karl Anton, *Umbruch der Zeit 1923–1930* (Berlin: Stilke, 1930).

Rosenberg, Alfred, *Der deutsche Ordensstaat: Ein neuer Abschnitt in der Entwicklung des nationalsozialistischen Staatsgedankens* (Munich: Zentralverlag der NSDAP, Eher, 1934).

Rosenberg, Alfred, *Der Kampf um die Weltanschauung: Rede, geh. am 22. Febr. 1934 im Reichstagssitzgssaal d. Kroll-Oper zu Berlin* (Munich: Eher, 1936).

Rosenberg, Alfred and Karlheinz Rüdiger, *Tradition und Gegenwart: Reden und Aufsätze 1936–1940* (Munich: F. Eher Nachf., 1941).

Rosenberg, Alfred and Thilo von Trotha, *Blut und Ehre: ein Kampf für Deutsche Wiedergeburt; Reden und Aufsätze von 1919–1933* (Munich: Zentralverlag der N.S.D.A.P., 1934).

Saint-Pierre, Abbé, *A Project for Settling an Everlasting Peace in Europe. First Proposed by Henry IV of France, and Approved by Queen Elizabeth, and Most of the Then Princes of Europe, and Now Discussed at Large, and Made Particable by the Abbot St. Pierre, of the French Academy* (London: J. Watts, 1714).

Salomo, Israel Rex and Eric Gill, *Das Hohe Lied: [Auf d. Handpressen d. Cranachpresse in 3 Farben gedr.]* (Leipzig: Insel-Verl., 1931).

Salomon, Ernst von, *Der Fragebogen* (Hamburg: Rowohlt, 1951).

Salomon, Ernst von, *Die Geächteten* (Berlin: Rowohlt, 1931).

Salomon, Ernst von, *The Outlaws* (London: Arktos, 2013), 301.

Salter, Sir Arthur, *The United States of Europe and Other Papers* (New York: Reynald and Hitchcock, 1933).

Saussure, Ferdinand de, *Cours de linguistique générale*, ed. Charles Bally and Albert Sechehaye (Paris: Payot, 1916).

Sazonoff, Sergei, *Vspominania* [Memoirs] (Paris: Siyalskaya, 1927).

Scelle, Georges and Boris Mirkine-Goutzevich, *L'union européenne* (Paris: Presses Universitaire, 1931).

Schmitt, Carl, *Unabhängigkeit der Richter, Gleichheit vor dem Gesetz und Gewährleistung des Privateigentums nach der Weimarer Verfassung. Ein Rechtsgutachten zu den Gesetzentwürfen über die Vermögensauseinandersetzung mit den früher regverenden Fürstenhäusern* (Berlin und Leipzig: de Gruyter, 1926).

Schreyvogl, Friedrich, *Die Entdeckung Europas* (Leipzig: Staackmann, 1931).

Shklovsky, Viktor, *O teorii prozy* (Moscow: Krug, 1925).

Simmel, Georg, 'Zur Soziologie des Adels. Fragment aus einer Formenlehre der Gesellschaft', in *Frankfurter Zeitung und Handelsblatt* (Neue Frankfurter Zeitung), 52:358, 1, Morgenblatt (27 December 1907), Feuilleton-Teil, 1–3.

Sosnosky, Theodor von, 'Erzherzog Franz Ferdinand', in Leopold Freiherr von Chlumetzky et al. (eds.), *Erzherzog Franz Ferdinand. Unser Thronfolger. Zum 50. Geburtstag* (Vienna and Leipzig: Illustriertes Sonderheft der Oesterreichischen Rundschau, 1913), 9–11.

Spengler, Oswald, *Der Mensch und die Technik* (Munich: Beck, 1931).

Spengler, Oswald, *Der Untergang des Abendlandes* (Wien: Braumülller, 1918; München: Beck, 1922).

Strachey, James (ed.), *The Standard Edition of the Complete Psychological Works of Sigmund Freud*, transl. James Strachey, in collaboration with Anna Freud, assisted by Alix Strachey and Alan Tyson, vol. 10 (London: The Hogarth Press, 1955).

Strachey, John, *The End of Empire* (New York: Random House, 1959).

de Taube, Baron M., *La politique russe d' avant guerre et la fin de l' empire des Tsars (1904–1917)* (Paris: Leroux, 1928).

von Taube, M., *Archiv des uradeligen Geschlechts Taube, sonst Tuve genannt* (Yuryev: Mattiesen, 1911).

von Taube, M., 'Beiträge zur baltischen Familiengeschichte', in *Jahrbuch für Genealogie, Heraldik und Sphragistik* (1899), 143–147; 1900, 85–89; 1903, 113–115; 1904, 115–120; 1905/06, 257–262; 1907/08, 65–73; 1909/10, 13.

von Taube, M., *Die von Uxkull; genealogische Geschichte des uradeligen Geschlechts der Herren, Freiherren und Grafen von Uxkull, 1229–1929* (Berlin: Julius Sittenfeld, 1930).

Taube, Michael von, articles in the *Collected Courses of the Hague Academy of International Law* (1926–35), e.g. *L'inviolabilité des traités*, in *Collected Courses of the Hague Academy of International Law*, 32 (1930); *Le statut juridique de la mer Baltique jusqu'au début du xixe siècle*, in *Collected Courses of the Hague Academy of International Law*, 53 (1935); *L'apport de Byzance au développement du droit international occidental*, 67 (1939).

Taube, Michiael Freiherr von, *Rußland und Westeuropa (Rußlands historische Sonderentwicklung in der europäischen Völkergemeinschaft)*, Institut für internationales Recht an der Universität Kiel (Berlin: Stilke, 1928).

Taube, Mikhail, *Der großen Katastrophe entgegen. Die russische Politik der Vorkriegszeit und das Ende des Zarenreiches (1904–1917)* (Berlin and Leipzig: Georg Neuner, 1929).

von Taube, Mikhail, Khristianstvo i mezhdunarodnyi mir, 2nd ed. (Moscow: Posrednik, 1905).

Taube, Mikhail, 'K istorii gerba Romanovykh (dogadka o proiskhozhdenii Romanovskogo grifa)', Lecture given at the Russian Genealogical Society on the occasion of the 300th anniversary of the Romanovs, 26 February 1913, in *Gerboved*, July 1913, 109–117. http://gerboved.ru/t/july1913.html, accessed 3 April 2014.

Taube, Prof. bar., *Vechnyi mir ili vechnaia voina? (Mysli o „Ligi Natsii")* (Berlin: Detinets, 1922).

Tocqueville, Alexis de, *The Old Regime and the Revolution*, ed. François Furet and Françoise Mélonio, transl. Alan S. Kahan (Chicago and London: The University of Chicago Press, 1998).

Trotsky, Leon, *Europe et Amérique* (Paris: Librairie de l'Humanité, 1926).

Trotsky, Leon, 'Is the Time Ripe for the Slogan: "The United States of Europe?"', in *Pravda* (30 June 1923).

Trubetskoi, Kn. N.S., *Evropa i Chelovechestvo* (Sofia: Rossiisko-bolgarskoe knigoizdatel'stvo, 1920)

Trubetzkoy, Nikita, *Europa und die Menschheit* (Munich: Drei Masken Verlag, 1922).

Vattel, Emil de, *Le droit des gens, ou Principes de la loi naturelle appliqués à la conduite et aux affaires des nations et des souverains*, Classics of International Law (Washington: Carnegie Institution, 1916).

Vergin, Fedor, *Psychoanalyse der europäischen Politik* (Wien: Hess, 1931).

Les Eclogues de Virgile, transl. and ed. Marc Lafargue, ill. by Eric Gill (Weimar: Cranachpresse, 1926).

Vitte, Sergei, *The Memoirs of Count Witte*, with an Introduction by Countess Witte, transl. from Russian original by Abraham Yarmolinsky (New York: Doubleday, 1921).

Voytinsky, Wladimir, *Die vereinigten Staaten von Europa* (Berlin: J.H.W. Dietz Nachf., 1926).

Weber, Max, ,Die „Objektivität" sozialwissenschaftlicher und sozialpolitischer Erkenntnis', in *Archiv für Sozialwissenschaft und Sozialpolitik*, 19 (1904), 22–88.

Weber, Max, *Gesamtausgabe*, 23 vols. (Tübingen: Mohr, 1988–2015). vol. I:15, Wolfgang Mommsen and Gangolf Hübinger (eds.), *Max Weber. Zur Politik im Weltkrieg* (Tübingen: Mohr, 1984); vol. I:16, *Zur Neuordnung Deutschlands. Schriften und Reden 1918–1920*, Wolfgang Mommsen and Gangolf Hübinger (eds.) (Tübingen: Mohr, 1988); vol. I:17, *Wissenschaft als Beruf. 1917/19. Politik als Beruf. 1919*, Wolfgang Mommsen and Wolfgang Schluchter, in collaboration with Birgitt Morgenbrod (eds.) (Tübingen: Mohr, 1992); vol. I:22–24, Edith Hanke, with assistance from Thomas Kroll (eds.), *Teilband 4: Herrschaft* (Tübingen: Mohr, 2005).

Weber, Max, 'The Nation State and Economic Policy', in Ronald Speirs and Peter Lassmann (eds.), *Political Writings* (Cambridge: Cambridge University Press, 1994).

Weber, Max, 'Politik als Beruf', in Max Weber, 'Geistige Arbeit als Beruf. Vier Vorträge vor dem Freistudentischen Bund. Zweiter Vortrag. München und Leipzig 1919', in Max Weber, *Politik und Gesellschaft. Politische Reden und Schriften* (Neu Isenburg: Zweitausendeins, 2006).

Wiese, Leopold von, *Europa als geistige Einheit* (Darmstadt: Otto Reichl, 1919).

Wilde, Oscar, *The Sphinx*, with decoratins by Charles Ricketts (London: E. Matthews and J. Lane, 1894).

Wilhelm, II, *Ereignisse und Gestalten, 1878–1918* (Leipzig and Berlin: Koehler, 1922).

Wirsing, Giselher, *Zwischeneuropa und die deutsche Zukunft* (Jena: Eugen Diederichs, 1932).

Woolf, Leonard, *International Government*, with an introduction by Bernhard Shaw (New York: Brentano's, 1916).

Woolf, Leonard, *The Village in the Jungle* (New York: Harcourt, 1937).

Ydewalle, Charles, *Vingt ans d'Europe, 1919–1939*. Vorwort v. André Tardie (Paris: Flammarion, 1939).

Zielinski, V., *L'Europe Unie. Essai de programme pacifiste pratique* (Constantinople: Esperanto, 1921).

Zinoviev, Grigory, *Der Krieg und die Krise des Sozialismus* (Vienna: Verlag für Literatur und Politik, 1924).

Biographica (Memoirs, biographies and autobiographies)

Alvensleben, Maximilian Baron von, *With Maximilian in Mexico* (London: Longmans, Green, & Co., 1867).

Anonymous, *The Fall of the Romanoffs. How the Ex-Empress and Rasputine Caused the Russian Revolution* (London: Henry Jenkins Limited, 1918, New York: E. P. Dutton & Co.).

Berberova, Nina, *The Italics are Mine*, transl. Ph. Radley (New York: Knopf, 1992).

Bismarck, Otto von, *Gedanken und Erinnerungen* (Stuttgart and Berlin: Cotta, 1898).

Blasio, José Luis, *Maximilian. Emperor of Mexico. Memoirs of His Private Secretary*, transl. Robert Hammond Murray, Introduction Carleton Beals (New Haven: Yale University Press, 1934).

Boehm, Max Hilderbert, *Wir Balten* (Salzburg: Akademischer Gemeinschaftsverlag, 1951).

Cantacuzène, Princess, *Revolutionary Days. Recollections of Romanoffs and Bolsheviki, 1914–17* (Boston: Small, Maynard and Company, 1919).

Cederholm, Boris, *In the Clutches of the Tcheka*, transl. F.H. Lyon (Boston and New York: Houghton Mifflin, 1929).

Chamisso, Adalbert von, *Reise um die Welt mit der Romanzoffischen Entdeckungs-Expedition in den Jahren 1815–18 auf der Brigg Rurik. Kapitain Otto v. Kotzebue* (Leipzig: Weidmann'sche Buchhandlung, 1836).

Clary-Aldringen, Alfons, *Geschichten eines alten Österreichers* (Berlin: Ullstein, 1977).

Corti, Egon Caesar Count, *Maximilian and Charlotte of Mexico*, transl. Catherine Alison Phillips, 2 vols. (1924, New York and London: Knopf, 1928).

Coudenhove-Kalergi, Mitsu, *Memoirs*, in Alena Vondrušová and Ladislava Váňová (eds.), Memoiren von Gräfin Mitsu Coudenhove-Kalergi, die auf dem Schloss in Ronsperg gelebt hat (Domažlice: Nakladatelství Českého lesa, 2006).

Eisenstein, Sergei, *Beyond the Stars*, 4 vols. (London: BFI, 1996).

Eliot, T.S., 'The Waste Land', in *The Criterion*, 1:1 (October 1922), 50–64.

Essad-Bey, Mohammed, *Nicholas II. Prisoner of the Purple* (London: Hutchinson & Co., 1936).

Graves, Robert, *Goodbye to All That* (London: Jonathan Cape, 1929).

Gul', Roman, *Les Maitres de la Tcheka. Histoire de la Terreur en URSS, 1917–1938* (Paris: Les Editions de France, 1938).

Gul', Roman, *Dzerzhinskiy (Nachalo terror)* (New York: Most, 1974).

Iswolsky, Alexander, *Recollections of a Foreign Minister*, transl. from French original by Charles Louis Seeger (New York: Doubleday, 1921).

Kerensky, Aleksandr, *The Prelude to Bolshevism*, transl. from Russian unknown (New York: Dodd, Mead and Company, 1919).

Kessler, Harry Graf, *Gesichter und Zeiten. 1. Band: Völker und Vaterländer* (Berlin: Fischer, 1935).

Kessler, Harry Graf, *Walther Rathenau. Sein Leben und sein Werk* (Berlin: Klemm, 1928).

Kessler, Harry Graf, *Walther Rathenau. His Life and Work* (London: Howe, 1929).

Kessler, Harry Graf, *Walther Rathenau, avec un Préface de Gabriel Marcel* (Paris: Grasset, 1933).

Kessler, Harry Graf (ed.), *Krieg und Zusammenbruch 1914–1918: aus Feldpostbriefen* (Weimar: Cranachpresse, 1921).

Kessler, Harry Graf, as printer of *Les Eclogues de Virgile*, transl. and ed. Marc Lafargue, ill. by Eric Gill (Weimar: Cranachpresse, 1926).

Kessler, Harry Graf, as printer of William Shakespeare, *The Tragedie of Hamlet Prince of Denmarke*, ed. J. Dover Wilson, ill. by Edward Gordon Craig and Eric Gill (Weimar: Cranachpresse, 1930).

Kojève, Alexandre, *Introduction to the Reading of Hegel. Lectures on the Phenomenology of Spirit* (1947; New York: Basic Books, 1980),

Kovalevskii, P.I., *Zarubezhnaia Rossia: Istoria i kul'turno-prosvetitel'skaia rabota russkogo zarubezh'ia za polveka (1920–1970)* (Paris: Libraire des Cinq Continents, 1971).

Leavis, F.R., *Mass Civilisation and Minority Culture* (Cambridge: Minority Press, 1930).

Löwenstein, Prince H., *A Catholic in Republican Spain* (London: Gollancz, 1937).

Ludwig, Emil, *Wilhelm Hohenzollern. The Last of the Kaisers* (New York and London: G.B. Putnam's, 1927).

Mann, Thomas, *Tagebücher*, ed. Peter de Mendelssohn (Frankfurt: S. Fischer, 1977).

Mannheim, Karl, 'Das konservative Denken I. Soziologische Beiträge zum Werden des politisch-historischen Denkens in Deutschland', in *Archiv für Sozialwissenschaft und Sozialpolitik*, 57:1 (1927), 68–143.

Maximilian I of Habsburg, *Recollections of My Life*, 3 vols. (London: Richard Bentley, 1868).

Mazzini, Giuseppe, 'Europe, Its Condition and Prospects', in *Westminster Review* (April 1852), 236–250.

Metternich, Prince Klemens von, *Memoirs of Prince Metternich*, ed. Prince Richard von Metternich, 2 vols. (London: Bentley & Son, 1880).

Musil, Robert *Der Mann ohne Eigenschaften* (Hamburg: Rowohlt, 1930–43).

Nabokov, Vladimir, *Conclusive Evidence* (New York: Harper, 1951).

Popovici, Aurel, *Die Vereinigten Staaten von Groß-Österreich. Politische Studien zur Lösung der nationalen Fragen und staatrechtlichen Krisen in Österreich-Ungarn* (Leipzig: B. Elisch, 1906).

Popovici, Aurel, *La Question Rumaine en Transylvanie et en Hongrie* (Lausanne and Paris: Payot, 1918).

Popper, Karl, *The Open Society*, 2 vols. (London and New York: Routledge, 2002).

Popper, Karl, *Unended Quest: An Intellectual Autobiography* (La Salle, Ill.: Open Court, 1982).

Reventlow, Ernst Graf von, 'Nemesis über dem Bürgertum', in *Nationalsozialistische Monatshefte*, 1 (1930), 5–11.

Rilke, Rainer Maria, 'Aus der Übertragung der altrussischen Dichtung «Das Igorlied»', *Insel-Almanach auf das Jahr 1931*.

Rilke, Rainer Maria, *Duineser Elegien. Elegies from the Castle of Duino*, transl. V. Sackville-West and Edward Sackville-West (London: The Hogarth Press, 1931).

Rilke, Rainer Maria, *The Notebook of Malte Laurids Brigge*, transl. John Linton (London: The Hogarth Press, 1931).

Rilke, Rainer Maria, *Poems*, transl. J.B. Leishman (London: The Hogarth Press, 1934).

Rohan, Karl Anton, *Heimat Europa* (Düsseldorf-Köln: Eugen Diederichs, 1954).

Sacher-Masoch, Leopold von, 'Don Juan von Kolomea', in *Westermann's Illustrirte Deutsche Monatshefte*, 121:25 (October 1866), 1–26.

Salm Salm, Felix zu, *Queretaro: Blätter aus meinem Tagebuch in Mexico: nebst einem Auszuge aus dem Tagebuche der Prinzessin Agnes zu Salm-Salm* (Leipzig: Körner, 1868).

Salomon, Ernst von, *Der Fragebogen* (Hamburg: Rowohlt, 1951).

Sazonoff, Sergei, *Vospominania* [Memoirs] (Paris: Siyalskaya, 1927).

Simmel, Georg, *Briefe 1912–18*, ed. Klaus Christian Köhnke, in *Gesamtausgabe*, 23 vols., vol. 23 (Frankfurt: Suhrkamp, 2005), Simmel to Keyserling, 18 May 1918.

Srbik, H. Ritter von, 'Franz Joseph I. Charakter und Regierungsgrundsätze', in *Historische Zeitschrift*, 144 (1931), 509.

Srbik, H. Ritter von, *Metternich. Der Staatsmann und der Mensch* (Munich: F. Bruckmann, 1957).

Stenbock-Fermor, Graf Alexander, *My Experiences as a Miner*, transl. Frances, Countess of Warwick (London and New York: Putnam, 1930).

Taube, Michael Freiherr von, *Der großen Katastrophe entgegen. Die russische Politik der Vorkriegszeit und das Ende des Zarenreiches* (Leipzig: Koehler, 1937).

Thelen, Albert Vigoleis, *Die Insel des zweiten Gesichts* (Amsterdam: van Oorshot, 1953).

Tolstoy, Leo, *The Kingdom of God is Within You*, transl. Constance Garnett (New York: Cassell, 1894).

Tolstoy, Leo, *Slavery of Our Times* (1890), transl. Aylmer Maude (New York: Oxford World Classics Edition, 1900), 9–63.

Vitte, Sergei, *The Memoirs of Count Witte*, with an Introduction by Countess Witte, transl. from Russian original by Abraham Yarmolinsky (New York: Doubleday, 1921).

Wilhelm II, *Ereignisse und Gestalten, 1878–1918* (Leipzig and Berlin: Koehler, 1922).

Wilton, Robert, *The Last Days of the Romanovs* (London: Thornton Butterworth Ltd., 1920).

Woolf, Leonard, *Sowing. An Autobiography of the Years 1880–1904* (New York: Harcourt & Brace, 1960).

Woolf, Virginia, 'Mr Bennett and Mrs Brown', in *The Hogarth Essays* (London: The Hogarth Press, 1924), 21–24.

Woolf, Virginia, *Three Guineas* (London: Hogarth, 1938; Florida: Harcourt, 1966).

Zweig, Stefan, *Decisive Moments in History. Twelve Historical Miniatures*, transl. Lowell A. Bangerter (Riverside: Ariadne Press, 1999).

Zweig, Stefan, *Marie Antoinette: The Potrait of an Average Woman* (New York: Garden City Publishing Co., 1933).

Zweig, Stefan, 'Wilson versagt' (1940), in Stefan Zweig (ed.), *Sternstuden der Menschheit. Vierzehn historische Miniaturen* (Stockholm: Bermann-Fischer, 1943, Frankfurt: Fischer, 2012), 368–394.

Geographica (Travelogues and psychogeography)

Churchill, Winston, *The Unknown War* (New York: Scribner's Sons, 1931).

Dawson, Daniel, *The Mexican Adventure* (London: G. Bell & Sons, 1935).

Dönhoff, Marion Gräfin, *Namen, die keiner mehr nennt. Ostpreußen – Menschen und Geschichte* (Düsseldorf und Köln: Eugen Diederichs, 1962).

Ferdinand, Franz, *Tagebuch meiner Reise um die Erde*, 2 vols., vol. 1. 1892–93. (Vienna: Hölder, 1895).

Fontane, Friedrich, *Jenseits des Tweed* (Frankfurt: Insel, 1860).

Haxthausen, August Baron von, *The Russian Empire: Its People, Institutions and Resources*, transl. Robert Farie (London: Chapman and Hall, 1856, reprinted in London: Cass, 1968).

Kessler, Harry Graf, *Notizen über Mexico* (Berlin: Fontane & Co., 1898).

Keyserling, Hermann Count, *Europe*, transl. Maurice Samuel (New York: Harcourt, Brace and Company, 1928).

Keyserling, Hermann Graf, *Das Reisetagebch eines Philosophen*, vol. 1 (Berlin: Duncker&Humblot, 1919); vol. 2 (Darmstadt: Otto Reichl, 1920).

Keyserling, Hermann Graf, *Südamerikanische Meditationen* (Stuttgart-Berlin: Deutsche Verlags-Anstalt, 1932).

Keyserling, Graf Hermann, *Das Spektrum Europas* (Heidelberg: Niels Kampmann, 1928).

Koestler, Arthur, *Spanish Testament* (London: Gollancz, 1937).

Popper, Karl, 'Zur Philosophie des Heimatgedankens', in *Die Quelle*, 77 (1927), 899–908.

Putlitz, Wolfgang Edler Hans zu, *Unterwegs in Deutschland* (Berlin: Verlag der Nation, 1956).

Renn, Ludwig, *In Mexiko* (Berlin: Aufbau, 1979).

Rilke, Rainer Maria, *Briefe in zwei Bänden*, 1. Bd. 1896 bis 1919, ed. Horst Nalewski (Frankfurt and Leipzig: Insel, 1991).

Rilke, Rainer Maria, *Briefe Zur Politik*, Hg. Joachim W. Storck. (Frankfurt/main und Leipzig: Insel, 1992),

Ritchie, Leitch, *A Journey to St. Petersburg and Moscow Through Courland and Livonia* (London: Longman, 1836).

Scherzer, Karl (ed.), *Reise der österreichischen Fregatte Novara um die Erde*, 3 vols. (Vienna: Carl Gerold, 1861–76).

Seton-Watson, Hugh, *Eastern Europe between the Wars: 1918–1941* (Cambridge: Cambridge University Press, 1945).

Shklovsky, Viktor, *A Sentimental Journey. Memoirs, 1917–1922*, transl. Richard Sheldon (Ithaca: Cornell University Press, 1970).

Templewood, Viscount [Sir Samuel Hoare], *Empire of the Air. The Advent of the Air Age 1922–29* (London: Collins, 1957).

Tocqueville, Alexis de, *Democracy in America*, vol. 1 (London: Random House, 1994).

Veltheim, Hans-Hasso von, *Bali* (Leipzig: Suhrkamp, 1943).

Veltheim, Hans-Hasso von, *Der Atem Indiens. Tagebücher aus Asien. Neue Folge. Ceylon und Südindien* (Hamburg: Claassen, 1954).

Veltheim, Hans-Hasso von, *Götter und Menschen zwischen Indien und China. Tagebücher aus Asien. Dritter Teil. Birma. Thailand. Kambodscha. Malaya. Java und Bali*. Unter Mitwirkung von Maria Stephan (Hamburg: Claassen, 1858).

Veltheim, Hans-Hasso von, *Tagebücher aus Asien. Erster Teil. Bombay. Kaljutta. Kashmir. Afghanistan. Die Himalayas. Nepal. Benares. 1935–1939* (Cologne: Greveb, 1951).

von Oesterreich, Rudolph, *Eine Orientreise vom Jahre 1881* (Vienna: Kaiserl.-Königl. Hof- u. Staatsdr., 1885).

Historical and general reference works

Almanach de Gotha (1763–1944).
Ahnentafel berühmter Deutscher, (Leipzig: Zentralstelle für Deutsche Personen- und Familiengeschichte, 1939).
Biographie universelle (Paris: Chez Madame Desplaces, 1843–63).
Dellingshausen, Eduard von, *Die Entstehung, Entwicklung und Aufbauende Tätigkeit der Baltischen Ritterschaften* (Langensalza: H. Beyer, 1928).
Dictionary of National Biography, ed. Leslie Stephen (London, 1885–).
Michelin Guide to the Battlefields of the World War. The First Battle of the Marne, Including the Operations on the Ourcq, in the Marshes of St. Gond and in the Revigny Pass, 1914 (Milltown, N.J.: Michelin, 1919).
Nationalsozialistische Monatshefte, 33, special issue on 'Krisis Europas' (December 1932).
Parkinson, Thomas and Anne Brannen (eds.), *'Michael Robartes and the Dancer' Manuscript Materials* (Ithaca: Cornell University Press, 1994).
Paris 1935. Erster Internationaler Schriftstellerkongreß zur Verteidigung der Kultur. Reden und Dokumente, ed. Akademie der Wissenschaften der DDR (Berlin: Akademie-Verlag, 1982).
Semigothasches Genealogisches Taschenbuch.
Stackelberg, Otto Magnus von, *Genealogisches Handbuch Der Estländischen Ritterschaft* (Görlitz: Verl. für Sippenforschung und Wappenkunde Starke, 1930).
Stavenhagen, Oskar, *Genealogisches Handbuch der Kurländischen Ritterschaft* (Görlitz: Verl. für Sippenforschung und Wappenkunde Starke, 1939).
Vereshchagin, Vasili, Second Appendix to *Catalogue of the Verestchagin Exhibition: Realism* (Chicago: The Art Institute, 1889).
Vereshchagin, Vassili, *Souvenirs. Enfance – Voyage – Guerre* (Paris: Albert Savine, 1888).
Vermeil, Edmond, *Doctrinaires de la révolution allemande (1918–1938): W. RathenauKeyserling–Th. Mann–O. Spengler–Mœller van den Bruck–Le groupe de la 'Tat'–Hitler–A. Rosenberg–Gunther–Darré–G. Feder–R. Ley–Gœbbels* (Paris: F. Sorlot, 1938).
Yeats, W.B., *Michael Robartes and the Dancer* (Dublin: Cuala Press, 1920).
Zonenberg, Kh., *Istoria goroda Brest-Litovska. 1016–1907, etc.* (Brest-Litovsk: Tipografia Kobrinca, 1908).

Secondary sources

'AHR Conversation: On Transnational History', with Chris Bayly, Sven Beckert, Matthew Connelly, Isabel Hofmeyr, Wendy Kozol, and Patricia Seed, in *The American Historical Review*, 111:5 (December 2006), 1441–1464.

Aichelburg, Wladimir, *Der Thronfolger und die Architektur* (Vienna: Neuer Wissenschaftlicher Verlag, 2003).

Anderson, Amanda, *The Powers of Distance: Cosmopolitanism and the Cultivation of Detachment* (Princeton: Princeton University Press, 2001).

Anderson, Benedict, *Imagined Communities* (1983, London: Verso 2006).

Anderson, Benedict, *The Spectre of Comparisons: Nationalism, Southeast Asia, and the World* (London: Verso, 1998).

Anderson, Benedict, *Under Three Flags. Anarchism and the Anti-Colonial Imagination* (London: Verso. 2005).

Anonymous, 'Das römische Recht in Russland', in Rudolf Leonhard (ed.), *Stimmen des Auslands über die Zukunft der Rechtswissenschaft*, series Studien zur Erläuterung des bürgerlichen Rechts, vol. 17 (Breslau: M&H Marcus, 1906), 105–106.

Anton, Florian and Leonid Luks (eds.), *Deutschland, Russland und das Baltikum: Beiträge zu einer Geschichte wechselvoller Beziehungen*. Festschrift zum 85. Geburtstag von Peter Krupnikow (Vienna, Weimar and Cologne: Böhlau, 2005).

Applegate, Celia, *A Nation of Provincials: The German Idea of Heimat* (Berkeley: University of California Press, 1990).

Arendt, Hannah, 'The Decline of the Nation State and the End of the Rights of Man' (1951), in Hannah Arendt, *The Origins of Totalitarianism* (New York: Harcourt and Brace, 1968), 267–303.

Armitage, David, *Foundations of Modern International Thought* (Cambridge: Cambridge University Press, 2013).

Arnold, Matthew, *Culture and Anarchy: An Essay in Political and Social Criticism* (London: Smith, Elder, and Co., 1896).

Arslan, Ahmet, *Das Exil vor dem Exil. Leben und Wirken deutscher Schriftsteller in der Schweiz während des Ersten Weltkrieges* (Marburg: Tectum, 2004).

Asch, Ronald, *Europe 1450–1789: Encyclopedia of the Early Modern World*, ed. Jonathan Dewald, 6 vols. (New York: Scribner, 2004).

Asch, Ronald G., "Aristocracy and Gentry"', entry in Jonathan Dewald (ed.), *Europe 1450–1789: Encyclopedia of the Early Modern World*, 6 vols. (New York: Scribner, 2004), 96–102.

Aschhheim, Steven E., *The Nietzsche Legacy in Germany, 1890–1990* (Berkeley and London: UCLA Press, 1992).

Assmann, Jan, *Das kulturelle Gedächtnis: Schrift, Erinnerung und politische Identität in frühen Hochkulturen* (Munich: C.H. Beck, 1992).

Attwood, Philipp and Felicity Powell (eds.), *Medals of Dishonour* (London: The British Museum, 2009).

Auerbach, Bertrand, *Les races et les nationalités en Autriche-Hongrie* (Paris: Alcan, 1898).

Aust, Martin, Alexei Miller, and Ricarda Vulpius, *Imperium Inter pares: Rol' transferov v istorii Rossiiskoi imperii (1700–1917)* (Moscow: Novoe Literaturnoe Obozrenie, 2010).

Ayo, Langley, J., 'Pan-Africanism in Paris, 1924–36', in *The Journal of Modern African Studies*, 7 (1969), 69–94.

Bach, Ulrich, 'Sacher-Masoch's Utopian Peripheries', in *The German Quarterly*, 80.2 (Spring 2007), 201–219.

Bachleitner, Norbert, Franz M. Eybl, and Ernest Fischer, *Geschichte des Buchhandels in Österreich* (Wiesbaden: Harassowitz, 2000).

Balibar, Etienne, *We, the People of Europe?* (Princeton: Princeton University Press, 2003).

Balibar, Etienne and Wallerstein, Immanuel, *Race, Nation, Class. Ambiguous Identities* (London: Verso, 1991).

Barabasz, Adam, 'Poland's Attitude to the Conception of European Integration in the Years 1918–1939', in *Western Review*, 2 (2007), 229–251.

Baranowski, Shelley, *The Sanctity of Rural Life: Nobility, Protestantism and Nazism in Weimar Prussia* (New York and Oxford: Oxford University Press, 1995).

Baranowsky, Shelley, *Nazi Empire. German Colonialism and Imperialism from Bismarck to Hitler* (Cambridge: Cambridge University Press, 2011).

Bariéty, Jacques (ed.), *Aristide Briand, la Société des Nations et l'Europe, 1919–1932* (Strasbourg: Presses Universitaires, 2007).

Barkey, Karen and Mark von Hagen (eds.), *After Empire: Multiethnic Societies and Nation-Building: The Soviet Union, and the Russian, Habsburg and Ottoman Empires* (Boulder, Co.: Westview Press, 1997).

Barkin, Kenneth D., 'Fritz K. Ringer's the Decline of the Mandarins', in *The Journal of Modern History*, 43 (1971), 276–286.

Barth, Boris, *Dolchstosslegenden und politische Deisntegration: Fas Trauma der deutschen Niederlage im Ersten Weltkrieg, 1914–1933* (Düsseldorf: Droste, 2003).

Barthes, Roland, *Camera Lucida: Reflections on Photography* (New York: Farrar, Straus and Giroux, 1981).

Bartov, Omer and Eric D. Weitz (eds.), *Shatterzone of Empires. Coexistence and Violence in the German, Habsburg, Russian, and Ottoman Borderlands* (Bloomington: Indiana University Press, 2013).

Barzantny, Tamara, 'Kessler, Harry und das Theater: Autor, Mäzen, Initiator, 1900–1933', in *Central European History*, 3 (2004), 423–429.

Bassin, Mark, *Horizons géographiques* (Rosny-sous-Bois: Bréal, 2004).

Bassin, Mark, 'Imperial Visions Nationalist Imagination and Geographical Expansion in the Russian Far East, 1840–1865', in *Cambridge Studies in Historical Geography*, 29 (Cambridge and New York: Cambridge University Press, 1999).

Bauer, Franz J., *Die Regierung Eisner 1918/19. Ministerratsprotokolle und Dokumente*, Series Quellen yur Geschichte des Parlamentarismus und der politischen Parteien (Düsseldorf: Droste, 1987).

Bauer, Otto, *The Question of Nationalities and Social Democracy*, transl. Joseph O'Donnell (Minneapolis and London: University of Minnesota Press, 2000).

Baur, Johannes, *Die russische Kolonie in München 1900–1945* (Wiesbaden: Harassowitz, 1998).

Bayly, C.A., *The Birth of the Modern World 1780–1914. Global Connections and Comparisons* (Oxford: Blackwell, 2004).

Bayly, C.A., *Imperial Meridian: The British Empire and the World 1780–1830* (London: Longmans, 1989).

Bayly, C.A., and Eugenio Biagini (eds.), *Giuseppe Mazzini and the Globalization of Democratic Nationalism, 1830–1920* (Oxford: Oxford University Press, 2008).

Bayly, C.A. and Tim Harper, *Forgotten Armies: Britain's Asian Empire and the War with Japan* (London: Penguin, 2004).

Behrends, Jan C., *Antiamerikanismus im 20. Jahrhundert Studien zu Ost- und Westeuropa* (Bonn: Dietz, 2005).

Bell, Duncan, *The Idea of Greater Britain: Empire and the Future of World Order, 1860–1900* (Princeton: Princeton University Press, 2011).

Benjamin, Walter, 'L'œuvre d'art à l'époque de sa reproduction mécanisée', transl. Pierre Klossowski, in *Zeitschrift für Sozialforschung*, 5:1 (1936), 40–66.

Bennett, Jill, *Empathic Vision: Affect, Trauma, and Contemporary Art* (Palo Alto: Stanford University Press, 2005).

Benton, Lauren. *Law and Colonial Cultures: Legal Regimes in World History, 1400–1900* (Cambridge: Cambridge University Press, 2002).

Benton, Lauren, *A Search for Sovereignty: Law and Geography in European Empires, 1400–1900* (Cambridge: Cambridge University Press, 2009).

Berdahl, Robert M., *The Politics of the Prussian Nobility: The Development of a Conservative Ideology, 1770–1848* (Princeton: Princeton University Press, 1988).

Berger, Peter, *Im Schatten der Diktatur: die Finanzdiplomatie des Vertreters des Völkerbundes in Österreich, Meinoud Marinus Rost van Tonningen 1931–1936* (Vienna: Böhlau, 2000).

Berger, Peter and Thomas Luckmann, *The Social Construction of Reality* (Garden City, N.Y.: Doubleday, 1966).

Berger, Stefan and Bill Niven (eds.), *Writing the History of Memory* (London: Bloomsbury, 2014).

Berlin, Isaiah, 'In Conversation with Steven Lukes', in *Salmagundi*, 120 (Fall 1998), 52–134.

Bertrams, Kurt U., *Der falsche Prinz und das Corps Saxo-Borussia: die Abenteuer des Hochstaplers Harry Domela* (Hilden: WJK-Verl., 2006).

Bhabha, Homi, *Nation and Narration* (New York: Routledege, 1990).

Bialas, Wolfgang and Burkard Stenzel (eds.), *Die Weimarer Republik zwischen Metropole und Provinz. Intellektuellendiskurse zur politischen Kultur* (Weimar, Cologne and Vienna: Böhlau, 1996).

Bideleux, Robert and Ian Jeffries, *A History of Eastern Europe: Crisis and Change* (London: Routledge, 1998).

Bill, Claus Heinrich, *Adelserlangung und Standes-Modifikation in Kurbrandenburg-Preußen: 1660–1918: eine Typologie, an ausgewählten Beispielen vornehmlich des 19. und 20. Jahrhunderts erläutert mit Namenweiser* (Owschlag: Inst. für Preußische Historiographie, 1997).

Billeter, Felix and Andrea Pophanken (eds.), *Die Moderne und ihre Sammler. Französische Kunst in deutschem Privatbesitz vom Kaiserreich zur Weimarer Republik* (Berlin: Akademie Verlag, 2001).

Billington, James H. *The Icon and the Axe: An Interpretive History of Russian Culture* (New York: Knopf, 1966).

Binder-Krieglstein, Reinhard, *Österreichisches Adelsrecht 1868–1918/19: von der Ausgestaltung des Adelsrechts der cisleithanischen Reichshälfte bis zum Adelsaufhebungsgesetz der Republik unter besonderer Berücksichtigung des adeligen Namensrechts* (Frankfurt/Main: Lang, 2000).

Blackbourn, David and Geoff Eley, *Mythen deutscher Geschichtsschreibung. Die gescheiterte bürgerliche Revolution von 1848* (Frankfurt/Main: Ullstein, 1980).

Blanning, T.C.W., *The Power of Culture and the Culture of Power: Old Regime Europe, 1660–1789* (Oxford and New York: Oxford University Press, 2002).

Blasius, Dirk, *Weimars Ende. Bürgerkrieg und Politik 1930–1933* (Göttingen: Vandenhoeck & Ruprecht, 2005).

Boehmer, Elleke, *Empire, the National and the Postcolonial, 1890–1920. Resistance in Interaction* (Oxford: Oxford University Press, 2002).

Bollinger, Stefan (ed.), *Imperialismustheorien. Historische Grundlagen für eine aktuelle Kritik* (Vienna: Promedia, 2004).

Bonneville, Georges, *Prophètes et témoins de l'Europe; essai sur l'idee d'Europe dans la litterature française de 1914 à nos jours* (Leyde: A.W. Sythoff, 1961).

Boorstin, Daniel J., *The Image: A Guide to Pseudo-Events in America* (New York: Atheneum, 1961).

Botz-Bornstein, Thorsten, 'European Transfigurations – Eurafrica and Eurasia: Coudenhove and Trubetzkoy Revisited', in *The European Legacy*, 12 (2007), 565–575.

Bourdieu, Pierre, *Homo academicus* (Paris: Éditions de Minuit, 1984).

Bourdieu, Pierre, *Language and Symbolic Power* (1982, translation 1991).

Bourdieu, Pierre, *Les règles de l'art. Genèse et structure du champ littéraire* (Paris: Seuil, 1998).

Bourke, Richard, 'Edmund Burke and Enlightenment Sociability: Justice, Honour and the Principles of Government', in *History of Political Thought*, 21:4 (Winter 2000), 632–656.

Bourke, Richard, *Empire and Revolution: The Political Life of Edmund Burke* (Princeton: Princeton University Press, 2015).

Bourquin, Laurent, *La noblesse dans la France moderne, XVIe-XVIIIe siècles* (Paris: Belin, 2002).

Boym, Svetlana, *The Future of Nostalgia* (New York: Basic Books, 2001).

Bracewell, Wendy (ed.), *Orientations. An Anthology of East European Travel Writing*, ca. 1550–2000 (Budapest: Central European University Press, 2009).

Bracher, Karl-Dietrich, *Die Auflösung der Weimarer Republik. Eine Studie zum Problem des Machtverfalls in der Demokratie* (Villingen/Schwarzwald: Ring, 1960).

Bracher, Karl-Dietrich, Wolfgang Sauer, and Gerhard Schulz, *Die nationalsozialistische Machtergreifung. Studien zur Errichtung des totalitären Herrschaftssystems in Deutschland*, 2nd ed. (Wiesbaden: Springer, 1962).

Braudy, Leo, *The Frenzy of Renown* (New York: Vintage, 1997).

Braun, Rudolf, 'Konzeptionelle Bemerkungen zum Obenbleiben. Der Adel im 19. Jahrhundert', in Hans-Ulrich Wehler (ed.), *Europäischer Adel 1750–1950* (Göttingen: Vandenhoeck&Ruprecht, 1989).

Breuer, Stefan, *Grundpositionen der deutschen Rechten 1871–1945* (Tübingen: discord, 1999).

Breuer, Stefan, *Ordnungen der Ungleichheit. Die deutsche Rechte im Widerstreit ihrer Ideen 1871–1945* (Darmstadt: Wissenschaftliche Buchgesellschaft, 2001).

Brinks, John Dieter, *The Book as a Work of Art: The Cranach Press of Count Kessler, Harry* (Laubach: Triton, 2005).

Brockington, Grace (ed.), *Internationalism and the Arts in Britain and Europe at the Fin de Siècle* (Oxford: Peter Lang, 2009).

Brockmann, Stephen, *Nuremberg: The Imaginary Capital* (Woobridge: Camdenhouse, 2006).

Bronner, Simon J., 'Pictorial Jokes: A Traditional Combination of Verbal and Graphic Processes', in *Tennessee Folklore Society Bulletin*, 44 (1978), 189–196.

Brook-Shepherd, Gordon, *The Last Habsburg* (New York: Weybright and Talley, 1969).

Brook-Shepherd, Gordon, *Uncrowned Emperor: The Life and Times of Otto von Habsburg* (London: Hambledon Continuum, 2007).

Broszat, Martin, *Alltagsgeschichte der NS-Zeit. Neue Perspektiven oder Trivialisierung?* (Munich: Oldenbourg, 1984).

Brown, Kate, *A Biography of No Place: From Ethnic Borderland to Soviet Heartland* (Cambridge, Mass.: Harvard University Press, 2004).

Brownlee, John S., *Japanese Historians and the National Myths, 1600–1945: The Age of the Gods* (Tokyo: University of Tokyo Press, 1999).

Brubaker, Rogers, *Ethnicity Without Groups* (Cambridge, Mass.: Harvard University Press, 2004).

Brückler, Theodor, 'Thronfolger Franz Ferdinand als Denkmalpfleger', in *Die 'Kunstakten' der Militärkanzlei im Österreichischen Staatsarchiv (Kriegsarchiv)* (Cologne, Weimar and Vienna: Böhlau, 2009).

Brugmans, H. (ed.), *Europe: Rêve–Aventure–Réalité* (Brussels: Elsevier, 1987).

Bruisch, K. and Nikolaus Katzer, *Bolshaia voina Rossii: Sotsial'nyi poriadok, publichnaia kommunikatsia i nasilie na rubezhe tsarskoi i sovetskoi epochi* (Moscow: NLO, 2014).

Brunner, Otto, Reinhart Koselleck, and Werner Conze (eds.), *Geschichtliche Grundbegriffe: historisches Lexikon zur politisch-sozialen Sprache in Deutschland* (Stuttgart: Klett-Cotta, 1972–97).

Budnitsky, Oleg, *Terrorizm v rossiiskom osvoboditel'nom dvizhenii* (Moscow: Rosspen, 2000).

Bues, Almut, *Zones of Fracture in Modern Europe: The Baltic Countries, the Balkans, and Northern Italy* (Wiesbaden: Harrassowitz, 2005).

Bullen, J.B., 'Byzantinism and Modernism 1900–14', in *The Burlington Magazine*, 141:1160 (November 1999), 665–675.

Burdick, Charles B., *Ralph H. Lutz and the Hoover Institution* (Stanford: Hoover Institution Press, Stanford University, 1974).

Burgard, Oliver, *Das gemeinsame Europa–von der politischen Utopie zum aussenpolitischen Programm: Meinungsaustausch und Zusammenarbeit pro-europäischer Verbände in Deutschland und Frankreich, 1924–1933* (Frankfurt am Main: Verlag Neue Wissenschaft, 2000).

Burke, Peter, 'Context in Context', in *Common Knowledge*, 8:1 (Winter 2002), 152–177.

Burks, Richard V., 'A Conception of Ideology for Historians', in *Journal of the History of Ideas*, 10 (1949), 183–198.

Cancik, Hubert and Hildegard Cancik-Lindemaier, *Philolog und Kultfigur. Friedrich Nietzsche und seine Antike in Deutschland* (Stuttgart and Weimar: J.B. Metzler, 1999).

Cancik, Hubert and Uwe Puschner, *Antisemitismus, Paganismus, Völkische Religion* (Munich: K.G. Saur, 2004).

Cannadine, David, *The Decline and Fall of the British Aristocracy* (New Haven: Yale University Press, 1990).

Cannadine, David, *The Decline and Fall of the British Aristocracy* (New Haven: Yale University Press, 1997).

Cardoza, Anthony, *Aristocrats in Bourgeois Italy* (Cambridge: Cambridge University Press, 1997).

Carr, E.H., *The Twenty Years' Crisis, 1919–1939: An Introduction to the Study of International Relations* (Basingbroke: Palgrave, 2001).

Caruso, Carla, *Oswaldo de Andrade* (São Paulo: Callis Editora, 2000).

Cassels, Alan, 'Repairing the Entente Cordiale and the New Diplomacy', in *The Historical Journal*, 23 (1980), 133–153.

Cassirer, Ernst, *An Essay on Man* (New Haven: Yale University Press, 1944).

Cassis, Youssef, 'Wirtschaftselite und Bürgertum. England, Frankreich und Deutschland um 1900', in Jürgen Kocka (ed.), *Bürgertum im 19. Jahrhundert. Deutschland im europäischen Vergleich* (Munich: dtv, 1988).

Casteel, James, 'The Politics of Diaspora: Russian German Émigré Activists in Interwar Germany', in Mathias Schulze et al. (eds.) *German Diasporic Experiences: Identity, Migration, and Loss* (Waterloo: Wilfrid Laurier University Press, 2008).

Castro-Klaren, Sara, 'A Genealogy for the "Manifesto Antropofago," or the Struggle between Socrates and the Caraibe', in *Nepantla: Views from South*, 4 (2000), 295–322.

Cecil, Lamar, 'The Creation of Nobles in Prussia, 1871–1918', in *American Historical Review*, 3 (1970), 757–795.

Cederholm, Boris, *In the Clutches of the Tcheka*, transl. F.H. Lyon (Boston and New York: Houghton Mifflin, 1929).

Cepl-Kaufmann, Gertrude, Gerd Krumeich, and Ulla Sommers, *Krieg und Utopie: Kunst, Literatur und Politik im Rheinland nach dem Ersten Weltkrieg* (Essen: Klartext, 2006).

Cesaire, Aimé, *Discours sur le colonialisme* (Paris: Réclame, 1950).

Chabod, Federico, *Storia dell'idea d'Europa* (Bari: Laterza, 1961).

Chandler, James, *An Archaeology of Sympathy. The Sentimental Mode in Literature and Cinema* (Chicago and London: University of Chicago Press, 2013).

Chapman, Mark D., 'Theology, Nationalism and the First World War: Christian Ethics and the Constraints of Politics', in *Studies in Christian Ethics*, 8 (1995), 13–35.

Charle, Christophe, *Les intellectuels ein Europe eu XIX siècle. Essai d'histoire comparée* (Paris: Seuil, 1996).

Chaubet, François, *Paul Desjardins et les Décades de Pontigny* (Villeneuve-d'Ascq (Nort): Presses universitaires du Septentrion, 2000).

Chinyaeva, Elena, *Russians outside Russia: The Émigré Community in Czechoslovakia 1918–1938* (Munich: R. Oldenbourg Verlag, 2001).

Claeys, Gregory, *Imperial Sceptics. British Critics of Empire, 1850–1920* (Cambridge: Cambridge University Press, 2010).

Clark, Christopher, *Iron Kingdom. The Rise and Downfall of Prussia* (London: Penguin, 2007).

Clark, Christopher, *The Sleepwalkers: How Europe Went to War in 1914* (London: Allen Lane, 2013).

Clark, Katerina, *Moscow, the Fourth Rome. Stalinism, Cosmopolitanism, and the Evolution of Soviet Culture, 1931–1941* (Cambridge, Mass: Harvard University Press, 2011).

Clark, T.J., 'Painting in the Year Two', in *Representations*, 47, Special Issue: National Cultures before Nationalism (Summer 1994), 13–63.

Clavin, Patricia, *The Reinvention of the League of Nations, 1920–1946* (Oxford: Oxford University Press, 2013).

Clough, Patricia Ticineto and Jean Galley (eds.), *The Affective Turn* (Durham: Duke University Press, 2007).

Cochet, François (ed.), *1916–2006. Verdun sous le regard du monde* (Saint-Cloud: Belin, 2006).

Coetzee, J.M., 'Emperor of Nostalgia', reviewing *The Collected Stories of Joseph Roth*, *The New York Review of Books* (28 February 2002).

Cœuré, Sophie, *La grande lueur à l'Est: les Français et l'Union soviétique, 1917–1939* (Paris: Éd. du Seuil, 1999).

Cœuré, Sophie, *La mémoire spoliée: les archives des Français, butin de guerre nazi puis soviétique, de 1940 à nos jours* (Paris: Payot, 2006).

Cohen, Chester G., *Shtetl Finder: Jewish Communities in the 19th and Early 20th Centuries in the Pale of Settlement of Russia and Poland, and in Lithuania, Latvia, Galicia, and Bukovina, with Names of Residents* (Bowie, M.D.: Heritage Books, 2003).

Cohen, Robin, *Global Diasporas, an Introduction* (London: Routledge, 1997).

Cole, Laurence and Daniel L. Unowsky (eds.), *The Limits of Loyalty: Imperial Symbolism, Popular Allegiances, and State Patriotism in the Late Habsburg Monarchy* (Oxford: Berghahn, 2005).

Colleville, Maurice, 'Le Comte Hermann Keyserling et son Ecole de la Sagesse de Darmstadt', in *Annales du Centre Universitaire Mediterrannéen* (1967–68), 21.

Collini, Stefan, *Absent Minds* (Oxford: Oxford University Press, 2006).

Collini, Stefan, 'Review: Liberalism and the Legacy of Mill', in *The Historical Journal*, 20 (1977), 237–254.

Collins, Michael, *Empire, Nationalism and the Postcolonial World. Rabindranath Tagore's Writings on History, Politics and Society* (London: Routledge, 2011).

Confino, Alon and Peter Fritzsche (eds.), *The Work of Memory. New Directions in the Study of German Society and Culture* (Chicago and Urbana: Illinois University Press, 2002).

Connerton, Paul, *How Societies Remember* (Cambridge: Cambridge University Press, 1989).

Connor, Walker, 'The Impact of Homelands upon Diasporas', in Gabriel Sheffer (ed.), *Modern Diasporas in International Politics* (New York: St. Martin's, 1986), 16–46.

Conway, Stephen, *The British Isles and the War of American Independence* (Oxford: Oxford University Press, 2000),

Conze, Eckart, *Kleines Lexikon des Adels. Titel, Throne, Traditionen* (Munich: Beck, 2005).

Conze, Eckart, *Von deutschem Adel: die Grafen von Bernstorff im zwanzigsten Jahrhundert* (Stuttgart: Deutsche Verlags-Anstalt, 2000).

Conze, Eckart and Monika Wienfort (eds.), *Adel und Moderne. Deutschland im europäischen Vergleich im 19. Und 20. Jh* (Cologne: Böhlau, 2004).

Conze, Vanessa, *Das Europa der Deutschen. Ideen von Europa in Deutschland zwischen Reichstradition und Westorientierung (1920–1970)* (Oldenbourg: Institut für Zeitgeschichte, 2005).

Conze, Vanessa, *Richard Codenhove-Kalergi: umstrittener Visionär Europas* (Gleichen: Muster-Schmidt, 2004).

Cooper, Frederick, 'Decolonizing Situations: The Rise, Fall, and Rise of Colonial Studies, 1951–2001', in *French Politics, Culture & Society*, 20:2, Special Issue: Regards croisés: Transatlantic Perspectives on the Colonial Situation (Summer 2002), 47–76.

Cooper, Frederick and Ann Stoler (eds.), *Tensions of Empire: Colonial Cultures in a Bourgeois World* (Berkeley: University of California Press, 1997).

Corney, Frederick C., *Telling October: Memory and the Making of the Bolshevik Revolution* (Ithaca: Cornell University Press, 2004).

Cotta, Maurizio and Heinrich Best (eds.), *Parliamentary Representatives in Europe 1848–2000. Legislative Recruitment and Careers in Eleven European Countries* (Oxford: Oxford University Press, 2000).

Craig, Alexander and Felix Gilbert, *The Diplomats: 1919–1939* (Princeton: Princeton University Press, 1953).

Davies, Douglas J. 'The Cremation Movement', in Clifton D. Bryant and Dennis L. Peck (eds.), *Encyclopedia of Death and the Human Experience* (London: Sage, 2009).

Davies, Norman, *Heart of Europe. A Short History of Poland* (Oxford: Clarendon Press, 1984).

Davies, Norman, *Vanished Kingdoms. The History of Half-Forgotten Europe* (London: Penguin, 2011).

D'Avray, David, *Rationalities in History. A Weberian Essay in Comparison* (Cambridge: Cambridge University Press, 2010).

Deák, István, *Beyond Nationalism. A Social and Political History of the Habsburg Officer Corps, 1848–1918* (Oxford: Oxford University Press, 1990).

Debord, Guy, *The Society of the Spectacle*, transl. Black & Red (Cambridge, Mass.: MIT Press, 2010).

Delanty, Gerard, *Inventing Europe: Idea, Identity, Reality* (London: Macmillan, 1995).

Demel, Walter, 'Die Spezifika des europäischen Adelp. Erste Überlegungen zu einem globalhistorischen Thema', in *zeitenblicke*, 4 (2005), Nr. 3 (13 December 2005), www.zeitenblicke.de/2005/3/Demel, accessed 1 November 2008.

Denison, George T., *A History of Cavalry from the Earliest Times. With Lessons for the Future* (London: Macmillan, 1877).

Descartes, René, *Mediations* (1641).

Dewald, Jonathan, *Aristocratic Experience and the Origins of Modern Culture. France, 1570–1715* (Berkeley: University of California Press, 1993).

Dewald, Jonathan, *The European Nobility, 1400–1800* (New York: Cambridge University Press, 1996).

Dmitrieva, Marina, *Italien in Sarmatien. Studien zum Kulturtransfer im östlichen Europa in der Zeit der Renaissance* (Stuttgart: Franz Steiner, 2008).

Dollinger, Hans (ed.), *Facsimile Querschnitt durch Signal* (Munich, Bern and Wien: Scherz, 1969).

Dönhoff, Marion Gräfin (ed.), *Die neue Mittwochsgesellschaft* (Munich: Knaur, 1998).

Dönhoff, Marion Gräfin, *Namen die keiner mehr kennt* (Düsseldorf and Cologne: Eugen Diederichs, 1980).

Dönhoff, Tatjana and J. Roettger, *Auf der Fluchtroute von Marion Gräfin Dönhoff* (Berlin: Nicolai-Verlag, 2004).

Douglas Carls, Stephen, *Louis Loucheur and the Shaping of Modern France, 1916–1931* (Baton Rouge: Louisiana State University Press, 1993).

Doyle, Michael W., *Empires* (Ithaca: Cornell University Press, 1986).

Doyle, William (ed.), *The Oxford Handbook of the Ancien Régime* (Oxford: Oxford University Press, 2011).

DuBois, W.E.B., *The Souls of Black Folk* (Chicago: McClurg, 1904).

Dudziak, Mary L., *War Time: An Idea, Its History, Its Consequences* (Oxford: Oxford University Press, 2012).

Dülmen, Richard von, *The Society of the Enlightenment: The Rise of the Middle Class and Enlightenment Culture in Germany* (Cambridge: Polity Press, 1992).

Dunn, Frederick Sherwood, *The Practice and Procedure of International Conferences* (Baltimore and London: The Johns Hopkins Press; H. Milford, Oxford University Press, 1929).

Dunning, Eric and Stephen Mennell, 'Elias on Germany, Nazism and the Holocaust: On the Balance between "Civilizing" and "Decivilizing" Trends in the Social Development of Western Europe', in *The British Journal of Sociology*, 49:3 (September 1998), 339–357.

Easton, Laird, *The Red Count. The Life and Times of Kessler, Harry* (Berkeley, Los Angeles and London: University of California Press, 2002).

Eisenstadt, Shmuel (ed.), *Max Weber on Charisma and Institution Building* (Chicago: University of Chicago Press, 1968).

Eisenstadt, Shmuel, 'Multiple Modernities', in *Daedalus*, 129 (Winter 2000), 1–26.

Eley, Geoff, 'Imperial Imaginary, Colonial Effect: Writing the Colony and the Metropole Together', in Catherine Hall and Keith McClelland (eds.), *Race, Nation and Empire. Making Histories, 1750 to the Present* (Manchester: Manchester University Press, November 2010).

Elias, Norbert, *The Civilizing Process* (Oxford: Blackwell, 1994) (originally Basel: Haus zum Falker, 1939).

Elias, Norbert, *Court Society* (Oxford: Blackwell, 1983).

Elias, Norbert, *The Germans. Power Struggles and the Development of Habitus in the Nineteenth and Twentieth Century* (Oxford: Oxford University Press, 1996).

Elias, Norbert, 'Group Charisma and Group Disgrace', in Norbert Elias, *Essays III. On Sociology and the Humanities* (Dublin: University College Dublin Press, 2009), 73–82.

Elias, Norbert, *Studien über die Deutschen. Machtkämpfe und Habitusentwicklung im 19. und 20. Jh* (Frankfurt: Suhrkamp, 1989).

Elias, Norbert and J.L. Scotson, *The Established and the Outsiders* (London: Frank Cass, 1965).

Endres, Franz Carl, 'Soziologische Struktur und ihr entsprechende Ideologien des deutschen Offizierkorps vor dem Weltkriege', in *Archiv für Sozialwissenschaft und Sozialpolitik*, 58:1 (1927), 282–319.

Espagne, Michel, 'Maßstab und Untersuchungsebene. Zu einem Grundproblem der Essner, Cornelia, and Winkelhane, Gerd, "Carl Heinrich Becker (1876–1933), Orientalist und Kulturpolitiker"', in *Die Welt des Islams*, 28 (1988), 154–177.

Etkind, Alexander, *Internal Colonization. Russia's Imperial Experience* (Cambridge: Polity Press, 2011).

Etkind, Alexander, Dirk Uffelman, and Ilya Kukulin (eds.), *Tam, vnutri. Praktiki vnutrennei kolonizatsii v kul'turnoi istorii Rossii* (Moscow: Novoe Literaturnoe Obozrenie, 2012).

Evans, Richard, 'Art in the Time of War', in *The National Interest*, 113 (May/June 2011), 16–26.

Evans, Richard, *The Coming of the Third Reich: How the Nazis Destroyed Democracy and Seized Power in Germany* (London: Penguin, 2003).

Evans, Richard, 'Introduction: Redesigning the Past: History in Political Transitions', in *Journal of Contemporary History*, 38:1, Redesigning the Past (January 2003), 5–12.

Faber, Richard and Christine Holste (eds.), *Kreise – Gruppen – Bünde. Zur Soziologie moderner Intellektuellenassoziation* (Würzburg: Königshausen & Neumann, 2000).

Faltin, Sigrid and Andreas Schäfler, *La Paloma – Das Lied* (Hamburg: Mare, 2008).

Fanon, Frantz, 'Concerning Violence', in *The Wretched of the Earth*, transl. Constance Farrington (New York: Grove, 1963).

Farrer, E. (ed.), *Portraits in Norfolk Houses*, 2 vols. (Norwich: Jarrold & Sons, 1929).

Febvre, Lucien, 'Civilisation: évolution d'un mot et d'un groupe d'idées', in Lucien Febvre (ed.), *Pour une histoire à part entière* (Paris: Sevpen, 1962).

Febvre, Lucien, 'De 1892 à 1933. Examen de conscience d'une histoire et d'un historien', in *Revue de Synthèse*, vii:2, Synthèse historique (June 1934), 93–128.

Febvre, Lucien, *Le problème historique du Rhin* (Strasbourg: Imprimerie Alsacienne, 1930).

Febvre, Lucien, *L'Europe. Genèse d'une civilisation. Cours professé au Collège de France en 1944–1945* (Paris: Perrin, 1999).

Fedor, Julie, *Russia and the Cult of State Security: The Chekist Tradition, from Lenin to Putin*, transl. Julie Fedor (London: Routledge, 2013).

Fehér, Ferenc, *The Frozen Revolution: An Essay on Jacobinism* (Cambridge et al.: Cambridge University Press and Editions de la Maison des Sciences de l'Homme, 1987).

Fénelon, François, 'Sentiments on the Ballance of Europe', in *Two Essays on the Balance of Europe* (London: n.p., 1720).

Finchelstein, Federico, *Transatlantic Fascism. Ideology, Violence, and the Sacred in Argentina and Italy, 1919–1945* (Chapel Hill: Duke University Press, 2010).

Finger, Stanley and Meredith P. Hustwit, 'Five Early Accounts of Phantom Limb in Context: Paré, Descartes, Lemos, Bell, and Mitchell', in *Neurosurgery*, 52:3 (2003), 675–686.

Fischer, Robert-Tarek, *Österreich im Nahen Osten: die Grossmachtpolitik der Habsburgermonarchie im Arabischen Orient, 1633–1918* (Vienna, Cologne and Weimar: Böhlau, 2006).

Flis, Andrzej, 'Bronislaw Malinowski's Cracow Doctorate', in Ernest Gellner, Roy Ellen, Grazyna Kubica, and Janusz Mucha (eds.), *Malinowski Between Two Worlds. The Polish Roots of an Anthropological Tradition* (Cambridge: Cambridge University Press, 1988), 195–200.

Forsbach, Ralf, 'Adel und Bürgertum im deutschen auswärtigen Dienst 1867–1950', in Franz Bosbach, Keith Robbins and Karina Urbach (eds.), *Geburt oder Leistung? Elitenbildung im deutsch-britischen Vergleich* (Munich: K.G. Saur, 2003).

Forster-Hahn, Françoise, 'Text and Display: Julius Meier-Graefe, the 1906 White Centennial in Berlin, and the Canon of Modern Art', in *Art History*, 38:1 (February 2015), 138–169.

Foucault, Michel, « *Il faut défendre la société* », *Cours au collège de France (1975–1976)* (Paris: Gallimard, 1997).

Foucault, Michel, *Surveiller et punir* (Paris: Gallimard, 1975).

François, Etienne, Marie-Claire Hoock-Demarle, Reinhart Meyer-Kalkus, and Michael Werner (eds.), *Marianne-Germania. Deutsch-französischer Kulturtransfer im europäischen Kontext 1789–1914* (Leipzig: Universitätsverlag, 1998).

Frank, Robert, 'Les contretemps de l'aventure européenne', in *Revue d'histoire*, Numéro spécial: Les engagements du 20e siècle, 60 (October–December 1998), 82–101.

Frankel, Nicholas, *Oscar Wilde's Decorated Books* (Ann Arbor: University of Michigan Press, 2000).

Fraser, Nancy and Axel Honneth, *Redistribution or Recognition?: A Political-Philosophical Exchange* (London: Verso, 2003).

Frazer, James, *The Golden Bough: A Study in Magic and Religion* (New York: Macmillan, 1925).

Frazer, James, 'The Killing of the Khazar Kings', in *Folk-lore*, xviii (1917), 382–407.

Freeden, Michael, 'Emotions, Ideology and Politics', in *Journal of Political Ideologies*, 18:1 (2013), 1–10.

Freeden, Michael, *Ideologies and Political Theory* (Oxford: Clarendon Press, 1998).

Freifeld, Alice, 'Empress Elisabeth as Hungarian Queen: The Uses of Celebrity Monarchism', in Laurence Cole and Daniel L. Unowsky (eds.), *The Limits of Loyalty: Imperial Symbolism, Popular Allegiances, and State Patriotism in the Late Habsburg Monarchy* (Oxford: Berghahn, 2005), 138–162.

Freud, Sigmund, *Zur Auffassung der Aphasien. Eine kritische Studie* (Leipzig and Vienna: Deuticke, 1891).

Frevert, Ute, *Emotions in History: Lost and Found* (New York: Central European University Press, 2011).

Fromm, Erich, Max Horkheimer, and Ludwig Marcuse (eds.), *Studien über Autorität und Familie* (Paris: Alcan, 1936).

Fussell, Paul, *The Great War and Modern Memory* (Oxford: Oxford University Press, 2005).

Fussell, Paul, *Wartime: Understanding and Behavior in the Second World War* (Oxford: Oxford University Press, 1989).

Gahlings, Ute, *Hermann Graf Keyserling. Ein Lebensbild*, Darmstädter Schriften 68 (Darmstadt: Justus von Liebig Verlag, 1997).

Gahlings, Ute, 'Hermann Keyserling', in Frank-Lothar Kroll (ed.), *Deutsche Autoren des Ostens als Gegner und Opfer des Nationalsozialismus*, in Beiträge zur Widerstandsproblematik (Berlin: Duncker und Humblot, 2000).

Gallo, Rubén, *Freud's Mexico. Into the Wilds of Psychoanalysis* (Cambridge, Mass.: MIT University Press, 2010).

Gandhi, Mahatma, *An Autobiography: Or, the Story of My Experiments with Truth*, transl. from Gujarati by Mahadev Desai, 2 vols. (Ahmedabad, 1927; London: Harmondsworth, 1982).

Garber, Marjorie, *Vested Interests: Cross-Dressing and Cultural Anxiety* (London: Routledge, 2011).

Garleff, Michael (ed.), *Deutschbalten. Weimarer Republik und Drittes Reich*, vol. 1 (Cologne, Weimar, and Vienna: Böhlau, 2001).

Gates, Skip G., 'Of Negroes Old and New', in *Transition*, 46 (1974), 44–58.

Gatrell, Peter, *Russia's First World War: A Social and Economic History* (London and New York: Routledge, 2005).

Gavin, Catherine Irvine, *The Cactus and the Crown* (New York: Doubleday, 1962).

Gay, Peter, *Bourgeois Experience. Victoria to Freud*, vol. 1 (New York: Oxford University Press, 1984).

Gay, Peter, *Freud for Historians* (Oxford: Oxford University Press, 1985).

Gay, Peter, *Weimar Culture: The Outsider as Insider* (London: Secker & Warburg, 1968).

Geertz, Clifford, 'Centers, Kings, and Charisma: Reflections on the Symbolics of Power', in Joseph Ben-David and Terry Nichols-Clark (eds.), *Culture and Its Creators. Essays in Honor of Edward Shils* (Chicago: Chicago University Press, 1971), 150–171.

Geertz, Clifford, 'Thick Description: Toward an Interpretive Theory of Culture', in *The Interpretation of Cultures. Selected Essays* (New York: Basic Books, 1973), 3–30.

Gehler, Michael, *Der Lange Weg nach Europa* (Innsbruck: StudienVerlag, 2002).

Gellner, Ernesst, *Culture, Identity, and Politics* (Cambridge: Cambridge University Press, 1987).

Gellner, Ernest, *Language and Solitude. Wittgenstein, Malinowski, and the Habsburg Dilemma* (Cambridge: Cambridge University Press, 1998).

Gellner, Ernest, *Nationalism* (London: Orion, 1997).

Gerasimov, Ilya, Sergey Glebov, Jan Kusber, Marina Mogilner, and Alexander Semyonov, *Empire Speaks Out. Languages of Rationalization and Self-Description in the Russian Empire* (Leiden: Brill, 2009).

Gernsheim, Helmut, *A Concise History of Photography*, 3rd ed. (Toronto: Courier Dover Publications, 1986).

Gerstner, Alexandra, *Neuer Adel: aristokratische Elitekonzeptionen zwischen Jahrhundertwende und Nationalsozialismus* (Darmstadt: Wissenschaftliche Buchgesellschaft, 2008).

Gerstner, Alexandra, *Rassenadel und Sozialaristokratie: Adelsvorstellungen in der völkischen Bewegung (1890–1914)* (Berlin: SuKuLTuR, 2003).

Gerstner, Alexandra, Barbara Könczöl, and Janina Nentwig (eds.), *Der neue Mensch. Utopien, Leitbilder und Reformkonzepte zwischen den Weltkriegen* (Frankfurt/Main: Peter Lang, 2006).

Gerwarth, Robert and Erez Manela (eds.), *Empires at War: 1911–1923* (Oxford: Oxford University Press, 2014).

Geuss, Raymond, *The Idea of a Critical Theory. Habermas and the Frankfurt School* (Cambridge: Cambridge University Press, 1981).

Geuss, Raymond, '*Kultur, Bildung, Geist*', in Raymond Geuss (ed.), *Morality, Culture, History* (Cambridge: Cambridge University Press, 1999).

Geuss, Raymond, 'Nietzsche and Genealogy', in Raymond Geuss (ed.), *Morality, Culture, and History: Essays on German Philosophy* (Cambridge: Cambridge University Press, 1999).

Geyer, Meyer and Sheila Fitzpatrick (eds.), *Beyond Totalitarianism: Stalinism and Nazism Compared* (Cambridge: Cambridge University Press, 2009).

Giacone, Alessandro and Bino Olivi, *L'Europe difficile* (Paris: folio, 2007).

Gilbert, Felix, *History: Choice and Commitment* (Cambridge, Mass.: Belknap Press of Harvard University Press, 1977).

Gilbert, Felix, *The 'New Diplomacy' of the Eighteenth Century* (Indianapolis: Bobbs-Merrill, 1951).

Giloi, Eva, *Monarchy, Myth, and Material Culture in Germany, 1750–1950* (Cambridge: Cambridge University Press, 2011).

Gilroy, Paul, *The Black Atlantic: Modernity and Double Consciousness* (Cambridge, M.A.: Harvard University Press, 1993).

Ginzburg, Carlo, 'Representing The Enemy: Historical Evidence and Its Ambiguities', in Andrew Bell, John Swenson-Wright, and Karin Tybjerg (eds.), *Evidence* (Cambridge: Cambridge University Press, 2008), 29–48.

Glassheim, Eagle, *Noble Nationalists. The Transformation of the Bohemian Aristocracy* (Cambridge, Mass.: Harvard University Press, 2005).

Goncharova, Natalia, Mezhdu vostokom i zapadom (Moscow: Tret'iakovskaia galereia, 2013).

Göbel, Wolfram, *Der Kurt Wolff Verlag, 1913–1930: Expressionismus als verlegerische Aufgabe: mit einer Bibliographie des Kurt Wolff Verlages und der ihm angeschlossenen Unternehmen, 1910–1930* (Munich: Buch & media, 2000).

Godsey, William, *Aristocratic Re-Doubt: The Austro-Hungarian Foreign Office on the Eve of the First World War* (West Lafayette, I.N.: Purdue University Press, 1999).

Godsey, William D., *Nobles and Nation in Central Europe Free Imperial Knights in the Age of Revolution, 1750–1850* (Cambridge: Cambridge University Press, 2004).

Goffman, Erving, 'On Face-Work', in Erving Goffman (ed.), *Interaction and Ritual* (New York: Doubleday, 1967).

Goguel, Rudi, *Antifaschistischer Widerstand und Klassenkampf: die faschistische Diktatur 1933 bis 1945 und ihre Gegner: Bibliographie deutschsprachiger Literatur aus den Jahren 1945 bis 1973* (Berlin: Militärverlag der Deutschen Demokratischen Republik, 1976).

Gorman, Daniel, *The Emergence of International Society in the 1920s* (Cambridge: Cambridge University Press, 2012).

Gorman, Daniel, *Imperial Citizenship: Empire and the Question of Belonging* (Manchester: Manchester University Press, 2006).

Gowing, Alain, *Empire and Memory. The Representation of the Roman Republic in Imperial Memory* (Cambridge: Cambridge University Press, 2005).

Gradmann, Christoph, *Historische Belletristik. Populäre historische Biographien in der Weimarer Republik* (Frankfurt/New York: Campus, 1993).

Gramsci, Antonio, 'The Formation of the Intellectuals', in Antonio Gramsci, *Selections from the Prison Notebooks*, Quintin Hoare and Jeffrey Nowell Smit (eds.) (New York: International Publishers, 2010), 5–17.

Griffin, Roger, *Modernism and Fascism: The Sense of a Beginning under Mussolini and Hitler* (Basingstoke: Palgrave Macmillan, 2007).

Grimstead, Patricia, *Trophies of War and Empire: The Archival Heritage of Ukraine, World War II, and the International Politics of Restitution* (Cambridge, Mass.: Harvard Ukrainian Research Institute, 2001).

Groß, Gerhard P. (ed.), *Die vergesse Front. Der Osten 1914/15. Ereignis, Wirkung, Nachwirkung.* (Paderborn, Munich, Wien, and Zürich: Ferdinand Schöningh, 2006).

Groppe, Carola, *Die Macht der Bildung. Das deutsche Bürgertum und der George-Kreis 1890–1933*, (Cologne, Weimar, and Vienna: Böhlau, 2001).

Grunewald, Michel, Uwe Puschner, and Hans Manfred Bock (eds.), *Le milieu intellectuel conservateur en Allemagne, sa presse et ses réseaux (1890–1960)* (Bern: P. Lang, 2003).

Grupp, Peter, *Harry Graf Kessler. Eine Biographie* (Munich: Beck, 1996; Frankfurt/Main, and Leipzig: Insel, 1999).

Grützmacher, Richard Heinrich and Viktor Schultze, *Kritiker und Neuschöpfer der Religion im zwanzigsten Jahrhundert: Keyserling, L. Ziegler, Blüher, Chamberlain, Steiner, Scholz, Scheler, Hauck* (Leipzig and Erlangen: A. Deichertsche Verlagsbuchhandlung Dr. Werner Scholl, 1921).

Gruzinski, Serge, *The Mestizo Mind: The Intellectual Dynamics of Colonization and Globalization* (New York: Routledge, 2002).

Gul', Roman, *Dzerzhinskiy (Nachalo Terrora)* (New York: Most, 1974).

Gusejnova, Dina, 'Concepts of Culture and Technology in Germany, 1916–1933: Ernst Cassirer and Oswald Spengler', in *Journal of European Studies*, 36 (March 2006), 5–30.

Gusejnova, Dina, 'Die russophile Fronde. Mit Kessler zur bibliographischen Internationale', in Roland Kamzelak (ed.), *Kessler, der Osten und die Literatur* (Münster: Mentis, 2015), 41–67.

Gusejnov, Gasan, *Karta nashei rodiny. Ideologema mezhdu slovom I telom* (Moscow: Tri kvadrata, 2005).

Gyorgy, Andrew, *Geopolitics, the New German Science* (Berkeley, Los Angeles: University of California Press, 1944).

Habermas, Jürgen, *Der Strukturwandel der Öffentlichkeit. Untersuchungen zu einer Kategorie der bürgerlichen Gesellschaft*, revised edition (Frankfurt: Suhrkamp, 1990).

Hacohen, Malachi Haim, 'Karl Popper, Jewish Identity, and "Central European Culture"', in *Journal of Modern History*, 71:1 (March 1999), 105–149.

Hadler, Frank, *Weg von Österreich!: das Weltkriegsexil von Masarýk und Beneš im Spiegel ihrer Briefe und Aufzeichnungen aus den Jahren 1914 bis 1918: eine Quellensammlung* (Berlin: Akad.-Verl., 1995).

Hahn, Barbara, *Encounters at the Margins: Jewish Salons around 1900* (Los Angeles: UCLA Press, 1999).

Halbwachs, Maurice, *On Collective Memory*, transl. Lewis Coser (Chicago: University of Chicago Press, 1992).

Hall, Catherine, *Civilising Subjects. Metropole and Colony in the English Imagination, 1830–1867* (Cambridge and Chicago: Polity and Chicago University Press, 2002).

Hall, Catherine and Keith McClelland (eds.), *Race, Nation and Empire. Making Histories, 1750 to the Present* (Manchester: Manchester University Press, November 2010).

Hamilton, Richard F., *Who Voted for Hitler?* (Princeton: Princeton University Press, 1982).

Hannaford, Ivan, *Race. The History of an Idea in the West* (Baltimore: The Johns Hopkins University Press, 1996).

Hansen, Miriam Bratu, 'Film, Medium of a Disintegrating World', in Miriam Bratu Hansen, *Cinema and Experience: Siegfried Kracauer, Walter Benjamin, and Theodor W. Adorno* (Berkeley and London: University of California Press, 2012), 3–40.

Hansen, Peo and Stefan Jonsson, *Eurafrica: the Untold History of European Integration and Colonialism* (London: Bloomsbury, 2014).

Hansen-Schaberg, Inge and Ulrike Müller, '*Ethik der Erinnerung' in der Praxis: zur Vermittlung von Verfolgungs- und Exilerfahrungen* (Wuppertal: Arco, 2005).

Harari, Yuval, *The Ultimate Experience. Battlefield Revelations and the Making of Modern War Culture, 1450–2000* (Basingstoke: Palgrave Macmillan, 2008).

Hardt, Michael and Antonio Negri, *Multitude. War and Democracy in the Age of Empire* (London: Penguin, 2005).

Hardtwig, Wolfgang (ed.), *Utopie und politische Herrschaft im Europa der Zwischenkriegszeit* (Munich: R. Oldenbourg, 2003).

Has-Ellison, Trygve John, 'Nobles, Modernism, and the Culture of fin-de-siècle Munich', in *German History*, 26 (2008), 1–23.

Hechter, Michael, *Alien Rule* (Cambridge: Cambridge University Press, 2013).

Hechter, Michael, *Internal Colonialism. The Celtic Fringe in British National Development* (1975, new edition New Brunswick: Transaction, 1999).

Heck, Kilian, 'Das Fundament der Machtbehauptung. Die Ahnentafel als genealogische Grundstruktur der Neuzeit', in Sigrid Weigel (ed.), *Genealogie und Genetik* (Berlin: Akademie-Verlag, 2002).

Heffernan, Michael J., *The Meaning of Europe: Geography and Geopolitics* (London and New York: Oxford University Press, 1998).

Heffter, August Wilhelm, *Das europäische Völkerrecht der Gegenwart, auf den bisherigen Grundlagen* (Berlin: Schroeder, 1844).

Heidegger, Martin, 'Die Zeit des Weltbildes' (1938), in Martin Heidegger (ed.), *Holzwege* (Frankfurt/Main: Klostermann, 1977), 87–88.

Heidegger, Martin, 'The Hand and the Typewriter' (1942–43), in Friedrich Kittler (ed.), *Gramophone, Film, Typewriter* (Stanford: Stanford University Press, 1999).

Heimböckel, Dieter, *Walther Rathenau und die Literatur seiner Zeit* (Würzburg: Königshausen & Neumann, 1996).

Heinz, Karl E., *Adel und Republik: Adelsname und Adelstitel unter den Garantien des deutschen Grundgesetz* (Bonn: IAIS, 2006).

Bernhard, Henry (ed.), *Gustav Stresemann, Vermächtnis. Der Nachlass in drei Bänden* (Berlin: Ullstein, 1933).

Herzfelde, Wieland, *Der Malik-Verlag*, Ausstellungskatalog (Berlin: Deutsche Akademie der Künste, 1967).

Hewitson, Mark, 'Violence and Civilization. Transgression in Modern Wars', in Mary Fulbrook (ed.), *Un-civilizing Processes?: Excess and Transgression in German Society and Culture: Perspectives Debating with Norbert Elias* (Amsterdam: Rodopi, 2007), 117–157.

Hewitson, Mark and Matthew D'Auria (eds.), *Europe in Crisis. Intellectuals and the European Idea, 1917–1957* (Oxford: Berghahn, 2012).

Heymel, Charlotte, *Touristen an der Front. Das Kriegserlebnis 1914–1918 als Reiseerfahrung in zeitgenössischen Reiseberichten* (Münster: LIT, 2007).

Hiden, John and Martyn Housden, *Neighbours or Enemies? Germans, the Baltic and Beyond* (Amsterdam: Rodopi, 2008).

Hirsch, Marianne, *Family Frames: Photography, Narrative, and Postmemory* (Cambridge, Mass.: Harvard University Press, 1997).

Hirsch, Marianne, *The Generation of Postmemory: Writing and Visual Culture after the Holocaust* (New York: Columbia University Press, 2012).

Hobbes, Thomas, *Leviathan*, ed. Richard Tuck (Cambridge: Cambridge University Press, 2001).

Hobsbawm, Eric, *The Age of Empire, 1875–1914* (London: Weidenfeld and Nicholson, 1987).

Hobsbawm, Eric, 'Gli intellettuali e l'antifascismo', in *Storia del marxismo*, 3:2 (Turin: Einaudi, 1981).

Hobsbawm, Eric, *Nations and Nationalism since 1780. Programme, Myth, Reality* (Cambridge: Canto, 1992).

Hobsbawm, Eric, *Primitive Rebels. Studies in the Archaic Forms of Social Movements in the Nineteenth and Twentieth Century* (Manchester: Manchester University Press, 1959).

Hobson, John, *Imperialism: A Study* (New York: James Pott, 1902).

Höpp, Gerhard, *Muslime in der Mark: als Kriegsgefangene und Internierte In Wünsdorf und Zossen, 1914–1924* (Berlin: das Arabische Buch, 1999).

Hofer, Hans-Georg, *Nervenschwäche und Krieg. Modernitätskritik und Krisenbewältigung in der österreichischen Psychiatrie (1880–1920)* (Cologne, Vienna, and Weimar: Böhlau, 2004).

Höfer, Regina (ed.), *Imperial Sightseeing. Die Indienreise von Franz Ferdinand Erzherzog von Österreich-Este* (Vienna: Museum für Völkerkunde, 2010).

Hoffmann, Peter, *Claus Schenk Graf von Stauffenberg* (Munich: Pantheon, 2007).

Holborn, Hajo, 'Diplomats and Diplomacy in the Early Weimar Republic', in Gordon Alexander Craig and Felix Gilbert (eds.), *The Diplomats: 1919–1939* (Princeton: Princeton University Press, 1953), 123–172.

Holborn, Hajo, *The Political Collapse of Europe* (Westport, Conn.: Greenwood Press, 1982).

Holquist, Peter, 'Dilemmas of a Progressive Administrator. Baron Boris Nolde', in *Kritika: Explorations in Russian and Eurasian History*, 7:2 (Spring 2006), 241–273.

Holzer. Anton (ed.), *Die andere Front: Fotografie und Propaganda im Ersten Weltkrieg: mit unveröffentlichten Originalaufnahmen aus dem Bildarchiv der Österreichischen Nationalbibliothek* (Vienna: Primus, 2007).

Honeth, Axel, *Kampf um Anerkennung. Zur moralischen Grammatik sozialer Konflikte* (Frankfurt/Main: Suhrkamp, 2003).

Hont, Istvan, *Jealousy of Trade. International Competition and the Nation-State in Historical Perspective* (Cambridge, Mass.: Harvard University Press, 2005).

Horne, John N. and Alan Kramer, *German Atrocities, 1914: A History of Denial* (New Haven: Yale University Press, 2001).

Horst and Lois Jarka (eds.), *The Others' Austria* (Riverside, Calif.: Ariadne Press, 2011).

Hoyningen-Huene, Iris von, *Adel in der Weimarer Republik: die rechtlich-soziale Situation des reichsdeutschen Adels 1918–1933* (Limburg: Starke, 1992).

Huber, Valeska, *Channelling Mobilities: Migration and Globalisation in the Suez Canal Region and Beyond, 1869–1914* (Cambridge: Cambridge University Press, 2013).

Hudemann, Rainer and Georges-Henri Soutou (eds.), *Eliten in Deutschland und Frankreich im 19. und 20. Jahrhundert. Strukturen und Beziehungen* (Munich: R. Oldenbourg, 1994).

Hull, Isabel V., *The Entourage of Kaiser Wilhelm II, 1888–1918* (Cambridge and New York: Cambridge University Press, 1982).

Hull, Isabel V., *A Scrap of Paper. Breaking and Making International Law during the Great War* (Ithaca: Cornell University Press, 2014).

Hunter, F. Robert, 'Tourism and Empire: The Thomas Cook & Son Enterprise on the Nile, 1868–1914', in *Middle Eastern Studies*, 40:5 (September 2004), 28–54.

Hyams, Barbara, 'The Whip and the Lamp: Leopold von Sacher-Masoch, the Woman Question, and the Jewish Question', in *Women in German Yearbook*, 13 (1997), 67–79.

Hymans, Jacques Louis, *Léopold Sédar Senghor: An Intellectual Biography* (Edinburgh: Edinburgh University Press, 1971).

Ikegami, Eiko, *Bonds of Civility. Aesthetic Networks and the Political Origins of Japanese Culture* (Cambridge: Cambridge University Press, 2005)

Ikegami, Eiko, *The Taming of the Samurai: Honorific Individualism and the Making of Modern Japan* (Cambridge, Mass.: Harvard University Press, 1995).

Iriye, Akira, *Cultural Internationalism and World Order* (Baltimore: Johns Hopkins University Press, 1997).

Irvine, William, 'Man and Superman, a Step in Shavian Disillusionment', in *The Huntington Library Quarterly*, 10 (1947), 209–224.

Isabella, Maurizio, 'Entangled Patriotisms: The Italian Diaspora and Spanish America', in G. Paquette and M. Brown (eds.), *Connections after Colonialism. Europe and Latin America in the 1820s* (Tuscaloosa: Alabama University Press, 2013).

Ishay, Micheline R., *Internationalism and Its Betrayal* (Minneapolis: University of Minnesota Press, 1995).

Israel, Jonathan, *Radical Enlightenment: Philosophy and the Making of Modernity, 1650-1750* (Oxford: Oxford University Press, 2001).

Jackson, Alvin, *Home Rule. An Irish History, 1800–2000* (London: Weidenfeld & Nicholson, 2003).

Jahn, Hubertus F., *Patriotic Culture in Russia During World War I* (Ithaca: Cornell University Press, 1995).

Jakobson, Roman, *Kindersprache, Aphasie und allgemeine Lautgesetze* (1941) (Frankfurt: Suhrkamp, 1969).

Jakubowska, Longina, *Patrons of History. Nobility, Capital and Political Transitions in Poland* (London: Ashgate, 2012).

James, Harold, *The Roman Predicament. How the Rules of International Order Create the Politics of Empire* (Princeton: Princeton University Press, 2006).

Jansen, Marius B., *The Making of Modern Japan* (Cambridge, Mass.: Harvard University Press, 2000).

Jarausch, Konrad, *Die Umkehr. Deutsche Wandlungen 1945–1995* (Munich: DVA, 2005).

Jelavich, Barbara, *Modern Austria. Empire and Republic, 1815–1986* (Cambridge: Cambridge University Press, 1987).

Johnston, Peter H., *New Mecca, New Babylon: Paris and the Russian Exiles, 1920–1945* (Canada: McGill University Press, 1988).

Judson, Pieter, 'Inventing Germans: Class, Nationality, and Colonial Fantasy at the Margins of the Hapsburg Monarchy', in Daniel A. Segal and Richard Handler (eds.), *Nations, Colonies, and Metropoles*, special issue of *Social Analysis*, 33 (2007), 47–67.

Judson, Pieter M. and Marsha L. Rozenblit (eds.), *Constructing Nationalities in East Central Europe* (Oxford: Berghahn, 2005).

Judt, Tony, *A Grand Illusion? An Essay on Europe* (New York and London: New York University Press, 2011).

Judt, Tony, *Postwar: A History of Europe since 1945* (New York: Penguin Press, 2005).

Junyk, Ihor, *Foreign Modernism: Cosmopolitanism, Identity, and Style in Paris* (Toronto: The University of Toronto Press, 2013).

Jussen, Bernhard, *Ordering Medieval Society: Perspectives on Intellectual and Practical Modes of Shaping Social Relations* (Philadelphia: University of Pennsylvania Press, 2001).

Jussen, Bernhard (ed.) *Signal: Christian Boltanski* (Göttingen: Wallstein, 2004).

Jussen, Bernhard, 'Zwischen lignage und Stand. Arbeit am Schema der "Treulosen Matrone" in den "Sieben weisen Meistern"', in Jan-Dirk Müller (ed.), *Text und Kontext. Fallstudien und theoretische Begründungen einer kulturwissenschaftlich angeleiteten Mediävistik* (Munich: Oldenbourg, 2007).

Kaiser, Wolfram, *Christian Democracy and the Origins of European Union* (Cambridge: Cambridge University Press, 2007).

Kaiser, Wolfram and Jan-Henrik Meyer, *Societal Actors in European Integration: Polity-Building and Policy-Making 1958–1992* (London: Palgrave Macmillan, 2013).

Kalm, Harald von, *Das preussische Heroldsamt, 1855–1920: Adelsbehörde und Adelsrecht in der preussischen Verfassungsentwicklung* (Berlin: Duncker & Humblot, 1994).

Kämpchen, Martin, *Rabindranath Tagore in Germany. Four Responses to a Cultural Icon* (Delhi: Institute of Advanced Study, 1999).

Kamzelak, Roland, Introduction to Roland Kamzelak (ed.), *Kessler, der Osten und die Literatur* (Münster: Mentis, 2015).

Kantorowicz, Ernst, *The King's Two Bodies: A Study in Medieval Political Theology* (Princeton: Princeton University Press, 1957).

Kaplun, Viktor, '"Zhit" Goratsiem ili umeret' Katonom': rossiiskaia traditsiia grazhdanskogo respublikanizma (konets xviii – pervaia tret' XIX veka)', in *Neprikosnovennyi zapas*, 5 (2007), 197–219.

Kaschuba, Wolfgang and Tsypylma Darieva (eds.), *Representations on the Margins of Europe: Politics and Identities in the Baltic and South Caucasian States* (Frankfurt/Main: Campus, 2007).

Kaufhold, Karl Heinrich, 'Fürstenabfindung oder Fürstenentschädigung? Der Kampf um das Hausvermögen der ehemals regierenden Fürstenhäuser im Jahre 1926 und die Innenüpolitik der Weimarer Republik', in Markus A. Denzel Günther Schulz (ed.), *Deutscher Adel im 19. und 20. Jahrhundert* (St. Katharinen: Scriptae Mercaturae, 2004).

Kauffmann, Kai, 'Slawische Exotik und Habsburger Mythos: Leopold von Sacher Masochs Galizische Erzählungen', in *Germanisch-Romanische Monatsschrift*, 52:1 (2002), 175–190.

Kinemann, Friedrich, *Vom Krummstab zur Republik: westfälischer Adel unter preußischer Herrschaft; 1802–1945* (Bochum: Brockmeyer, 1997).

Kellmann, Steven G., *The Translingual Imagination* (Lincoln: University of Nebraska Press, 2000).

Kellogg, Michael, *The Russian Roots of Nazism: White Emigrés and the Making of National Socialism* (Cambridge: Cambridge University Press, 2005).

Kelly, Duncan, 'Revisiting the Rights of Man: Georg Jellinek on Rights and the State', in *Law and History Review*, 22:3 (Autumn, 2004), 493–529.

Kershaw, Ian, *Making Friends with Hitler: Lord Londonderry, the Nazis and the Road to World War II* (New York: Allen Lane/Penguin Press, 2004).

King, Greg, *The Fate of the Romanovs* (Hoboken, N.J.: Wiley, 2003).

Kirchner-Reill, Dominique, *Nationalists Who Feared the Nation. Adriatic Multi-Nationalism in Habsburg Dalmatia, Trieste, and Venice* (Palo Alto: Stanford University Press, 2012).

Klautke, Egbert, *The Mind of the Nation: Völkerpsychologie in Germany, 1851–1955* (New York and Oxford: Berghahn Books, 2013).

Klemperer, Klemens von, *Ignaz Seipel: Christian Statesman in a Time of Crisis* (Princeton: Princeton University Press, 1972).

Klemperer, Victor, *Man möchte immer weinen und Lachen in Einem. Revolutionstagebuch 1919* (Berlin: Aufbau, 2015).

Knodt, Manfred, *Ernst Ludwig. Großherzog von Hessen und bei Rhein*, 3rd ed. (Darmstadt: H.L. Schlapp, 1997).

Kocka, Jürgen, 'Asymmetrical Historical Comparison: The Case of the German Sonderweg', in *History and Theory*, 38 (1999), 40–50.

Kocka, Jürgen, 'Wege zur politischen Identität Europas. Europäische Öffentlichkeit und europäische Zivilgesellschaft', in www.fes-online-akademie.de/mo dul.php?md=5&c=texte&id=59, accessed 1 August 2008.

Koerner, Joseph Leo, *Caspar David Friedrich and the Subject of Landscape*, 2nd ed. (London: Berghahn, 2009).

Kogan, Vivian, *The 'I' of History. Self-Fashioning and National Consciousness in Jules Michelet* (Chapel Hill, N.C.: University of North Carolina Press, 2006).

Kojève, Alexandre, *Introduction to the Reading of Hegel. Lectures on the Phenomenology of Spirit* (New York: Basic Books, 1980).

Kolakowski, Leszek, *Main Currents of Marxism* (Oxford and New York et al.: Oxford University Press, 1978).

Kolonitskii, Boris, *Tragicheskaya erotika. Obrazy imperatorskoi sem'i v gody Pervoi mirovoi voiny* (Moscow: Novoe Literaturnoe Obozrenie, 2010).

Konràd, George and Ivan Szelényi, *The Intellectuals on the Road to Class Power* (Brighton: Harvester Press, 1979).

Kopke, Christoph and Werner Treß (eds.), *Der Tag von Potsdam* (Berlin: Walter de Gruyter, 2013).

Korbel, Josef, *Twentieth-Century Czechoslovakia: The Meanings of Its History* (New York: Columbia University Press, 1977).

Körner, Axel, *1848: A European Revolution? International Ideas and National Memories of 1848*, 2nd revised ed. (Basingstoke: Palgrave Macmillan, 2004).

Koschorke, Albrecht, *Leopold von Sacher-Masoch: Die Inszenierungeiner Perversion* (Munich: Piper, 1988).

Koselleck, Reinhart, *Kritik und Krise: eine Studie zur Pathogenese der bürgerlichen Welt* (Freiburg: Alber, 1959).

Koselleck, Reinhart, *Vergangene Zukunft. Zur Semantik geschichtlicher Zeiten* (Frankfurt/Main: Suhrkamp, 1988).

Kostka, Alexandre and Irving Wohlfarth, *Nietzsche and 'an Architecture of Our Minds'* (Los Angeles, Calif.: Getty Research Institute for the History of Art and the Humanities, 1999).

Kozlov, Vladimir, Vladimir M. Khrustalëv, and Alexandra Raskina (eds.), *The Last Diary of Tsaritsa Alexandra* (New Haven: Yale University Press, 1997).

Kracht, Klaus Große, 'Ein Europa im kleinen. Die Sommergespräche von Pontigny und die deutsch-französische Intellektuellenverständigung in der

Zwischenkriegszeit', in *Internationales Archiv für Sozialgeschichte der deutschen Literatur*, 27 (2002), 144–169.

Kramer, Cheryl, 'Natalia Goncharova. Her Depiction of Jews in Tsarist Russia', in *Woman's Art Journal*, 23:1 (Spring–Summer, 2002), 17–23.

Kratz-Kessemeier, Kristina, *Kunst für die Republik: die Kunstpolitik des preussischen Kultusministeriums 1918 bis 1932* (Berlin: Akademie-Verl., 2008).

Kraus, Hans-Christof, *Konservative Zeitschriften zwischen Kaiserreich und Diktatur* (Berlin: Duncker & Humblot, 2003).

Kredov, Sergei, *Dzerzhinskiy*, series Zhizn Zamechatel'nykh ludei (Moscow: Molodaia Gvardia, 2013).

Kühn, Rolf, *Atmosphäre und Lebensform die kulturpolitische und traditionshermeneutische Bedeutung Frankreichs bei Graf Hermann Keyserling* (Heidelberg: Winter, 1990).

Kuisel, Richard F. and Ernest Mercier, *French Technocrat* (Berkeley: University of California Press, 1967).

Kunz, Josef L., 'Pan Europe, the Marshall Plan Countries and the Western European Union', in *The American Journal of International Law*, 42:4 (October 1948), 868–877.

Kusch, Martin, *Knowledge by Agreement: The Programme of Communitarian Epistemology* (Oxford: Oxford University Press, 2002).

Lane, Melissa and Martin Ruehl (eds.), *A Poet's Reich: Politics and Culture in the George Circle* (London: Camden House, 2011).

Laqua, Daniel (ed.), *Internationalism Reconfigured: Transnational Ideas and Movements between the World Wars* (London: Tauris Academic Studies, 2011).

Laqua, Daniel, 'Transnational Intellectual Cooperation, the League of Nations, and the Problem of Order', in *Journal of Global History*, 6:2 (2011), 223–247.

Laqueur, Walter, *Deutschland und Russland* (Berlin: Propyläen, 1965).

Latour, Bruno, *Reassembling the Social. An Introduction to Actor-Network Theory* (Oxford: Oxford University Press, 2005).

Laubner, Jürgen, 'Zwischen Industrie und Landwirtschaft. Die oberschlesischen Magnaten – aristokratische Anpassungsfähigkeit und "Krisenbewältigung"', in Andreas Heinz Lawaty and Hubert Orlowski (eds.), *Deutsche und Polen. Geschiche – Kultur – Politik* (Munich: Siedler, N6, 2003).

Launay, Robert, 'Montesquieu: The Specter of Despotism and the Origin of Modern Comparative Law', in Annelise Riles (ed.), *Rethinking the Masters of Comparative Law* (Oxford: Hart, 2001).

Lee, Eun-Jeung, *Anti-Europa: die Geschichte der Rezeption des Konfuzianismus und der konfuzianischen Gesellschaft seit der frühen Aufklärung; eine ideengeschichtliche Untersuchung unter besonderer Berücksichtigung der deutschen Entwicklung* (Hamburg: LIT, 2003).

Lefèbvre, Henri, *La production de l'espace* (Paris: Anthropos/Economica, 1999).

Lehmann, Hartmut and Otto Gerhard Oexle, *Nationalsozialismus in den Kulturwissenschaften* (Göttingen: Vandenhoeck & Ruprecht, 2004).

Lemon, Robert, *Imperial Messages. Orientalism as Self-Critique in the Habsburg Fin de Siècle* (London: Camden House, 2011).

Lenin, Nikolai, *Imperialism, the Highest Stage of Capitalism* (Petrograd: Zhizn' i Znanie, 1917).

Levenson, Alan T., *Between Philosemitism and Antisemitism: Defense of Jews and Judaism in Germany, 1871–1932* (Lincoln: University of Nebraska Press, 2004).

Levin, Yuri and Evgeny Soshkin (eds.), *Imperia N. Nabokov I nasledniki* (Moscow: Novoe literaturnoe obozrenie, 2006).

Levinas, Emmanuel, *Othewise than Being: Or, Beyond Essence*, transl. Alphonso Lengis (Pittsburgh: Duquesne University Press, 2005).

Levine, Barbara and Kirsten M. Jensen (eds.), *Around the World: The Grand Tour in Photo Albums* (New York: Princeton University Press, 2007).

Lewis, Gordon K., 'Fabian Socialism; Some Aspects of Theory and Practice', in *The Journal of Politics*, 14 (1952), 442–470.

Lewis, Martin W. and Karen E. Wigen, *The Myth of Continents: A Critique of Metageography* (Berkeley and Los Angeles: University of California Press, 1997).

Liebersohn, Harry, 'Discovering Indigenous Nobility: Tocqueville, Chamisso, and Romantic Travel Writing', in *The American Historical Review*, 99 (1994), 746–766.

Lieven, Dominic, *The Aristocracy in Europe, 1815–1914* (New York: Columbia University Press, 1993).

Lieven, Dominic, 'The Russian Empire and the Soviet Union as Imperial Polities', in *Journal of Contemporary History*, 30 (1995), 607–636.

Lilti, Antoine, *Figures publiques. L'invention de la célébrité 1750–1850* (Paris: Fayard, 2014).

Lilti, Antoine, 'Reconnaissance et célébrité: Jean-Jacques Rousseau et la politique du nom propre', in *Orages, Littérature et culture*, n° 9, mars 2010, 77–94.

Lindsay, Franklin, *Beacons in the Night: With the OSS and Tito's Partisans in Wartime Yugoslavia* (Stanford: Stanford University Press, 1993).

Loader, Colin and David Kettler, *Karl Mannheim's Sociology as Political Education* (New Brunswick, N.J.: Transaction Publishers, 2002).

Lohmann-Hinrichs, Dagmar, 'Review of Bialas, Wolfgang, and Stenzel, Burkhard (eds.): Die Weimarer Republik zwischen Metropole und Provinz. Intellektuellendiskurse zur politischen Kultur', in *Jahrbuch zur Literatur der Weimarer Republik*, 1 (1997), 239–247.

Losev, Alexei, *Problema simvola i realisticheskoe iskusstvo*, 2nd ed. (Moscow: Iskusstvo, 1995).

Losev, Alexei, *Znak, simvol, mif* (Moscow: Izd-tvo moskovskogo un-ta, 1982).

Lotman, Yuri, *Besedy o russkoi kul'ture: byt i traditsii russkogo dvorianstva XVIII-nachalo XIX veka/ Conversations on Russian culture: the habits and traditions of the Russian court nobility of the 18th – beginning of the 19th centuries* (Sankt-Peterburg: "Iskusstvo-SPB", 1994).

Lotman, Yuri, *Semiotika kul'tury i poniatie teksta* (Tallinn: University Press, 1992).

Löwenthal, Leo, 'German Popular Biographies: Culture's Bargain Counter', in Barrington Moore, Jr. and Kurt H. Wolff (eds.), *The Critical Spirit. Essays in Honor of Herbert Marcuse* (Boston: Beacon Press, 1967), 267–287.

Lubenow, W.C., *The Cambridge Apostles, 1820–1914. Liberalism, Imagination, and Friendship in British Intellectual and Professional Life* (Cambridge: Cambridge University Press, 1998).

Ludwig, Emil, *Wilhelm Hohenzollern, The Last of the Kaisers* (New York and London: G.B. Putnam's, 1927).

Lukács, Georg, *Die Zerstörung der Vernunft* (Berlin: Aufbau, 1984).

Lukács, Georg, *Geschichte und Klassenbewusstsein* (Berlin: Malik, 1923).

MacCarthy, John A., *Zensur und Kultur: zwischen Weimarer Klassik und Weimarer Republik mit einem Ausblick bis heute: from Weimar Classicism to Weimar Republic and beyond* (Tübingen: Niemeyer, 1995).

Machthan, Lothar, *Die Abdankung. Wie Deutschlands gekrönte Haeupter fielen* (Berlin: Propyläen, 2008).

Magun, Artemy, *La révolution négative. Deconstruction du sujet politique* (Paris: L'Harmatte, 2009).

Malinowski, Stephan, 'Geschichte von oben. Autobiographien als Quelle einer Sozial- und Kulturgeschichte des deutschen Adels in Kaiserreich und Weimarer Republik', in *Historische Anthropologie. Kultur, Gesellschaft, Alltag*, 7 (1999), 236–270.

Malinowski, Stephan, *Vom König zum Führer: Sozialer Niedergang und politische Radikalisierung im deutschen Adel zwischen Kaiserreich und NS-Staat* (Berlin: Akademie-Verlag, 2003).

Malinowski, Stephan and Markus Funck, 'Masters of Memory: The Strategic Use of Autobiographical Memory by the German Nobility', in Alon Confino and Peter Fritzsche (eds.), *The Work of Memory. New Directions in the Study of German Society and Culture* (Chicago and Urbana: Illinois University Press, 2002).

Mälksoo, Lauri, 'The History of International Legal Theory in Russia: A Civilizational Dialogue with Europe', in *The European Journal of International Law*, 19:1 (2008), 211–232.

Mandler, Peter, *The Fall and Rise of the Stately Home* (New Haven: Yale University Press, 1997).

Manela, Erez, *The Wilsonian Moment: Self-Determination and the International Origins of Anticolonial Nationalism* (New York: Oxford University Press, 2007).

Manias, Chris, *Race, Science, and the Nation: Reconstructing the Ancient Past in Britain* (London: Routledge, 2013).

Mann, Michael, *The Sources of Social Power, vol. 2: The Rise of Classes and Nation-States, 1760–1914* (Cambridge and New York: Cambridge University Press, 1993).

Marburg, Silke and Josef Matzerath, 'Vom Stand zur Erinnerungsgruppe. Zur Adelsgeschichte des 18. und 19. Jahrhunderts', in Silke Marburg and

Josef Matzerath (eds.), *Der Schritt in die Moderne. Sächsischer Adel zwischen 1763 und 1918* (Cologne, Weimar, and Vienna: Böhlau, 2001).

Marchand, Suzanne, 'German Orientalism and the Decline of the West', in *Proceedings of the American Philosophical Society*, 145 (2001), 465–473.

Marchand, Suzanne, *German Orientalism in the Age of Empire: Religion, Race, and Scholarship* (New York: Cambridge University Press, 2009).

Marchand, Suzanne, *Germany at the Fin de Siecle Culture. Politics and Ideas* (Baton Rouge: Louisiana State University Press, 2004).

Marchand, Suzanne, 'Leo Frobenius and the Revolt Against the West', in *Journal of Contemporary History*, 32 (1997), 153–170.

Marchand, Suzanne, 'The Rhetoric of Artifacts and the Decline of Classical Humanism: The Case of Josef Strzygowski', in *History and Theory*, 33, (1994), 106–130.

Margalit, Avishai, *The Ethics of Memory* (Cambridge, Mass.: Harvard University Press, 2002).

Marshall, David, *Celebrity and Power: Fame in Contemporary Culture* (Minneapolis: University of Minnesota Press, 1997).

Martin, Nicholas, '"Fighting a Philosophy": The Figure of Nietzsche in British Propaganda of the First World War', in *The Modern Language Review*, 98:2 (1 April 2003), 367–380.

Martynkewicz, Wolfgang, *Salon Deutschland* (Berlin: Aufbau, 2009).

Maslov, Boris, 'Tradicii literaturnogo diletantisma i esteticheskaia ideologia romana "Dar"', in Yuri Leving and Evgeny Soshkin (eds.), *Imperiya N. Nabokov I nasledniki* (Moscow: Novoe literaturnoe obozrenie, 2006), 37–73.

Matera, Mark, 'Colonial Subjects: Black Intellectuals and the Development of Colonial Studies in Britain', in *The Journal of British Studies*, 49:2 (April 2010), 388–418.

Maurer Zenk, Claudia, *Ernst Krenek – ein Komponist im Exil* (Vienna: Elisabeth Lafite, 1980).

Mayall, James, 'Nationalism and Imperialism', in Terence Ball and Richard Bellamy (eds.), *The Cambridge History of Twentieth-Century Political Thought* (Cambridge: Cambridge University Press, 2005), 104–123.

Mayer, Arno J., *The Persistence of the Old Regime* (London: Croom Helm, 1981).

Mayer, Arno J., *Political Origins of the New Diplomacy, 1917–1918* (New Haven, Conn.: Yale University Press, 1959).

Mazower, Mark, *The Dark Continent: Europe's Twentieth Century* (London: Allen Lane, 1998).

Mazower, Mark, *Governing the World. The History of an Idea* (London: Allen Lane, 2012).

McClelland, Keith and Sonya Rose (eds.), *At Home with the Empire. Metropolitan Culture and the Imperial World* (Cambridge: Cambridge University Press, 2006).

Mehler, Jacqueline Amati, Simona Argentieri, and Jorge Canestri (eds.), *The Babel of the Unconscious Mother Tongue and Foreign Languages in the Psychoanalytic Dimension* (Madison, Conn.: International Universities Press, 1993).

Meier-Graefe, *Julius, Edouard Manet* (Munich: Piper, 1912).

Merkle, Judith A., *Management and Ideology. The Legacy of the International Scientific Management Movement* (Berkeley: University of California Press, 1980).

Metcalf, Thomas R., *Ideologies of the Raj* (Cambridge: Cambridge University Press, 1997).

Meteling, Wencke, 'Adel im preussisch-deutschen Weltkriegsoffizierkorps', in Eckart Conze et al. (eds.), *Aristokratismus und Moderne. Adel als politisches und kulturelles Konzept, 1890–1945* (Weimar, Cologne, and Vienna: Boehlau, 2013), 215–239.

Metz, Joseph, 'Austrian Inner Colonialism and the Visibility of Difference in Stifter 's "Die Narrenburg"', *Proceedings of the Modern Languages Association*, 121:5 (October 2006), 1475–1492.

Middell, Matthias (ed.), *Comparativ*, 10:1, issue on Kulturtransfer und Vergleich (2000).

Middell, Matthias, Transnationale Geschichte als transnationales Projekt? Zur Einführung in die Diskussion, in: geschichte.transnational 11 Januar 2005, www.hsozkult.de/article/id/artikel-571.

Mienert, Marion, *Grossfürstin Marija Pavlovna: ein Leben in Zarenreich und Emigration; vom Wandel aristokratischer Lebensformen im 20. Jahrhundert* (Frankfurt am Main: Lang, 2005).

Mikkeli, H., *Europe as an Idea and an Identity* (Basingbroke: Macmillan, 1998).

Miller, Nicola, *In the Shadow of the State: Intellectuals and the Quest for National Identity in Twentieth-Century Spanish America* (London and New York: Verso, 1999).

Miller, Peter N., 'Review: Citizenship and Culture in Early Modern Europe', in *Journal of the History of Ideas*, 57 (1996), 725–742.

Mills, Charles Wright, *White Collar. The American Middle Classes* (London, Oxford, and New York: Oxford University Press, 1956).

Misztal, Barbara, *Theories of Social Remembering* (Philadelphia: Open University Press, 2003).

Mitchell, Stanley W., 'Phantom Limbs', in *Lippincott's Magazine of Popular Literature and Science*, 8 (1871), 563–569.

Mitrany, David, for the Carnegie Endowment for International Peace. 'Division of Economics and History', in *The Land & the Peasant in Rumania; the War and Agrarian Reform (1917–21)* (New Haven: Yale University Press, 1930).

Mitscherlich, Alexander and Margarete, *Die Unfähigkeit zu trauern. Grundlagen kollektiven Verhaltens*, transl. Beverley R. Placzek (Munich: Piper, 1965).

Mommsen, Wolfgang J. (ed.), *Imperialismustheorien* (Göttingen: Vandenhoeck & Ruprecht, 1987).

Mommsen, Wolfgang J., 'Max Weber and the Regeneration of Russia', in *The Journal of Modern History*, 69 (1997), 1–17.

Moody, Vernon Alton, 'Agrarian Reform before Post-War European Constituent Assemblies', in *Agricultural History*, 7 (1933), 81–95.

Moody, Vernon Alton, 'Europe's Recurrent Land Problem', in *Agricultural History*, 22 (1948), 220–232.

Moore, Bob, Martin Thomas, and L.J. Butler (eds.), *Crises of Empire. Decolonization and Europe's Imperial States, 1918–1975* (London: Hodder, 2008).

Morris, David B., *The Culture of Pain* (Berkeley: University of California Press, 1993).

Moses, Wilson Jeremiah, *Afrotopia: The Roots of African American Popular History* (Cambridge and New York: Cambridge University Press, 1998).

Mosse, Werner, 'Adel und Bürgertum im Europa des 19. Jahrhundertp. Eine vergleichende Betrachtung', in Jürgen Kocka (ed.), *Bürgertum im 19. Jahrhundert. Deutschland im europäischen Vergleich* (Munich: dtv, 1988).

Mothander, Carl, *Barone, Bauern und Bolschewiken in Estland* (Weißenhorn: Konrad, 2005).

Mühlendahl, Ernst von and Hoyningen gennant Huene, Heinrich, *Die baltischen Ritterschaften: Übersicht über d. in d. Matrikeln d. Ritterschaften von Livland, Estland, Kurland u. Oesel verzeichneten Geschlechter* (Limburg (Lahn): Starke, 1973).

Müller, Guido, '"Europa" als Konzept adlig-bürgerlicher Elitendiskurse', in Heinz Reif (ed.), *Adel und Bürgertum in Deutschland II. Entwicklungslinien und Wendepunkte im 20. Jahrhundert* (Berlin: Akademie Verlag, 2001), 235–268.

Müller, Guido, *Europäische Gesellschaftsbeziehungen nach dem Ersten Weltkrieg das Deutsch-Französische Studienkomitee und der Europäische Kulturbund* (Munich: Oldenbourg, 2005).

Müller, Guido, 'Von Hugo von Hofmannsthals "Traum des Reiches" zum Europa unter nationalsozialistischer Herrschaft – Die "Europäische Revue" 1925–1936/44', in Hans-Christof Kraus (ed.), *Konservative Zeitschriften zwischen Kaiserreich und Diktatur. Fünf Fallstudien* (Berlin: Duncker&Humblot, 2003), 155–186.

Müller, Lothar, 'Sekretär seiner Zeit: Harry Kessler', in *Merkur. Deutsche Zeitschrift für europäisches Denken*, 43 (1989), 174–181.

Müller, Mathias F., *Der Orden vom Goldenen Vlies und das Haus Habsburg im Heiligen Römischen Reich: ein (kultur-)geschichtlicher Rückblick* (Vienna: Gesellschaft für vergleichende Kunstforschung, 2009).

Müller, Michael, 'In cerca dell'Europa: realtà e rappresentazioni di un continente', *Contemporanea*, 1 (January 1999), 81–87.

Müller, O.W., *Intelligencija. Untersuchungen zur Geschichte eines politischen Schlagwortes* (Frankfurt: Athenäum, 1971).

Münkler, Herfried, *Imperien* (Berlin: Rowohlt, 2005).

Münster, Sebastian, *Cosmographey oder Beschreibung aller Länder, Herrschafftenn und fürnemesten Stetten des gantzen Erdbodens* (Basel, 1588; Munich: Kölbl, 1977).

Naimark, Norman M., *Terrorists and Social Democrats: The Russian Revolutionary Movement under Alexander III* (Cambridge, Mass.: Harvard University Press, 1983).

Nekliudov, Sergei (ed.), *Moskovsko-Tartuskauia semioticheskaia shkola. Istoria, vospominania, razmyshlenia* (Moscow: Shkola 'Yazyki russkoi kul'tury', 1998).

Neumann, Gerhard, 'Erkennungsszene und Opferritual in Goethes "Iphigenie" und in Kleists "Penthesilea"', in Anton Philipp Knittel and Günther Emig (eds.), *Käthchen und seine Schwestern. Frauenfiguren im Drama um 1800* (Heilbronn: Stadtbücherei, 2000).

Neumann, Manfred and Helga Neumann, *Maximilian Harden (1861–1927) Ein unerschrockener deutsch-jüdischer Kritiker und Publizist* (Würzburg: Königshausen & Neumann, 2003).

Zur Nieden, Susanne, *Homosexualität und Staatsräson: Männlichkeit, Homophobie und Politik in Deutschland 1900–1945* (Frankfurt and New York: Campus, 2005).

Nietzsche, Friedrich, *On the Genealogy of Morality*, ed. Keith Ansell-Pearson (Cambridge: Cambridge University Press, 2001).

Nietzsche, Friedrich, *Sämtliche Werke: Kritische Studienausgabe in 15 Bänden*, ed. Giorgio Colli and Mazzino Montinari (eds.) (Munich Berlin; New York: Deutscher Taschenbuch Verlag; W. de Gruyter, 1999).

Nora, Pierre, 'Between Memory and History: Les Lieux de mémoire', in *Representations*, No. 26 (Spring 1989).

Norton, Robert, *Secret Germany: Stefan George and His Circle* (New York: Cornell University Press, 2002).

Nye, Joseph, 'Soft Power', in *Foreign Policy*, 80 (Autumn 1990), 153–171.

Obolensky, Dimitri, *Bread of Exile: A Russian Family*, transl. Harry Willetts (London: Harvill Press, 1999).

Oexle, Otto Gerhard, 'Das Mittelalter und das Unbehagen an der Moderne. Mittelalterbeschwörungen in der Weimarer Republik', and 'Das Mittelalter als Waffe. Ernst H. Kantorowicz' "Kaiser Friedrich der Zweite" in den politischen Kontroversen der Weimarer Republik', in O.G. Oexle, (ed.), *Geschichtswissenschaft im Zeichen des Historismus* (Göttingen: Vandenhoeck & Ruprecht, 1996), 137–216.

Oexle, Otto Gerhard and Jörn Rüsen (eds.), *Historismus in den Kulturwissenschaften. Geschichtskonzepte, historische Einschätzungen, Grundlagenprobleme* (Cologne, Weimar and Vienna: Böhlau, 1996).

Oldenburg, Veena T., *Colonial Lucknow, 1856–1877* (Oxford: Oxford University Press, 1990).

O'Loughlin, John, Colin Flint, and Luc Anselin, 'The Geography of the Nazi Vote', in *Annals of the Association of American Geographers*, 84:3 (September 1994), 351–380.

Osterhammel, Jürgen, *Colonialism. A Theoretical Overview* (Princeton: Markus Wiener, 2005).

Osterhammel, Jürgen, *Die Entzauberung Asiens: Europa und die asiatischen Reiche im 18. Jahrhundert* (Munich: C.H. Beck, 1998).

Osterhammel, Jürgen, 'Die Wiederkehr des Raumes: Geopolitik, Geohistorie und historische Geographie', in *Neue Politische Literatur* 4:3 (1998), S. 374–397.

Osterhammel, Jürgen, 'Europamodelle und imperial Kontexte', in *Journal of Modern European History*, 2 (2004), S. 157–181.

Osterhammel, Jürgen, *Geschichtswissenschaft jenseits des Nationalstaats* (Göttingen: Vandenhoeck & Ruprecht, 2001).

Osterhammel, Jürgen, 'Imperien', in Gunilla Budde, Sebastian Conrad, and Oliver Janz (eds.), *Transnationale Geschichte: Themen, Tendenzen und Theorien* (Göttingen: Vandenhoeck & Ruprecht, 2004).

Osterhammel, Jürgen, *The Transformation of the World: A Global History of the Nineteenth Century* (Princeton: Princeton University Press, 2014)

Osterhammel, Jürgen and Sebastian Conrad (eds.), *Das Kaiserreich Transnational: Deutschland in der Welt, 1871–1914* (Göttingen: Vandenhoeck & Ruprecht, 2004).

Oushakine, Sergei, *The Patriotism of Despair. Nation, War, and Loss in Russia* (Ithaca and London: Cornell University Press, 2009).

Owen, Roger and Bob Sutcliffe (eds.), *Studies in the Theory of Imperialism* (London: Longman, 1972).

Pagden, Anthony (ed.), *The Idea of Europe: From Antiquity to the European Union* (Washington, D.C.: Woodrow Wilson Center; New York: Cambridge University Press, 2002).

Palatini, John and Georg Rosentreter (eds.), *Alter Adel, neuer Geist. Studien zur Biographie und zum Werk Hans-Hasso von Veltheims* (Halle: Mitteldeutscher Verlag, 2012).

Palatini, John and Georg Rosentreter (eds.), *Das Erbe der Veltheims. Schloss, Park und Kirche Ostrau* (Halle/Saale: Mitteldeutscher Verlag, 2014).

Palmer, James, *The Bloody White Baron* (London: Faber & Faber, 2008).

Palmier, Jean Michel, *Weimar in Exile: The Antifascist Emigration in Europe and America* (London and New York: Verso, 2006).

Paret, Peter, *The Berlin Secession: Modernism and Its Enemies in Imperial Germany* (Cambridge, Mass.: Belknap Press of Harvard University Press, 1980).

Peter, Paret and Beth Irwin Lewis, 'Art, Society, and Politics in Wilhelmine Germany', in *The Journal of Modern History*, 57 (1985), 696–710.

Passerini, Luisa, *Europe in Love, Love in Europe: Imagination and Politics between the Wars* (Washington Square, N.Y.: New York University Press, 1999).

Passerini, Luisa, *Europe in Love, Love in Europe. Imagination and Politics in Britain between the Wars* (London: I.B.Tauris, 1999).

Patijn, S, *Landmarks in European Unity: 22 Texts on European Integration* (Leyden: A.W. Sijthoff, 1970).

Patterson, Orlando, *Slavery and Social Death: A Comparative Study* (Cambridge, Mass: Harvard University Press, 1982).

Paul, Ina Ulrike, 'Konservative Milieus und die *Europäische Revue (1925–1944)*', in Michel Grunewald, Uwe Puschner, and Hans Manfred Bock, *Le milieu intellectuel conservateur en Allemagne, sa presse et ses réseaux (1890–1960)* (Bern: P. Lang, 2003).

Pessoa, Fernando and Pedro Teixeira da Mota, *A grande alma portuguesa: a carta ao Conde de Keyserling e outros dois textos inéditos* (Lisboa: Edições Manuel Lancastre, 1988).

Peterson, Walter F., *The Berlin Liberal Press in Exile. A History of the Pariser Tageblatt-Pariser Tageszeitung* (Tübingen: Niemeyer, 1987).

Petropoulos, Jonathan, *Royals and the Reich: The Princes von Hessen in Nazi Germany* (Oxford and New York: Oxford University Press, 2006).

Pierremont, E., *Tche-Ka. Matériaux et documents sur la terreur bolcheviste recueillis par le bureau central du parti socialiste révolutionnaire russe* (Paris: J. Povolozky, n.d.).

Pietsch, Martina, *Zwischen Verachtung und Verehrung: Marschall Jósef Pilsudski im Spiegel der deutschen Presse 1926–1935* (Vienna, Cologne and Weimar: Böhlau, 1995).

Pietsch, Tamson, *Empire of Scholars. Universities, Networks and the British Academic World 1850–1939* (Manchester: Manchester University Press, 2013).

Pike, Frederick B., 'Visions of Rebirth: The Spiritualist Facet of Peru's Haya de la Torre', in *The Hispanic American Historical Review*, 63:3 (August 1983), 479–516.

Piper, Ernst, *Alfred Rosenberg. Hitlers Chefideologe* (Munich: Pantheon, 2007).

Pitts, Jennifer, *A Turn to Empire. The Rise of Imperial Liberalism in Britain and France* (Princeton: Princeton University Press, 2005).

Plakans, Andrejs, *The Latvians: A Short History* (Stanford: Hoover Institution Press, 1995).

Plamper, Jan, *Geschichte und Gefühl. Grundlagen der Emotionsgeschichte* (München: Siedler, 2012).

Pokrovac, Zoran, *Juristenausbildung in Osteuropa bis zum Ersten Weltkrieg. Rechtskulturen des modernen Osteuropa. Traditionen und Transfers* (Frankfurt: Klostermann, 2007).

Pollard, Sidney, *Marginal Europe. The Contribution of Marginal Lands since the Middle Ages* (Oxford: Clarendon Press, 1997).

Porombka, Stephan (ed.), *Harry Domela, Der falsche Prinz: Leben und Abenteuer von Harry Domela* (Berlin: Bostelmann & Siebenhaar, 2000).

Pratt, Marie-Luise, *Imperial Eyes: Studies in Travel Writing and Transculturation* (London and New York: Routledge, 1992).

Pugh, Martin (ed.), *A Companion to Modern European History. 1871–1945* (Oxford: Blackwell, 1997).

Puschner, Uwe, *Die völkische Bewegung im wilhelminischen Kaiserreich: Sprache-Rasse-Religion* (Darmstadt: WBG, Wissenschaftliche Buchgesellschaft, 2001).

Puschner, Uwe, Walther Schmitz, and Justus H. Ulbricht, *Handbuch zur 'Völkischen Bewegung' 1871–1918* (Munich; New Providence: K.G. Saur, 1996).

Raabe, Paul, *Die Autoren und Bücher des literarischen Expressionismup. Ein biblio-graphisches Handbuch in Zusammenarbeit mit Ingrid Hannich-Bode* (Stuttgart: Metzler, 1992).

Raabe, Paul, *Index Expressionismus Bibliographie der Beiträge in den Zeitschriften und Jahrbüchern des literarischen Expressionismus 1910–1925* (Nendeln, Liechtenstein: Kraus-Thomson Organization Limited, 1972).

Raßloff, Steffen, '"Der falsche Prinz". Harry Domela zu Gast im „Erfurter Hof" 1926', in Steffen Raßloff (ed.), *Das Erfurter Gipfeltreffen 1970 und die Geschichte des „Erfurter Hofes"* (Jena: Schriften des Vereins für die Geschichte und Altertumskunde von Erfurt, 2007).

Radcliffe-Brown, Andrew, 'A Further Note on Joking Relationships', in *Africa: Journal of the International African Institute*, 19:2 (April 1949), 133–140.

Radcliffe-Brown, Andrew, 'On Joking Relationships', in *Africa: Journal of the International African Institute*, 13:3 (July 1940), 195–210.

Radcliffe-Brown, Andrew, *Structure and Function in Primitive Societies* (Glencoe: The Free Press, 1952).

Raeff, Marc, *Russia Abroad: A Cultural History of the Russian Emigration, 1919–1939* (New York: Oxford University Press, 1990).

Raschauer, Bernhard, *Namensrecht: eine systematische Darstellung des geltenden österreichischen und des geltenden deutschen Rechts* (Vienna and New York: Springer, 1978).

Redondo, Gonzalo, *Las empresas politicas de Jose Ortega y Gasset: 'El Sol', 'Crissol', 'Luz' (1917–1934)*, 2 vols. (Madrid: Ediciones Rialp, 1970).

Rees, Tim and Andrew Thorpe (eds.), *International Communism and the Communist International, 1919–43* (Manchester: Manchester University Press, 1998).

Reif, Heinz (ed.), *Adel im 19. und 20. Jahrhundert* (Munich: R. Oldenbourg, 1999).

Reif, Heinz (ed.), *Entwicklungslinien und Wendepunkte im 19. Jahrhundert* (Berlin: Akad.-Verl., 2000).

Reif, Heinz (ed.), *Entwicklungslinien und Wendepunkte im 20. Jahrhundert* (Berlin: Akad.-Verl., 2001).

Reif, Heinz (ed.), *Ostelbische Agrargesellschaft im Kaiserreich und in der Weimarer Republik. Agrarkrise, junkerliche Interessenpolitik, Modernisierungsstrategien* (Berlin: Akademie-Verlag, 1994), 251–266.

Reif, Heinz, *Westfälischer Adel 1770–1860: vom Herrschaftsstand zur regionalen Elite* (Göttingen: Vandenhoeck und Ruprecht, 1979).

Repp, Kevin, *Reformers, Critics, and the Paths of German Modernity: Anti-Politics and the Search for Alternatives, 1890–1914* (Cambridge, Mass.: Harvard University Press, 2000).

Retallack, James and Geoff Eley, *Wilhelminism and Its Legacies. German Modernities, Imperialism, and the Meaning of Reform, 1890–1930* (Oxford: Berghahn Books, 2003).

Reynolds, Michael A., *Shattering Empires. The Clash and Collapse of the Ottoman and Russian Empires, 1908–1918* (Cambridge: Cambridge University Press, 2011).

Reytier, Marie-Emmanuelle, 'Die Fürsten zu Löwenstein an der Spitze der deutschen Katholikentage. Aufstieg und Untergang einer Dynastie (1868–1968)', in Günther Schulz and Markus Denzel (eds.), *Deutscher Adel im 19. und 20. Jahrhundert*, Büdinger Forschungen zur Sozialgeschichte 2002 und 2003 (St. Katharinen: Scripta Mercaturae, 2004).

Reytier, Marie-Emmanuelle, 'Hubertus zu Löwenstein et Karl zu Löwenstein. Deux itinéraires', unpublished paper delivered at the 5th German-French summer workshop at the German Historical Institute in Paris on 'La noblesse en mutation (XVIe–XXe siècle)', 25 June 2008, forthcoming in www .perspectivia.net (2009).

Ribera, Alain, *Keyserling 1980, ou, la révolution inutile: méditations sur une tradition élitaire* (Monteil à Pessac, Gironde: Du Monteil, 1978).

Ribot, Théodoule, *Les Maladies de la mémoire* (Paris: Alcan, 1895).

Richard, Anne-Isabelle, 'The Limits of Solidarity. Europeanism, Anti-Colonialism and Socialism at the Congress of the Peoples of Europe, Asia and Africa at Puteaux, 1948', in *European Review of History*, 21:4 (2014), 519–537.

Ricoeur, Paul, *Oneself as Another*, transl. Katherine Blamey (Chicago: The University of Chicago Press, 1992).

Riederer, Günter, Introduction to G. Riederer et al. (eds.), *Harry Graf Kessler. Das Tagebuch, Sechster Band 1916–18* (Stuttgart: Klett-Cotta, 2006).

Ringer, Fritz K., *The Decline of the German Mandarins; The German Academic Community, 1890–1933* (Cambridge, Mass.: Harvard University Press, 1969).

Rittersporn, Gábor Tamás, Malte Rolf, and Jan C. Behrends, *Sphären von Öffentlichkeit in Gesellschaften sowjetischen Typs: zwischen partei-staatlicher Selbstinszenierung und kirchlichen Gegenwelten* (Berlin: Akademie-Verlag, 2003).

Robinson, Roland, 'Non-European Foundations of European Imperialism: Sketch for a Theory of Collaboration', in R. Owen and B. Sutcliffe (eds.), *Studies in the Theory of Imperialism* (London: Longman, 1972), 117–140.

Roediger, David, *Towards the Abolition of Whiteness: Essays on Race, Politics, and Working Class History* (New York: Verso, 1994).

Rojek, Chris, *Celebrity* (London: Reaktion, 2001).

Rosanvallon, Pierre, *The Society of Equals*, transl. Arthur Goldhammer (Cambridge, Mass.: Harvard University Press, 2013).

Rose, Peter Isaac (ed.), *The Disposessed: An Anatomy of Exile* (New York: Doubleday, 2005).

Rosenbaum, S.P. and James H. Haule (eds.), *The Bloomsbury Group. A Collection of Memoirs and a Commentary* (Toronto: University of Toronto Press, 1995).

Rosenwein, Barbara, 'Worrying About Emotions in History', in *American Historical Review*, 107:3 (June 2002), 821–845.

Rostagno, Irene, 'Waldo Frank's Crusade for Latin American Literature', in *The Americas*, 46 (1989), 41–69.

Rothberg, Michael, *Multidirectional Memory. Remembering the Holocaust in the Age of Decolonization* (Stanford: Stanford University Press, 2009).

Rothman, Natalie E., *Brokering Empire. Trans-Imperial Subjects between Venice and Istanbul* (Ithaca: Cornell University Press, 2013).

Rudnev, Daniil, *Viktor Kingissepp Moskvas* (Tallinn: Eesti Riiklik Kirjastus, 1963).

Ruehl, Martin, 'Death in Florence: Thomas Mann and the Ideologies of Renaissancismus at the Fin de Siècle', in D. Lindenfeld and Suzanne Marchand (eds.), *Germany at the Fin de Siècle: Culture, Politics and Ideas* (Baton Rouge: Louisiana State University Press, 2004).

Ruehl, Martin, '"In This Time Without Emperors": The Politics of Ernst Kantorowicz's Kaiser Friedrich der Zweite Reconsidered', in *Journal of the Warburg and Courtauld Institutes*, 63 (2000), 187–242.

Safran, William, 'Diasporas in Modern Societies: Myths of Homeland and Return', in *A Journal of Transnational Studies*, 1:1 (Spring 1991), 83–99.

Said, Edward, *Freud and the Non-European* (London: Verso. 2003).

Said, Edward, 'Invention, Memory and Place', in *Critical Inquiry*, 26:2 (Winter 2000), 175–192.

Saint Martin, Monique de, *L'espace de la noblesse* (Paris: Éditions Métailié, 1993).

Sassen, Saskia, *Territory, Authority, Rights. from Medieval to Global Assemblages* (Princeton: Princeton University Press, 2006).

Saussure, Ferdinand de, *Cours de linguistique générale*, ed. Charles Bally and Albert Sechehaye (Paris: Payot, 1916).

Sauvy, Alfred, 'Trois mondes, une planète', in *L'Observateur* (14 August 1952).

Schenk, Rafael, 'Höfische Intrige als Machtstrategie in der Weimarer Republik. Paul v. Hindenburgs Kandidatur zur Reichspräsidentschaft 1925', in Eckart Conze and Monika Wienfort (eds.), *Adel und Moderne. Deutschland im europäischen Vergleich im 19. und 20. Jahrhundert* (Cologe, Weimar, and Vienna: Böhlau, 2004).

Schiffer-Ekhart, Armgard, *Sebastianutti & Benque – Fünf Fotografen. Vier Generationen. DreiKontinente* (Graz: Steiermärkisches Landesmuseum Joanneum, 1997).

Schilmar, Boris, *Der Europadiskurs im deutschen Exil 1933–1945* (Munich: R. Oldenbourg, 2004).

Schlieben, Olaf Schneider and Kerstin Schulmeyer (eds.), *Geschichtsbilder im George-Kreis* (Göttingen: Wallstein, 2004).

Schlingensiepen, Georg Hermann, *Der Strukturwandel des baltischen Adels in der Zeit vor dem ersten Weltkrieg* (Marburg/Lahn: Herder-Institut, 1959).

Schlögel, Karl, *Im Raume lesen wir die Zeit: Über Zivilisationsgeschichte und Geopolitik* (Frankfurt am Main: Fischer Taschenbuch, 2007).

Schlotheuber, Eva, 'Das Privilegium maius – eine habsburgische Fälschung im Ringen um Rang und Einfluss', in *Die Geburt Österreichs. 850 Jahre Privilegium minus* (Regensburg: Schnell and Schnell, 2007), 143–165.

Schneede, Uwe M. (ed.), *Die Avantgarden im Kampf* (Bonn: Bundeskunsthalle Bonn, 2014).

Schneidmüller, Bernd, *Heilig – Römisch – Deutsch das Reich im mittelalterlichen Europa* (Dresden: Sandstein, 2006).

Scholder, Klaus (ed.), *Die Mittwochsgesellschaft. Protokolle aus dem geistigen Deutschland 1932 bis 1944* (Berlin: Severin und Siedler, 1982).

Schönpflug, Daniel and Jürgen Voss, *Révolutionnaires et émigrés: Transfer und Migration zwischen Frankreich und Deutschland 1789–1806* (Stuttgart: Jan Thorbecke Verlag, 2002).

Schreiber, Georg, *Habsburger auf Reisen* (Vienna: Ueberreuter, 1994).

Schüddekopf, Otto-Ernst, *Linke Leute von rechtp. Die nationalrevolutionären Minderheiten und der Kommunismus in der Weimarer Republik* (Stuttgart: W. Kohlhammer, 1960).

Schuhmann, Klaus, *Walter Hasenclever, Kurt Pinthus und Franz Werfel im Leipziger Kurt Wolff Verlag (1913–1919): ein verlags- und literaturgeschichtlicher Exkurs ins expressionistische Jahrzehnt* (Leipzig: Leipziger Universitätsverlag, 2000).

Schulz, Günther and Markus Denzel (eds.), *Deutscher Adel im 19. und 20. Jahrhundert*, Büdinger Forschungen zur Sozialgeschichte 2002 und 2003 (St. Katharinen: Scripta Mercaturae, 2004).

Schumacher, Martin (ed.), *Die Reichstagsabgeordneten der Weimarer Republik in der Zeit des Nationalsozialismup. Politische Verfolgung, Emigration und Ausbürgerung 1933–1945* (Düsseldorf: Droste, 1991).

Schuster, Gerhard et al. (eds.), *Kessler, Harry: Ein Wegbereiter der Moderne* (Freiburg i.Br.: Rombach Litterae, 1997).

Scott, David, *Conscripts of Modernity. The Tragedy of Colonial Enlightenment* (Durham: Duke University Press, 2004).

Searle, John R., *The Construction of Social Reality* (New York: Free Press, 1990).

Searle, John R., *Making the Social World: The Structure of Human Civilization* (Oxford: Oxford University Press, 2010).

Searle, John R., *Speech Acts: An Essay in the Philosophy of Language* (Cambridge: Cambridge University Press, 1969).

Sennett, Richard, *The Corrosion of Character* (New York: Norton, 1998).

Seton-Watson, Hugh, *Eastern Europe between the Wars: 1918–1941* (Cambridge: Cambridge University Press, 1945).

Sherwood Dunn, Frederick, *The Practice and Procedure of International Conferences* (Baltimore and London: The Johns Hopkins Press; H. Milford, Oxford University Press, 1929).

Shils, Edward, 'Charisma, Order, and Status', in *American Sociological Review*, 30:2 (April 1965), 199–213.

Shine, Mary L., 'Review of Textor', in *The Journal of Land & Public Utility Economics*, 2 (1926), 472–473.

Shklar, Judith, *American Citizenship: The Quest for Inclusion* (Cambridge, Mass.: Harvard University Press, 1991).

Simmel, Georg, *Soziologie. Untersuchungen über die Formen der Vergesellschaftung* (Berlin: Duncker&Humblot, 1908).

Simmonds, Alan G.V., *Britain and World War One* (London and New York: Routledge, 2012).

Singh, Gajendra, *The Testimonies of Indian Soldiers and the Two World Wars* (London: Bloomsbury Academic, 2014).

Sismondi, J.C.L., *Etudes sur les Constitutions des peoples libres* (Bruxelles: Société, 1839).

Sked, Alan, *The Decline and Fall of the Habsburg Empire, 1815–1918* (London and NewYork: Longman, 1989).

Skinner, Elliot P., 'The Dialectic between Diasporas and Homelands', in Joseph E. Harris, (ed.), *Global Dimensions of the African Diaspora* (Washington: Howard University Press, 1982), 17–45.

Skinner, Quentin, 'The Art of Theory', conversation with Teresa Bejan (2013), in www.artoftheory.com/quentin-skinner-on-meaning-and-method/.

Skinner, Quentin, *The Foundations of Modern Political Thought*, vol. 2, The Age of Reformation (Cambridge: Cambridge University Press, 1978).

Skinner, Quentin, 'From the State of Princes to the Person of the State', in Quentin Skinner (ed.), *Visions of Politics*, 3 vols., vol. 2 (Cambridge: Cambridge University Press, 2002), 368–414.

Skinner, Quentin, 'Meaning and Understanding in the History of Ideas', in *History and Theory*, 8:1 (1969), 3–53.

Skinner, Quentin, *Visions of Politics*, vol. 1, Regarding Method (Cambridge: Cambridge University Press, 2002).

Skocpol, Theda, *States and Social Revolutions. A Comparative Analysis of France, Russia and China* (Cambridge: Cambridge University Press, 1979).

Slatkin, Wendy, 'The Genesis of Maillol's La Mediterrannée', in *Art Journal*, 38 (1979), 184–189.

Sluga, Glenda, *Internationalism in the Age of Nationalism* (Philadelphia: University of Pennsylvania Press, 2013).

Smele, Jonathan (ed. and annot.), *The Russian Revolution and Civil War, 1917–1921: An Annotated Bibliography* (London and New York: Continuum, 2003).

Smith, Anthony D., 'National Identity and the Idea of European Unity', in *International Affairs*, 68:1 (1992), 55–76.

Smith, Douglas, *Former People: The Last Days of the Russian Aristocracy* (New York: Macmillan, 2012).

Smith, Helmut Walser, 'When the Sonderweg Debate Left Us', in *German Studies Review*, 31:2 (May 2008), 225–240.

Snyder, Timothy, *Bloodlands: Europe between Hitler and Stalin* (New York: Basic Books, 2011).

Snyder, Timothy, *The Red Prince. The Fall of a Dynasty and the Rise of Modern Europe* (London: Vintage, 2009).

Sonnabend, Gaby, *Pierre Viénot (1897–1944): ein Intellektueller in der Politik* (Munich: R. Oldenbourg, 2005).

Sontheimer, Kurt, *Antidemokratisches Denken in der Weimarer Republik* (Munich: Nymphenburger Verlagshandlung, 1962).

Sontheimer, Kurt, 'Antidemokratisches Denken in der Weimarer Republik', in *Vierteljahrshefte für Zeitgeschichte*, 5:1 (January 1957), 42–62.

Sorabji, Richard, *Gandhi and the Stoics. Modern Experiments on Ancient Values* (Oxford: Oxford University Press, 2012), 78–99.

Sorkin, David, *The Religious Enlightenment: Protestants, Jews, and Catholics from London to Vienna* (Princeton: Princeton University Press, 2011).

Spang, Christian and Rolf-Harald Wippich, *Japanese–German Relations, 1895–1945: War, Diplomacy and Public Opinion* (New York: Routledge, 2006).

Spekke, Arnolds, *History of Latvia. An Outline* (Stockholm: M. Goppers, 1951).

Spengler, Oswald, *Der Mensch und die Technik* (Munich: Beck, 1931).

Spengler, Oswald, *Der Untergang des Abendlandes*, vol. 1 (Munich: Beck, 1918).

Spenkuch, Hartwin, *Das Preußische Herrenhaup. Adel und Bürgertum in der Ersten Kammer des Landtages 1854–1918* (Düsseldorf: Droste, 1998).

Sperlings Zeitschriften- und Zeitungs-Adreßbuch. Handbuch der deutschen Presse. Leipzig 1902–1939 (Leipzig: Börsenverein der Deutschen Buchhändler, 1939).

Spivak, Gayatri Chakravorty, 'Can the Subaltern Speak?', in C. Nelson and L. Grossberg (eds.), *Marxism and the Interpretation of Culture* (Basingstoke: Macmillan, 1988), 271–313.

Spöttel, Michael, *Die ungeliebte 'Zivilisation': Zivilisationskritik und Ethnologie in Deutschland im 20. Jahrhundert* (Frankfurt am Main [u.a.]: Lang, 1995).

Ssorin-Chaikof, Nikolai, *Topografia schast'ia: etnograficheskie karty moderna* (Moscow: NLO, 2013).

Stark, Gary D., 'Publishers and Cultural Patronage in Germany, 1890–1933', in *German Studies Review*, 1:1 (February 1978), 56–71.

Stedman Jones, Gareth, *Languages of Class: Studies in English Working Class History, 1832–1982* (Cambridge: Cambridge University Press, 1983).

Stedman Jones, Gareth, 'Radicalism and the Extra-European World: The Case of Marx', in Duncan Bell (ed.), *Victorian Visions of Global Order: Empire and International Relations in Nineteenth Century Political Thought* (Cambridge: Cambridge University Press, 2008), 186–214.

Stedman Jones, Gareth, 'Saint-Simon and the Liberal Origins of the Socialist Critique of Political Economy', in Sylvie Aprile and Fabrice Bensimon (eds.), *La France et l'Angleterre au XIXe siècle. Échanges, représentations, comparaisons* (Paris: Créaphis, 2006), 21–47.

Steinberg, Michael P., *The Meaning of the Salzburg Festival: Austria as Theater and Ideology, 1890–1938* (Ithaca: Cornell University Press, 1990).

Steiner, George, *Antigones: How the Antigone Legend Has Endured in Western Literature, Art, and Thought* (New Haven: Yale University Press, 1984).

Steiner, Zara, *The Lights that Failed: European International History, 1919–1933* (Oxford: Oxford University Press, 2007).

Steinfeld, Thomas, 'Als die Moderne nach Weimar wollte: Harry Kessler, die Kunstdiplomatie und der Skandal um Auguste Rodin', in *Frankfurter Allgemeine Zeitung*, No. 26 (31 January 1998).

Stekl, Hannes, *Adel und Bürgertum in der Habsburgermonarchie 18. bis 20. Jahrhundert* (Vienna and Munich: Verlag für Geschichte und Politik, Oldenbourg, 2004).

Stenzel, Burkard and Bialas, Wolfgang (eds.), *Die Weimarer Republik zwischen Metropole und Provinz. Intellektuellendiskurse zur politischen Kultur* (Weimar, Cologne, and Vienna: Böhlau, 1996).

Stern-Rubarth, Edgar, *Drei Männer suchen Europa; Briand, Chamberlain, Stresemann* (Munich: W. Weismann, 1947).

Steveling, Lieselotte, *Juristen in Münster: Ein Beitrag zur Geschichte der Rechts- und Staatswissenschaftlichen Fakultät der Westfälischen Wilhelms-Universität Münster/Westf*, Beiträge zur Geschichte der Soziologie, 10 (Münster: LIT-Verlag, 1999).

Stoler, Ann Laura (ed.), *Imperial Debris. On Ruins and Ruination* (Durham and London: Duke University Press, 2013).

Strayer, Robert W. (ed.), *The Making of the Modern World. Connected Histories, Divergent Paths. 1500 to the Present* (New York: St. Martin's Press, 1989).

Struve, Walter, *Elites Against Democracy. Leadership Ideals in Bourgeois Political Thought in Germany, 1890–1933* (Princeton: Princeton University Press, 1973).

Stümke, Hans-Georg, *Homosexuelle in Deutschland: eine politische Geschichte* (Munich: Beck, 1989).

Suppan, Arnold, *Jugoslawien und Österreich 1918–1938. BIlaterale Aussenpolitik im europäischen Umfeld* (Vienna and Munich: Verlag für Geschichte und Politik, Oldenbourg, 1996).

Sussman, Herbert, *Victorian Masculinities: Manhood and Masculine Poetics in Early Victorian Literature and Art* (Cambridge: Cambridge University Press, 1995).

Swenson, Astrid, *The Rise of Heritage. Preserving the Past in France, Germany and England, 1789–1914* (Cambridge: Cambridge University Press, 2013).

Talmon, Stefan, *Recognition of Governments in International Law: With Particular Reference to Governments in Exile* (Oxford: Clarendon Press, 1998).

Tanner, Marie, *The Last Descendant of Aeneas: The Hapsburgs and the Mythic Image of the Emperor* (New Haven: Yale University Press, 1993).

Taylor, Charles, 'The Politics of Recognition', in Charles Taylor and Amy Gutmann (eds.), *Multiculturalism: Examining the Politics of Recognition* (Princeton: Princeton University Press, 1994).

Taylor, Charles, *The Sources of the Self. The Making of Modern Identity* (Cambridge, Mass.: Harvard University Press, 1989).

Tchouikina, Sofia, *Dvorianskaia pamiat': 'byvshye' v sovetskom gorode (Leningrad, 1920e–30e gody)* (St. Petersburg: Izd-vo Evropeiskogo universiteta v StPb, 2006).

Textor, Lucy Elizabeth, *Land Reform in Czechoslovakia* (London: G. Allen & Unwin Ltd., 1923).

Théry, Franck, *Construire l'Europe dans les Années Vingt: L'Action de l'Union Paneuropéenne sur la Scène Franco-Allemande, 1924–1932* (Genève: Institut Européen de l'Université de Genève, 1998).

Thomas, Martin, Bob Moore, and L.J. Butler (eds.), *Crises of Empire. Decolonization and Europe's Imperial States, 1918–1975* (London: Hodder, 2008).

Thompson, E.P., *The Making of the English Working Class* (New York: Vintage, 1963).

Thompson, E.P., *Whigs and Hunters: The Origin of the Black Act* (New York: Pantheon, 1975).

Thompson, Kenneth W., 'The New Diplomacy and the Quest for Peace', in *International Organization*, 19 (1965), 394–409.

Thompson, Sarahelen, 'Agrarian Reform in Eastern Europe Following World War I: Motives and Outcomes', in *American Journal of Agricultural Economics*, 75 (1993), 840–844.

Tilly, Charles, *European Revolutions, 1492–1992* (Oxford: Blackwell, 1993).

Tilly, Charles, *Roads from Past to Future* (Lanham, M.D.: Rowman & Littlefield Publishers, 1997).

Todorov, Tzvetan, *On Human Diversity. Nationalism, Racism, and Exoticism in French Thought* (Cambridge, Mass.: Harvard University Press, 1993).

Tsagourias, Nicholas, 'Nicholas Politis' Initiatives to Outlaw War and Define Aggression, and the Narrative of Progress in International Law', in *The European Journal of International Law*, 23:1 (2012), 255–266.

Ulbricht, Justus H., *Justus H. Ulbricht, Klassikerstadt und Nationalsozialismus: Kultur und Politik in Weimar 1933 bis 1945* (Jena: Glaux, 2002).

Ungern-Sternberg, Walther von, *Geschichte der baltischen Ritterschaften* (Limburg a. d. Lahn: C.A. Starke, 1960).

Urbach, Karina, 'Adel versus Bürgertum. Überlebens- und Aufstiegschancen im deutsch-britischen Vergleich', in Franz Bosbach, Keith Robbins, and Karina Urbach (eds.), *Geburt oder Leistung? Elitenbildung im deutsch-britischen Vergleich* (Munich: K.G. Saur, 2003).

Urbach, Karina (ed.), *European Aristocracies and the Radical Right 1918–1939* (Oxford: Oxford University Press, 2007).

Urbach, Karina, *The Go-Betweens* (Oxford: Oxford University Press, 2015).

Urbach, Karina, Franz Bosbach, and Keith Robbins (eds.), *Geburt oder Leistung? Elitenbildung im deutsch-britischen Vergleich* (Munich: K.G. Saur, 2003).

Uscatescu, George, *Profetas de Europa* (Madrid: Editora Nacional, 1962).

Vaget, H. Rudolf, 'Der Dilettant: eine Skizze der Wort- und Begriffsgeschichte', in *Jahrbuch der deutschen Schillergesellschaft*, 14 (1970), 131–158.

Vedyuškin, V.A., *Evropeiskoe dvoryanstvo XVI – XVII vv.: granicy sosloviya* (Moskva: Archeografičeskij Centr, 1997).

Verdery, Katherine, *The Political Lives of Dead Bodies. Reburial and Postsocialist Change* (New York: Columbia University Press, 1999).

Volkelt, Johannes, *Ästhetik des Tragschen* (1896) (Munich: Beck, 1923).

Volkmann, Hans-Erich, *Die deutsche Baltikumspolitik zwischen Brest-Litovsk und Compiègne: ein Beitrag zur 'Kriegszieldiskussion'* (Vienna, Weimar and Cologne: Böhlau, 1970).

Vridaghiri, Ganeshan, *Das Indienbild deutscher Dichter um 1900. Dauthendey, Bonsels, Mauthner, Gjellerup, H. Keyserling und St. Zweig* (Bonn: Bouvier, 1972).

Wahl, Dieter v., 'Die Verzeichnisse der Umsiedler aus Estland (1939/1940)', in Verband der Baltischen Ritterschaften (ed.), *Nachrichtenblatt der Baltischen Ritterschaften*, vol. xxxiv:135 (September 1992), 49–50.

Wallas, Armin A., *Zeitschriften und Anthologien des Expressionismus in Österreich: analytische Bibliographie und Register* (Munich: K.G. Saur, 1995).

Walser-Smith, Helmut, *The Continuities of German History* (Cambridge: Cambridge University Press, 2008).

Walters, E. Garrison, *The Other Europe. Eastern Europe to 1945* (Syracuse, N.Y.: Syracuse University Press, 1988).

Walterskirchen, Gudula, *Blaues Blut für Österreich: Adelige im Widerstand gegen den Nationalsozialismus* (Vienna and Munich: Amalthea, 2000).

Walther, Karl-Kraus, *Hans-Hasso von Veltheim. Eine Biographie* (Halle: Mitteldeutscher Verlag, 2014).

Watson, Alexander, *Ring of Steel: Germany and Austria-Hungary at War, 1914–1918* (London: Penguin, 2015).

Watt, Richard, *The Kings Depart: The Tragedy of Germany. Versailles and the German Revolution* (New York: Simon and Schuster, 1968).

Wattenbach, Wilhelm, 'Die österreichischen Freiheitsbriefe. Prüfung ihrer Echtheit und Forschungen über ihre Entstehung', in *Archiv für Kunde Österreichischer Geschichtsquellen*, 8 (1852), 77–119.

Weber, Thomas, *Hitler's First War: Adolf Hitler, the Men of the List Regiment, and the First World War* (Oxford: Oxford University Press, 2011).

Wehler, Hans-Ulrich, *Deutsche Gesellschaftsgeschichte*, vol. 4 (Munich: C.H. Beck, 2003).

Wehler, Hans-Ulrich, *Gesellschaftsgeschichte*, vol. 3 (Munich: Beck, 1995).

Weidle, Barbara, *Kurt Wolff: ein Literat und Gentleman* (Bonn: Weidle, 2007).

Weigel, Sigrid, *Genealogie und Genetik: Schnittstellen zwischen Biologie und Kulturgeschichte* (Berlin: Akademie Verlag, 2002).

Weigel, Sigrid, *Generation: zur Genealogie des Konzepts, Konzepte von Genealogie* (Munich: Fink, 2005).

Weindling, Paul J., 'Race, Eugenics, and National Identity in the Eastern Baltic: From Racial Surveys to Racial States', in Björn M. Felder and Paul J. Weindlin (eds.), *Baltic Eugenics: Bio-Politics, Race and Nation in Interwar Estonia, Latvia and Lithuania 1918–1940* (Amsterdam: Rodopi, 2013).

Weinrich, Uriel, *Languages in Contact: Findings and Problems* (The Hague: Mouton, 1953).

Weinstein, Valerie, 'Reise um die Welt: The Complexities and Complicities of Adelbert von Chamisso's Anti-Conquest Narratives', in *The German Quarterly*, 72:4 (Autumn 1999), 377–395.

Werner, Michael and Bénédicte Zimmermann, 'Penser l'histoire croisée: entre empirie et réflexivité', in *Annales. Histoire, Sciences Sociales*, 1: 58 (2003), 7–36 (11).

Westad, Odd Arne, *The Global Cold War. Third World Interventions and the Making of Our Times* (Cambridge: Cambridge University Press, 2007).

Whelan, Heide W., *Adapting to Modernity: Family, Caste and Capitalism among the Baltic German Nobility* (Köln: Böhlau, 1999).

Wienfort, Monika, *Der Adel in der Moderne* (Göttingen: Vandenhoeck & Ruprecht, 2006).

Wiese, Benno von, 'Goethes und Schillers Schemata über den Dilettantismus', in Benno von Wiese (ed.), *Von Lessing bis Grabbe: Studien zur deutschen Klassik und Romantik* (Düsseldorf: Babel, 1968).

Wiezbicka, Anna, *Semantics, Culture and Cognition: Universal Human Concepts in Culture-Specific Configurations* (Oxford: Oxford University Press, 1992).

Willcock, Sean, 'Aesthetic Bodies: Posing on Sites of Violence in India, 1857–1900', in *History of Photography*, 39:2 (2015), 142–159.

Williams, Raymond, 'The Bloomsbury Fraction', in Raymond Williams (ed.), *Culture and Materialism: Selected Essays* (London: Verso, 2005), 148–170.

Wilson-Bareau, Juliet, *Manet, the Execution of Maximilian: Painting, Politics and Censorship* (London: National Gallery, 1992).

Winnicott, Donald W., *The Maturational Processes and the Facilitating Environment: Studies in the Theory of Emotional Development* (London: Karnac Press, 1990).

Winock, Michel, *Le siècle des intellectuels* (Paris: Seuil, 1997).

Winter, Jay (ed.), *The Cambridge History of the First World War*, vol. III Civil Society (Cambridge: Cambridge University Press, 2014).

Wintzer, Joachim, *Deutschland und der Völkerbund 1918–1926* (Paderborn: Schöningh, 2006).

Wita, Béatrix le, *Mémoire familiale et mémoire généalogique dans quelques familles de la bourgeoisie parisienne* (Paris: Ministére de la Culture, 1983).

Wollkopf, Roswitha, 'Das Nietzsche-Archiv im Spiegel der Beziehungen Elisabeth-Förster Nietzsches zu Kessler, Harry', in *Jahrbuch der deutschen Schillergesellschaft*, 34 (1990), 125–167.

Wollkopf, Roswitha, 'Die Gremien des Nietzsche-Archivs und ihre Beziehungen zum Faschismus bis 1933', in Karl-Heinz Hahn (ed.), *Im Vorfeld der Literatur. Vom Wert archivalischer Überlieferung für das Verständnis von Literatur und ihrer Geschichte* (Cologne, Weimar, and Vienna: Böhlau, 1991).

Woolf, Stuart, 'Europe and Its Historians', in *Contemporary European History*, 12:3 (2003), 323–337.

Woollacott, Angela, Desley Deacon, and Penny Russell (eds.), *Transnational Lives. Biographies of Global Modernity, 1700-Present* (New York: Palgrave Macmillan 2010).

Woolmer, J. Howard, *A Checklist of the Hogarth Press, 1917–1938* (Andes, N.Y.: Woolmer & Brotherson, 1987).

Wordsworth, William, *Tract on the Convention of Sintra* (1808) (London: Humphrey Milford, 1915).

Wundt, Wilhelm, *Völkerpsychologie: Eine Untersuchung der Entwicklungsgesetze von Sprache, Mythus, und Sitte*, 10 vols. (Leipzig: Engelmann, 1900–20).

Wurgaft, Lewis D., 'The Activists: Kurt Hiller and the Politics of Action on the German Left 1914–1933', in *Transactions of the American Philosophical Society*, 67 (1977), 1–114.

Wynne Newhall, Nancy (ed.) *The Daybooks of Edward Weston* (New York: Aperture, 1990).

Yates, Frances, *The Art of Memory* (London and New York: Routledge, 1999).

Yates, Frances, *Astraea. The Imperial Theme in the Sixteenth Century* (London: Routledge, 1975).

Yun Casalilla, Bartolomé and Paul Janssens (eds.), *Aristocracies and Colonial Elites. Patrimonial Management Strategies and Economic Development, 15th–18th Centuries* (Aldershot: Ashgate, 2005).

Zahra, Tara, 'Imagined Noncommunities: National Indifference as a Category of Analysis', in *Slavic Review*, 69:1 (Spring 2010), 93–119.

Zantop, Suzanne, *Colonial Fantasies. Conquest, Family, and Nation in Precolonial Germany, 1770–1870* (Durham: Duke University Press, 1997).

Zeller, Bernhard, *Harry Kessler. Zeuge und Chronist seiner Epoche*, in *Abhandlungen der Klasse der Literatur* (Wiesbaden and Stuttgart: Franz Steiner, 1989).

Ziegerhofer-Prettenthaler, Anita, *Botschafter Europas: Richard Nikolaus Coudenhove-Kalergi und die Paneuropa-Bewegung in den zwanziger und dreissiger Jahren* (Vienna: Böhlau, 2004).

Ziegler, Herbert, *Nazi Germany's New Aristocracy: The SS Leadership, 1925–1939*, 2nd ed. (Princeton: Princeton University Press, 2014).

Zielonka, Jan, *Europe as Empire. The Nature of the Enlarged European Union* (Oxford: Oxford University Press, 2007).

Ziemann, Benjamin, *Contested Commemorations: Republican War Veterans and Weimar Political Culture* (Cambridge: Cambridge University Press, 2009).

Zinnenburg Carroll, Khadija von, *Fragile Crown: Empire, Collection, Repatriation*, (Chicago: Chicago University Press, forthcoming).

Zuber, Otto, *Richard Graf Coudenhove-Kalergi als Freimaurer* (Bayreuth: Quatuor coronati, 1995).

Zunz, Oliver (ed.), *Alexis de Tocqueville and Gustave de Beaumont in America: Their Friendship and Their Travels*, transl. Arthur Goldhammer (Danver, Mass.: University of Virginia Press, 2011).

Index